Impossibility in Modern Private Law

Hüseyin Can Aksoy

Impossibility in Modern Private Law

A Comparative Study of German, Swiss and Turkish Laws and the Unification Instruments of Private Law

Springer

Hüseyin Can Aksoy
Faculty of Law
Bilkent University
Ankara
Turkey

ISBN 978-3-319-34817-9 ISBN 978-3-319-01704-4 (eBook)
DOI 10.1007/978-3-319-01704-4
Springer Cham Heidelberg New York Dordrecht London

Softcover reprint of the hardcover 1st edition 2014

Printed on acid-free paper

Springer is part of Springer Science+Business Media (www.springer.com)

For my beloved wife, Pınar

Foreword

Comparative legal research works best when scholars from different jurisdictions collaborate. That is why I was happy to supervise the doctoral thesis of Hüseyin Can Aksoy, whom I met in the course of a guest lectureship at Bilkent University in Ankara and who—as I soon realized—was one of the most promising young scholars at the excellent law faculty there.

Dr. Aksoy approached his thesis with great enthusiasm. His eagerness and rigor were tangible, and he soon received the opportunity to conduct research at the Max Planck Institute for Comparative and International Private Law in Hamburg. As there is no better place for comparative legal research, Dr. Aksoy readily accepted the Institute's invitation, and we remain thankful that the Max Planck Institute opened its doors for him.

Most notably, we would like to thank the faculty of Martin Luther University in Halle-Wittenberg—especially Prof. Matthias Lehmann and Prof. Armin Höland—for their kind support and their willingness to participate in Dr. Aksoy's doctoral examination. Their assistance enabled Dr. Aksoy's thesis defence to be conducted entirely in English.

Dr. Aksoy's doctoral thesis deals with Turkish, Swiss and German rules on impossibility in contractual performance and with related provisions in unification instruments such as the Convention on the International Sale of Goods (CISG) or the Unidroit principles. From the viewpoint of a German reader, it provides an unbiased outside view on German law. From a more general perspective, it aims at building bridges between the so-called civil law and common law and finally Unification Instruments—which is possibly one of the most important and challenging tasks of our times.

Dr. Aksoy will pursue his academic career at Bilkent University in Ankara, which will be of great benefit to the faculty there. My best wishes accompany him and his future endeavours.

Mainz, Germany

Urs Peter Gruber

Preface

This book is a slightly revised version of the Ph.D. Thesis (Dissertation), which was accepted at the oral examination at the Law Faculty of Martin-Luther-Universität Halle-Wittenberg (Germany) in April 2013 held by the exam committee consisting of Prof. Dr. Armin Höland, Prof. Dr. Urs Peter Gruber and Prof. Dr. Matthias Lehmann.

It is not very common for a foreign student to write a dissertation in English at a German law faculty. Accepting me as a Ph.D. student under these circumstances is enough reason that I am deeply grateful to my "Doktorvater" Prof. Dr. Urs Peter Gruber. On top of that he has fully supported me and made invaluable contributions to my entire doctoral study. In addition to giving remarkably thorough and helpful comments on the former drafts of the thesis, he was never tired of encouraging me and explaining to me the German academic system and the procedures which I was unfamiliar with. I find myself very lucky to have met him as a research assistant, when he was teaching at Bilkent University in 2008.

I must also thank Prof. Dr. Matthias Lehmann for his precious comments to the thesis as the "Zweitgutachter" and also Prof. Dr. Armin Höland for his valuable contributions during the oral examination as the chairman of the oral exam committee.

I am indebted to Prof. Dr. Osman Berat Gürzumar and Prof. Dr. Erden Kuntalp for their faith in me since the beginning of my academic life. The chances you have given me are rarely bestowed. It is my biggest desire to be worthy of your trust.

I also owe particular thanks to Max Planck Institute for Comparative and International Private Law for having granted me a fellowship to conduct part of my research in Hamburg. In my opinion, every scholar should have the privilege of studying there at least once in his/her academic carreer.

I am also thankful to my editor Ms. Anke Seyfried for her interest and guidance in the publication of this book.

Finally, I would like to thank my family, and especially my wife, Pınar Çağlayan Aksoy, for all the support they have shown during each and every phase of this study. Thank you for supporting my decisions and being proud of me even more than I deserve.

This book is dedicated to my beloved wife...

Ankara, Turkey
June 2013

Hüseyin Can Aksoy

Abbreviations

Abs.	Absatz
AcP	Archiv für die civilistische Praxis
AJCL	American Journal of Comparative Law
AJP	Aktuelle Juristische Praxis
Art.	Article
AÜHFD	Ankara Üniversitesi Hukuk Fakültesi Dergisi
AÜSBFD	Ankara Üniversitesi Siyasal Bilgiler Fakültesi Dergisi
Bd.	Band
BGE	Bundesgerichtsentscheid (Decision of Swiss Federal Court)
Art.	Article
Batıder	Banka ve Ticaret Hukuku Dergisi
BeckOK	Beck'scher Online-Kommentar
BGB	Bürgerliches Gesetzbuch (German Civil Code)
BGH	Bundesgerichtshof (German Federal Supreme Court)
BGHZ	Entscheidungen des Bundesgerichtshofes in Zivilsachen (Decision of Federal Court in Civil Matters)
CC	Code Civil des Français (French Civil Code)
CESL	Common European Sales Law
CHK	Handkommentar zum Schweizer Privatrecht
CISG or Convention	United Nations Convention on the Contracts for the International Sale of Goods
DB	Der Betrieb
DCFR	Draft Common Frame of Reference
E.	Esas (File Number of the Turkish Court of Appeals)
EBLR	European Business Law Review
EC	European Council
ed.	Editor
eds.	Editors
e.g.	*exampli gratia*/example
EJLE	European Journal of Law and Economics

EJLR	European Journal of Law Reform
ELR	Edinburgh Law Review
ERPL	European Review of Private Law
et seq.	*et sequence*/and the following
EU	European Union
ff.	On the following pages
fn.	Footnote
HD.	Hukuk Dairesi (Legal Chamber)
HGK	Hukuk Genel Kurulu (Assembly of Civil Chambers)
HICLR	Hastings International and Comparative Law Review
Hk-BGB	Bürgerliches Gesetzbuch Handkommentar
i.e.	*id est*/that is
IBR	Zeitschrift IBR Immobilien- & Baurecht
IRLE	International Review of Law and Economics
İÜHFM	İstanbul Üniversitesi Hukuk Fakültesi Mecmuası
JJ	Jherings Jahrbücher für die Dogmatik des bürgerlichen Rechts
JLC	Journal of Law and Commerce
JR	Juristische Rundschau
JurionRS	Jurion Rechtsprechung Database
jurisPK-BGB	Juris Praxis Kommentar, BGB, Schuldrecht
JuS	Juristiche Schulung
JZ	Juristen Zeitung
K.	Karar (Decision Number of the Turkish Court of Appeals)
LQR	Law Quarterly Review
MDR	Monatsschrift für Deutsches Recht
MMR	Multimedia und Recht
MüKo	Münchener Kommentar zum Bürgerliches Gesetzbuch
N.	Note
NJCL	Nordic Journal of Commercial Law
NJW	Neue Juristische Wochenschrift
Nr./No.	Number
OR	Schweizerisches Obligationenrecht (Swiss Code of Obligations)
p.	Page
pp.	Pages
para.	Paragraph
PECL	Principles of European Contract Law
PICC	UNIDROIT Principles of International Commercial Contracts
PILR	Pace International Law Review
PWW	Prütting/Wegen/Weinrich BGB Kommentar
Rdnr.	Randnummer
recht	Zeitschrift für juristische Ausbildung und Praxis

RLR	Ritsumeikan Law Review
s.	Sentence
TCO	Turkish Code of Obligations
TLR	Tulane Law Review
ULR	Uniform Law Review
ULF	Uniform Law on the Formation of Contracts for the International Sale of Goods
ULIS	Uniform Law on the International Sale of Goods
UN	United Nations
UNCITRAL	United Nations Commission on International Trade Law
UNIDROIT	International Institute for the Unification of Private Law
v.	Versus
VJ	Vindobona Journal of International Commercial Law and Arbitration
Vol.	Volume
VUWLR	Victoria University Wellington Law Review
Yarg.	Yargıtay (Turkish Court of Appeals)
ZGB	Schweizerisches Zivilgesetzbuch (Swiss Civil Code)
ZIP	Zeitschrift für Wirtschaftsrecht
ZEuP	Zeitschrift für Europäisches Privatrecht
ZfBR	Zeitschrift für deutsches und internationales Bau- und Vergaberecht
ZSR	Zeitschrift für Schweizerisches Recht

Contents

Part I
Introduction

1) Introduction

Impossibility is a concept dating back to Roman law. Therefore at first sight it seems that there is really not much to write about impossibility anymore. However, the treatment of impossibility in the modern private law and the reactions of national lawmakers (specifically, German, Swiss and Turkish lawmakers) to such treatment show that impossibility is still an item of interest in the study of contemporary private law.

The Roman lawyers accepted the principle of *impossibilium nulla obligation est*: the impossible is no obligation. This lead to the result that if performance of an obligation was already objectively impossible at the time of contract formation (*i.e.*, initial objective impossibility),[1] no obligation would arise. However, if performance of an obligation became impossible after formation of the contract (*i.e.*, subsequent impossibility), the obligation would be extinguished. Such distinctions are still used in some modern jurisdictions including Swiss and Turkish laws, but there is also a developing divergence from such approach.

Although the foundations of the impossibility doctrine can be traced back to the Roman times, recently the general rules on the contractual duties of parties have been reformed by several national legislators. The German and Turkish legislators, especially, have made law of obligations reforms in their domestic laws in 2002 and 2012, respectively. During the reforms, the concept of impossibility has been questioned, particularly in Germany. It was even debated whether or not to abolish impossibility as a dogmatic concept from the German Bürgerliches Gesetzbuch (BGB). Although in the end, the lawmakers decided to keep impossibility as a category of non-performance, it deserves to be taken into account that impossibility was on the verge of abolishment.[2]

---

[1] Initial subjective impossibility did not cause voidness of the contract. **Zimmermann**, Law of Obligations, p. 687; **Immenhauser**, p. 290; **Mousourakis**, p. 191.

[2] The unofficial translation of the provision, which was proposed in the Discussion Draft (Diskussionsentwurf) reads as follows: "*If the obligation is not money debt, the debtor may refuse the performance to the extent that and as long as he is unable to provide these with the effort,*

H.C. Aksoy, *Impossibility in Modern Private Law*, DOI 10.1007/978-3-319-01704-4_1,

The debates in Germany with regard to the abolishment of impossibility were parallel to the modern legal trend in private law. More specifically, the modern private law diverges from the traditional approach and does not recognize impossibility as a dogmatic concept. Rather than referring to the concept of impossibility and its results, modern private law instruments regulate *non-performance* in general. In fact, *(i)* the United Nations Convention on International Sale of Goods (CISG or Convention), *(ii)* UNIDROIT Principles of International Commercial Contracts (PICC), *(iii)* Principles of European Contract Law (PECL also known as the Lando-Principles), *(iv)* Draft Common Frame of Reference (DCFR) and *(iv)* Common European Sales Law (CESL), (altogether the Unification Instruments) have designated impossibility only as an excuse to the debtor's non-performance. Moreover, modern private law does not accept initial objective impossibility as a reason of invalidity of a contract.

The divergent attitudes of the modern laws towards the institution of impossibility raise the following questions *prima facie*: Why do Unification Instruments prefer to abolish impossibility as a dogmatic category and regulate more general exemption provisions with no distinction of initial objective or subjective impossibility? To what extent do the German, Swiss and Turkish lawmakers prefer to follow Unification Instruments? Is it better to directly use clear-cut impossibility rules (as in German, Swiss or Turkish laws) or is it preferable to use more general exemption clauses (as in Unification Instruments)?

Despite dating back to the Roman law, impossibility remains a contemporary topic, which deserves a comparative analysis. The main objective of this book is to analyze **the treatment of impossibility in modern private law**. Within this scope, the treatment of impossibility in German law, Swiss and Turkish laws and Unification Instruments will be appraised in Part II. This will be followed in Part III by a comparative analysis of the legal instruments studied in the previous part. In this part, rather than the application of general exemption/*force majeure* clauses, the utility of impossibility as a dogmatic concept will be specifically evaluated. Within this scope, the significance of impossibility for modern legislation will be explored. The book will elaborate the "ideal" scope of impossibility and discuss if—and to what extent—there is a necessity to classify impossibility into different types. Part IV of the book is reserved for the compilation of the conclusions.

References

Der Bundesminister der Justiz: Diskussionsentwurf eines Schuldrechtsmodernisierungsgesetzes, Der Bundesminister der Justiz, Berlin 2000. (Cited as Discussion Draft)

Immenhauser, Martin: Das Dogma von Vertrag und Delikt, Böhlau, Köln 2006.

Mousourakis, George: Fundamentals of Roman Private Law, Springer, Berlin/Heidelberg 2012.

Zimmermann, Reinhard: Law of Obligations: Roman foundations of the civilian tradition, Oxford University Press, Oxford 1996. (Cited as: Zimmermann, Law of Obligations)

which he is obliged according to the content and nature of the obligatory relationship. The rights of the creditor are determined in accordance with §§ 280 to 282 and 323."

Part II
Treatment of Impossibility in Modern Laws and Unification Instruments

2) Treatment of Impossibility in German Law

I) German Law of Contracts in General

In 2002, Germany reformed its law of obligations (Schuldrechtsreform) and amended the German Civil Code (BGB) dated 1 January 1900. The Act on the Modernization of the Law of Obligations (Gesetz zur Modernisierung des Schuldrechts), was published on 26 November 2001 and it is effective since 1 January 2002.

The idea of a comprehensive reform of the German law of obligations reaches back to the late 1970s. Respectively in 1981 and 1983, a number of academic opinions were published in three volumes at the request of the German Ministry of Justice. This was followed by the formation of a study commission in 1984, which completed its studies and published a final report in 1992. However, the final report of the reform commission was not widely discussed.[1]

In 2002, an amendment to the BGB, which was more than 100 years old, was put forward. This mainly resulted from the aim of fulfilling the objective of transforming several European Union (EU) Directives into German law.[2] However, German legislators accepted this as a chance to adjust the main provisions of the BGB in order to meet modern demands. Thus, the legislator has gone far beyond a simple transformation of the EU Directives.[3]

---

[1] **Zimmermann**, Breach of Contract, p. 2.

[2] In 1999, the EC enacted three Directives, which were required to be transposed into German law. These were: the Consumer Sales Directive No. 1999/44/EC; the E-Commerce Directive No. 2000/31/EC and Late Payment Directive No. 2000/35/EC. The German legislator accepted such transposition as a chance to improve the reform proposal of 1992 in accordance with the Directives. The result was the Government Draft (Regierungsentwurf) of an Act to Modernize the Law of Obligations of May 9, 2001, which was approved by the German Parliament in July in its first reading. For a historical background of the reform, see **Schlechtriem**, German Act, p. 1 ff.

[3] **Zimmermann**, Breach of Contract, p. 2.

H.C. Aksoy, *Impossibility in Modern Private Law*, DOI 10.1007/978-3-319-01704-4_2,

The 2002 amendments, which are considered the most important reform of the BGB since its enactment, have dramatically changed German law.[4] Although BGB has not been completely rewritten, it has been subject to major changes as a result of the reform.[5] Within this stance, contract law was one of the fields that were subject to significant changes. The provisions regarding breach of contract and its results have been drastically altered.[6] As a result, the new BGB has incorporated a uniform concept of breach of duty (Pflichtverletzung) and it has been structured according to various remedies available for breach of contract.[7] Under the current BGB, the cause and characterization of a breach becomes relevant only with regard to specific remedies such as for a primary claim (Primäranspruch), damages or termination, which depend on additional pre-requisites.[8] In addition to the provisions transposed from EU Directives, the following also deserve to be emphasized among various changes: (*i*) the harmonization of prescription periods; (*ii*) liability for defective performance in sales contract; and (*iii*) integration of various acts regarding civil law—especially acts on consumer protection—into BGB.[9]

II) Regulation of Impossibility Before the Reform of the German Law of Contracts

Prior to the reform of 2002, the German doctrine of impossibility was dealt with BGB of the year 1900. Although between 1900 and 2002, BGB was subject to various amendments, its regime of breach of obligation followed the traditional Roman law understanding. Within this stance, BGB had acknowledged a chronological and fault-based approach regarding impossibility of performance.

Before the reform, BGB had different provisions for different types of breaches. In other words, cases of impossibility, default and non-conformity were regulated

---

[4] **Schulte-Nölke**, p. 1; **Zimmermann**, Breach of Contract, p. 1.

[5] For a study on the problematic aspects of the reform of the German law of obligations, see **Lorenz**, NJW 2005, 1889, 1889 ff.

[6] The amendments include a reform of the provisions regarding impossibility of performance as well.

[7] **Zimmermann**, New German Law, p. 40. According to Huber, the concept of "Pflichtverletzung" is identical to the term "non-performance" (which is recognized by the Unification Instruments). Author argues that the concept of non-performance is not appropriate for use in German law, since BGB has accepted fault-liability system. **Huber**, ZIP 2000, 2273, 2278 ff. For a critique of the term "Pflichtverletzung" and also "Nichterfüllung" (non-performance) as an alternative term, see **Schwingenheuer**, p. 44; **Fikentscher/Heinemann**, § 42 II, Nr. 361. For the conceptual difference between the terms, see **Berghoff**, p. 19 ff.

[8] **Brunner**, p. 81; **Schlechtriem**, German Act, p. 1 ff.

[9] For a detailed description of the changes brought by the reform, see, **Mathias**, TLR 2009, 877, 877 ff.; **Löwisch**, RLR 2003, 157, 157 ff.; **Krajewski**, EBLR 2003, 201, 201 ff.; **Lorenz**, ELR 1997, 317, 317 ff.

under different sections of the law. However, impossibility of performance was the central notion of breach of contract.[10]

The impossibility regime of BGB was based on the distinction of initial and subsequent impossibility. Accordingly, objective initial impossibility caused the contract to be void.[11] On the other hand, subsequent impossibility—either objective or subjective—resulted in extinguishment of the debtor's obligation. However, subsequent impossibility was subject to a distinction by considering the debtor's responsibility for impossibility. If the debtor had responsibility for the occurrence of impossibility, he had to compensate the damages of the creditor. Otherwise, he was not required to pay compensation.

Initial subjective impossibility was not really dealt with in the old BGB. Pursuant to the German courts and doctrine, it did not lead to the voidness of the contract, but to a strict liability of the debtor for damages.

III) Regulation of Impossibility After the Reform of the German Law of Contracts

One of the most significant changes in the 2002 BGB reform is in the field of impossibility. In fact, German lawmakers have almost rewritten the impossibility regime of the law. Within this scope, both the distinctions based on types of impossibility and the results of impossibility of performance have been amended.

Unlike the former BGB, which had the notion of impossibility as the central legal institution in the law for the breach of contract, the new BGB refers to the concept of *breach of duty*.[12] Within this stance, the concept of breach includes impossibility as well.[13]

---

[10] **Lorenz**, ELR 1997, 317, 318; **Huber**, ZIP 2000, 2137, 2139.

[11] The logic behind the voidness of contracts due to initial impossibility was that in such cases the law assumed that the parties have made a mistake regarding ability to perform; hence the contract is not in uniformity with their free wills. In other words, parties would not conclude the contract should they be aware of the impossibility. **Mitzkait**, p. 210; **Huber**, Leistungsstörungen I, § 4 IV 2, p. 122, fn. 91. However, the former BGB did not limit voidness of the contract to the cases of mistake on initial impossibility. In other words, initial impossibility caused voidness of the contract regardless of the knowledge of the parties on the existence of initial impossibility at the time of contract formation. **Mitzkait**, p. 210. As a result, the distinction of initial and subsequent impossibility was highly criticized in the former BGB.

[12] **Lorenz**, ELR 1997, 317, 327; **Schwingenheuer**, p. 43; **Kaiser**, ZfBR 2001, 147, 148. According to Mitzkait, in cases of impossibility § 275 BGB eliminates the debtor's duty to perform regardless of his responsibility for impossibility. Therefore, once such duty is eliminated, it is a contradiction to base the creditor's compensation claim to a *breach of duty*. **Mitzkait**, p. 249 ff.

[13] Canaris argues that in the new BGB, the significance of the concept of impossibility has rather increased as an exemption from the obligation to perform the primary claim, but it has decreased as regard to claim for damages. **Canaris**, Schuldrechtsmodernisierung, p. XIII.

Since Roman times, impossibility of performance has been accepted as a limit of the debtor's duty to perform. However, the scope of impossibility has always been a matter of dispute. Such discussions find no room under § 275 BGB, which regulates the results of impossibility on the primary claim. More specifically, this provision deals with all kinds of impossibility without a distinction of the time of occurrence of impossibility and the responsibility of the debtor for the occurrence of impossibility.

The first three paragraphs of § 275 BGB regulate the types of impossibility: (*i*) real impossibility, (*ii*) practical impossibility; and (*iii*) moral impossibility, respectively.[14] The effects of real, practical and moral impossibility on the debtor's duty to perform are also dealt with under these three paragraphs. Such effects are exclusion of the primary claim (§ 275 I BGB) or a right of defense to refuse performance (Einrede, § 275 II and III BGB). On the other hand, the fourth paragraph of the provision makes reference to the rights of the creditor. § 275 BGB, titled as "*Exclusion of the duty of performance*" reads as follows[15]:

> (1) A claim for performance is excluded to the extent that performance is impossible for the obligor or for any other person.
> (2) The obligor may refuse performance to the extent that performance requires expense and effort which, taking into account the subject matter of the obligation and the requirements of good faith, is grossly disproportionate to the interest in performance of the obligee. When it is determined what efforts may reasonably be required of the obligor, it must also be taken into account whether he is responsible for the obstacle to performance.
> (3) In addition, the obligor may refuse performance if he is to render the performance in person and, when the obstacle to the performance of the obligor is weighed against the interest of the obligee in performance, performance cannot be reasonably required of the obligor.
> (4) The rights of the obligee are governed by sections 280, 283 to 285, 311a and 326.

1) Impossibility and Unexpectedness of Performance Under German Law

a) Impossibility of Performance (§ 275 I BGB)

§ 275 I BGB states that "*A claim for performance is excluded to the extent that performance is impossible for the obligor or for any other person.*" The provision covers the cases, where the verdict of performance would be meaningless, since

[14] However, impossibility in technical and traditional sense falls under § 275/I BGB. **Fikentscher/ Heinemann**, § 43 II 6, Nr. 402. In fact, the term "impossible" is only used in the first paragraph of the provision.

[15] For the English translation of § 275 BGB, see <http://www.gesetze-im-internet.de/englisch_bgb/>.

performance cannot be maintained by enforcement of such decision against the debtor.[16]

In accordance with § 275 I BGB, impossibility under the provision corresponds to real impossibility.[17] Within this meaning, the term refers to impossibility of all primary performances with no distinction of main and side obligations.[18] Moreover cases of legal impossibility[19] fall under the scope of § 275 I BGB as well.[20] Finally there might be cases where the purpose of the contract is accomplished (Zweckerreichung) or destructed (Zweckfortfall). In the first case, the creditor is satisfied prior to the performance by the debtor, whereas in the latter performance becomes impossible in the sphere of control of the creditor.[21] Such cases are covered by § 275 I BGB.[22]

Under the provision, the scope of impossibility is quite wide. In fact § 275 I BGB does not make any distinction between objective-subjective impossibility, the impossibility for which the debtor is responsible or not, and initial-subsequent impossibility. In other words, the provision is applicable to all such types of impossibility, regardless of the responsibility[23] of the debtor for

---

[16] **MüKo/Ernst**, § 275, Rdnr. 32.

[17] Reasoning of BGB, Drucksache 14/6040, p. 129, available at <http://dipbt.bundestag.de/dip21/btd/14/060/1406040.pdf>. The term impossibility under § 275 I BGB corresponds to the cases termed as "echte Unmöglichkeit" or "wirkliche Unmöglichkeit". **Brox/Walker**, § 22, Nr. 3; **Fehre**, p. 22; **Vogt**, p. 29; **Blank**, p. 47; **Jousssen**, Nr. 351; **Wagner**, p. 97; **Dörner/Staudinger**, p. 32; **Looschelders**, Nr. 456; **Schimmel/Buhlmann**, p. 240.

[18] **Palandt/Grüneberg**, § 275, Rdnr. 2; **Gauch/Schluep**, Band I, Nr. 632.

[19] "Legal impossibility occurs, when performance cannot be provided due to legal reasons." MMR 2012, 89, 91. For the differences between logical and legal impossibility, see **Berckemeyer**, p. 8 ff.

[20] **Staudinger**, Eckpfeiler, p. 309; **Vogt**, p. 31; **Medicus**, Nr. 367; **Fikentscher/Heinemann**, § 42 III 2, Nr. 369; **Mitzkait**, p. 45; **Blank**, p. 47; **Jousssen**, Nr. 358; **Dörner/Staudinger**, p. 32.

[21] **Palandt/Grüneberg**, § 275, Rdnr. 18–19; **Fikentscher/Heinemann**, § 43 II 2, Nr. 393; **Koller**, § 53, Nr. 14; **Hirse**, in: Tonner/Willingmann/Tamm, § 275, Rdnr. 26. For a detailed explanation on accomplishment and destruction of purpose, see, **Beuthien**, p. 1 ff. On the concept of destruction of purpose, also see **Quass**, p. 1 ff. on the accomplishment of purpose, also see **Sarrazin**, p. 1 ff.

[22] **Staudinger**, Eckpfeiler, p. 309; **Looschelders**, Nr. 459; **Fikentscher/Heinemann**, § 43 II 2, Nr. 393; **Palandt/Grüneberg**, § 275, Rdnr. 13; **Maile-Zinser**, p. 16. The notion of performance under § 275 is not the *act of performance*, but the *result of performance*. In other words, if the performance would not yield any results, there exists impossibility even if the debtor can act to perform. **BeckOK/Unberath**, § 275, Rdnr. 41. However, such cases must be separated from frustration of purpose (Zweckstörung), where there is an impossibility of use (Verwendungsunmöglichkeit), since the creditor has no interest in performance as he cannot use the performance as intended. In fact, in cases where the impossibility of use occurs, the performance is still possible, despite being useless for the creditor. For instance, if a bride breaks up with the groom a short time before the wedding and the wedding gown that she ordered becomes useless, there is impossibility of use. **Koller**, § 53, Nr. 15; **Looschelders**, Nr. 460; **Hütte/Helbron**, Nr. 384; **MüKo/Ernst**, § 275, Rdnr. 160. For detailed information on frustration of purpose, see **Köhler**, p. 17 ff.

[23] Former § 275/I BGB required debtor not be responsible for the occurrence of impossibility, otherwise he would not be released from his obligation to perform. Such provision was based on the Roman understanding that each obligation has a duplicate content: One party owes the primary

impossibility.[24] This is clear from the text of the provision, which states that performance cannot be claimed if performance "*is impossible*".[25] As a matter of fact, even if impossibility is caused by the debtor, it would be illogical to grant the creditor a primary claim, since the debtor would be unable to perform and performance could not be enforced in any way.[26] Considering the above view, German lawmakers have accepted that impossibility of performance causes extinguishment of the debtor's obligation to perform and this is independent from the availability of secondary (compensatory) claims of the creditor—hence the debtor's responsibility of impossibility.

Since § 275 I BGB refers to impossibility "*for the obligor or for any other person*", it is clear that the provision applies both to subjective impossibility and objective impossibility.[27] However, it is necessary to clarify which cases of subjective impossibility are covered by the said provision. Within this stance, it is arguable that under circumstances that he is not responsible for, if the debtor loses his physical disposal on the subject matter good, his obligation to perform would be extinguished.[28] However, as expressed in the reasoning of the BGB[29] and also by German courts,[30] it must be accepted that there is no subjective

claim and the other owes to make payment. Accordingly, it was argued that the debtor who is responsible for impossibility must not be relieved from his obligation to perform, otherwise the legal ground for the monetary compensation would disappear as well. Therefore the former § 275 I BGB accepted that the debtor's obligation to perform would be extinguished only if he was not responsible for impossibility. In such case, the creditor would not ask for compensation instead, and therefore no legal ground would be necessary for compensation claim. However, if the debtor was responsible for impossibility, he would still be under the obligation to perform and this would enable the monetary compensation claim of the creditor. **Fehre**, p. 30.

[24] **Fehre**, p. 22; **Blank**, p. 47; **Kötz**, Nr. 789; **Dauner/Lieb**, in: Dauner-Lieb/Heidel/Lepa/Ring, Schuldrecht, § 275, Rdnr. 4; **Zimmermann**, New German Law, p. 44; **Brunner**, p. 82; **Kollmann**, Nr. 172; **Vogt**, p. 29; **Lutz**, p. 8; **Medicus**, Nr. 378; **Fikentscher/Heinemann**, § 43 II 1, Nr. 390–391; **Finn**, p. 130; **BeckOK/Unberath**, § 275, Rdnr. 8; **Palandt/Grüneberg**, § 275, Rdnr. 5; **Schlechtriem/Schmidt-Kessel**, Nr. 474; **Knütel**, JR 2001, 353, 353 ff. **Zimmer**, NJW 2002, 1, 2; **Dörner/Staudinger**, p. 31; **Schmidt-Räntsch**, Nr. 275–277.

[25] **Huber/Faust**, Section 2, Nr. 9; **Fehre**, p. 25; **Mitzkait**, p. 39; **Palandt/Grüneberg**, BGB, § 275 Rdnr. 4; **Jousssen**, Nr. 362.

[26] **Canaris**, JZ 2001, 499, 500; **Schwingenheuer**, p. 40; **Finn**, p. 132; **Palandt/Grüneberg**, § 275, Rdnr. 5; Reasoning of BGB, Drucksache 14/6040, p. 128, available at <http://dipbt.bundestag.de/dip21/btd/14/060/1406040.pdf>.

[27] The former § 275 II BGB contained the same provision as well. However, the former distinction between subjective and objective impossibility was caused by the provision of the former § 306 BGB, which was applicable to objective impossibility only. **Fehre**, p. 23.

[28] **Huber**, Leistungsstörungen I, § 3I3a, p. 69. Also see, **Wilhelm/Deeg**, JZ 2001, 223, 226 ff.; **Zimmer**, NJW 2002, 1, 2.

[29] Reasoning of BGB, Drucksache 14/6040, p. 129, available at <http://dipbt.bundestag.de/dip21/btd/14/060/1406040.pdf>.

[30] For instance, see OLG Brandenburg, Urteil v. 31.07.2008 5 U 107/07 - JurionRS: "*It is not necessary that the debtor, alone, cannot currently make dispositions on the subject of the obligation, in order to accept impossibility in terms of § 275 paragraph 1 BGB. It must be certain that the debtor can no longer obtain disposition on the subject of the obligation, in the future as well. The*

impossibility in accordance with § 275 I BGB, when the debtor can overcome an existing obstacle to the performance, and therefore he can generate or regenerate his ability to perform through procurement or replacement.[31] As a matter of fact, if it were accepted that the loss of physical disposition on the subject-matter good would solely cause an extinguishment of the debtor's primary obligation (Primärleistungspflicht), this would end up in an unlimited release of the debtor and an extensive erosion of the right to primary claim.[32] More specifically, since § 275 I BGB applies regardless of the debtor's responsibility of the impossibility, transfer of ownership to a third party would easily enable the debtor to replace his primary obligation with a secondary (compensatory) obligation.[33]

In cases, where the debtor is obliged to perform in kind (Gattungschuld), he may obtain the subject matter goods from a third party. Therefore, in such cases, it is clear that there is no real impossibility.[34] However, in some cases the debtor may have no chance to obtain the goods from the third parties. For instance, if the third party refuses to cooperate or if he is untraceable,[35] the obstacle to the performance cannot be overcome and this constitutes real impossibility under § 275 I BGB.[36] In any case, it is required that the debtor cannot perform by spending all efforts.[37]

In an assessment about whether the debtor can overcome an obstacle to the performance through cooperation of third parties, in principle, only the financial means that have been offered may be taken into consideration. Such financial means include payments offered to third parties, or offers to release the third parties from their compensation liabilities to other persons. Within this scope, other legal actions that are not regarded as financial offers would not be usually taken into consideration. Immoral offers, or the possibility of illegal or even criminal acts

impediment must be almost insurmountable for the debtor. This can happen, for instance, in the case where the third party has definitely refused to participate in the performance."

[31] **Finn**, p. 141; **Zimmer**, NJW 2002, 1, 2; **Mitzkait**, p. 47; **MüKo/Ernst**, § 275, Rdnr. 52; **Staudinger/Löwisch**, § 275, Rdnr. 69; **Palandt/Grüneberg**, § 275, Rdnr. 23.

[32] **Finn**, p. 140; **Fehre**, p. 24.

[33] **Fehre**, p. 24. "*If the debtor gives the promised object to a third party, the performance is not automatically impossible for the debtor due to the fact that he cannot dispose on the object anymore and has no right of claim for it. However, if it is determined that the debtor cannot get his power of disposal back and cannot satisfy the claim raised for the object, impossibility occurs. As long as there is a possibility that third party grants the debtor the power of disposal again or consents to disposal, the inability for the debtor is not definite.*" MDR 2006, 79, 80.

[34] **MüKo/Ernst**, § 275, Rdnr. 51. However, such cases may lead to practical impossibility which is dealt with under § 275 II BGB. **Fehre**, p. 23; **Barta**, p. 14; **Zimmer**, NJW 2002, 1, 2. For a study on impossibility in obligation in kind, see **Rohde**, p. 1 ff.

[35] According to Ernst, the debtor would be released from his primary obligation if the third party is regarded as absolutely untraceable. However, if there is reasonable possibility for reaching the third party, no such release would take place. In such cases, § 275 II BGB may apply, if there is gross disproportion between the expenses to be made by the debtor to trace the third party and the interest of the creditor. **MüKo/Ernst**, § 275 Rdnr. 52.

[36] **Fehre**, p. 24; **Brox/Walker**, § 22, Nr. 7; **Finn**, p. 141; **BeckOK/Unberath**, § 275, Rdnr. 42.

[37] **Mitzkait**, p. 47.

against the third party (such as coercion, extortion, etc.) would not be taken into consideration as well.[38] If the debtor fails to overcome a surmountable obstacle since he lacks the required financial means, this would not also extinguish his primary obligation.[39] In fact it is a well-accepted principle that no impossibility may occur regarding monetary obligations.[40]

§ 275 I BGB applies without any distinction of partial or total impossibility. In case of partial impossibility, § 275 BGB releases the debtor from his obligation to perform the impossible part only, but the debtor is still under the obligation to perform the part which can be performed.[41] However, partial impossibility requires that the performance is divisible.[42] Therefore, if performance is indivisible in nature, or considering the content and purpose of the contract if partial performance would not satisfy the creditor, partial impossibility would be deemed to be equivalent to total impossibility.[43]

In some cases, performance may be impossible temporarily.[44] However, there is no special provision in BGB regarding temporary impossibility. The lawmakers have left the matter to the courts and the doctrine.[45] Within this stance, it is a well accepted principle that for an exemption under § 275 I BGB, performance must be permanently impossible.[46] However, under § 275 I BGB—temporary impossibility only causes the postponement of the performance on the date of maturity.[47] This being the fact, the prevailing doctrine states that—as also accepted at the time of the former law, there are some cases where temporary impossibility may be deemed as

---

[38] **Finn**, p. 143.

[39] IBR 2009, 388, 388; **Finn**, p. 141; **Staudinger/Löwisch**, § 275, Rdnr. 72; **Dedek**, in: Henssler/Graf von Westphalen, § 276, Rdnr. 12; **Willingmann/Hirse** in: Kohte/Micklitz/Rott/Tonner/Willingmann, § 276, Rdnr. 14.

[40] **Kötz**, Nr. 797; **Lorenz/Riehm**, Nr. 315. For a study on impossibility regarding monetary obligations see, **Ahrens**, p. 1 ff.

[41] **Emmerich**, § 10, Nr. 32; **BeckOK/Unberath**, § 275, Rdnr. 48; **Jauernig**, § 275, Rdnr. 7; **MüKo/Ernst**, § 275, Rdnr. 127. For studies on the partial impossibility, see **Marquardt**, p. 1 ff. **Kaplan**, p. 1 ff. For a study on initial partial impossibility during the former BGB, see **Kaplan**, Ürsprüngliche, p. 1 ff.

[42] BGHZ 116, 334, 337.

[43] **Emmerich**, § 10, Nr. 32; **BeckOK/Unberath**, § 275, Rdnr. 48; **Jauernig**, § 275, Rdnr. 7; **MüKo/Ernst**, § 275, Rdnr. 123–124; **Palandt/Grüneberg**, § 275, Rdnr. 7; **Schwab/Löhnig**, Nr. 888; **Schwarze**, § 4, Nr. 32.

[44] For detailed analysis on temporary impossibility in German law, see **Canaris**, Die einstweilige Unmöglichkeit, p. 144 ff.; **Kuhlmann/Nauen**, p. 31 ff.; **Schmidt**, p. 13 ff.; **Scheer**, p. 1 ff.; **Lenczyk**, p. 1 ff.; **Scheller**, p. 1 ff. For the distinction between default and temporary impossibility, see **Stelzer**, p. 1 ff.; **Stipanski**, p. 29 ff.

[45] **Brox/Walker**, § 22, Nr. 16. According to Canaris, the phrase "*to the extent that*" (soweit) covers temporary impossibility, in addition to partial impossibility. According to the author, any confusions regarding the scope of the provision could be avoided by inclusion of the phrase "as long as" (solange) in addition to the phrase "to the extent that" (soweit). **Canaris**, JZ 2001, 499, 500, fn. 19.

[46] BGHZ 174, 61, 65.

[47] **Kaiser**, Zeitweilige, p. 143.

permanent impossibility. Accordingly, if temporary impossibility prevents the accomplishment of the purpose of the contract (Vertragszweck) and adherence to the contract cannot be expected under principles of good faith, temporary impossibility is deemed as permanent impossibility.[48] Especially in cases that the performance time has become an element/subject of the agreement and the creditor cannot be satisfied after a certain time interval (absolute definite due date/absolutes Fixgeschäft), impossibility occurs after the lapse of such time. [49]

Once temporary impossibility is deemed as permanent impossibility, the debtor's obligation to perform would be extinguished *ipso iure*.[50] Therefore, if such obstacle disappears later on, this does not result in an automatic revival of the obligation to perform. If temporary impossibility is not equated with permanent impossibility, performance claim of the creditor is temporarily prevented during the time of impossibility.[51]

§ 275 I BGB has also eliminated the distinction of initial and subsequent impossibility. Unlike the former law, which accepted initial impossibility as a reason to void the contract, § 275 BGB applies to all cases of impossibility, including initial impossibility. This is also made clear by the first paragraph of § 311a BGB, which is titled as "*Obstacle to performance when contract is entered into*".[52] The provision reads as follows:

> (1) A contract is not prevented from being effective by the fact that under section 275 (1) to (3) the obligor does not need to perform and the obstacle to performance already exists when the contract is entered into.[53]

---

[48] **Fikentscher/Heinemann**, § 42 III 2, Nr. 377; **Finn**, p. 148. "*Namely a temporary impossibility is equal to the permanent impossibility, if it challenges the attainability of the purpose of the transaction and the other party's adherence to the contract cannot be expected until the abolition of the obstacle to the performance.*" NJW 2005, 989, 990. Similarly see MMR 2012, 89, 91.

[49] **Mitzkait**, p. 45; **Kötz**, Nr. 802; **Ród**, p. 35; **Staudinger/Otto**, § 326, Rdnr. B 24; **PWW/Schmidt-Kessel**, § 275, Rdnr. 6; **Kuhlmann/Nauen**, p. 48; **Klausch**, p. 183; **MüKo/Emmerich**, § 275, Rdnr. 46; **BeckOK/Unberath**, § 275, Rdnr. 34; **Jauernig**, § 275, Rdnr. 14; **Däubler**, p. 57; **Westermann/Bydlinski/Weber**, § 7 II 2, Rdnr. 7/8; **Palandt/Grüneberg**, § 275, Rdnr. 11; **Schwenzer**, Obligationenrecht, Nr. 63.04; **Förster**, Nr. 211; **Blank**, p. 49; **Zerres**, p. 135; **Hirse**, in: Tonner/Willingmann/Tamm, § 275, Rdnr. 15; **Maile-Zinser**, p. 14.

[50] The burden of proof regarding the length of the term of impossibility is carried by the debtor. **Gsell**, p. 280.

[51] **Finn**, p. 157. However, if the obstacle to the performance is surmountable, there exists no impossibility at all (not even temporarily). **Finn**, p. 158.

[52] On the other hand, § 311a II BGB is relevant when the debtor is responsible. However, in such cases, the requirement of the debtor's responsibility is not with regard to the occurrence of impossibility. In other words, the provision requires that the debtor knows the impossibility while concluding the contract or that the debtor is responsible for not knowing the impossibility. The provision reads as follows: "*The obligee may, at his option, demand damages in lieu of performance or reimbursement of his expenses in the extent specified in section 284. This does not apply if the obligor was not aware of the obstacle to performance when entering into the contract and is also not responsible for his lack of awareness. Section 281 (1) sentences 2 and 3 and (5) apply with the necessary modifications.*"

[53] The provision eliminates the discussions regarding the time for the assessment of initial and subsequent impossibility. Accordingly, the time to be considered for such distinction is the time

The distinction in the former BGB regarding the effects of initial and subsequent impossibility was highly criticized due to the coincidental nature of the time of occurrence of impossibility.[54] Therefore courts followed a restrictive interpretation of the former § 306 BGB,[55] which ruled the voidness of the contract[56] in case of initial objective impossibility.[57] Following such criticism, § 311a BGB, has explicitly set forth that neither subjective nor objective impossibility under § 275 BGB prevents the contract from being effective due to[58] initial impossibility.[59]

Actually, it is unusual that BGB explicitly regulates when a contract is valid. In other words, the lawmakers accept as a principle that all contracts are valid and sets the exceptional cases which make a contract invalid.[60] However, in § 311a I BGB, the lawmakers have made an exception and preferred to set forth that initial impossibility is *not* a reason of voidness. This preference is based on the aim to prevent future discussions regarding the effect of initial impossibility on the validity of a contract.[61]

---

when the contract is entered into. **Fehre**, p. 25. This is also valid for contracts with condition and term. **Fehre**, p. 25; **Palandt/Grüneberg**, BGB, § 311a, Rdnr. 4.

[54] See, **Harke**, p. 54 ff. **Kley**, p. 140.

[55] For a detailed study on initial impossibility from the perspective of former § 306 BGB see **Arp**, p. 35 ff. also see **Reinke**, p. 1 ff. **Pakuscher**, p. 1 ff.

[56] For a study on the impossibility as a reason of voidness, see **Fischer**, Unmöglichkeit, p. 1 ff.

[57] **Grunewald**, JZ 2001, 433, 434; **Fehre**, p. 25. For initial impossibility from the perspective of the former BGB, see **Pels Leusden**, p. 49 ff. For the results of initial impossibility in former BGB regarding unilateral obligations, see **Schweitzer**, p. 1 ff.

[58] If the contract is null and void for another reason (such as breach of a legal prohibition or immorality), § 311a BGB would not change such legal result. **MüKo/Ernst**, § 311a, Rdnr. 25; **Fehre**, p. 28; **BeckOK/Gehrlein**, § 311a, Rdnr. 4; **Staudinger/Löwisch**, § 311a, Rdnr. 56; **Palandt/Grüneberg**, § 311a, Rdnr. 5; Reasoning of BGB, Drucksache 14/6040, p. 165, available at <http://dipbt.bundestag.de/dip21/btd/14/060/1406040.pdf>.

[59] As a result, the lawmakers have shifted the risk against the debtor. Since the contract is valid, the debtor would be obliged to compensate the creditor's positive interest, in case of the responsibility of the debtor. **Motsch**, JZ 2001, 428, 430. However, the provision of § 311a I is in principle fully dispositive. The parties may accept in the contract that a specific impediment must not exist at the time of the formation of the contract, otherwise the debtor or the creditor would be entitled to revocation. **MüKo/Ernst**, § 311a, Rdnr. 102.

[60] **Fehre**, p. 26.

[61] **Fehre**, p. 26; **MüKo/Ernst**, § 311a, Rdnr. 2. In case of initial impossibility, the primary obligations of the parties are excluded. As a matter of fact, § 275 BGB eliminates the debtor's obligation to perform and § 326/I eliminates the creditor's counter-obligation. As a result, the contract lacks primary obligations of the parties. **Brox/Walker**, § 22, Nr. 11; **Jauernig**, § 311a, Rdnr. 4; **BeckOK/Gehrlein**, § 311a, Rdnr. 4; **Fehre**, p. 27; **Fikentscher/Heinemann**, § 43 II 1, Nr. 389; **Staudinger**, Eckpfeiler, p. 309; Reasoning of BGB, Drucksache 14/6040, p. 164, available at <http://dipbt.bundestag.de/dip21/btd/14/060/1406040.pdf>. However, since the contract is still valid, it still constitutes a basis for the secondary claims (Sekundäransprüche) of the parties. **Canaris**, JZ 2001, 499, 506; **Fikentscher/Heinemann**, § 43 II 1, Nr. 389. Moreover, since the contract is valid, the parties are bound with their side obligations (Nebenpflichten). **Staudinger/Löwisch**, § 311a, Rdnr. 21. Accordingly, if the debtor is responsible for the occurrence of impossibility, this creates an obligation to compensate the damages of the creditor.

As it has been explained above, § 275 I BGB applies to objective impossibility and subjective impossibility equally. As a result of the reference to § 275 I BGB in § 311a BGB, the provision of § 311a BGB covers both the cases of objective and subjective *initial* impossibility (initial inability).[62] Similarly, the references to § 275 II and III reflect that initial unexpectedness of performance does not prevent the validity of the contract from the perspective of § 311a BGB.[63]

Finally, in principle, § 275 BGB applies both to debt in kind (Gattungsschuld) and specific obligations (Stücksschuld/Speziesschuld).[64] However, in debt in kind, where the debtor is obliged to deliver one thing among the entire kind, real impossibility under § 275 I BGB occurs rarely because of the principle of *genus non perit*. In fact, it is a well established principle that in cases, where the subject of the obligation is determined to be in kind, damage or destruction of the goods does not constitute impossibility (*genus non perit*)—unless there is limited debt in kind (begrenzte Gattungsschuld/Vorratsschuld) and the entire stock is destroyed.[65] In other words, in case of debt in kind, the obligation of the debtor does not include a guarantee that the debtor will perform *what he has* from the in kind good, but he will perform by providing the alternative good from that kind.[66] As long as it is possible for the debtor to obtain the goods belonging to the same kind from other sources, there is no impossibility.[67]

However, there are secondary claims which are available even in cases where the debtor is not responsible for impossibility. For instance even if the debtor is not responsible for the occurrence of impossibility, the creditor is entitled to demand substitutes from the debtor. **Fehre**, p. 27; Reasoning of BGB, Drucksache 14/6040, p. 165, available at <http://dipbt.bundestag.de/dip21/btd/14/060/1406040.pdf>. If the contract were invalid, no substitutes could be claimed. The validity regime of § 311a BGB, which entitles the creditor to substitutes, enables the contract to fulfill its purpose. **Fehre**, p. 27. This is basically a result of the fact that in case of initial impossibility, a valid contractual relationship is established, but only the obligation to perform is eliminated. **Staudinger/Löwisch**, § 311a, Rdnr. 20.

[62] **Staudinger/Löwisch**, § 311a, Rdnr. 14. For information on the liability for initial inability, see **Sutschet**, NJW 2005, 1404, 1404 ff.; **Hohmeister**, p. 1 ff. Also see **Krückmann**, p. 127 ff.; **Kleineidam**, p. 45 ff. For the difference between inability and impossibility, see **Haake**, p. 1 ff. also see **Asendorf**, p. 1 ff. Specifically on the differences between initial inability and initial impossibility under the former BGB, see **Jagielski**, p. 1 ff.

[63] **Staudinger/Löwisch**, § 311a, Rdnr. 16.

[64] For a study on impossibility without the responsibility of the debtor regarding sale of a specific good and its treatment under § 275 II BGB, see **Canaris**, JZ 2004, 214, 214 ff.

[65] In case of limited debt in kind, impossibility occurs if the entire stock is destroyed. **Looschelders**, Nr. 289; **Zerres**, p. 135; **Kötz**, Nr. 793; **Huguenin**, Nr. 557; **Bucher**, p. 421.

[66] **Dural**, Sonraki İmkansızlık, p. 138.

[67] Unless there is limited debt in kind, objective real impossibility may occur if the subject-matter good is destroyed after the *concretization* of a particular piece of such kind. Within this stance, concretization refers to everything that the debtor must do as required by him for performance. **Looschelders**, Nr. 290; **Hütte/Helbron**, Nr. 97 ff. See § 243 II BGB: "*If the obligor has done what is necessary on his part to supply such a thing, the obligation is restricted to that thing.*" If there is not any concretization as well, then impossibility occurs only when the entire kind is destroyed. **MüKo/Ernst**, § 275, Rdnr. 34; **Förster**, Nr. 213; **Blank**, p. 48; **Westermann/Bydlinski/Weber**, § 7, Nr. 7/29 - 7/30; **Dullinger**, § 3, Nr. 3/52; **Jousssen**, Nr. 366; **Zerres**, p. 135; **Hütte/Helbron**,

b) Unexpectedness of Performance due to Gross Disproportionality (§ 275 II BGB)

Before the reform of BGB, there was an effort to equate certain cases of performance difficulty with real impossibility.[68] As a result of the regulation of § 275 II BGB, real impossibility, the so-called practical impossibility and collapse of the basis of transaction have found different provisions in the law. Within this stance, unexpectedness of performance due to gross disproportionality is regulated under § 275 II BGB as another boundary of the debtor's obligation to perform.[69]

§ 275 II BGB covers the cases, which are termed as practical impossibility.[70] These are the cases, where performance is theoretically possible, but no reasonable person would consider attempting performance.[71] More precisely, § 275 II BGB deals with surmountable obstacles, but insurmountable obstacles to performance are covered by § 275 I BGB as real and legal impossibility.[72] The classical example of practical impossibility is illustrated by a ring which falls to the ocean.[73]

In the assessment of surmountability, the law of nature, the boundaries of science and technology, logic and the applicable legal system would be decisive.[74] In other words, the differentiating factors between surmountable and

Nr. 385; **Markesinis/Unberath/Johnston**, p. 410. On the other hand, subjective real impossibility takes place when the debtor may have neither a thing of the kind, nor is it possible to obtain such a thing under any effort whatsoever. For instance, there is subjective real impossibility when the subject-matter good is available abroad, but the debtor cannot obtain such good due to an import ban. **Mitzkait**, p. 61. Such cases fall under § 275 BGB as well.

[68] **Fehre**, p. 32.

[69] For an analysis of § 275 II BGB from the perspective of law and economics doctrine, see **Köndgen**, p. 275 ff.

[70] Reasoning of BGB, Drucksache 14/6040, p. 129, available at <http://dipbt.bundestag.de/dip21/btd/14/060/1406040.pdf>; **Canaris**, Schuldrechtsmodernisierung, p. XII.

[71] NJW 1983, 2873, 2874.

[72] It is argued that it may be difficult to distinguish § 275/I BGB from § 275 II BGB in case of subjective impossibility. **Schlechtriem**, German Act, p. 1 ff.; **Zimmermann**, New German Law, p. 47; **Staudinger**, Eckpfeiler, p. 310. Zimmermann argues that applying the parameters of § 275 II BGB to subjective impossibility sometimes leads to unsatisfactory results. **Zimmermann**, New German Law, p. 48.

[73] Reasoning of BGB, Drucksache 14/6040, p. 130–131, available at <http://dipbt.bundestag.de/dip21/btd/14/060/1406040.pdf>.

[74] Finn, p. 137. "*Performance is objectively impossible and therefore cannot be demanded or enforced (§ 275 paragraph 1 BGB), if, under the laws of nature, or existing knowledge of science and technology it cannot be absolutely provided. It is so in case of the promise of using supernatural, 'magical' or psychic powers and abilities.*" BGHZ 188, 71, 73. According to Fehre, sometimes the obligation arising from the contract may be nonsensical according to the views of third parties at the time of contract formation. For instance, an obligation to convert a car into an airplane by using magical powers is a nonsensical obligation. Similarly, an obligation to beam someone from one place to another might be accepted as a nonsensical one. It is quite difficult to concretize which obligations are nonsensical and which are sensible. Therefore, it would be more appropriate to accept that the contract is valid in accordance with § 311a/I BGB. In other words, in accordance with the intentions of the parties, the contract must be deemed valid. **Fehre**, p. 29.

insurmountable obstacles are whether the debtor has a rational option between performing and refusing the performance.[75] Therefore the first question to be asked is a factual one, which objectively asks whether the debtor can overcome the obstacle by technical means. If the answer is negative, the obligation would be extinguished under § 275 I BGB. However, if the answer is positive, in order words if the obstacle is surmountable, a legal assessment is to be made to determine whether the debtor must spend the required efforts and expenses.[76]

§ 275 II BGB sets forth that the debtor may refuse to perform, provided that the required expenses and efforts are grossly disproportionate to the creditor's interest in performance.[77] This requires a review of the concepts of (*i*) required expenses and efforts, (*ii*) creditor's interest in performance, and (*iii*) gross disproportion.

aa) Required Expenses and Efforts

§ 275 II BGB first of all requires an assessment of the expenses and efforts required by the debtor to perform. Within this stance, the efforts and expenses refer to the expenses, which are required for the procurement or manufacturing of the subject-matter of the obligation.[78] In this stance, it must be underlined that the provision not only focuses on the financial aspect of the issue but also on the activities and personal efforts to be made by the debtor.[79] However, only the actual expenses to be made are covered by this provision, not the loss of other opportunities.[80]

In principle, the expenses and efforts that are required for performance at the time of the *last* oral negotiation must be taken into consideration.[81] In other words, any expenses and efforts that have been made *during* the time of negotiation must

---

[75] **Medicus**, Nr. 376.

[76] **Finn**, p. 135.

[77] § 275 II BGB: "*The obligor may refuse performance to the extent that performance requires expense and effort which, taking into account the subject matter of the obligation and the requirements of good faith, is grossly disproportionate to the interest in performance of the obligee. When it is determined what efforts may reasonably be required of the obligor, it must also be taken into account whether he is responsible for the obstacle to performance.*"

[78] **Staudinger/Löwisch**, § 275, Rdnr. 93.

[79] **Fehre**, p. 40; **Klausch**, p. 87; **Mitzkait** p. 49; **BeckOK/Unberath**, § 275, Rdnr. 55; **Jauernig**, § 275, Rdnr. 25; **Canaris**, JZ 2001, 499, 501; **Hirse**, in: Tonner/Willingmann/Tamm, § 275, Rdnr. 38; **Dauner/Lieb**, in: Dauner-Lieb/Heidel/Lepa/Ring, Schuldrecht, § 275, Rdnr. 15; **jurisPK-BGB/Alpmann**, § 275, Rdnr. 28; **Maile-Zinser**, p. 34.

[80] Opportunity costs are not taken into consideration within the scope of the assessment of required expenses and efforts. Opportunity costs are profits that could be acquired through other transactions that could be made by the debtor, if he had not concluded the contract with the creditor. The debtor cannot claim to be released from his duty to perform with an argument based on opportunity costs because when concluding the contract with the creditor, the debtor has already relinquished from other transactions which may bring profit. **Fehre**, p. 41; **MüKo/Ernst**, § 275 Rdnr. 85; **Huber/Faust**, Section 2, Nr. 60.

[81] **Fehre**, p. 41; **MüKo/Ernst**, 275 Rdnr. 84; **Huber/Faust** Section 2, Nr. 33.

be disregarded from the scope of § 275 II BGB. However, before refusing the performance by claiming practical impossibility, the debtor might have commenced the performance process and he might have already incurred some expenses and efforts. Here, the question is the following: when claiming gross disproportionality, can a debtor also count the expenses and efforts that he has already made, or only the *future* efforts and expenses that are required to perform? It would be appropriate to accept that not only additional efforts and expenses, but also past efforts and expenses must be considered.[82] However, only the justified efforts and expenses of the debtor must be taken into consideration. In other words, all efforts and expenses, which are not objectively required must be disregarded regardless of the time they are (to be) made.[83]

Pursuant to § 275 II s. 2 BGB, the debtor's responsibility for impossibility increases the limits of the efforts and expenses to be expected from the debtor for overcoming the impediment.[84] In fact, when the debtor is responsible for the obstacle to the performance, more efforts and expenses would be expected from the debtor making it more difficult to be released from the obligation to perform.[85] Moreover, in cases where the debtor, either by culpable error or in knowledge of the legal situation, transfers the subject matter of the contract to a third party, the debtor must spend considerably more than the market price to repurchase the good in order to be released from his primary obligation.[86] It must also be noted that, although it is not explicitly stated in the law, not only the existence of the debtor's fault but the type of such fault must be considered as well.[87] In other words, intention, gross negligence, and light negligence of the debtor would make difference in such assessment.

Finally, in cases, where the debtor has undertaken to spend specific amount of efforts to perform, he cannot argue that there is disproportion between his concretized efforts and the creditor's interest in performance. Similarly, in cases where the debtor has undertaken to make unlimited amounts of expenses, in order words when he has undertaken the expense risk, he cannot ask to be released from his obligation in accordance with § 275 II.[88]

---

[82] **Mitzkait**, p. 49; **MüKo/Ernst**, § 275, Rdnr. 84.

[83] **Fehre**, p. 41–42; **MüKo/Ernst**, § 275, Rdnr. 84.

[84] **Mitzkait**, p. 56.

[85] **Fehre**, p. 43; **Mitzkait**, p. 56; **Dedek**, in: Henssler/Graf von Westphalen, § 275, Rdnr. 15; **Schmidt-Räntsch**, Nr. 289; **MüKo/Ernst**, § 275, Rdnr. 72; Reasoning of BGB, Drucksache 14/6040, p. 131, available at <http://dipbt.bundestag.de/dip21/btd/14/060/1406040.pdf>.

[86] **Canaris**, JZ 2001, 499, 502; **BeckOK/Unberath**, § 275, Rdnr. 56.

[87] **Mitzkait**, p. 57.

[88] **MüKo/Ernst**, § 275, Rdnr. 77.

bb) Creditor's Interest in Performance

The reference in § 275 II BGB to the creditor's interest is made to the creditor's interest in the *primary claim*. The provision requires a comparison of the creditor's interest in primary claim with the efforts and expenses to be made by the debtor. However, the point of reference is the individual situation of the specific/concrete creditor.[89]

A calculation of the creditor's interest in performance requires a distinction between the material and immaterial interests of the creditor. In cases where the interest of the creditor has a material nature, creditor's interest in performance corresponds to the amount of compensation that he would receive instead of specific performance.[90] This includes for example, consequential damages or any resale profit that could be achieved by the creditor if the debtor had performed.[91] However, it is possible that the subject matter of the good has a sentimental value to the creditor, which is even higher than the economic value of the good. In this stance, in the doctrine it is argued that when calculating the interest of the creditor in performance, such sentimental value of the good to the creditor must also be taken into consideration.[92] This is necessary to maintain an efficient protection of the creditor.[93]

The creditor's interest in performance must be assessed at the time of maturity, which is the time, when the creditor must receive the performance.[94] However, the legal results (compensation claims), which arise from the debtor's release from the obligation to perform would not be considered in calculation of the creditor's interest in performance.[95]

---

[89] **MüKo/Ernst**, § 275, Rdnr. 78.

[90] **MüKo/Ernst**, § 275, Rdnr. 79; **Fehre**, p. 42.

[91] **MüKo/Ernst**, § 275, Rdnr. 79.

[92] **MüKo/Ernst**, § 275 Rdnr. 80; **Staudinger/Löwisch**, § 275, Rdnr. 92; **Fehre**, p. 42; **Huber/Faust**, Section 2, Nr. 27; **BeckOK/Unberath**, § 275, Rdnr. 54.

[93] **Mitzkait**, p. 50

[94] **MüKo/Ernst**, § 275 Rdnr. 80.

[95] If these legal results are taken into consideration in comparison of interests, the creditor's interest in performance would be comparatively higher, whenever he had no compensation claim against the debtor; because, when the creditor is entitled to compensation due to non-performance, this would decrease his interest in performance. In other words, the gap between the creditor's interest and the required efforts and expenses of the debtor would be higher when the debtor is responsible for impossibility. As a result, it would be easier for the debtor, who is responsible for the obstacle to be released from his obligation to perform under § 275 II BGB. **Fehre**, p. 43; **MüKo/Ernst**, § 275, Rdnr. 81; **Huber/Faust**, Section 2 Nr. 31. On the other hand, when the debtor is not responsible for impossibility, since the creditor will not receive compensation due to non-performance, he would be better-off if the debtor performed. In other words, the creditor would have higher interest in performance. In such cases the disproportion between the creditor's interest in performance and the debtor's interest in non-performance would be lower. Therefore it would be harder for the debtor to rely on § 275 II BGB to be released from his

cc) Gross Disproportion

Gross disproportion exists, when a reasonable person would not obviously spend the required efforts and expenses to perform, even when he could perform.[96] As rightfully argued by Faust, if any change in external circumstances takes place after the conclusion of the contract, the required expenses of the debtor and the creditor's interest in performance at the time of assessment are to be compared. However, how much the *proportion* between the expense and interest has changed due to the obstacle to performance would not be decisive.[97] In other words, the fact that there is a change in the proportion cannot be regarded as gross disproportion as long as the debtor's expenses are still less than the creditor's interest in performance.[98] In fact, at all times, the creditor's interest in performance is the lower threshold of the expenses and efforts to be required from the debtor.[99] Therefore, when the value of the expenses and efforts required from the debtor is below the value of the creditor's interest in performance, there is no disproportion under § 275 II BGB. [100]

Existence of disproportion is not sufficient under § 275 II BGB to release the debtor from his obligation to perform. As a matter of fact the law sets forth that the disproportion must be "gross" "*taking into account the subject matter of the obligation and the requirements of good faith*".[101] In other words, to claim release

---

obligation. This would contradict with the logic and also the intention of the lawmakers. **Fehre**, p. 43.

[96] **MüKo/Ernst**, § 275 Rdnr. 89.

[97] Huber/Faust name this as absolute approach. **Huber/Faust**, Section 2, Nr. 43–44. On the other hand, relative approach considers how the proportion between the required expenses of the debtor and the creditor's interest in performance has changed within time. **Huber/Faust**, Section 2, Nr. 43. In other words, according to the relative approach only the change is decisive. Within this context, there is disproportion if the proportion between the expenses and efforts of the debtor and the creditor's interest in performance has changed against the benefit of one of the parties. **Fehre**, p. 44.

[98] **Huber/Faust**, Section 2, Nr. 43.

[99] **Fehre**, p. 45; **Huber/Faust**, Section 2, Nr. 45.

[100] **Fehre**, p. 45.

[101] In case of defective performance, § 439 I BGB entitles the buyer to "*demand that the defect is remedied or a thing free of defects is supplied.*" However, if the defect cannot be cured under § 275 I - III BGB, this constitutes qualitative impossibility (qualitative Unmöglichkeit). In case of qualitative impossibility, the debtor's release from his obligation to perform may occur under any of the paragraphs of § 275 BGB, including paragraph 2. However, § 439 III BGB, which deals with defective goods, enables the seller's release from his obligation under lower standards than § 275 II BGB. The said provision reads as follows: "*Without prejudice to section 275 (2) and (3), the seller may refuse to provide the kind of cure chosen by the buyer, if this cure is possible only at disproportionate expense. In this connection, account must be taken in particular, without limitation, of the value of the thing when free of defects, the importance of the defect and the question as to whether recourse could be had to the alternative kind of cure without substantial detriment to the buyer. The claim of the buyer is restricted in this case to the alternative kind of cure; the right of the seller to refuse the alternative kind of cure too, subject to the requirements of sentence 1 above, is unaffected.*" For a study on the competition between the rules of impossibility and the rules on defective performance, see **Lehmann**, Unmöglichkeit, p. 1 ff.

from the obligation to perform under § 275 II BGB, the lack of proportionality must be so drastic that the claim of specific performance must appear pointless and quite abusive.[102] Therefore, an assessment of gross disproportion requires a case-by-case analysis.[103]

Pursuant to § 275 II BGB, the subject matter of the obligation is a decisive factor in the assessment of disproportionality. Accordingly, the subject matter of the obligation refers to all rights and duties of the parties.[104] Within this scope, the content of the contract could either lead to a tightening of the scale (if there is an assumption of risk), or a mitigation result (in case of a restriction of a contractual obligation).[105]

The first obligation of the debtor is to show all efforts that he has undertaken under the contract. This requires an assessment of the fact if any foreseeable difficulty of performance has already been taken into consideration in calculation of the counter-obligation.[106] Gross disproportion can only occur if an obstacle has occurred after the formation of the contract or if the debtor considered the obstacle thereafter.[107] As it has been explained above, if the debtor has undertaken a specific risk or expense risk, he cannot be released from his obligation to perform with a claim of disproportion.[108]

In an evaluation of gross disproportion, the type of the obligation plays an important role. For instance, if the subject matter of the obligation is a unique good (Stückschuld/Speziesschuld) and it has been stolen, the efforts to be expected from the debtor to re-procure the good would not be set too high because it is unlikely that the debtor would be able to recover and deliver the stolen specific good to the creditor. On the other hand, in case of a debt in kind, the debtor must perform by re-obtaining goods.[109]

Another principle to be considered in assessment of gross disproportion is the requirements of good faith. In the doctrine, the reference to good-faith is criticized to be highly superfluous.[110] Therefore there are some attempts to set some specific cases when gross disproportion is to be accepted due to the requirements of good faith. For instance, Faust argues that when a *creditor* is responsible for an obstacle, which strongly increases the expenses and efforts required by the debtor, or when such increase takes place during the *creditor's* default of acceptance, gross disproportionality must be accepted.[111]

---

[102] **MüKo/Ernst**, § 275, Rdnr. 70.

[103] **Staudinger/Löwisch**, § 275, Rdnr. 96.

[104] **Staudinger/Löwisch**, § 275, Rdnr. 100.

[105] **BeckOK/Unberath**, § 275, Rdnr. 55.

[106] **Canaris**, JZ 2001, 499, 502; **Fehre**, p. 46.

[107] **Mitzkait**, p. 51–52.

[108] **Mitzkait**, p. 51; **Fehre**, p. 47; **MüKo/Ernst**, § 275, Rdnr. 87.

[109] **Canaris**, JZ 2001, 499, 502; **Fikentscher/Heinemann**, § 43 II 3. Nr. 397.

[110] **MüKo/Ernst**, § 275 Rdnr. 88.

[111] **Huber/Faust**, Section 2, Nr. 50; **Fehre**, p. 49.

The analysis of gross disproportion requires making a cost-benefit analysis between the expenses to be made for performance and the creditor's interest in performance. Therefore, the subject matter of the obligation and the requirements of good faith must be taken into consideration only to the extent that they affect the expenses to be made, or the interest in performance, or the proportion between the two.[112] Moreover, the provision does not cover all cases where performance cannot be expected from the debtor, but only those cases where performance cannot be expected as a result of the cost-benefit analysis and due to the gross inefficiency of performance.[113]

Due to the existence of various criteria regarding the assessment of gross disproportion, in the doctrine there is a tendency for concretization of the ratio for gross disproportion. Accordingly, Faust proposes that there is gross disproportion between the required expenses of the debtor and the creditor's interest in performance, if the required expenses and efforts exceed the creditor's interest in performance by: [114]

i. 110 %, when the debtor is not responsible for the obstacle to the performance;
ii. 120 %, when the debtor is responsible for the obstacle to the performance, despite the lack of his fault;
iii. 130 %, when the debtor has light negligence;
iv. 140 %, when the debtor has gross negligence; and
v. 150 %, when the debtor has intention.

Fehre uses the same criteria with Faust, but proposes that the ratios must be 180, 190, 200, 210 and 220 % respectively.[115] Despite being against a numerical determination, Medicus proposes that there is gross disproportion if the required expenses are equal to 300 % of the creditor's interest in performance.[116]

According to above proposals, the existence of gross disproportion is directly correlational to the responsibility of the debtor. Most probably this is based on the second sentence of § 275 II BGB, which states that "*When it is determined what efforts may reasonably be required of the obligor, it must also be taken into account whether he is responsible for the obstacle to performance.*" It has already been explained that when the debtor is responsible for the obstacle, an increased effort would be expected from him to overcome such obstacle.[117]

---

[112] **MüKo/Ernst**, § 275, Rdnr. 69.

[113] **MüKo/Ernst**, § 275, Rdnr. 74.

[114] **Huber/Faust**, Section 2, Nr. 68.

[115] **Fehre**, p. 51–52.

[116] **Medicus**, Rdnr. 370.

[117] **MüKo/Ernst**, § 275, Rdnr. 72; **Staudinger/Löwisch**, § 275, Rdnr. 102; Reasoning of BGB, Drucksache 14/6040, p. 131, available at <http://dipbt.bundestag.de/dip21/btd/14/060/1406040.pdf>.

It must be noted that the second sentence of § 275 II BGB would only apply in case of subsequent obstacles to performance.[118] As it has been explained above, the new BGB has eliminated the difference between initial and subsequent impossibility, and § 275 BGB applies regardless of the time of occurrence of impossibility. However, a distinction must be made between these two types of impossibility from the perspective of the responsibility of the debtor because in cases of initial impossibility it is not considered if the debtor is responsible for the *occurrence* of impossibility. In such cases, it matters if the debtor was *aware* or should have been aware of the occurrence of impossibility while concluding the contract.[119] Such awareness of the debtor completely eliminates the claim of gross disproportion because such obstacles have been included in the equilibrium of the contract at the time of contract formation.[120]

The efforts to concretize the criteria of gross disproportion is based on good-intentions to create uniformity in application of law. However, if it was possible to concretize the border of gross disproportion, lawmakers would set such values in the law.[121] Lawmakers have preferred to accept a provision, which is flexible enough to cover the characteristics of each specific case. In the provision, there is reference to both the subject matter of the obligation and the requirements of good faith. Therefore an attempt to make such concretization would only undermine the functioning of § 275 II BGB. As a matter of fact even the authors who propose ratios to concretize the border of gross disproportion accept that such ratios may be changed in specific cases.[122]

Finally, it must be noted that the cases dealt with under § 275 II BGB have more of a theoretical importance. In a proper assessment of the creditor's interest, it is generally seen that there is no disproportion within the scope of § 275 II BGB. In fact, in an obligation to deliver goods in kind, a price increase which increases the expenses and efforts to be made by the debtor, also increases the creditor's interest in performance in the same ratio.[123] In fact, if the debtor fails to perform, the debtor would have to purchase the good from the market at its increased price. Therefore, in such cases there is no disproportion within the scope of § 275 II BGB between the required efforts and expenses of the debtor and the creditor's interest in performance.[124] However, as it will be explained below in further details, depending on the features of the case, the debtor may rely on § 313 BGB.

---

[118] **MüKo/Ernst**, § 275 Rdnr. 103.

[119] **Mitzkait**, p. 56–57; **Klausch**, p. 104; **Wallow**, p. 26.

[120] **Mitzkait**, p. 56–57.

[121] Medicus also states that setting such ratios to determine gross disproportion fails. **Medicus**, Nr. 372.

[122] For instance, see **Fehre**, p. 52.

[123] **Zimmermann**, New German Law, p. 46; **MüKo/Ernst**, § 275, Rdnr. 93; **Fehre**, p. 45.

[124] **Brunner**, p. 83; **Fehre**, p. 45; **Huber/Faust**, Section 2, Nr. 41.

dd) Difference Between Practical Impossibility and the Interference with the Basis of the Transaction (§ 313 BGB)

After World War I, long-term contracts were rendered ruinous for one of the parties due to inflation in Germany. The former *Reichsgericht* applied the provisions of impossibility to such cases. However, after 1923, the doctrine of the collapse of the basis of transaction (Wegfall der Geschäftsgrundlage) was created and regularly applied by the German courts to decide cases of the so-called economic impossibility.[125] The new BGB has explicitly regulated such cases under § 313 BGB, which is titled as "*Interference with the basis of the transaction*".[126] The provision reads as follows:

(1) If circumstances which became the basis of a contract have significantly changed since the contract was entered into and if the parties would not have entered into the contract or would have entered into it with different contents if they had foreseen this change, adaptation of the contract may be demanded to the extent that, taking account of all the circumstances of the specific case, in particular the contractual or statutory distribution of risk, one of the parties cannot reasonably be expected to uphold the contract without alteration.
(2) It is equivalent to a change of circumstances if material conceptions that have become the basis of the contract are found to be incorrect.
(3) If adaptation of the contract is not possible or one party cannot reasonably be expected to accept it, the disadvantaged party may revoke the contract. In the case of continuing obligations, the right to terminate takes the place of the right to revoke.

§§ 275 II, 313 BGB have some similarities. In fact, the legal results of performance difficulty and the boundaries of the debtor's obligation to perform is dealt with not only under § 275 II BGB, but also under § 313 BGB regarding the interference with the basis of the transaction. However, there are also important differences between these two provisions.

One of the major differences between §§ 313 BGB and § 275 II BGB is that § 275 II BGB focuses on the relationship between the required expenses by the debtor and the creditor's interest in performance.[127] In other words, it concentrates solely on the interest of the creditor, but not the debtor's interest.[128] However, the doctrine of interference with the basis of the transaction makes an interest assessment from the debtor's side.[129] It concentrates on the expenses of the debtor and burdens associated with such expenses or the disturbance of the balance between the

---

[125] **Brunner**, p. 79.

[126] For a procedure law approach to § 313 BGB, see **Schmidt-Kessel**, NJW 2002, 2076, 2076 ff.

[127] Reasoning of BGB, Drucksache 14/6040, p. 130, available at <http://dipbt.bundestag.de/dip21/btd/14/060/1406040.pdf>; **Brox/Walker**, § 22, Nr. 21; **Maile-Zinser**, p. 48.

[128] **Canaris**, JZ 2001, 499, 501; **Finn**, p. 515; **Mitzkait**, p. 50; **BeckOK/Unberath**, § 275, Rdnr. 53; **Eckert**, Nr. 306; **Petersen**, Nr. 263; **Schmidt-Recla**, p. 662. For a critique of § 275 II BGB in comparison with § 313 BGB, see **Schmidt-Recla**, p. 641 ff. **jurisPK-BGB/Alpmann**, § 275, Rdnr. 34.

[129] **Brox/Walker**, § 22, Rdnr. 21; **Finn**, p. 515; **Mitzkait**, p. 50; **Maile-Zinser**, p. 48; **Lorenz/Riehm**, Nr. 408.

obligations of the parties.[130] In other words, interference with the basis of the transaction deals with the difference between the expenses that have been priorly calculated by the debtor and those that are actually required at the time of performance.[131] It is examined if the performance of the obligation is "worth" the counter-obligation that the debtor would receive in return [132]

As explained above, in case of interference with the basis of the transaction, the performance has become burdensome at the expense of the debtor, but there is no gross disproportion as in § 275 II BGB.[133] More specifically, when the value of the performance increases, the creditor's interest in receiving performance increases proportionally as well; hence the performance which has become burdensome to the debtor is not disproportionate to the interest of the creditor.[134] Therefore an objective increase in the market price of the good may cause collapse of the basis of transaction under § 313 BGB. However, § 275 II BGB cannot be used when the market price of the subject-matter good has increased, but only when the procurement of the good has become particularly costly for the specific debtor.[135]

The results of the provisions are different as well. § 275 II BGB grants the debtor a right of defense to refuse performance. On the other hand, under § 313 BGB the debtor may firstly demand adaptation of the contract.[136] In other words, in principle § 313 BGB does not eliminate the debtor's obligation to perform completely. However, "*if adaptation of the contract is not possible or one party cannot reasonably be expected to accept it, the disadvantaged party may revoke the contract.*"[137]

In comparison to the rigid all-or-nothing approach of the impossibility regime in § 275 II BGB, § 313 BGB has more flexible legal results.[138] Therefore in the prior drafts of the BGB, it was assumed that the collapse of the basis of transaction has priority before the impossibility regime of § 275 II BGB.[139] However, application of § 313 BGB requires the existence of an obligation to perform, so that it can be

---

[130] **Canaris**, JZ 2001, 499, 501.

[131] **Fehre**, p. 44.

[132] **MüKo/Ernst**, § 275, Rdnr. 75.

[133] **Fikentscher/Heinemann**, § 43 II 3, Nr. 398; **Canaris**, Neuregelung, p. 14.

[134] **Fehre**, p. 45; **Brunner**, p. 83; **MüKo/Ernst**, § 275, Rdnr. 93; **Huber/Faust**, Section 2, Nr. 41.

[135] **Finn**, p. 519. Even for this reason, when compared to § 313 BGB, the cases dealt with under § 275 II BGB have more of a theoretical importance. In fact it is comparatively unlikely to experience cases, which fall under the so-called practical impossibility.

[136] For a study on the adaptation request and the obligation to negotiate (Verhandlungspflichten) under § 313/I BGB, see **Lüttringhaus**, p. 266 ff.

[137] For the relationship between revocation of the contract due to impossibility and revocation due to collapse of the basis of transaction, see **Feldhahn**, NJW 2005, 3381, 3382.

[138] **Brox/Walker**, § 22, Nr. 21; **Fehre**, p. 54; **BeckOK/Unberath**, § 275, Rdnr. 33.

[139] **Fehre**, p. 54. For the opinion that the debtor must be given the right to choose between refusing performance under § 275 and using his rights under § 313 BGB, see **Emmerich**, § 3, Nr. 68; **MüKo/Ernst**, § 275, Rdnr. 23; **Huber/Faust**, Section 2, Nr. 79; **Staudinger/Löwisch**, § 275, Rdnr. 115; **Palandt/Grüneberg**, § 275, Rdnr. 29.

subject to adaptation. Therefore in the Government Draft, the priority has been given to the impossibility doctrine.[140] In other words, in cases where §§ 275 II, 313 BGB coincide, firstly it must be assessed whether the debtor can refuse performance due to practical impossibility. If the answer is positive, there would be no ground to apply § 313 BGB. However, in cases where the answer is negative, it must be determined whether the debtor may demand adaptation or revocation of the contract due to collapse of the basis of transaction.

c) Unexpectedness of Performance due to Personal Reasons (§ 275 III BGB)

§ 275 III BGB[141] deals with unexpectedness of performance due to personal reasons, *i.e.*, moral impossibility.[142] The provision covers performances that must be rendered by the debtor in person. In such cases, since personal qualifications of the debtor are very important, the debtor cannot perform through an agent. This is generally the case in employment contracts.[143] The classical example of moral impossibility is the soprano who refuses to sing after she has learnt that her son has a life-threatening disease.[144]

The difference between § 275 I and III BGB is not always very clear. Especially a distinction needs to be made between the two provisions with regard to the employee's inability to work (disability). Accordingly, if the performance is personal in nature and it is definitely excluded due to the disease of the employee, this

[140] **Fehre**, p. 54; **Finn**, p. 516; Reasoning of BGB, Drucksache 14/6040, p. 176, available at <http://dipbt.bundestag.de/dip21/btd/14/060/1406040.pdf>.

[141] § 275 III BGB: "*In addition, the obligor may refuse performance if he is to render the performance in person and, when the obstacle to the performance of the obligor is weighed against the interest of the obligee in performance, performance cannot be reasonably required of the obligor.*"

[142] In the former BGB, moral impossibility was dealt with under the rules concerning change of circumstances. **Zimmermann**, New German Law, p. 49. For a study on the unexpectedness of performance due to personal reasons, see **Joachim**, p. 49 ff.

[143] **MüKo/Ernst**, § 275, Rdnr. 112. For a case on moral impossibility, where a Turkish employee is called for his compulsory military service in Turkey and the employee was granted the right to refuse performing the employment contract for the duration of military service, see NJW 1983, 2782.

[144] **Canaris**, Schuldrechtsmodernisierung, p. XIII; **Zimmermann**, New German Law, p. 49; **Brunner**, p. 84; **Staudinger**, Eckpfeiler, p. 310; **Fikentscher/Heinemann**, § 43 II 4, Nr. 400; **Klausch**, p. 112; **BeckOK/Unberath**, § 275, Rdnr. 34; **MüKo/Ernst**, § 275, Rdnr. 118. It is debated in the doctrine, if § 275 III BGB covers performance difficulty arising from reasons of conscience. For instance, it is debatable if a catholic doctor may refuse to participate in an abortion, or a female publisher may refuse to publish a misogynistic paper. **Fikentscher/Heinemann**, § 43 II 5, Nr. 401. In such cases the reasoning of the law makes reference to § 313 BGB, dealing with collapse of the basis of transaction or § 242 BGB on performance in good faith. See Reasoning of BGB, Drucksache 14/6040, p. 130, available at <http://dipbt.bundestag.de/dip21/btd/14/060/1406040.pdf>.

constitutes real impossibility. On the other hand, if the employee can theoretically perform despite his illness but expecting the performance would be excessive, the employee may only be released from his obligation to perform in accordance with § 275 III BGB.[145]

The distinction between § 275 II and III BGB is not very clear as well.[146] The main reason for inclusion of a special provision in addition to § 275 II is that practical impossibility requires a pure cost-benefit analysis, which is objectified in financial terms and thus abstracted from the personality of the debtor. However, such analysis is not appropriate for performances that must be rendered personally.[147]

In cases, where the performance can only be rendered by personal sacrifice, the debtor must be given the chance to be released from his obligation to perform in an easier way than in § 275 II BGB.[148] § 275 III BGB requires a comparison between the creditor's interest in performance and the debtor's obstacle to performance.[149] In contrast to § 275 II BGB, § 275 III BGB does not consider the quantity of the expenses required by the debtor and it also does not require the existence of gross disproportion.[150]

The provision of § 275 III BGB equates impossibility with unreasonableness. Accordingly, under the provision, the debtor is released from the obligation to perform in any case that expecting such sacrifice is unreasonable.[151] Contrary to § 275 II BGB, the responsibility of the debtor for impossibility is not a decisive factor in assessment of what can reasonably be expected of the debtor.[152] As a matter of fact, the idea behind § 275 III BGB is that the debtor must be released from his obligation to perform even if he is responsible for the occurrence of moral impossibility.[153]

---

[145] **MüKo/Ernst**, § 275, Rdnr. 39; **Staudinger/Löwisch**, § 275, Rdnr. 108; **jurisPK-BGB/Alpmann**, § 275, Rdnr. 39.

[146] **Fehre**, p. 55; **Zimmermann**, New German Law, p. 49.

[147] **MüKo/Ernst**, § 275, Rdnr. 107.

[148] **Huber/Faust**, Section 2, Nr. 87. When the obstacles may be overcome by the use of financial means, § 275 II BGB would apply; if § 275 II BGB is not relevant, § 313 BGB may apply. **Fehre**, p. 57.

[149] **Fikentscher/Heinemann**, § 43 II 4, Nr. 400.

[150] **Medicus**, Nr. 375.

[151] Within this stance, expecting performance is unreasonable, when the negative results of performance for the debtor are highly burdensome in comparison to the interest of creditor in performance. **Fehre**, p. 56.

[152] **Zimmermann**, New German Law, p. 49; **Fehre**, p. 55.

[153] **Jauernig**, § 275, Rdnr. 30. For instance, the soprano may refuse to sing even if she, herself, has caused the illness of her child. **Zimmermann**, New German Law, p. 49. The responsibility of the debtor for moral impossibility rather affects the claims of counter-obligation and compensation. **Fehre**, p. 56.

Similar to practical impossibility, in case of moral impossibility both material and immaterial interests of the creditor are taken into consideration.[154] Within this scope, in case of a conflict of interests, the creditor's interest in performance may be higher. For instance, a nurse may have to leave her sick child alone in order to give a life-saving medicine to a patient.[155] However, the creditor's interest in performance is only one aspect to be considered in determining the issue of unreasonableness on the basis of a general balancing of interests, rather than a decisive criterion.[156]

Although it is not explicitly stated in the law, similar to § 275 II BGB, when making an assessment of unexpectedness under § 275 III BGB, subject matter of the obligation and the requirements of good faith would be considered.[157] Moreover, the criteria accepted by the court decisions regarding employment contracts (§ 606 BGB) may be helpful.[158]

2) Legal Results of Impossibility Under German Law

a) In General

During the reform of 2002, the German lawmakers did not diverge from the civil law tradition of fault-liability. Accordingly, impossibility of performance is subject to different legal results depending on the existence of the debtor's responsibility for the occurrence of impossibility. Therefore prior to explaining the legal results of impossibility, the issue of responsibility of the debtor must be examined.

b) Responsibility of the Debtor

The responsibility of the debtor is regulated under § 276 BGB. The provision with the heading "*Responsibility of the obligor*" reads as follows:

> (1) The obligor is responsible for intention and negligence, if a higher or lower degree of liability is neither laid down nor to be inferred from the other subject matter of the obligation, including but not limited to the giving of a guarantee or the assumption of a procurement risk. The provisions of sections 827 and 828 apply with the necessary modifications.
> (2) A person acts negligently if he fails to exercise reasonable care.
> (3) The obligor may not be released in advance from liability for intention.

---

[154] **Mitzkait**, p. 59; **Klausch**, p. 135.

[155] **Staudinger/Löwisch**, § 275, Rdnr. 106.

[156] **Zimmermann**, New German Law, p. 49. According to the author, § 275 III BGB is a specific manifestation of the rules regarding change of circumstances and therefore "*undermines the subtle line the law has drawn in § 275 II between impossibility and change of circumstances.*"

[157] **Mitzkait**, p. 59; **MüKo/Ernst**, § 275 Rdnr. 113; **Wagner**, p. 101.

[158] See **Fehre**, p. 56.

As it is clearly seen in the provision, above all, the debtor is responsible for fault either in the form of intention or negligence. In this stance, negligence covers the cases where the debtor fails to exercise reasonable care. According to § 278 BGB, when he is in default, the debtor is responsible for all negligence.[159] Moreover, if the debtor has given a guarantee or assumed the procurement risk, he would be responsible regardless of his fault. Finally, the reference to §§ 827, 828 points to another requirement for the debtor's responsibility. Accordingly, the debtor must have the capacity of responsibility [160]

In civil law, until proven otherwise, the debtor is accepted to be at fault for non-performance. In fact, this is clearly expressed in the wording of § 280 I s. 1. The said provision sets forth that:

> If the obligor breaches a duty arising from the obligation the obligee may demand damages for the damage caused thereby. In this stance, the creditor does not need to prove that the debtor is at fault in the occurrence of impossibility.

However, according to § 280 I s. 2, which is phrased as an exception to the preceding sentence, "*This does not apply if the obligor is not responsible for the breach of duty.*" When evaluated as a whole, the provision shows that in order to be released from his obligation, the debtor carries the burden of proof that he is not at fault in the occurrence of impossibility.[161] In other words, unless the debtor can prove that he is not at fault in the occurrence of impossibility, he would be deemed responsible. The reason why the burden of proof is placed on the debtor is that usually the debtor is in a position to know and explain the circumstances, which caused impossibility of performance.[162]

In an attempt to prove that he is not at fault with regard to impossibility, the debtor has two options. Firstly, the debtor may prove that he has no fault in the occurrence of the circumstance which rendered the performance impossible. Secondly, the debtor may choose to prove that there is no causal link between the said circumstance (for which the debtor is faulty) and the occurrence of impossibility.[163] In the first case, the debtor may prove that the creditor or a third party is responsible for impossibility; in the second case, the debtor may prove that impossibility is caused by an accident (unexpected situation/Zufall/cas fortuit) or *force majeure*.[164] If the debtor can prove either of the above stated facts, he would be accepted to lack responsibility for the occurrence of impossibility.

---

[159] § 278 BGB: "*While he is in default, the obligor is responsible for all negligence. He is liable for performance in the case of chance as well, unless the damage would have occurred even if performance had been made in good time.*"

[160] **Looschelders**, Nr. 519.

[161] **Emmerich**, § 9, Nr. 22; **Mitzkait**, p. 119.

[162] **Emmerich**, § 9, Nr. 23; **Medicus**, Nr. 385.

[163] **Emmerich**, § 9, Nr. 25.

[164] The terms cas fortuit and *force majeure* are mentioned under Article 1148 CC as reasons which prevent damage claim for non-performance. The terms are used equivalently in French law to refer to cases, where the performance is prevented without the fault of the debtor. **Zweigert/Kötz**, p. 498; **Brunner**, p. 67.

At this point it is necessary to underline that the debtor's responsibility may arise also due to his responsibility for third parties. In fact, according to § 278 BGB, the debtor is responsible also for the fault of "*his legal representative, and of persons whom he uses to perform his obligation.*"[165] § 278 BGB s. 2 indicates that the debtor may be released in advance from such liability.

An assessment of the debtor's responsibility for the occurrence of impossibility is particularly important because the lawmakers have bound some legal results to the debtor's responsibility. First of all, legal results of impossibility for which the debtor is not responsible would be studied below.

c) Legal Results of Impossibility for Which the Debtor Is Not Responsible

aa) Extinguishment of the Primary Obligation (§ 275 I, II and III BGB)

As explained above, the debtor's obligation to perform is eliminated in all cases of impossibility dealt with under § 275 BGB.[166] Although there are slight differences regarding extinguishment of the primary obligation under § 275 I–III BGB, in all cases the debtor who refuses to perform in accordance with § 275 BGB carries the burden of proof regarding impossibility of performance.[167]

Extinguishment of the debtor's primary obligation will be explained below for each case separately.

(1) Extinguishment of the Primary Obligation Under § 275 I BGB

Under § 275 I BGB, the extinguishment of the debtor's primary obligation refers to an objection (Einwendung) that the judge must consider *ex officio*. In fact, the debtor is not obliged to apply to the court or the creditor to be released from his obligation to perform. The effects of objection take place *ipso iure* at the time of the occurrence of impossibility.[168] In case of impossibility under § 275 I BGB, such extinguishment is the only logical solution,[169] because in cases of real impossibility there is no chance for the debtor to perform under any circumstances.[170]

---

[165] § 278 BGB: "*The obligor is responsible for fault on the part of his legal representative, and of persons whom he uses to perform his obligation, to the same extent as for fault on his own part. The provision of section 276 (3) does not apply.*"

[166] "*... the impossibility applies only to the sole obligation to perform, not the obligatory relationship (Schuldverhältnis) in its entirety.*" MMR 2012, 89, 91.

[167] **Finn**, p. 173; **Fikentscher/Heinemann**, § 43 IV 4, Nr. 459; **MüKo/Ernst**, § 275, Nr. 162; **Staudinger/Otto**, § 326, Nr. B 69.

[168] **Fehre**, p. 31; **Vogt**, p. 29; **Finn**, p. 154.

[169] **Fehre**, p. 32.

[170] Schlechtriem states that in the Discussion Draft of BGB, it was proposed that the debtor must refuse performance in order to be released from his obligation to perform. However, in the final draft it was accepted that § 275 I BGB automatically eliminates the debtor's obligation. This is

(2) Extinguishment of the Primary Obligation Under § 275 II BGB

Similar to § 275 I BGB, § 275 II BGB enables the debtor to be released from his obligation to perform. However, unlike § 275 I BGB, which sets forth the automatic extinguishment of the primary obligation, § 275 II BGB gives a right of defense to refuse performance (Einrede) to the debtor.[171]

The solution, which grants an objection right to the debtor, gives the debtor the chance to perform his obligation, even when it requires excessive efforts.[172] This is logical in cases, where the debtor has the alternative to perform.[173] For instance, the debtor may prefer to perform so that he can receive the counter-obligation. Similarly the debtor may choose to perform if the capacity will remain unused otherwise or if he wants to prove his ability to perform in cases where he expects to receive further profitable orders from the same customer in the future. [174]

(3) Extinguishment of the Primary Obligation Under § 275 III BGB

§ 275 III BGB enables the debtor to refuse performance in case of moral impossibility. Similar to § 275 II BGB, § 275 III BGB gives a right of defense to refuse performance to the debtor due to unreasonableness of expecting performance. In fact, generally the creditor is unaware of the personal obstacles faced by the debtor. Therefore, in order to inform the creditor, the condition for the debtor's release from his obligation to perform is that the debtor relies on his right of refusal against the creditor.[175]

bb) Counter-Obligation

It has been explained that in cases falling under § 275 BGB, the debtor is released from his obligation to perform. At this point appears the question, whether the creditor who cannot receive the subject-matter of the contract must still perform the counter-obligation. Such question is answered under § 326 BGB. Accordingly, § 326 I s. 1 BGB sets forth that "*If, under section 275 (1) to (3), the obligor is not*

criticized as an influence of the former BGB's approach: no obligation in case of impossibility. **Schlechtriem**, German Act, p. 1 ff.

[171] Reasoning of BGB, Drucksache 14/6040, p. 129, available at <http://dipbt.bundestag.de/dip21/btd/14/060/1406040.pdf>.

[172] **Fehre**, p. 52; **Brunner**, p. 84; **Medicus**, Nr. 376; **Förster**, Nr. 233; **MüKo/Ernst**, § 275, Rdnr. 96; **BeckOK/Unberath**, § 275, Rdnr. 61; **Huber/Faust**, Section 2, Nr. 6.

[173] **Canaris**, Kategorie der Unmöglichkeit, p. 48; **Medicus**, Unmöglichkeit, p. 349.

[174] **Fehre**, p. 52; **Medicus**, Nr. 376.

[175] **Fehre**, p. 57.

obliged to perform, there is no entitlement to consideration; in the case of part performance, section 441 (3) applies with the necessary modifications."[176]

The basis of § 326 I BGB is the *synallagma* between the obligations of the parties.[177] Therefore first condition of § 326 I BGB is the existence of a reciprocal contract.[178] Pursuant to § 326 I BGB, in cases where the debtor is released from his obligation to perform, the creditor is released from his obligation of counter-performance as well. In other words, the counter-obligation risk (Gegenleistungsgefähr) is carried by the debtor, but the performance risk (Leistungsgefähr) belongs to the creditor.[179] However, statutory obligations, in addition to unilateral contracts and imperfect reciprocal contracts (unvollkommen zweiseitige Verträge) such as donation, gratuitous loan, mandate and suretyship are excluded from the scope of the provision.[180]

The second condition of § 326 I BGB is exclusion of the performance in accordance with § 275 I–III BGB.[181] In cases where the debtor is released from his obligation to perform, the creditor is released from his obligation of counter-performance *ipso iure*. In cases which fall under § 275 II and III BGB, the counter-obligation claim collapses when the debtor uses his right of refusal to perform.[182] When the creditor refuses to perform the counter-obligation in accordance with § 326 I BGB, he carries the burden of proof that performance of the primary obligation has become impossible under § 275 I–III BGB.[183]

The provision makes a distinction between full and partial impossibility. Accordingly, in case of partial performance by the debtor, the creditor is not released from the counter-obligation in full. In such cases, by reference to §

---

[176] As it will be explained below, § 326/I s. 2 BGB sets forth that "*Sentence 1 does not apply if the obligor, in the case of failure to perform in conformity with the contract, does not, under section 275 (1) to (3), have to effect cure.*"

[177] **Palandt/Grüneberg**, § 326, Rdnr. 2; **BeckOK/Grothe**, § 326, Rdnr. 2.

[178] **Staudinger/Otto**, § 326, Rdnr. B 18; **BeckOK/Grothe**, § 326, Rdnr. 4; **MüKo/Ernst**, § 326, Rdnr. 7.

[179] **Palandt/Grüneberg**, § 275, Rdnr. 33. However, exceptionally in some cases the law has placed the price risk beforehand on the creditor. Accordingly, §§ 326 II, 446, 447, 616, 644, 645, 2380 BGB and § 56 I ZVG (Foreclosure Law) are examples of such exceptional provisions. In such cases, the creditor is obliged to perform the counter-obligation, even if he does not receive the performance of the debtor. **Emmerich**, § 9, Nr. 6; **Staudinger, Eckpfeiler**, p. 311; **Fikentscher/Heinemann**, § 43 IV 3, Nr. 454.

[180] **Brox/Walker**, § 22, Nr. 32. In imperfect reciprocal contracts, the creditor's counter obligation arises after the birth of the obligation of the debtor. Therefore in such contracts, when the first obligation becomes impossible to perform, the second obligation does not come to existence at all. As a result, in such contracts, there is no room to apply the provision.

[181] **BeckOK/Grothe**, § 326, Rdnr. 5; **Brox/Walker**, § 22, Nr. 31; **Staudinger/Otto**, § 326, Rdnr. B 21.

[182] **Huber/Faust**, Section 5, Nr. 51; **Schlechtriem/Schmidt-Kessel**, Nr. 493; **Fikentscher/Heinemann**, § 43 IV 1, Nr. 447; **MüKo/Ernst**, § 326, Rdnr. 8; **Staudinger/Otto**, § 326, Rdnr. B 21.

[183] **Fikentscher/Heinemann**, § 43 IV 4, Nr. 459.

441 III BGB, the creditor's counter-obligation would be proportionally reduced[184] and the reduction would take place *ipso iure*.[185] If the creditor has objectively no interest in partial performance and wants to be fully released from the counter-obligation, he must revoke the contract under § 326 BGB.[186] In fact this is completely logical, when it is considered that in case of partial impossibility, § 275 BGB releases the debtor from his obligation to perform the impossible part only, but the debtor is still under the obligation to perform the part which can be performed.[187]

At this point specific emphasis must be given to § 326 I s. 2 BGB, which sets forth an exception to the above-explained first sentence of the same provision in cases of qualitative impossibility.[188] According to the provision, unlike partial impossibility, in case of qualitative impossibility, where the debtor cannot recover the defect and perform as undertaken in the contract, the counter-obligation would not be reduced *ipso iure*. The logic behind the provision is to grant the creditor the right to choose between reduction of the counter-obligation and revocation of the contract (Rücktritt).[189] In fact, in warranty law, reduction is a right that should be used by declaration.[190] Therefore, the creditor must not be forced by law to choose

---

[184] § 326 I sets forth that "*in the case of part performance, section 441 (3) applies with the necessary modifications.*" § 441 III reads as follows: "*In the case of a price reduction, the purchase price is to be reduced in the proportion in which the value of the thing free of defects would, at the time when the contract was entered into, have had to the actual value. To the extent necessary, the price reduction is to be established by appraisal.*"

[185] **MüKo/Ernst**, § 326, Rdnr. 18. Such provision regarding partial impossibility would also apply to temporary impossibility. This means that as long as temporary impossibility exists, the creditor is entitled not to perform the counter-obligation. Provided that the creditor loses his interest in the performance in case of delay, the creditor is also entitled to terminate the contract. Reasoning of BGB, Drucksache 14/6040, p. 189, available at <http://dipbt.bundestag.de/dip21/btd/14/060/1406040.pdf>.

[186] **Fikentscher/Heinemann**, § 43 IV 2, Nr. 448; **Huber/Faust**, Section 5, Nr. 59; **Emmerich**, § 10, Nr. 33; **Wieser**, MDR 2002, 858, 861; **Staudinger/Otto**, § 326, Rdnr. B 40; Reasoning of BGB, Drucksache 14/6040, p. 188, available at <http://dipbt.bundestag.de/dip21/btd/14/060/1406040.pdf>. However, it must be underlined that such loss of interest does not cause partial impossibility revert into full impossibility. This means that the creditor's obligation is not extinguished *ipso iure*, and the counter-obligation is not fully eliminated. In case of loss of interest in partial performance, the creditor is given a right to revoke the contract. This might then end up in full extinguishment of the obligations of both parties. **Wieser**, MDR 2002, 858, 861. According to Ernst, in such cases the *debtor* does not have the right of revocation, since partial impossibility has affected the performance of the debtor. Hence the debtor must bear its consequences in the first place. **MüKo/Ernst**, § 326, Rdnr. 25.

[187] However, an application of § 441 III requires that the counter-obligation is divisible; otherwise the provision would not apply. **MüKo/Ernst**, § 326, Rdnr. 28. If performance is indivisible in nature, partial impossibility would be deemed to be equivalent to full impossibility. **Emmerich**, § 10, Nr. 32; **Staudinger/Otto**, § 326, Nr. B 40.

[188] **MüKo/Ernst**, § 326, Rdnr. 32 ff. **Staudinger/Otto**, § 326, Rdnr B 57 ff.

[189] **Staudinger/Otto**, § 326, Rdnr. B 66; **Lorenz/Riehm**, Nr. 327.

[190] **Hütte/Helbron**, Nr. 441.

the reduction option. Hence his right to revoke the contract is protected.[191] As a result, the creditor's counter-obligation remains in full, but the creditor may choose to revoke the contract under §§ 326 V, 323 V s. 2 BGB, or decrease the counter-obligation under §§ 441, 638 BGB.[192]

In case of temporary impossibility, the debtor is not obliged to perform under § 275 II BGB as long as impossibility exists. Similarly, during that period the counter-obligation cannot be claimed from the creditor. However, if impossibility disappears within time, the counter-obligation of the creditor reappears.[193] Finally, in cases where temporary impossibility is deemed as permanent impossibility, and the debtor's obligation to perform is extinguished permanently, the counter-obligation of the creditor is extinguished permanently as well.[194]

§ 326 II BGB sets forth some exceptions to the principle accepted in the first paragraph of the same provision. The logic behind § 326 II BGB is that no one may derive rights from his legally deprecated behavior, which makes the performance by the other party impossible or difficult.[195] Accordingly, in the following two cases indicated under § 326 II BGB, the debtor retains the entitlement to the counter-obligation, although the creditor cannot receive the debtor's performance:

i. If the creditor is "*solely or very predominantly responsible for the circumstance*" which eliminates the debtor's obligation to perform under § 275 BGB; and
ii. "*If the circumstance for which the obligor is not responsible occurs at a time when the obligee* (creditor) *is in default of acceptance*".

If the creditor is "*solely or very predominantly responsible for the circumstance*" which eliminates the debtor's obligation to perform, the counter-obligation risk is shifted to the creditor.[196] However, the lawmakers do not state the reasons which cause responsibility of the *creditor*.[197] Within this stance, §§ 276, 278 BGB are not directly applicable since they regulate the responsibility of the *debtor*.[198] Therefore, it is necessary to concretize some cases where the creditor is solely or predominantly responsible. In the first place the creditor may be deemed responsible due to the contractual risk distribution.[199] Moreover, the creditor's responsibility may arise due to an intentional or negligent breach of his contractual primary obligations or side obligations. By analogy to § 278 BGB, the creditor may be responsible for

---

[191] **Staudinger/Otto**, § 326, Rdnr. B 58.

[192] **Staudinger/Otto**, § 326, Rdnr. B 59.

[193] **Canaris**, JZ 2001, 499, 500; **Schwingenheuer**, p. 42.

[194] **Canaris**, JZ 2001, 499, 500.

[195] **BeckOK/Grothe**, § 326, Rdnr. 3; **MüKo/Ernst**, § 326, Rdnr. 41.

[196] **MüKo/Ernst**, § 326, Rdnr. 11.

[197] For a detailed study on the responsibility of the creditor, see **Dötterl**, p. 19 ff. For a study on impossibility for which both the debtor and the creditor are responsible, see **Reinhard**, p. 16 ff. Also see **Seichter**, p. 1 ff.

[198] **Fikentscher/Heinemann**, § 43 IV 2, Nr. 451.

[199] **MüKo/Ernst**, § 326, Rdnr. 52.

the acts of the third parties, *i.e.*, "*his legal representative, and of persons whom he uses to perform his obligation*" (Hilfspersonen).[200] On the other hand, "very predominant" responsibility of the creditor would be assessed in a comparison with the responsibility of the debtor.[201] In any case, the debtor carries the burden of proof regarding responsibility of the creditor.[202]

The creditor's default of acceptance also shifts the counter-obligation risk to the creditor. In such cases, the risk is carried by the creditor prior to the due date of the full performance.[203] However, this requires the lack of debtor's responsibility for the occurrence of impossibility.[204] The debtor's responsibility in case of default of acceptance is regulated by § 300 I BGB.[205] Accordingly, the debtor is held responsible only for his intentional or grossly negligent behaviour. In other words, in case of light negligence of the debtor, no responsibility would occur.[206] As a result, if the debtor has only light negligence, he can still claim the counter-obligation.[207]

§ 326 II BGB intends to put the debtor in such position as if the contract had been properly carried out. In other words, the debtor's position would neither be better nor worse as a result of a circumstance for which the creditor is solely or very predominantly responsible.[208] Although in the two cases listed under § 326 II BGB, the creditor must perform the counter-obligation even if he cannot receive the subject-matter of the contract,[209] the second sentence of § 326 II BGB protects the creditor, who is obliged to perform the counter-obligation without receiving the debtor's performance. Accordingly, in such cases the debtor "*must allow to be credited against him what he saves due to release from performance or acquires or wilfully fails to acquire from other use of his labour.*" To be more specific, the counter-obligation of the creditor must be reduced firstly in the amount of the saving the debtor has made due to non-performance of the contractual obligation.

---

[200] **Brox/Walker**, § 22, Nr. 39; **Fikentscher/Heinemann**, § 43 IV 2, Nr. 451.

[201] **Brox/Walker**, § 22, Nr. 40. The lawmakers have not regulated in detail the results of impossibility, for which both the debtor and creditor are responsible. Within this stance, § 326 II BGB is a rare case, where the lawmakers have regulated the effects of impossibility caused by both parties of a contract. **Staudinger/Otto**, § 326, Rdnr. C 73.

[202] **Fikentscher/Heinemann**, § 43 IV 4, Nr. 459.

[203] **Palandt/Grüneberg**, § 326, Rdnr. 10; **MüKo/Ernst**, § 326, Rdnr. 12.

[204] **Fikentscher/Heinemann**, § 43 IV 2, Nr. 453; **MüKo/Ernst**, § 326, Rdnr. 69.

[205] § 300/I BGB reads as follows: "*The obligor is, during the period of the default of the obligee, only responsible for intent and gross negligence.*"

[206] **MüKo/Ernst**, § 326, Nr. 69.

[207] **Brox/Walker**, §22, Nr. 44; **Fikentscher/Heinemann**, § 43 IV 2, Nr. 453.

[208] **MüKo/Ernst**, § 326, Rdnr. 80.

[209] If the creditor's act constitutes a breach of duty under § 280 I BGB (or a tortuous act), the debtor can ask for compensation in addition to the counter-performance. **Staudinger/Otto**, § 326, Rdnr. C 72; **MüKo/Ernst**, § 326, Rdnr. 83.

These include transportation and postage costs as well as fees, wear and tear of machinery and equipment, and the residual value of the non-transferred matter.[210] In fact, even if the contract was performed as stipulated in the contract, the debtor would have to make such expenses to receive the counter-obligation of the creditor. In this case the debtor would be excessively protected if he received the counter-obligation in addition to saving the expenses required for his performance. The second item, which must be reduced from the creditor's counter-obligation is the earnings that the debtor makes due to using his labor otherwise. Again in this case, the debtor would not be able to use his labor to make such earnings if he performed the contract as negotiated. Similarly, if he has willfully failed to use his labor otherwise, this must be deducted from the counter-obligation that he will receive. It is not required in such failure that the debtor has intended to harm the creditor. It is enough that the debtor willfully chooses to stay idle, when he is aware of a reasonable earning opportunity and the disadvantages of staying idle to the creditor.[211] In any case, the said deduction would take place automatically without a claim of the creditor.[212] However, the creditor carries the burden of proof regarding existence of savings, acquisitions, etc.[213]

cc) Substitutes

In some cases, where the performance of the obligation becomes impossible, the debtor may acquire substitutes or a claim of substitute.[214] For instance, if the subject matter good is damaged or destroyed by a third party in the sphere of control of the debtor, the debtor acquires compensation claim from the third party. Similarly, the debtor might have insured the good so that he would receive compensation from the insurance company, or compensation in case of expropriation (*commodum ex re*).[215] § 285 I BGB sets forth that in such cases, if the debtor is released from his obligation to perform under § 275 BGB,[216] the creditor "*may demand return of what has been received in reimbursement or an assignment of the claim to reimbursement.*"[217] § 285 I BGB is based on the idea that when the debtor

[210] **BeckOK/Grothe**, § 326, Rdnr. 21.

[211] **BeckOK/Grothe**, § 326, Rdnr. 21.

[212] If the debtor was unaware of the availability of such deduction and has performed the entire counter-obligation, he may request return of the deductable amount through the provisions of unjust enrichment (§ 812/I BGB). **MüKo/Ernst**, § 326, Nr. 84.

[213] **Fikentscher/Heinemann**, § 43 V, Nr. 459.

[214] For a study on surrogation principle in case of impossibility, see **Kalbhen**, p. 1 ff.

[215] **Emmerich**, § 10, Nr. 20.

[216] As explained above, in cases, which fall under § 275 II and III BGB, the debtor must first of all use his right to refuse performance. Reasoning of BGB, Drucksache 14/6040, p. 145, available at <http://dipbt.bundestag.de/dip21/btd/14/060/1406040.pdf>.

[217] "*Since such obligation of the claimant has become impossible within the meaning of § 275 BGB, in principle, as compensation, the claimant owes according to the leasing contract,*

is released from performing the primary claim (under § 275 BGB), he must at least transfer to the creditor the substitute of the promised performance. This would prevent an improper distribution of assets.[218]

According to § 285 I BGB, subject matter of the obligation must be an object; hence acts and omissions cannot be accepted as object in accordance with the provision.[219] Moreover, § 285 I BGB requires that the debtor "*obtains reimbursement or a claim to reimbursement for the object owed*".[220] Therefore, it is not enough that the debtor could have obtained the substitute. The creditor can only claim what the debtor has actually obtained.[221] Within this stance, the debtor is not obliged to care for receiving a substitute in case of impossibility, especially through insurance of the good.[222] Anyway, the creditor carries the burden of proof regarding existence of a substitute.[223]

In cases where the debtor sells and delivers the subject-matter good to a third party, the counter-obligation that he receives (*commodum ex negotiatione*) is subject to § 285 I BGB as well.[224] Otherwise such breach of the contract by the debtor would be risk free.[225] This applies even in cases where the counter-obligation received by the debtor exceeds the value of the subject-matter good. This aims to prevent a speculation by the debtor at the expense of the creditor.

In order for the creditor to claim the substitutes, there must be a causal link between the obstacle to the performance and acquisition of the substitute.[226] In other words, the debtor must have received the substitute (or a claim of substitutes)

---

the surrogate of the amortization or transfer on account of performance of the claim on the insurance claim assigned to the defendant." AG Hamburg-Altona, Urteil v. 11.08.2004 319B C 79/04 - JurionRS. For an evaluation on the availability of the claim of substitutes in cases of initial impossibility, see **Hammen**, Stellvertretendes, p. 41 ff.

[218] **Fikentscher/Heinemann**, § 43 III 5, Nr. 442; **Mitzkait**, p. 117; **BeckOK/Unberath**, § 285, Rdnr. 1; **MüKo/Emmerich**, § 285, Rdnr. 2; **Palandt/Grüneberg**, § 285, Rdnr. 2.

[219] **Palandt/Grüneberg**, § 285, Rdnr. 3.

[220] **Emmerich**, § 10, Nr. 19; **Mitzkait**, p. 117. § 285 BGB sets fort that the substitute of the "object owed" may be demanded by the creditor. Therefore, it is argued that the provision would not apply when the debtor is released from his obligation due to moral impossibility because in such cases the subject matter of the obligation is not an object but services. **BeckOK/Unberath**, § 285, Rdnr. 7.

[221] **BeckOK/Unberath**, § 285, Rdnr. 14; **Palandt/Grüneberg**, § 285, Rdnr. 9.

[222] **Staudinger/Löwisch**, § 285, Rdnr. 8.

[223] **Fikentscher/Heinemann**, § 43 V, Nr. 459; **BeckOK/Unberath**, § 285, Rdnr. 21; **MüKo/Emmerich**, § 285, Rdnr. 39; **Staudinger/Löwisch**, § 285, Rdnr. 60; **Palandt/Grüneberg**, § 285, Rdnr. 13.

[224] **Kötz**, Nr. 808; **Förster**, Nr. 288; **Fikentscher/Heinemann**, § 43 III 5, Nr. 443; **Emmerich**, § 10, Nr. 21; **Mitzkait**, p. 117; **Brox/Walker**, § 22, Nr. 27; **BeckOK/Unberath**, § 285, Rdnr. 10; **Jauernig**, § 285, Rdnr. 7; **jurisPK-BGB/Alpmann**, § 285, Rdnr. 17.

[225] **Mitzkait**, p. 117; **MüKo/Emmerich**, § 285, Rdnr. 22.

[226] **BeckOK/Unberath**, § 285, Rdnr. 8; **Mitzkait**, p. 117; **MüKo/Emmerich**, § 285, Rdnr. 17; **Staudinger/Löwisch**, § 285, Rdnr. 30.

as a result of the circumstance, which renders performance impossible.[227] Finally, the object that the debtor had initially undertaken to perform and the object that the debtor is later on released to perform must be identical.[228]

In the doctrine it is accepted that the scope of § 285 I BGB is restricted to the contractual and legal relationships concerning delivery of goods and rights, including immaterial rights.[229] Moreover, unlike the former law, it is not relevant whether impossibility is initial or subsequent.[230] Similarly the provision applies to full and partial impossibility without any distinction. In other words it is irrelevant whether the subject matter of the contract is partially damaged or completely destroyed.[231] Finally, the creditor's right to claim substitutes is independent from the debtor's responsibility for impossibility. In other words, such right is available both in cases where the debtor is not required to pay compensation to the creditor,[232] and even in cases where the creditor is responsible for impossibility.[233]

§ 285/I BGB only grants the creditor the right to claim the substitutes from the debtor. In other words, the substitutes are not automatically acquired by the creditor.[234] In case of uncertainty as to whether the creditor will exercise his rights under § 285 BGB, the debtor may set a reasonable deadline to the creditor for deciding whether to proceed under § 285 BGB or not. After expiry of such period, the liability of the debtor would be mellowed. In other words, the debtor would not be obliged to deliver the full amount of substitute, but only the amount that remains.[235]

---

227 **Palandt/Grüneberg**, § 285, Rdnr. 7; **Staudinger/Löwisch**, § 285, Rdnr. 30. § 285 II further sets forth that "*If the obligee may demand damages in lieu of performance, then, if he exercises the right stipulated in subsection (1) above, the damages are reduced by the value of the reimbursement or the claim to reimbursement he has obtained.*" This prevents the enrichment of the creditor at the expense of the debtor. **Emmerich**, § 10, Nr. 23.

228 **Palandt/Grüneberg**, § 285, Rdnr. 8. If impossibility is caused by the damage or destruction of the raw material that is required for the subject matter of the contract, § 285 I BGB would not apply. Similarly, § 285 I BGB is excluded when the leased property is destroyed because in such cases the lessor is under an obligation to leave the leased property to the lessee only for use. However, the compensation received by the lessor from the third party is given due to the destruction of the good and it pertains to the total value of the leased property. **Emmerich**, § 10, Nr. 21.

229 **MüKo/Emmerich**, § 285, Rdnr. 4; **Emmerich**, § 10, Nr. 16.

230 **Staudinger/Löwisch**, § 285, Rdnr. 28; **Emmerich**, § 10, Nr. 16; **MüKo/Emmerich**, § 285, Nr. 3.

231 **Emmerich**, § 10, Nr. 17; **MüKo/Emmerich**, § 285, Rdnr. 12.

232 **Fehre**, p. 27; **Emmerich**, § 10, Nr. 17.

233 **BeckOK/Unberath**, § 285, Rdnr. 7; **Emmerich**, § 10, Nr. 17; **MüKo/Emmerich**, § 285, Nr. 14.

234 **Fikentscher/Heinemann**, § 43 III 5, Nr. 443; **Emmerich**, § 10, Nr. 24; **MüKo/Emmerich**, § 285, Rdnr. 29; **BeckOK/Unberath**, § 285, Rdnr. 13; **Palandt/Grüneberg**, § 285, Rdnr. 9. However, in cases where the creditor is entitled to compensation, the debtor cannot force the creditor to demand substitutes under § 285 I BGB. **Emmerich**, § 10, Nr. 24.

235 **MüKo/Emmerich**, § 285, Rdnr. 34.

Despite the request of the creditor, if the debtor does not transfer the substitutes to the creditor, the creditor may apply to the guarantors and pledgers. In fact, their responsibility still exists, since it is based on the original performance that the guarantors and pledgers have guaranteed.[236] Similarly, the claim of substitutes is subject to the same prescription period with the claim of performance.However, it begins when the substitute claim arises.[237] If the delivery of the substitutes becomes impossible due to a reason for which the debtor is responsible, the debtor must compensate the value of such substitute to the creditor.[238]

The claim of substitutes is independent from the amount of damages suffered by the creditor due to non-performance. In other words, the value of the substitutes might be more or less than the damages suffered.[239] In each case, the debtor must transfer to the creditor anything that he has received as substitute.[240] The amount to be transferred to the creditor includes the emoluments and interests incurred, but requires the subtraction of the expenses, which are made to obtain the substitute.[241]

Finally, as set forth under § 326 III BGB, if the creditor demands the substitutes or assignment of the claim to the substitutes, "*he remains obliged to render consideration*". In other words, in bilateral contracts when the creditor receives the substitutes from the debtor, then he must also perform the counter-obligation stipulated under the contract. Within this stance, if the value of the substitutes is more than the value of the original performance owed by the debtor, the amount of consideration (the creditor's counter-obligation) would be reserved as in the contract.[242] On the other hand, if the value of the substitutes is less than the value of the original performance owed by the debtor, the amount of consideration (the creditor's counter-obligation) would be proportionally reduced.[243]

dd) Return of Already Performed Counter-Obligation

As explained above, in cases where the debtor is released from his obligation to perform under § 275 BGB, § 326 I BGB eliminates the creditor's obligation of

[236] **Palandt/Grüneberg**, § 285, Rdnr. 9; **Emmerich**, § 10, Nr. 25.

[237] **Emmerich**, § 10, Nr. 25.

[238] **MüKo/Emmerich**, § 285, Rdnr. 32

[239] **Emmerich**, § 10, Nr. 26; **MüKo/Emmerich**, § 285, Rdnr. 30.

[240] **MüKo/Emmerich**, § 285, Rdnr.30.

[241] **Emmerich**, § 10, Nr. 26.

[242] § 326 III BGB indicates that § 441 III would apply to such reduction of consideration. **BeckOK/Grothe**, § 326, Rdnr. 10. "*... any further claim on the payment of additional profits through the substitute is not available, according to the value judgment of the law. According to the value judgment of the law, the creditor can, instead, reclaim the substitute, when it has a higher value than the provided performance.*" AG Hamburg-Altona. Urteil v. 11.08.2004 319B C 79/04 – JurionRS.

[243] **Staudinger**, Eckpfeiler, p. 359; **BeckOK/Grothe**, § 326, Rdnr. 10; **Huber/Faust**, Section 5, Nr. 55.

counter-performance. However, it is possible that the creditor might have already performed the counter-obligation prior to the occurrence of impossibility. § 326 IV BGB regulates that in cases where the counter-obligation is excluded (as a result of the extinguishment of the primary claim), but the creditor has already performed the counter-obligation, "*what is performed may be claimed back.*" According to the provision, the return would take place under the provisions of §§ 346 to 348, which regulate the return of performance received and emoluments taken in case of revocation.[244]

The creditor's claim of return appears *ipso iure*. However, in cases covered by § 275 II and III, it is required that the debtor uses his right to refuse performance.[245] When the creditor claims return under § 326 IV BGB, he must both prove that the obligation is extinguished under § 275 BGB and he has already performed.[246]

In cases where impossibility is partial, the creditor's counter-obligation would be reduced proportionally. In such cases, the creditor is entitled to demand partial return of the counter-obligation.[247] In other words, the creditor may only demand the amount which exceeds the proportionally reduced counter-obligation.[248]

ee) Creditor's Right to Revocation

§ 326 V BGB sets forth that "*If, under section 275 (1) to (3), the obligor does not have to perform, the obligee may revoke*" the contract. Moreover, the provision makes reference to the application of § 323 "*with the necessary modifications to the revocation, subject to the proviso that it is not necessary to specify a period of time*".[249]

The former § 325 I enabled the creditor to revoke bilateral contracts only when the debtor was responsible for subsequent impossibility.[250] In contrast, the current BGB grants the creditor the right of revocation, even in cases where the debtor is not responsible for impossibility.[251] This is a very successful choice of the German

[244] This provision regulates the return of what has been performed before extinguishment of the counter-obligation. However, if performance has taken place after extinguishment of the counter-obligation, return would take place in accordance with the provisions regarding unjust enrichment (§ 812 BGB). **MüKo/Ernst**, § 326, Rdnr. 99.

[245] **Staudinger/Otto**, § 326, Rdnr. E 3.

[246] **Staudinger/Otto**, § 326, Rdnr. E 16.

[247] **Staudinger**, Eckpfeiler, p. 331; **MüKo/Ernst**, § 326, Rdnr. 18.

[248] **Staudinger**, Eckpfeiler, p. 331.

[249] In fact, in such cases it would be meaningless to specify a certain amount of time. **Staudinger/Otto**, § 326, Rdnr. F 8.

[250] **Emmerich**, § 10, Nr. 27. In the former BGB, initial impossibility was a reason of voidness of the contract. Therefore in such cases there existed no contract that could be revoked.

[251] **Dörner/Staudinger**, p. 38; **Rüssmann**, p. 285. According to Emmerich, such amendment has importance only in limited cases because in cases where the debtor has no responsibility for

lawmakers. In fact, there may be some cases, where the creditor may prefer to revoke the contract, even if the debtor is not responsible for impossibility.

Within this scope, the said amendment has importance in three cases. First case is the following: As a result of the reference in the second half of the first sentence of § 326 I BGB to § 441 BGB, partial impossibility is not enough to release the creditor from his entire counter-obligation, but in such cases the counter-obligation of the creditor would only be proportionally reduced. In such cases, the creditor may be released from the entire contract only through revocation.[252]

Since, the new provision enables the creditor to revoke the contract even if debtor has no responsibility, the second case that the said amendment has importance is where the creditor is unaware if the debtor is responsible for non-performance or not. Creditor may use his right to revocation in any case. For revocation under § 323 I BGB, it bears even no significance whether there exists impossibility or not, as the provision refers to non-performance in general.[253] As a matter of fact, if there is impossibility and the debtor is released from his obligation to perform under § 275 BGB, § 326 V BGB eliminates the requirement to specify additional time for revocation. However, even in cases where the creditor is unaware of the reason of non-performance, the creditor may always specify an additional period for performance and revoke the contract directly under § 323 I BGB.[254]

The third case where such amendment has importance is qualitative impossibility. In case of qualitative impossibility, the debtor's obligation to perform is eliminated under § 275 I–III BGB. This is very logical since the debtor cannot recover the defect and perform as undertaken in the contract. However, as explained above, pursuant to § 326 I s. 2 BGB, in case of an unrecoverable defect, the counter-obligation is not automatically reduced or eliminated. In other words, the creditor is still obliged to perform the counter-obligation. At this point, the creditor may be released from his entire obligation to perform only through revocation.[255]

---

impossibility, § 326 I BGB releases the creditor from his counter-obligation. Therefore there would generally be no need for the creditor to revoke the contract. **Emmerich**, § 10, Nr. 28.

[252] **Emmerich**, § 10, Nr. 28; **Staudinger**, Eckpfeiler, p. 311; **Staudinger/Otto**, § 326, Rdnr. F 2; **Brox/Walker**, § 22, Nr. 82; **Fikentscher/Heinemann**, § 43 IV 4, Nr. 457; **Klausch**, p. 245; **BeckOK/Grothe**, § 326, Rdnr. 35; **Huber/Faust**, Section 5, Nr. 66; **Köhler/Lorenz**, p. 40.

[253] **Emmerich**, § 10, Nr. 29; **Staudinger**, **Eckpfeiler**, p. 311; **Köhler/Lorenz**, p. 41; **Staudinger/Otto**, § 326, Rdnr. F 2; **Brox/Walker**, § 22, Nr. 85–86; **Fikentscher/Heinemann**, § 43 IV 4, Nr. 457; **Klausch**, p. 245; **BeckOK/Grothe**, § 326, Rdnr. 36; **Huber/Faust**, Section 5, Nr. 64.

[254] § 323 I reads as follows: "*If, in the case of a reciprocal contract, the obligor does not render an act of performance which is due, or does not render it in conformity with the contract, then the obligee may revoke the contract, if he has specified, without result, an additional period for performance or cure.*"

[255] **Brox/Walker**, § 22, Nr. 83; **Köhler/Lorenz**, p. 40; **Fikentscher/Heinemann**, § 43 IV 4, Nr. 457; **BeckOK/Grothe**, § 326, Rdnr. 34; **Staudinger/Otto**, § 326, Rdnr. F 2; **Huber/Faust**, Section 5, Nr. 67. Since § 326/V BGB makes reference to § 323 BGB, a valid revocation requires the breach of contract, namely the defect, not being trivial. **Fikentscher/Heinemann**, § 43 IV 4, Nr. 457.

The legal results of the revocation by the creditor are governed by §§ 346 ff. BGB.[256] Accordingly, § 346 I BGB requires that "*performance received and emoluments taken are to be returned*" upon revocation. Additionally, § 346 BGB also sets forth the specific cases when "*in lieu of restitution or return, the obligor must provide compensation for value*". Anyway, the creditor carries the burden of proof that all requirements of revocation (and also in principle the requirements of § 275 BGB) are met.[257]

Finally, it must be mentioned that the creditor's right to revocation is excluded under some certain cases. § 323 VI BGB indicates that:

> Revocation is excluded if the obligee is solely or very predominantly responsible for the circumstance that would entitle him to revoke the contract or if the circumstance for which the obligor is not responsible occurs at a time when the obligee is in default of acceptance.

The legal result of such provision is that in said cases the creditor cannot revoke the contract; hence the debtor reserves his right to the counter-obligation.[258]

d) Legal Results of Impossibility for Which the Debtor Is Responsible

aa) Extinguishment of the Primary Obligation (§ 275 I, II and III BGB)

As explained above, § 275 BGB rules that the debtor's primary obligation is extinguished in all cases of impossibility. Within this stance, the provision contains no distinction based on the responsibility of the debtor. Therefore, even in cases, when the debtor is responsible for the occurrence of impossibility, the primary claim is extinguished.[259]

bb) Compensation Payment

The most significant result of the debtor's responsibility for the occurrence of impossibility is that it enables the creditor to claim compensation for his damages.[260] As explained above, in 2002 the German lawmakers have abolished the difference between initial and subsequent impossibility and objective initial impossibility is no

---

[256] Also applicable to revocation under § 323 BGB, § 324 BGB and § 326 BGB. **Emmerich**, § 10, Nr. 31.

[257] **Staudinger/Otto**, § 326, Rdnr. F 29.

[258] **Fikentscher/Heinemann**, § 43 IV 4, Nr. 458.

[259] **Fehre**, p. 22; **Blank**, p. 47; **Zimmermann**, New German Law, p. 44; **Brunner**, p. 82; **Vogt**, p. 29; **Medicus**, Nr. 378; **Fikentscher/Heinemann**, § 43 II 1, Nr. 390–391; **Finn**, p. 130; **BeckOK/Unberath**, § 275, Rdnr. 8; **Palandt/Grüneberg**, § 275, Rdnr. 5; **Schlechtriem/Schmidt-Kessel**, Nr. 474; **Knütel**, JR 2001, 353, 353 ff.; **Zimmer**, NJW 2002, 1, 2.

[260] For a study on the foundations of the liability doctrine – also in relation with impossibility doctrine, see **Hamburger**, p. 23 ff.

longer a reason to void the contract. However, when it comes to the compensation for damages, the lawmakers have made a differentiation between initial and subsequent impossibility. The compensation claim of the creditor would be explained below for subsequent impossibility and initial impossibility separately.

(1) Compensation Claim for Subsequent Impossibility

The creditor's compensation claims are dealt with under § 280 BGB, in general. According to the first paragraph of the provision: "*If the obligor breaches a duty arising from the obligation, the obligee may demand damages for the damage caused thereby. This does not apply if the obligor is not responsible for the breach of duty.*"

As seen above, for any kind of compensation claim arising from the breach of contract, § 280 BGB requires the existence of the debtor's responsibility. This is, in fact, a result of the adoption of the fault-liability requirement of the civil law systems. As explained above, unless the debtor can prove that he is not responsible for the occurrence of impossibility, he would be deemed responsible.[261]

For claim of damages in lieu of performance, § 280 BGB makes reference to § 283 BGB, which is titled as: "*Damages in lieu of performance where the duty of performance is excluded.*"[262] § 283 BGB once again makes reference to the fault requirement of § 280 BGB and finally states that "*Section 281 (1) sentences 2 and 3 and (5) apply with the necessary modifications.*"[263]

The second and third sentences of § 281 I deal with partial performance and defective performance. These provisions would apply to partial impossibility and qualitative impossibility as well. Firstly, according to § 281 I s. 2, "*If the obligor has performed only in part, the obligee may demand damages in lieu of performance only if he has no interest in the part performance.*" However, in such cases, § 281 V[264] rules that the creditor must return the already performed partial

[261] As explained above, the burden of proof can be derived from § 280 I s. 2 BGB.

[262] According to Fikentscher/Heinemann, although it is not explicit in the BGB, § 283 applies solely to subsequent impossibility because compensation of damages has been specially regulated under § 311a II BGB for the cases of initial impossibility. **Fikentscher/Heinemann**, § 43 III 3, Nr. 419.

[263] The second, third and fourth paragraphs of § 281 deal with setting a period of time (Fristsetzung) prior to claiming damages so that the debtor can perform. However, these provisions are inapplicable to cases, which fall under § 275 BGB. In fact, in such cases, either there is impossibility that the debtor cannot perform, or he cannot be expected to perform due to gross disproportionality or personal reasons. In all cases, it is clear that setting a period of time would not result in performance. **Medicus**, Nr. 386; **Fikentscher/Heinemann**, § 43 III 3, Nr. 420; **Brox/Walker**, § 22, Nr. 56; MDR 2006, 858, 858. For a critique of § 281 I BGB, see **Altmeppen**, DB 2001, 1131, 1131 ff. For the responses of Canaris to the critique of **Altmeppen**, see **Canaris**, DB 2001, 1815, 1815 ff. For Altmeppen's counter-response to Canaris, see **Altmeppen**, DB 2001, 1821, 1821 ff.

[264] According to the § 281 V: "*If the obligee demands damages in lieu of complete performance, the obligor is entitled to claim the return of his performance under sections 346 to 348.*" This

performance, if any. Secondly, according to § 281 I s. 3, in case of qualitative impossibility, the creditor may claim damages in lieu of performance only if the breach is material. In other words, in cases of qualitative impossibility, the importance of the defect is decisive.[265] Therefore, in case of immaterial breach, the creditor may not claim damages in lieu of performance.[266]

The compensation damages in lieu of performance aim to put the creditor in a position as if the performance has been rendered as owed.[267] In other words, the damages to be compensated under §§ 280 ff. BGB are the creditor's positive interest.[268] However, if the occurrence of impossibility is preceded by default of the debtor, the creditor may also claim his damages arising from default.[269] In principle, the time for the calculation of damages is the time of occurrence of impossibility.[270]

(2) Compensation Claim for Initial Impossibility

Compensation claims arising from initial impossibility is separately dealt with under the second paragraph of § 311a BGB. Accordingly:

> The obligee may, at his option, demand damages in lieu of performance or reimbursement of his expenses in the extent specified in section 284. This does not apply if the obligor was not aware of the obstacle to performance when entering into the contract and is also not responsible for his lack of awareness. Section 281 (1) sentences 2 and 3 and (5) apply with the necessary modifications.

Compensation claims under the provision require the debtor's awareness of the impossibility at the time of the conclusion of the contract or his responsibility[271] for his unawareness.[272] Otherwise, the creditor cannot ask for the compensation

---

shows that the creditor cannot rely on the provisions of unjust enrichment (§ 818 f.). **Medicus**, Nr. 387.

[265] **Hirse**, in: Tonner/Willingmann/Tamm, § 311a, Rdnr. 11.

[266] According to § 281/I s. 2: "*If the obligor has not rendered performance as owed, the obligee may not demand damages in lieu of performance if the breach of duty is immaterial.*"

[267] **Brox/Walker**, § 22, Nr. 57; **Fikentscher/Heinemann**, § 43 III 3, Nr. 419.

[268] **Hk-BGB/Schulze**, § 283, Rdnr. 4. According to Koller, in case of subsequent impossibility for which the debtor is responsible, the creditor has a right to choose between his negative or positive interest. **Koller**, Leistungssörungen, p. 46. According to the author, a claim of negative interest makes sense when the creditor has lost his interest in the performance. **Koller**, Leistungssörungen, p. 54.

[269] **MüKo/Ernst**, § 283, Nr. 10.

[270] **MüKo/Ernst**, § 283, Nr. 11.

[271] In an assessment of the debtor's responsibility, the provision of § 276 BGB would apply. NJW 2005, 989, 990.

[272] In cases, which fall under § 275 II BGB, the awareness must be with regard to all circumstances giving rise to gross disproportionality. **MüKo/Ernst**, § 311a, Rdnr. 44. For the problem of knowledge-attribution to the debtor (Wissenszurechnung) when the people in the domain of the debtor have access to knowledge, but the debtor lacks access to information, see **MüKo/Ernst**, § 311a, Rdnr. 58 ff.

of his damages unless the debtor has given a warranty that there is no initial impossibility.[273] Under any circumstances, it does not matter if the debtor is responsible for the *occurrence* of impossibility. It only matters, if the debtor was aware of impossibility or he is responsible for his unawareness.[274] The creditor only carries the burden of proof regarding the occurrence of initial impossibility. In order to reject the compensation claim, the debtor carries the burden of proof that he was unaware of impossibility and that he could not be aware of it.[275]

If the debtor was already aware of the impossibility when concluding the contract, or if he may be held responsible for his lack of awareness, the creditor may claim compensation. Within this scope, the compensation covers the positive damages of the creditor.[276] However, it is argued that it is difficult to explain the dogmatic background of such compensation.[277] More specifically, an opinion in the doctrine asserts that in case of initial impossibility there is a breach of the *trust* relationship between the parties because the debtor has undertaken an obligation, which he cannot perform. According to this opinion, since § 280 BGB deals with the compensation claims arising from breach of *contractual* obligations, compensation claims arising from initial impossibility cannot be dealt with under § 280 BGB.[278] Accepting this opinion has an important practical result. If it is agreed that the legal reason of such compensation is a breach of trust, the creditor can only claim his negative interest (reliance interest). Therefore, against such arguments, the prevailing opinion in the doctrine argues that in such cases of breach, the reason for liability is the breach of the promise to perform

---

[273] **Looschelders**, Nr. 660.

[274] **Fikentscher/Heinemann**, § 43 III 2, Nr. 407; **Looschelders**, Nr. 661.

[275] **Hk-BGB/Schulze**, § 311a, Rdnr. 6; **Sy**, p. 163; **Palandt/Grüneberg**, § 311a, Rdnr. 10; **Dedek**, in: Henssler/Graf von Westphalen, § 311a, Rdnr. 16; **Fikentscher/Heinemann**, § 43 III 2, Nr. 414; **Petersen**, Nr. 313; **Hirse**, in: Tonner/Willingmann/Tamm, § 311a, Rdnr. 10. If it can be argued that the *creditor* was aware of initial impossibility or he must have been aware of it, this constitutes contributory negligence (Mitverschulden). Therefore, the compensation to be paid to the creditor would be reduced proportionally with his fault (in accordance with § 254 BGB) and then the counter-obligation that he would perform under § 326 II would be offset. **Fikentscher/Heinemann**, § 43 III 2, Nr. 412.

[276] **Staudinger/Löwisch**, § 311a, Rdnr. 3; **Hk-BGB/Schulze**, § 311a, Rdnr. 7; **Sy**, p. 160; **Canaris**, AGB, p. 1084; **Medicus**, Nr. 390c; **Schimmel/Buhlmann**, p. 251; **Hirsch**, Nr. 663; **Palandt/Grüneberg**, § 311a, Rdnr. 7; **jurisPK-BGB/Alpmann**, § 311a, Rdnr. 29; **Koller**, Leistungssörungen, p. 45; **PWW/Medicus/Stürner**, § 311a, Rdnr. 16; **Brieskorn**, p. 49; **Dauner-Lieb/Heidel/Lepa/Ring**, Das neue Schuldrecht, § 2, Nr. 88; **Schultz**, p. 75; **Fikentscher/Heinemann**, § 43 III 2, Nr. 407; **Lorenz**, Schuldrechtsmodernisierung, p. 27; **Dauner/Lieb**, in: Dauner-Lieb/Heidel/Lepa/Ring, Schuldrecht, § 311a, Rdnr. 14.

[277] According to Popescu, dogmatically the liability of the debtor under § 311a II cannot be positive interest. The author argues that positive damages may only be compensated under § 311a II if the debtor already knew the existence of an impediment that can be overcome. **Popescu**, p. 135–135.

[278] **Palandt/Grüneberg**, § 311a, Rdnr. 6. For the discussion, whether § 311a II is necessary in addition to §§ 280 I and II, 283 BGB, see **Käunicke**, 78 ff. **Canaris**, Grundlagen, p. 11 ff.; **Cekovic-Vuletic**, p. 32 ff.

(Leistungsversprechen), which is valid under § 311a BGB; not the breach of the obligation, which is extinguished under § 275 BGB.[279]

Since initial impossibility may be regarded as an error (Eigenschaftsirrtum), the relationship between initial impossibility and error must be discussed. In the doctrine it is argued that in cases where the creditor is entitled to his positive interest (expectation interest) under § 311a II, the debtor cannot avoid the contract under § 119 BGB (regarding voidability for mistake) based on error because in such cases the debtor would only compensate the negative interest of the creditor and avoidance due to error would therefore constitute an abuse of right.[280] However, it is argued that if the debtor is not responsible for initial impossibility—hence the creditor would not be entitled to any compensation under § 311a II BGB—the debtor may avoid the contract (Anfechtung) due to error and compensate the creditor's negative damages accordingly.[281] In fact, § 122 BGB regarding compensation of the damages of the addressee of the avoidance is not based of fault-requirement. Without a distinction of fault, such principle rules that the party, who avoids the contract due to error must compensate the damages of the addressee of such avoidance. Therefore, it is argued that only if the creditor is not entitled to claim his positive damages under § 311a II BGB, § 122 BGB may apply by analogy. [282]

Although § 280 BGB refrains from referring to the notion of impossibility, it must be noted that impossibility is also a useful concept with regard to secondary claim. Accordingly, impossibility bears special importance under §§ 283, 311a II BGB. More specifically, unlike any other types of breach of duty, (only) in cases of impossibility, there is no need to set additional time (Frist) prior to claiming damages in lieu of damages. Therefore, the differentiation between cases of impossibility and other types of breach still makes sense in the field of damage claims.

---

[279] **Canaris**, DB 2001, 1815, 1818; **Grunewald**, JZ 2001, 433, 435; **Looschelders**, Nr. 657; **Dauner-Lieb/Heidel/Lepa/Ring**, Das neue Schuldrecht, § 2, Nr. 88; **Dedek**, in: Henssler/Graf von Westphalen, § 311a, Rdnr. 13; **Brieskorn**, p. 49–50. In fact, § 311a II functions as an explicit provision, which enables the positive interest claims of the debtor. Otherwise the creditor could only claim his negative damages based on *culpa in contrahendo*. **Schlechtriem**, Unmöglichkeit, p. 131. According to Canaris, there is a warranty in the promise of the debtor. **Canaris**, Grundlagen, p. 35.

[280] For a study on the differences between the application of rules of impossibility and mistake in case of initial impossibility, see **Schneider**, p. 1 ff.

[281] **Dörner/Staudinger**, p. 36.

[282] **Dörner/Staudinger**, p. 36; **Hk-BGB/Schulze**, § 311a, Rdnr. 9; **Dedek**, in: Henssler/Graf von Westphalen, § 311a, Rdnr. 20. Hirse rejects such opinion since the option of claiming compensation based on *culpa in contrahendo* is already theoretically available. **Hirse**, in: Tonner/Willingmann/Tamm, § 311a, Rdnr 13. Similarly, Dauner/Lieb reject the option of analogy to § 122 BGB, since there is not a gap in the law. **Dauner/Lieb**, in: Dauner-Lieb/Heidel/Lepa/Ring, Schuldrecht, § 311a, Rdnr. 18.

cc) Reimbursement of Futile Expenses

Reimbursement of futile expenses is one of the rights of the creditor, which require the existence of the debtor's responsibility. Accordingly, if the creditor has made expenses in order to conclude the contract (such as certification expenses) or to use the subject matter of the contract (such as preparation of a frame for the subject matter painting), the creditor may claim these from the debtor in case of performance impossibility.[283] § 284 BGB, which regulates reimbursement of futile expenses reads as follows:

> In place of damages in lieu of performance, the obligee may demand reimbursement of the expenses which he has made and in all fairness was entitled to make in reliance on receiving performance, unless the purpose of the expenses would not have been achieved, even if the obligor had not breached his duty.

The claim of futile expenses is an alternative to the claim of damages in lieu of performance, *i.e.*, positive interest. Within this stance, the creditor is free to choose between damages in lieu of performance and reimbursement of futile expenses.[284] However, under all circumstances it is necessary that the creditor satisfies the conditions of claiming damages in lieu of performance because reimbursement of futile expenses is an alternative of claiming damages in lieu of performance.[285]

Compensation of damages in lieu of performance especially covers the creditor's loss of profit. The burden of proof regarding the loss of profit is carried by the creditor. However, such proof is generally difficult to make. Within this stance, § 284 BGB gives the creditor the chance to recover at least his futile expenses.[286] Moreover, the expenses covered by the provision would be made also in the event that the contract was performed as negotiated. Therefore they cannot be claimed in lieu of performance (under the scope of positive interest).[287] As a result, § 284 BGB functions as a basis to claim such expenses.

---

[283] **Brox/Walker**, § 22, Nr. 71.

[284] **Looschelders**, Nr. 683. According to Fikentscher/Heinemann, rather than as an alternative to positive damages, reimbursement of futile expenses must have been designated as a cumulative remedy. Authors think that there is a construction mistake with regard to § 284 BGB. **Fikentscher/Heinemann**, § 43 III 4, Nr. 440.

[285] **Looschelders**, Nr. 678; **Brox/Walker**, § 22, Nr. 74.

[286] Prior to the reform of 2002, to ease such difficulty of proof, the courts have applied a *presumption of profitability* (Rentabilitätsvermutung). Accordingly, it was presumed that the expenses made by one party for the performance of the contract are first palpable damages (ersten handgreiflichen Schaden). Therefore, even if the creditor cannot prove his lost profit, he can at least cover his expenses. However, this presumption applies only if the creditor has concluded the contract with a purpose of making profit. Unlike the presumption of profitability, the new provision of § 284 BGB does not require that the creditor has the purpose of making profit. **Medicus**, Nr. 388; **Looschelders**, Nr. 675–676; **Brox/Walker**, § 22, Nr. 72; **Dedek**, in: Henssler/Graf von Westphalen, § 284, Rdnr. 1; **Willingmann/Hirse,** in: Kohte/Micklitz/Rott/Tonner/Willingmann, § 284, Rdnr. 1; **Hk-BGB/Schulze**, § 284, Rdnr. 2; **Dauner-Lieb,** in: Dauner-Lieb/Langen, § 281, Rdnr. 64.

[287] **Brox/Walker**, § 22, Nr. 71.

Although the creditor can obtain the futile expenses from the debtor, § 284 BGB does not entitle the creditor to claim his entire negative damages. The following example by Brox/Walker illustrates the case very well: In case of a sale of a living room set, the buyer can request the disbursed delivery costs as his expenses under § 284 BGB. However, he cannot claim that in the meantime he could obtain the same set for cheaper from Furniture Store X but he failed to do so in reliance on the performance by the seller because non-utilization of an opportunity is not an expense. [288]

The expenses to be claimed by the creditor under § 284 BGB must have been already incurred. Moreover, there must be a voluntary asset transfer, which is performed in the creditor's own interest, not for the interest of a third party.[289] Under all circumstances, the creditor may only claim the expenses that he was entitled to make in all fairness and the expenses must be proportionate to the purpose pursued.[290] Fairness must be determined on a case-by-case basis by weighing the interests of the parties against each other while considering the content of the contract and the principle of good faith.[291]

Reimbursement under § 284 BGB also requires that the creditor makes such expenses by trusting in the preservation of the contract, *i.e.*, acquisition of the performance by the debtor.[292] For instance, expenses for the contract documentation, or registration expenses regarding land purchase and brokerage may be claimed under the provision.[293] In principle, such expenses must be made after the establishment of the obligation and before its extinguishment. Within this scope, it is argued that priorly made expenses are not reimbursable under the provision, if the creditor could postpone them or if there was strong evidence for the failure of the contract.[294] More specifically, costs of contract negotiations are not covered by the provision.[295]

According to one opinion, since the creditor's futile expenses are claimed on the basis of his trust in the preservation of the contract, the amount of such expenses may be as much as the creditor's negative interest. However, it is argued that even in cases where such futile expenses exceed the creditor's negative interest, the amount to be claimed must not exceed his positive interest. Otherwise, the creditor would be better-off than the performance of the contract.[296] According to another

[288] **Brox/Walker**, § 22, Nr. 80.

[289] **Looschelders**, Nr. 678.

[290] **Medicus**, Nr. 389; **Fikentscher/Heinemann**, § 43 III 4, Nr. 441.

[291] **Fikentscher/Heinemann**, § 43 III 4, Nr. 441. For instance, bribes paid by the creditor cannot be accepted within the scope of *fair* expenses. **Fehre**, p. 127.

[292] Arnold, in: **Dauner-Lieb/Langen**, § 284, Rdnr. 1; **MüKo/Ernst**, § 284, Rdnr. 18.

[293] **Staudinger/Löwisch**, § 311a, Rdnr. 40; **Fikentscher/Heinemann**, § 43 III 4, Nr. 439; **Fehre**, p. 125; **Arnold,** in: Dauner-Lieb/Langen, § 284, Rdnr. 1.

[294] **Canaris**, JZ 2001, 499, 517.

[295] **MüKo/Ernst**, § 284, Rdnr. 18.

[296] **Fehre**, p. 131.

opinion in the doctrine, the amount of compensation cannot be restricted to the creditor's positive damages, unless the *fairness* requirement requires such restriction.[297]

Reimbursement of futile expenses is available as an option to the creditor both in case of subsequent impossibility and initial impossibility. In fact, § 311a BGB, regarding initial impossibility also makes reference to § 284 BGB and states that the creditor may choose between damage compensation (positive damages) and the "*reimbursement of his expenses in the extent specified in section 284*".

According to one opinion in the doctrine, in the former BGB, where initial objective impossibility caused voidness of the contract, the creditor was entitled to his negative interest based on *culpa in contrahendo*. However, after the reform, if the creditor does not claim his positive damages, the only option left is compensation of his futile expenses. However, as explained above futile expenses fail to cover the full negative interest of the creditor. Consequently, the creditor is in a worse position than in the former law because, in cases, where the creditor's negative damages exceed his positive damages, the creditor has no option to claim his negative damages.[298] According to another opinion, in case of initial impossibility, a claim of negative damages based on *culpa in contrahendo* is still possible.[299]

Finally, if the purpose of the expenses would not have been achieved anyway (even if the debtor had not breached the contract), the creditor cannot claim such expenses. Such restriction aims to prevent the creditor shift the expenses of a loss involving transaction to the debtor.[300]

dd) Counter-Obligation

In synallagmatic contracts, there are two different methods of calculation of damages. The faith of the counter-obligation against compensation claims is bound to the application of either of these theories. According to the exchange theory (Surrogationstheorie), the party who requests compensation from the breaching party, must also perform his counter-obligation. On the other hand, the difference theory (Differenztheorie) argues that the party, who claims compensation, does not have to perform the counter-obligation. Instead, the value of his counter-obligation would be deducted from the amount of compensation to be

---

[297] **MüKo/Ernst**, § 284, Rdnr. 28.

[298] **Cekovic-Vuletic**, p. 46.

[299] In this opinion, see **Canaris**, DB 2001, 1815, 1816. Peres argues that compensation claim arising from *culpa in contrahendo* and § 311a II are concurring claims. **Peres**, p. 55. According to Fehre, in addition to the claim based on § 311a II, a claim based on *culpa in contrahendo* may also be possible, when the debtor has failed to immediately inform the creditor about the impediment to the performance. **Fehre**, p. 146.

[300] **Brox/Walker**, § 22, Nr. 79.

paid.[301] In practice, the difference between the application of either theory is important in barters, where the creditor has interest in reserving or performing his own obligation.[302]

The basis of § 326 I BGB, which regulates the extinguishment of counter-obligation in case of impossibility, is the *synallagma* between the obligations of the parties.[303] Therefore, provision makes no distinction between the results of impossibility depending on the existence of the debtor's responsibility. Hence the creditor's release from the counter-obligation takes place regardless of the existence of the responsibility of the debtor for impossibility.[304] Within this stance, under § 326 I BGB the creditor's release from his counter-obligation takes place *ipso iure*.[305] Therefore, one opinion argues that in cases of impossibility, when the creditor claims compensation from the debtor, there is no possibility for the application of the exchange theory.[306] On the other hand, according to another theory, the creditor must be entitled to choose exchange theory while claiming compensation.[307] According to the third opinion, which is argued by Ernst, when the debtor is responsible for the occurrence of impossibility, and the creditor's performance is a performance in-kind, Ernst finds the application of § 326 I BGB *ipso iure* inappropriate. According to the author, in such cases, the provision must be subject to teleological reduction and the creditor must be given the option to choose if he wants to perform the counter-obligation. Otherwise, the creditor would be unrightfully deprived of his chance to "sell" the relevant counter-obligation to a third party.[308]

ee) Substitutes

Acquisition of substitutes by the debtor as a result of impossibility is dealt with under § 285 I BGB, regardless of the debtor's responsibility for impossibility. In other words, § 285 I BGB is applicable even in cases where the creditor is responsible for the occurrence of impossibility.[309]

---

301 **Fikentscher/Heinemann**, § 43 IV 3, Nr. 456; **Dauner-Lieb,** in: Dauner-Lieb/Langen, § 281, Rdnr. 61; **Looschelders**, Nr. 666 ff.

302 **Willingmann/Hirse,** in: Kohte/Micklitz/Rott/Tonner/Willingmann, § 283, Rdnr. 8; **Looschelders**, Nr. 672.

303 **Palandt/Grüneberg**, § 326, Rdnr. 2; **BeckOK/Grothe**, § 326, Rdnr. 2.

304 **Gruber**, JuS 2002, 1066, 1067; **Fikentscher/Heinemann**, § 43 IV 1, Nr. 447; **Schlechtriem/Schmidt-Kessel**, Nr. 495.

305 **Laimer**, p. 44.

306 **Looschelders**, Nr. 672.

307 **BeckOK/Unberath**, § 326, Rdnr. 5; **Staudinger/Otto**, § 326, Rdnr. B6.

308 For the relevant criticism, see **MüKo/Ernst**, § 326, Rdnr. 13.

309 **BeckOK/Unberath**, § 285, Rdnr. 7; **Emmerich**, § 10, Nr. 17; **MüKo/Emmerich**, § 285, Nr. 14; **Medicus**, Nr. 390; **Ergüne**, İÜHFM 2004, 351, 369.

When the creditor is also entitled to request compensation for impossibility for which the debtor is responsible, the creditor has a right of choice between requesting compensation and the substitute.[310] However, the creditor's choice of the substitute does not result in loss of the right to claim damages, which exceed the value of the substitute. In other words, the value of the substitute is deducted from the compensation that the creditor may request.[311] Therefore, if the value of the substitute fails to cover the damages of the creditor, he may additionally claim his remaining damages from the debtor. However, if the value of the substitute exceeds the damages of the creditor, he should be entitled to the entire substitute in exchange of his contractually agreed upon counter-obligation.

ff) Return of Already Performed Counter-Obligation

It has been explained above that in cases where the debtor is released from his obligation to perform under § 275 BGB, § 326 I BGB also eliminates the creditor's obligation of counter-performance. Therefore, if the creditor has performed the counter-obligation prior to the occurrence of impossibility, § 326 IV BGB regulates that "*what is performed may be claimed back.*" This principle applies also in cases, where the debtor is responsible for the occurrence of impossibility.[312]

gg) Creditor's Right to Revocation

As explained above, § 326 V BGB sets forth that "*If, under section 275 (1) to (3), the obligor does not have to perform, the obligee may revoke*" the contract. Such right is also available regardless of the debtor's responsibility for the occurrence of impossibility.[313] Accordingly, the creditor may revoke the contract and at the same time claim compensation of his damages.[314] It must be underlined that, after the reform of 2002, BGB entitles the creditor to his positive damages also in case of revocation.[315] However, rather than claiming his positive damages, the debtor also has the right to claim his futile expenses.

---

[310] **MüKo/Emmerich**, § 285, Rdnr. 35; **Palandt/Grüneberg**, § 285, Rdnr. 10.

[311] **Brox/Walker**, § 22, Nr. 26; **Fikentscher/Heinemann**, § 43 III 5, Nr. 445. "*The value of the obtained substitute is to be deducted in accordance with § 285 para. 2 BGB from an additionally given compensation, if any.*" AG Hamburg-Altona, Urteil v. 11.08.2004 319B C 79/04 – JurionRS.

[312] **Palandt/Grüneberg**, § 326, Rdnr. 2a; MüKo/Ernst, § 284, Rdnr. 13.

[313] **Rüssmann**, p. 285; **Laimer**, p. 44; **Fikentscher/Heinemann**, § 43 IV 4, Nr. 458; **Dauner-Lieb/Arnold**, p. 31.

[314] **Fikentscher/Heinemann**, § 43 IV 4, Nr. 458; **MüKo/Gaier**, § 345, Rdnr. 66.

[315] **Döll**, p. 63; **Lorenz**, Kaufrecht, p. 9.

References

Ahrens, Martin: Der mittellose Geldschuldner: Unmöglichkeit zur Leistung und Verzug des Zahlungsverpflichteten, Duncker & Humblot, Berlin 1994.

Altmeppen, Holger: Schadenersatz wegen Pflichtverletzung, anfängliche Unmöglichkeit und Aufwendungsersatz im Entwurf des Schuldrechtsmodernisierungsgesetzes, DB 2001, pp. 1821–1824.

Altmeppen, Holger: Schadenersatz wegen Pflichtverletzung – Ein Beispiel für die Überhastung der Schuldrechtsreform, DB 2001, pp. 1131–1133.

Arp, Torsten: Anfängliche Unmöglichkeit, Ferdinand Schöningh, Paderborn 1988.

Asendorf, Hermann: Unmöglichkeit und Unvermögen, Triltsch & Huther, Berlin 1936.

Bamberger, Heinz Georg/Roth, Herbert: Beck'scher Online-Kommentar, C.H. Beck, München 2012. (Cited as: BeckOK)

Barta, Sebastian: BGB Allgemeines Schuldrecht, Grin, Norderstedt 2011.

Berckemeyer, Wolfgang: Die Behebung der Unmöglichkeit, Unger, Berlin 1930.

Berghoff, Erhard: Die Unmöglichkeit und ihre Rechtsfolgen nach dem BGB und dem einheitlichen Kaufrecht, Dissertation, Münster 1980.

Beuthien, Volker: Zweckerreichung und Zweckstörung im Schuldverhältnis, J.C.B. Mohr, Tübingen 1969.

Blank, Wladimir: Das allgemeine Leistungsstörungsrecht in Deutschland und in der Ukraine, Lit Verlag, Berlin 2009.

Brieskorn, Konstanze: Vertragshaftung und responsabilité contractuelle, Mohr Siebeck, Tübingen 2010.

Brox, Hans/Walker, Wolf-Dietrich: Allgemeines Schuldrecht, C.H. Beck, München 2009.

Brunner, Christoph: Force majeure and Hardship Excuse Under General Contract Principles, Wolters Kluwer, Alphen aan den Rijn 2009.

Bucher, Eugene: Schweizerisches Obligationenrecht, Allgemeiner Teil, Schulthess, Zürich 1988. (Cited as: Bucher)

Canaris, Claus-Wilhelm: Die Reform des Rechts der Leistungsstörungen, JZ, 2001, pp. 499–524. (Also available at: <http://uni-leipzig.de/wirtschaftsrecht/alt/dokumente/reform.pdf>).

Canaris, Claus-Wilhelm: Schadenersatz wegen Pflichtverletzung, anfängliche Unmöglichkeit und Aufwendungsersatz im Entwurf des Schuldrechtsmodernisierungsgesetzes, DB 2001, pp. 1815–1821.

Canaris, Claus-Wilhelm: Zur Bedeutung der Kategorie der "Unmöglichkeit" für das Recht der Leistungsstörungen, in: Schulze, Reiner/Schulte-Nölke, Hans, Die Schuldrechtsreform vor dem Hintergrund des Gemeinschaftsrechts, Mohr Siebeck, Münster 2001, pp. 43–67. (Cited as: Canaris, Kategorie der Unmöglichkeit)

Canaris, Claus-Wilhelm: Schuldrechtsmodernisierung 2002, C.H. Beck, München 2002. (Cited as: Canaris, Schuldrechtsmodernisierung)

Canaris, Claus-Wilhelm: Die AGB-rechtliche Leitbildfunktion des neuen Leistungsstörungsrechts, in: Habersack, Mathias/Hommelhoff, Peter/Hüffer, Uwe/Schmidt, Karsten, Festschrift für Peter Ulmer, De Gruyter Recht, Berlin 2003, pp. 1073–1096. (Cited as: Canaris, AGB)

Canaris, Claus-Wilhelm: Die Neuregelung des Leistungsstörungs- und des Kaufrechts-Grundstrukturen und Problemschwerpunkte, in: Lorenz, Egon, Karlsruher Forum 2002: Schuldrechtsmodernisierung, Verlag Versicherungswirtschaft, Karlsruhe 2003, pp. 5–100. (Cited as: Canaris, Neuregelung)

Canaris, Claus-Wilhelm: Die Behandlung nicht zu vertretender Leistungshindernisse nach § 275 Abs. 2 BGB beim Stückkauf, JZ, 2004, pp. 214–255.

Canaris, Claus-Wilhelm: Grundlagen und Rechtsfolgen der Haftung für anfängliche Unmöglichkeit nach § 311a Abs. 2 BGB, in: Lorenz, Stephan/Trunk, Alexander/Eidenmüller, Horst/Wendehorst, Christiane/Adolff, Johannes, Festschrift für Andreas Heldrich, C.H. Beck, München 2005, pp. 12–38. (Cited as: Canaris, Grundlagen)

Canaris, Claus-Wilhelm: Die einstweilige Unmöglichkeit der Leistung, in: Baums, Theodor/Huber, Ulrich/Wertenbruch, Johannes/Lutter, Marcus/Schmidt, Karsten, Festschrift Für Ulrich Huber Zum Siebzigsten Geburtstag, Mohr Siebeck, Tübingen 2006, pp. 144–164. (Cited as: Canaris, Die einstweilige Unmöglichkeit)

Cekovic-Vuletic, Simonida: Haftung wegen Unmöglichkeit nach dem Schuldrechtsmodernisierungsgesetz, C.H. Beck, München 2003.

Däubler, Wolfgang: Die vorübergehende Unmöglichkeit der Leistung, in: Lorenz, Stephan/Trunk, Alexander/Eidenmüller, Horst/Wendehorst, Christiane/Adolff, Johannes, Festschrift für Andreas Heldrich, C.H. Beck, München 2005, pp. 55–66.

Dauner-Lieb, Barbara/Arnold, Arnd: Kein Rücktrittsrech des Käufers bei von ihm verschuldeter Unmöglichkeit der Nacherfüllung?, in: Häuser, Franz/Steinbeck, Anja/Hammen, Horst/Siebel, Ulf R./Hennrichs, Joachim/Welter, Reinhard, Festschrift für Walter Hadding, De Gruyter Recht, Berlin 2004, pp. 25–31.

Dauner-Lieb, Barbara/Langen, Werner: BGB Schuldrecht, Nomos, Baden-Baden 2012. (Cited as: Author, in: Dauner-Lieb/Langen)

Dauner-Lieb, Barbara/Heidel, Thomas/Lepa, Manfred/Ring, Gerhard: Das neue Schuldrecht in der anwaltlichen Praxis, Deutscher Anwaltverlag, Bonn 2002. (Cited as: Dauner-Lieb/Heidel/Lepa/Ring, Das neue Schuldrecht)

Dauner-Lieb, Barbara/Heidel, Thomas/Lepa, Manfred/Ring, Gerhard: Schuldrecht, Deutscher Anwaltverlag, Bonn 2002. (Cited as: Author, in: Dauner-Lieb/Heidel/Lepa/Ring, Schuldrecht)

Der Bundesminister der Justiz: Diskussionsentwurf eines Schuldrechtsmodernisierungsgesetzes, Der Bundesminister der Justiz, Berlin 2000. (Cited as Discussion Draft)

Döll, Yves: Rückgewährstörungen beim Rücktritt, Mohr Siebeck, Tübingen 2011.

Dörner, Heinrich/Staudinger, Ansgar: Schuldrechtsmodernisierung systematische Einführung und synoptische Gesamtdarstellung, Nomos, Baden-Baden 2002.

Dötterl, Sebastian: Wann ist der Gläubiger für die Unmöglichkeit verantworlich?, Nomos, Baden-Baden 2008.

Dullinger, Silvia: Bürgerliches Recht, Band II, Schuldrecht Allgemeiner Teil, Springer, Wien 2008.

Dural, Mustafa: Borçlunun Sorumlu Olmadığı Sonraki İmkansızlık (BK. 117), Fakülteler Matbaası, İstanbul 1976. (Cited as: Dural, Sonraki İmkansızlık)

Eckert, Jörn: Schuldrecht, Allgemeiner Teil, Nomos, Baden-Baden 2003.

Emmerich, Volker: Das Recht der Leistungsstörungen, C.H. Beck, München 2005.

Ergüne, Mehmet Serkan: Reform Sonrasında Alman Medeni Kanununda İmkansızlık Halleri ve Sonuçları, İÜHFM, Vol. 62, No. 1–2, 2004, pp. 351–380.

Fehre, Andrea: Unmöglichkeit und Unzumutbarkeit der Leistung, Voraussetzungen und Rechtsfolgen nach Inkrafttreten des Schuldrechtsmodernisierungsgesetzes, Duncker & Humblot, Berlin 2005.

Feldhahn, Peer: Die Störung der Geschäftsgrundlage im System des reformierten Schuldrechts, NJW 2005, pp. 3381–3383.

Fikentscher, Wolfgang/Heinemann, Andreas: Schuldrecht, De Gruyter Recht, Berlin 2006.

Finn, Markus: Erfüllungspflicht und Leistungshindernis, die Bestimmung der Grenzen vertraglicher Primärpflichten nach §§ 275 Abs. 1 und 2, 313 BGB, Duncker & Humblot, Berlin 2007.

Fischer, Otto: Unmöglichkeit als Nichtigkeitsgrund bei Urteilen und Rechtsgeschäften, C.H. Beck, München 1913. (Cited as: Fischer, Unmöglichkeit)

Förster, Christian: Schuldrecht Allgemeiner Teil, Eine Einführung mit Fällen, C.F. Müller, Heidelberg 2011.

Gauch, Peter/Schluep, Walter R.: Schweizerisches Obligationenrecht, Allgemeiner Teil, Band I, Schulthess, Zürich/Basel/Genf 2008. (Cited as: Gauch/Schluep, Band I)

Gruber, Urs Peter: Schuldrechtsmodernisierung 2001/2002 – Die beiderseits zu vertretende Unmöglichkeit, JuS 2002, pp. 1066–1071.

Grunewald, Barbara: Vorschläge für eine Neuregelung der anfänglichen Unmöglichkeit und des anfänglichen Unvermögens, JZ 2001, pp. 433–436.

Gsell, Beate: Zeitweilige Unmöglichkeit und prozessuale Durchsetzung des Leistungsanspruchs, in: Bauer, Jobst-Hubertus/Kort, Michael/Möllers, Thomas M.J./Sandmann, Bernd, Festschrift für Herbert Buchner, C.H. Beck, München 2009, pp. 267–280.

Haake, Benno: Inwieweit steht das Unvermögen des Schuldners zur Leistung der Unmöglichkeit der Leistung gleich?, Dissertation, Rostock 1903.

Hamburger, Georg: Das Recht aus der Haftung und die Unmöglichkeit der Leistung, Vahlen, Berlin 1915.

Hammen, Horst: Stellvertretendes commodum bei anfänglicher Unmöglichkeit für jedermann?, in: Häuser, Franz/Steinbeck, Anja/Hammen, Horst/Siebel, Ulf R./Hennrichs, Joachim/Welter, Reinhard, Festschrift für Walter Hadding, De Gruyter Recht, Berlin 2004, pp. 41–56. (Cited as: Hammen, Stellvertretendes)

Harke, Jan Dirk: Unmöglichkeit und Pflichtverletzung: Römisches Recht, BGB und Schuldrechtsmodernisierung, in: Helms, Thobias/Neumann, Daniela/Caspers, Georg/Sailer, Rita/Schmidt-Kessel, Martin, Das neue Schuldrecht, Richard Boorberg Verlag, Stuttgart 2001, pp. 29–61.

Henssler, Martin/Graf von Westphalen, Friedrich: Praxis der Schuldrechtreform, ZAP Verlag, Recklinghausen 2001. (Cited as: Author, in: Henssler/Graf von Westphalen)

Hirsch, Christoph: Allgemeines Schuldrecht, Carl Heymanns Verlag, Köln 2009.

Hohmeister, Frank Udo: Die Einordnung anfänglichen Unvermögens des Schuldners zur Leistung in die Unmöglichkeitslehre des BGB, Dissertation, Göttingen 1982.

Huber, Peter/Faust, Florian: Schuldrechtsmodernisierung Einführung in das neue Recht, C.H. Beck, München 2002.

Huber, Ulrich: Handbuch des Schuldrechts, Leistungsstörungen, Band I, Die allgemeinen Grundlagen; Der Tatbestand des Schuldnersverzug; Die vom Schuldner zu vertretenden Umstände, Mohr Siebeck, Tübingen 1999. (Cited as: Huber, Leistungsstörungen I)

Huber, Ulrich: Handbuch des Schuldrechts, Leistungsstörungen, Band II, Die Folgen des Schuldnerverzugs – Die Erfüllungsverweigerung und die vom Schuldner zu vertretende Unmöglichkeit, Mohr Siebeck, Tübingen 1999. (Cited as: Huber, Leistungsstörungen II)

Huber, Ulrich: Die Pflichtverletzung als Grundtatbestand der Leistungsstörung im Diskussionsentwurf eines Schuldrechtsmodernisierungsgesetzes, ZIP 2000, pp. 2273–2284.

Huber, Ulrich: Die Unmöglichkeit der Leistung im Diskussionsentwurf eines Schuldrechtsmodernisierungsgesetzes, ZIP 2000, pp. 2137–2151.

Huguenin, Claire: Obligationenrecht, Allgemeiner Teil, Schulthess, Zürich/Basel/Genf 2006.

Hütte, Felix/Helbron, Marlena: Schuldrecht, Allgemeiner Teil, Verlag Dr. Rolf Schmidt, Grasberg bei Bremen 2005.

Jagielski, Boleslaus: Die Grundsätze über die ursprüngliche Unmöglichkeit und das ursprüngliche Unvermögen in dem Bürgerlichen Gesetzbuche, Noske, Borna-Leipzig 1910.

Jauernig, Othmar: Bürgerliches Gesetzbuch mit Allgemeinen Gleichbehandlungsgesetzes, C.H. Beck, München 2011.

Joachim, Willi: "Personale" Unmöglichkeit – Die Zumutbarkeit pflichtgemässen Verhaltens, in Zivil- und Wirtschaftsrecht im Europäischen und Globalen Kontext, De Gruyter Recht, Berlin 2006, pp. 49–65.

Joussen, Jacob: Schuldrecht I - Allgemeiner Teil, Kohlhammer, Stuttgart 2008.

Junker, Markus/Beckmann, Roland Michael/Rüssmann, Michael: juris PraxisKommentar, BGB, Schuldrecht, juris, Saarbrücken 2004. (Cited as: jurisPK-BGB/Author)

Kaiser, Dagmar: Zeitweilige Unmöglichkeit, in: Häuser, Franz/Steinbeck, Anja/Hammen, Horst/ Siebel, Ulf R./Hennrichs, Joachim/Welter, Reinhard, Festschrift für Walter Hadding, De Gruyter Recht, Berlin 2004, pp. 121–143. (Cited as: Kaiser, Zeitweilige)

Kaiser, Gisbert A.: Das allgemeine Leistungsstörungsrecht als Kernpunkt des Diskussionsentwurfs eines Schuldrechtsmodernisierungsgesetzes. Die Bedeutung für das Private Baurecht, ZfBR 2001, pp. 147–154.

Kalbhen, Kurt: Das Surrogationsprinzip bei Unmöglichkeit der Leistung, Dissertation, Erlangen 1937.

Kaplan, Felix: Die ürsprüngliche teilweise Unmöglichkeit der versprochenen Leistung, insbesondere die teilweise Nichtexistenz des geschuldeten Gegenstandes nach dem Gemeinen Recht und dem Recht des Bürgerlichen Gesetzbuches, Schade, Berlin 1903. (Cited as: Kaplan, Ürsprüngliche)

Kaplan, Felix: Die teilweise Unmöglichkeit der Leistung nach dem Recht des Bürgerlichen Gesetzbuches, Struppe & Winckler, Berlin 1904. (Cited as: Kaplan)

Käunicke, Anja: Die Schadensersatzpflicht des Rückgewährschuldners wegen anfänglicher Unmöglichkeit, Duncker & Humblot, Berlin 2011.

Klausch, Sebastian: Unmöglichkeit und Unzumutbarkeit im system des allgemeinen Leistungsstörungsrecht nach der Schuldrechtsmodernisierung 2002, Peter Lang, Frankfurt am Main 2004.

Kleineidam, Feodor: Unmöglichkeit und Unvermögen nach dem Bürgerlichen Gesetzbuche für das Deutsche Reich, Fischer, Jena 1900.

Kley, Britta: Unmöglichkeit und Pflichtverletzung, Duncker & Humblot, Berlin, 2001.

Knütel, Christian: Zur Gleichstellung von zu vertretender und nicht zu vertretender Unmöglichkeit in § 275 BGB im Regierungsentwurf zur Schuldrechtsmodernisierung, JR 2001, pp. 353–355.

Köhler, Helmut: Unmöglichkeit und Geschäftsgrundlage bei Zweckstörungen im Schuldverhältnis, C.H. Beck, München 1971.

Kohte, Wolfhard/Micklitz, Hans-W/Rott, Peter/Tonner, Klaus/Willingmann, Armin: Das neue Schuldrecht, Kompaktkommentar, Luchterhand, München 2003. (Cited as: Author, in: Kohte/Micklitz/Rott/Tonner/Willingmann)

Koller, Alfred: Schweizerisches Obligationenrecht, Allgemeiner Teil, Handbuch des allgemeinen Schuldrechts, Stämpfli, Bern 2009. (Cited as: Koller)

Koller, Ingo: Recht der Leistungsstörungen, in: Koller, Ingo/Roth, Herbert/Zimmermann, Reinhard, Schuldrechtsmodernisierungsgesetz 2002, C.H. Beck, München 2002, pp. 45–65. (Cited as: Koller, Leistungssörungen)

Kollmann, Andreas: Allgemeines Geschäftsbedingungen und Individualvereinbarungen, in: Kroiss, Ludwig, Klausel Schuldrecht, Deutscher Anwaltverlag, Bonn 2003, pp. 19–163.

Köhler, Helmut/Lorenz, Stephan: Schuldrecht I, Allgemeiner Teil, C.H. Beck, München 2005.

Köndgen, Johannes: Die Entlastung des Schuldners wegen Unmöglichkeit der Leistung - Versuch einer Ehrenrettung des § 275 Abs. 2 BGB, in: Eger, Thomas/Ott, Claus/Bigus, Jochen/von Wangenheim, Georg, Internationalisierung des Rechts und seine ökonomische Analyse, Festschrift für Hans-Bernd Schäfer zum 65. Geburtstag, Gabler, Wiesbaden 2008, pp. 275–298.

Kötz, Hein: Vertragsrecht, Mohr Siebeck, Tübingen 2009.

Krajewski, Markus: The New German Law of Obligations, EBLR, Vol. 14, No. 2, 2003, pp. 201–216.

Krückmann, Paul: Unmöglichkeit und Unmöglichkeitsprozess, Mohr Siebeck, Tübingen 1907.

Kuhlmann, Kai/Nauen, Bernd: Neues und Altes von der vorübergehenden Unmöglichkeit – Primärleistungspflicht und Sekundäransprüche, in: Sutschet, Holger, Tradition und Moderne - Schuldrecht und Arbeitsrecht nach der Schuldrechtsreform, Duncker & Humblot, Berlin 2005, pp. 31–94.

Laimer, Simon: Durchführung und Rechtsfolgen der Vertragsaufhebung bei nachträglichen Erfüllungsstörungen, Mohr, Tübingen 2009.

Lehmann, Berthold: Inwieweit können die allgemeinen Vorschriften des BGB über die Unmöglichkeit der Leistung mit den speziellen über die Gewährleistung des Verkäufers für Sachmängel gegebenen Normen konkurrieren?, Dissertation, Greifswald 1910. (Cited as: Lehmann, Unmöglichkeit)

Lenczyk, Harry: Teilweise Unmöglichkeit, Dissertation, Breslau 1936.

Looschelders, Dirk: Schuldrecht, Allgemeiner Teil, Carl Heymanns Verlag, Köln 2006.

Lorenz, Stephan: Schuldrechtsmodernisierung- Erfahrungen seit dem 1. Januar 2002, in: Lorenz, Egon, Karlsruher Forum 2005: Schuldrechtsmodernisierung- Erfahrungen seit dem 1. Januar

2002, Verlag Versicherungswirtschaft, Karlsruhe 2006, pp. 5–139. (Cited as: Lorenz, Schuldrechtsmodernisierung)
Lorenz, Stephan: Neues Leistungsstörungs- und Kaufrecht: Eine Zwischenbilanz, De Gruyter Recht, Berlin 2004. (Cited as Lorenz, Kaufrecht)
Lorenz, Stephan: Schuldrechtsreform 2002: Problemschwerpunkte drei Jahre danach, NJW 2005, pp. 1889–1896.
Lorenz, Stephan/Riehm, Thomas: Lehrbuch zum neuen Schuldrecht, C.H. Beck, München 2002.
Lorenz, Werner: Reform of the German Law of Breach of Contract, ELR, Vol. 1, No. 3, 1997, pp. 317–344.
Löwisch, Manfred: Neues Schuldrecht in Deutschland, RLR, No. 20, 2003, pp. 157–179, <www.ritsumei.ac.jp/acd/cg/law/lex/rlr20/Manfred157.pdf>.
Lüttringhaus, Jan D.: Verhandlungspflichten bei Störung der Geschäftsgrundlage – Ein Beitrag zur Dogmatik und Durchsetzung von Anpassungsanspruch und Verhandlungspflichten nach § 313 Abs. 1 BGB, AcP, Vol. 213, No. 2, 2013, pp. 266–298.
Lutz, Achim: Die Berücksichtigung persönlicher Leistungshindernisse in vertraglichen Schuldverhältnissen, Cuvillier Verlag, Göttingen 2002.
Maile-Zinser, Tanja: Auswirkungen der Unmöglichkeit auf den Erfüllungsanspruch, Logos Verlag, Berlin 2006.
Markesinis, Sir Basil/Unberath, Hannes/Johnston, Angus: The German Law of Contract, A Comparative Treatise, Hart, Oregon 2006.
Marquardt, Rudolf: Die teilweise Unmöglichkeit der Leistung nach deutschem bürgerlichem Recht, Vater, Breslau 1925.
Mathias, Reimann: The Good, the Bad, and the Ugly: The Reform of the German Law of Obligations, TLR, Vol. 83, No. 4, 2009, pp. 877–919.
Medicus, Dieter: Bemerkungen zur "vorübergehenden Unmöglichkeit", in: Lorenz, Stephan/Trunk, Alexander/Eidenmüller, Horst/Wendehorst, Christiane/Adolff, Johannes, Festschrift für Andreas Heldrich, C.H. Beck, München 2005, pp. 347–357. (Cited as: Medicus, Unmöglichkeit)
Medicus, Dieter: Schuldrecht I, Allgemeiner Teil, C.H. Beck, München 2006. (Cited as: Medicus)
Mitzkait, Anika: Leistungsstörung und Haftungsbefreiung, Mohr Siebeck, Tübingen 2008.
Motsch, Richard: Risikoverteilung im allgemeinen Leistungstörungsrecht, JZ 2001, pp. 428–433.
Pakuscher, Ernst: Die allgemeinen Grundsätze des Bürgerlichen Gesetzbuchs über die anfängliche Unmöglichkeit der Leistung, J. Pakuscher, Berlin 1907.
Palandt, Otto: Bürgerliches Gesetzbuch, C.H. Beck, München 2010. (Cited as: Palandt/Author)
Pels Leusden, Hans Heinrich: Besteht ein Anspruch auf Leistung trotz Unmöglichkeit der Erfüllung?, Trute, Quakenbrück 1929.
Peres, Daniel: Haftung, Zurechnung und Beweisführung bei anfänglicher und nachträglicher Unmöglichkeit, Duncker & Humblot, Berlin 2012.
Petersen, Jens: Examens-Repetitorium, Allgemeines Schuldrecht, C.F. Müller, Heidelberg 2002.
Popescu, Paul: Kein positives Interesse bei anfänglicher Unmöglichkeit und anfänglich unbehebbaren Mängeln, Nomos, Baden-Baden 2012.
Prütting, Hanns/Wegen, Gerhard/Weinreich, Gerd: BGB Kommentar, Luchterhand, Köln 2011. (Cited as: PWW/Author)
Quass, Guido: Die Nutzungsstörung, Duncker & Humblot, Berlin 2003.
Reinhard, Thorsten: Die beiderseits zu vertretende Unmöglichkeit im Synallagma, Duncker & Humblot, Berlin 1998.
Reinke, Alwin: Die allgemeinen Grundsätze über die anfängliche Unmöglichkeit der Leistung, R. Noske, Borna-Leipzig 1905.
Rohde, Gerd: Die Unmöglichkeit der Leistung bei Gattungsschulden, P & S Sofortdr., Würzburg 1972.
Rödl, Julia: Die Spannung der Schuld, Duncker & Humblot, Berlin 2002.

Rüssmann, Helmut: Die vom Gläubiger und vom Schuldner zu vertretende Unmöglichkeit, in: Brüggemeier, Gert, Liber Amicorum Eike Schmidt, C.F. Müller, Heidelberg 2005, pp. 281–301.

Säcker, Franz Jürgen/Rixecke, Roland: Münchener Kommentar zum Bürgerlichen Gesetzbuch, Band 2, Schuldrecht, Allgemeiner Teil §§ 241–432, C.H. Beck, München 2012. (Cited as: MüKo)

Sarrazin, Wilfried: Die Zweckerreichung als Erlöschungsgrund des Schuldverhältnisses : Zugleich ein Beitrag zur Lehre von der Abgrenzung der Zweckerreichung von der Unmöglichkeit, Vater, Breslau 1935.

Scheer, Günther: Die zeitweilige und die beseitigte Unmöglichkeit der Vertragsleistung, R. Noske, Borna-Leipzig 1906.

Scheller, Adolf: Die zeitweilige Unmöglichkeit der Leistung nach dem Rechte des Bürgerlichen Gesetzbuches, Dissertation, Heidelberg 1908.

Schimmel, Roland/Buhlmann, Dirk: Frankfurter Handbuch zum neuen Schuldrecht, Luchterland, Neuwied/Kriftel 2002.

Schlechtriem, Peter: Die Unmöglichkeit – ein Wiedergänger, in: Coester, Michael/Martiny, Dieter/von Sachsen Gessaphe, Karl August Prinz, Privatrecht in Europa, C.H. Beck, München 2004, pp. 125–133. (Cited as: Schlechtriem, Unmöglichkeit)

Schlechtriem, Peter: The German Act to Modernize the Law of Obligations in the Context of Common Principles and Structures of the Law of Obligations in Europe, <http://ouclf.iuscomp.org/articles/schlechtriem2.shtml>. (Cited as: Schlechtriem, German Act)

Schlechtriem, Peter/Schmidt-Kessel, Martin: Schuldrecht Allgemeiner Teil, Mohr Siebeck, Tübingen 2005.

Schmidt, Patrick: Die Unmöglichkeit der Erfüllung in Ansehung der Zeit, Duncker & Humblot, Berlin 2007.

Schmidt-Kessel, Baldus: Prozessuale Behandlung des Wegfalls der Geschäftsgrundlage nach neuem Recht, NJW 2002, pp. 2076–2078.

Schmidt-Räntsch, Jürgen: Das neue Schuldrecht, Carl Heymanns Verlag, Köln 2002.

Schmidt-Recla, Adrian: Echte, faktische, wirtschaftliche Unmöglichkeit und Wegfall der Geschäftsgrundlage, in: Kern, Bernd-Rüdiger/Wadle, Elmar/Schroeder, Klaus-Peter/Katzenmeier, Christian, Humaniora, Springer, Berlin 2006, pp. 641–668.

Schneider, Susanne: Wechselwirkungen zwischen Irrtum und Unmöglichkeit: ein Beitrag zur Haftung des Schuldners bei anfänglichen Leistungshindernissen, Duncker & Humblot, Berlin 2008.

Schulte-Nölke, Hans: The New German Law of Obligations: an Introduction, <http://www.iuscomp.org/gla/literature/schulte-noelke.htm>.

Schultz, Michael: Leistungsstörungsrecht, in: Westermann, Harm Peter, Das Schuldrecht 2002, Richard Boorberg Verlag, Stuttgart 2002, pp. 17–105.

Schulze, Reiner/Dörner, Heinrich/Ebert, Ina/Hoeren, Thomas/Kemper, Rainer/Saenger, Ingo/Schreiber, Klaus/Schulte-Nölke, Hans/Staudinger, Ansgar: Bürgerliches Gesetzbuch, Handkommentar, Nomos, Baden-Baden 2012. (Cited as: Hk-BGB/Author)

Schwab, Dieter/Löhnig, Martin: Einführung in das Zivilrecht: Einschliesslich BGB- Allgemeiner Teil, C.F. Müller, Heidelberg 2010.

Schwarze, Roland: Das Recht der Leistungsstörungen, de Gruyter, Berlin 2008.

Schweitzer, Herbert: Die ursprüngliche Unmöglichkeit der Leistung bei einseitigen Verpflichtungen nach dem Rechte des Bürgerlichen Gesetzbuches, Henning, Greiz 1911.

Schwenzer, Ingeborg: Schweizerisches Obligationenrecht Allgemeiner Teil, Stämpfli, Bern 2006. (Cited as: Schwenzer, Obligationenrecht)

Schwingenheuer, Yasmine-Lee: Die Geschichte der Unmöglichkeitslehre - Die Unmöglichkeit im Wandel der Zeit, Grin, Norderstedt 2001.

Seichter, Detlef Karl-Heinz: Beiderseits zu vertretende Unmöglichkeit beim Gegenseitigen Vertrag, Schmacht, Bamberg, Hamburg 1971.

Staudinger, Julius von: Kommentar zum Bürgerlichen Gesetzbuch mit Einführungsgesetz und Nebengesetzen, Buch 2, Recht der Schuldverhältnisse, §§ 311, 311a, 312, 312a - f, (Vertragsschluss), Neuarbeitung 2005, Sellier de Gruyter, Berlin 2005. (Cited as: Staudinger/ Author)

Staudinger, Julius von: BGB Eckpfeiler des Zivilrechts, Sellier de Gruyter, Berlin 2005. (Cited as: Staudinger, Eckpfeiler)

Staudinger, Julius von: Kommentar zum Bürgerlichen Gesetzbuch mit Einführungsgesetz und Nebengesetzen, Buch 2, Recht der Schuldverhältnisse, §§ 255–304, (Leistungsstörungsrecht 1), Neuarbeitung 2009, Sellier de Gruyter, Berlin 2009. (Cited as: Staudinger/Author)

Staudinger, Julius von: Kommentar zum Bürgerlichen Gesetzbuch mit Einführungsgesetz und Nebengesetzen, Buch 2, Recht der Schuldverhältnisse, §§ 315–326, (Leistungsstörungsrecht 2), Neuarbeitung 2009, Sellier de Gruyter, Berlin 2009. (Cited as: Staudinger/Author)

Stelzer, Alfred: Die Abgrenzung zwischen Verzug und zeitweiliger Unmöglichkeit der Leistung, Mauser, Forchheim Ofr., 1933.

Stipanski, Eckart: Die zeitweilige und die beseitigte nachfolgende Unmöglichkeit der Leistung nach dem Recht des bürgerlichen Gesetzbuches, Höfer & Limmert, Erlangen 1931.

Sutschet, Holger: Haftung für anfängliches Unvermögen, NJW 2005, pp. 1404–1406.

Sy, Ilaria: Pflichtverletzung und Vertretenmüssen beim Schadensersatz statt der Leistung, Dr. Kovač, Hamburg 2010.

Tonner, Klaus/Willingmann, Armin/Tamm, Marina: Vertragsrecht, Kommentar: Luchterhand, Köln 2010. (Cited as: Author, in: Tonner/Willingmann/Tamm)

Vogt, Patrick: Gesetzliche und rechtsgeschäftliche Beschränkungen der Mängelrechte des Käufers, Unmöglichkeit und Unzumutbarkeit der Leistung im kaufrechtlichen Mängelrecht und rechtsgeschäftliche Disponibilität der 437 ff. BGB, Peter Lang, Frankfurt am Main 2005.

Wagner, Eric: Studien zum Recht der Unmöglichkeit, Nomos, Baden-Baden 2007.

Wallow, Astrid: Risikozuweisung und Vertragshaftung: Anfängliche Leistungshindernisse vor den Gerichten in den U.S.A. und in Deutschland, Lit Verlag, Berlin 2008.

Westermann, Harm Peter/Bydlinski, Peter/Weber, Ralph: BGB-Schuldrecht Allgemeiner Teil, C.F. Müller, Heidelberg 2010.

Wieser, Eberhard: Schuldrechtsreform – Die Unmöglichkeit der Leistung nach neuem Recht, MDR 2002, pp. 858–862.

Wilhelm, Jan/Deeg, Peter: Nachträgliche Unmöglichkeit und nachträgliches Unvermögen, JZ 2001, pp. 223–233.

Zerres, Thomas: Bürgerliches Recht, Ein einführendes Lehrbuch in das Zivil- und Zivilprozessrecht, Springer, Berlin/Heidelberg 2005.

Zimmer, Daniel: Das neue Recht der Leistungsstörungen, NJW 2002, pp. 1–12.

Zimmermann, Reinhard: The New German Law of Obligations, Oxford University Press, Oxford/ New York 2005. (Cited as: Zimmermann, New German Law)

Zimmermann, Reinhard: Breach of Contract and Remedies under the New German Law of Obligations, <http://www.cisg.law.pace.edu/cisg/biblio/zimmerman.html>. (Cited as: Zimmermann, Breach of Contract)

Zweigert, Konrad/Kötz, Hein: Einführung in die Rechtsvergleichung auf dem Gebiete des Privatrechts, Mohr Siebeck, Tübingen 1996.

3) Treatment of Impossibility in Swiss and Turkish Laws

I) Swiss Law of Contracts in General

In 1883, Switzerland codified a law to maintain unification of the law of obligations in different cantons of the country. Despite being a big step of unification of law, not long after 1883, such law was abolished by the current Swiss Code of Obligations (OR) dated 30 March 1911. Within years, OR has been subject to some amendments, but it is still in effect without any cardinal changes to the former OR of 1883.[1]

Unlike the dualistic system in Germany, the Swiss lawmakers preferred to regulate the law of obligations and the commercial law in one single code, *i.e.*, OR. Within this stance, in addition to the law of obligations, which also includes the law of contracts, OR covers commercial law, company law and negotiable documents law. However, matters such as copyright law, patent law, private insurance law and the antitrust laws are excluded from the scope of the OR.[2]

The OR has been influential on a number of subsequent legislation. For instance, the codes of obligation of Italy, Greece, Hungary, Mexico, Montenegro, and Liechtenstein are influenced by the OR. Some influences are also seen on China, Near East and North Africa.[3] Moreover, Turkish lawmakers have *collectively* adopted the Swiss Civil Code (ZGB) and OR from Switzerland.

[1] **Honsell**, ZSR 2011 II, 5, 9.

[2] **Honsell**, ZSR 2011 II, 5, 16.

[3] **Honsell**, ZSR 2011 II, 5, 15 ff.

H.C. Aksoy, *Impossibility in Modern Private Law*, DOI 10.1007/978-3-319-01704-4_3,

II) Turkish Law of Contracts in General

Until the World War I, the law in the Ottoman Empire was based on Islamic principles. Exceptionally, Christians and Jews were entitled to resolve the disputes between each other in accordance with their own law.[4] As a result of the Lausanne Peace Treaty dated 24 July 1923, which confirmed the decline of the Ottoman Empire and the birth of the Republic of Turkey, Turkey undertook to maintain unification of its law.[5] Therefore, the Turkish lawmakers opted-for the adoption of ZGB and OR[6] on 17 February 1926 and 22 April 1926 respectively.[7] Both of the codes were adopted with very minor changes.[8] It would not even be wrong to say that the codes were almost identical to their Swiss equivalents.

Since their entry into force both of the codes have been amended several times. However, most of these amendments were minor and could not overcome the fact that the codes were outdated and failed to answer the needs of the modern world. Therefore reform studies began to fully replace both of the codes. Firstly, the Turkish Civil Code was abolished and replaced in 2001 (effective as of 1 January 2002). Secondly, the new Turkish Code of Obligations (TCO) was accepted in 11 January 2011 (effective as of 1 July 2012).

According to the preamble of the TCO, the international instruments regarding unification of the law have been considered in preparation of the new TCO. However, the amendments to the law were not based on the provisions of Unification Instruments. Moreover, the reforms of German and Dutch Civil Codes have been taken into consideration during the reform studies. However, it is specifically emphasized that none of these texts have significant effects on the provisions or structure of the TCO.[9]

The new TCO generally contains the former provisions with a simplification of the language of the former code, which was outdated. Moreover, there are some systematical changes and also amendments regarding the institutions, which were already accepted by the doctrine and the courts in Switzerland and Turkey—*e.g.*, regulation of the excessive performance difficulty. Actually, due to the continuous influence of the Swiss law in Turkey, the scholarly developments in the field of law of obligations have been parallel. Therefore, the new TCO may easily be regarded

---

[4] **Oğuz**, AÜHFD 2006, 195, 197.

[5] **Oğuz**, AÜHFD 2006, 195, 200.

[6] Except for the Commercial Code, which was adopted from Germany.

[7] During the discussions about modernization of the civil law, adoption of one of the three major civil codes were considered: ZGB, BGB and French Civil Code (CC). However, ZGB was chosen for adoption, as it was believed to be more modern and democratic than its alternatives. In particular, ZGB was found to be more modern than CC and more adaptable and concrete than BGB. **Oğuz**, AÜHFD 2006, 195, 201; **Oğuzman/Barlas**, p. 22.

[8] **Oğuz**, AÜHFD 2006, 195, 201; **Bucher**, p. 217.

[9] See the Preamble of the law, p. 2–3, available at: <http://www.tbmm.gov.tr/sirasayi/donem23/yil01/ss321.pdf>.

as an "update" of the former law in accordance with the jurisprudence and scholarly opinions in Switzerland.

Article 1/III of Turkish Civil Code rules that when making a decision, judges would consider scientific opinions and court decisions. Within this stance, the said sources do not only refer to doctrine and court decisions in Turkish law but also the Swiss doctrine and the jurisprudence. In fact, in its several decisions, the Turkish Court of Appeals makes reference to the Swiss doctrine and jurisprudence. Therefore, in this study, the regulation of impossibility under Swiss and Turkish laws will be evaluated together.

III) Mommsen's Impossibility Doctrine

The legal regime of impossibility in Swiss and Turkish laws is based on Mommsen's doctrine of impossibility, which the author revealed in his book of 1853.[10] Actually, Mommsen's impossibility doctrine has not only been highly influential on the OR and consequently on TCO. In fact, such influence could also be seen in the former BGB.[11] However, during the reform of 2002 such influence has been removed from the BGB to a large extent. This being the fact the Swiss and the Turkish laws still follow Mommsen's doctrine of impossibility.[12] More specifically, (objective) initial impossibility still causes the contract to be void and the sanction of voidness is based on the "*impossibilium nulla obligatio est*" principle accepted in the Roman law.[13]

Mommsen's perception of the breach of contract was shaped around the notion of impossibility. The author first of all separated between real impossibility (wahre Unmöglichkeit) and arbitrary non-performance (willkürlichen Nichterfüllung). According to the author, all cases, where impossibility caused the contract to be void or released the debtor from his obligation were termed as real impossibility. On the other hand, all the remaining cases, which had no effect on the debtor's obligation were termed as arbitrary non-performance.[14] Therefore, Mommsen's notion of impossibility was a very broad conceptual abstraction.[15]

---

[10] For the book: "Die Unmöglichkeit der Leistung in ihrem Einfluss auf obligatorische Verhältnisse", see **Mommsen**, p. 1 ff. For a critique of Mommsen's doctrine of impossibility, see **Wollschläger**, p. 159 ff.

[11] According to Zimmermann, if Mommsen's doctrine did not manage to impress Bernhard Windscheid and through him the fathers of BGB, such doctrine would probably be largely forgotten. **Zimmermann**, Law of Obligations, p. 810.

[12] In fact, Turkish lawmakers have adhered to such doctrine even after the reform of TCO.

[13] **von Büren**, p. 120; **Serozan**, § 14, Nr. 17; **Esser/Schmidt**, § 22, III; **Huber**, Leistungsstörungen I, § 4 III 3, p. 115.

[14] **Mommsen**, p. 2.

[15] **Zimmermann**, Law of Obligations, p 810; **Immenhauser**, p. 290.

The roots of Mommsen's doctrine of impossibility reaches to the Roman principle of *impossibilium nulla obligatio est.*[16] Therefore Mommsen was not the first person to state that initial objective impossibility caused the contract to be void. However, until the middle of the nineteenth century, this institution was understood in a very narrow way.[17] Mommsen's purpose was to reach a complete system from various individual rules of the *Corpus Iuris Civilis* and especially the *Digest.*[18] This being the fact, as a result of Mommsen's theory, subsequent impossibility became the essential dogmatic cornerstone of the law of breach of contract.[19]

In his book, Mommsen focused on identifying the requirements for the existence of impossibility; and when there exists real impossibility, which would enable the debtor's release from the results of non-performance.[20] Moreover, in his work, the author categorized impossibility as natural and legal, absolute and relative, objective and subjective, permanent and temporary, total and partial, initial and subsequent.[21] Such categorization was important because—in Mommsen's doctrine—legal consequences on a given situation depended on its place within such types of impossibility.[22]

As appropriately expressed by Zimmermann: "*Mommsen's book is characterized by that abstract and excessive conceptualism which is so typical of pandectist writing. It forced the sources into a scheme which was alien to the Roman lawyers and which, today, fails to appeal to legal historians and modern lawyers alike.*"[23] Although Mommsen tried to conceptualize and categorize all cases of impossibility, the distinctions between the types of impossibility are not easy to draw. Therefore, such classification of Mommsen is inappropriate for determining if the debtor should be released from his obligation and/or responsibility.[24]

Despite several criticisms made to his classification of impossibility, many of the propositions of Mommsen may still be found in Swiss and Turkish laws. For instance, in his book, the author introduced the systematical differentiation between the cases of initial and subsequent impossibility and emphasized that initial objective impossibility caused the contract to be void: *impossibilium nulla obligation est.*[25] On the other hand, the result of subsequent impossibility was twofolded: it differed when the debtor was responsible for the occurrence of impossibility and when the debtor was not responsible for such incident. Accordingly, only in the

---

[16] **Immenhauser**, p. 289.

[17] **Poszewiecki**, p. 4.

[18] **Emmert**, p. 11.

[19] **Zimmermann**, Law of Obligations, p. 810.

[20] **Mommsen**, p. 2 ff. **Sutschet**, Garantiehaftung, p. 84.

[21] **Mommsen**, p. 3 ff.

[22] **Zimmermann**, Law of Obligations, p. 810.

[23] **Zimmermann**, Law of Obligations, p. 810.

[24] **Brunner**, p. 87.

[25] **Mommsen**, p. 6 and p. 103 ff.

latter case the debtor could be released from his obligation to perform.[26] However, these were not the only propositions of the author, which survives until today. For instance, the author also stated that in principle temporary impossibility does not eliminate the debtor's obligation to perform,[27] and in principle no impossibility occurs regarding debt in kind[28] and monetary debt.[29]

IV) Regulation of Impossibility in Swiss and Turkish Laws

1) In General

Following Mommsen's doctrine, in Swiss and Turkish laws, the first criterion for the classification of the types of impossibility is the chronological distinction.[30] Accordingly it is considered whether impossibility occurred before the formation of the contract, or after the formation of the contract. Accordingly, (*i*) initial (objective) impossibility does not create obligation (*impossibilium nulla obligation est*), and (*ii*) subsequent impossibility eliminates the obligation to perform (*casus a nulla praestunt*).[31]

Similar to BGB, the Swiss law—as well as Turkish law—follow the fault-liability system of the civil law. Therefore, in addition to a time based-distinction, impossibility is subject to another distinction based on the responsibility[32] of the debtor on the occurrence of the impossibility. More specifically, as in German law, such responsibility is necessary to entitle the creditor to claim compensation from the debtor.

The provisions of the Swiss law—and Turkish law—regarding impossibility are very brief. Similar to BGB, neither OR nor TCO defines the concept of impossibility. Despite the detailed and complex nature of the types and effects of impossibility, the OR contains only three simple articles regarding impossibility of performance:

(i) Article 20 about voidness of contracts, which includes voidness due to initial impossibility;

[26] **Mommsen**, p. 228 ff.

[27] **Mommsen**, p. 295.

[28] **Mommsen**, p. 47.

[29] **Mommsen**, p. 232.

[30] **Poszewiecki**, p. 1 ff.

[31] **Serozan**, § 14, Nr. 17.

[32] "*Impossibility should not be classified based on the debtor's fault but in general whether the debtor can be held responsible for such impossibility or not.*" Yarg. HGK., 2010/14-386 E., 2010/427 K., 29.9.2010.

(ii) Article 97 about non-performance, which includes subsequent impossibility for which the debtor is responsible; and
(iii) Article 119 about the subsequent impossibility for which the debtor is not responsible.

The above stated provisions are also found in the TCO under Articles 27, 112 and 136 respectively. Moreover, during the reform of the TCO, the lawmakers regulated the partial impossibility of performance under Article 137. As it will be explained below, such provision is merely a restatement of the principle already accepted in Swiss and Turkish legal doctrines.

2) *Initial Impossibility of Performance*

a) The General Principle

Unlike German law, OR still preserves the distinction between initial impossibility and subsequent impossibility. Similarly, despite the criticism in the doctrine and the modern legal trend, which accepts that the time of occurrence of the impossibility has no relevance as to the results of impossibility, the Turkish lawmakers preferred to preserve the distinction of initial and subsequent impossibility in the new TCO.

The effects of initial impossibility of performance are dealt with under Article 20/I OR. Accordingly, "*A contract is void if its terms are impossible, unlawful or immoral.*"[33] In general, such provision is a restriction of the party autonomy and the freedom of contract.[34] Party autonomy is one of the most important principles, which constitutes the basis of the modern private law. It means that the parties have the authority to directly regulate their private law relationships in accordance with their free wills.[35] Within this scope, parties are free to conclude any contract they like within the boundaries permitted by law. Such freedom, which is derived from the principle of party autonomy is termed as the freedom of contract.

Article 20 OR—as Article 27/I TCO—is a brief provision with very important results. It restricts the parties' freedom to conclude contracts which are impossible to perform at the time of contract formation, and sets forth heavy legal sanctions for such cases. Accordingly, if the parties behave against the restriction of the law, the result is voidness of their contract.

---

[33] Similarly, Article 27/I TCO, titled as "*Voidness*" states that "*. . .where the subject of a contract is impossible, such contract is null and void.*"

[34] **Keller/Schöbi**, p. 79; **Basler/Huguenin**, Art. 19–20, N. 1; **Schwarz**, p. 358; **Topuz/Canbolat**, AÜHFD 2008, 673, 681; **Eren**, p. 295; **Altunkaya**, p. 47.

[35] **Altunkaya**, p. 66.

b) Elements of Initial Impossibility

Elements of initial impossibility are not revealed under Article 20 OR—or Article 27/I TCO. Therefore the elements of initial impossibility are concretized by jurisprudence and the doctrine.

Firstly, the subject of the contract must be impossible. Each contract consists of one or more obligations, which must be performed by the debtor. The subject of the contract refers to the obligations undertaken by the parties of the contract. For a contract to be void due to initial impossibility, the performance of one or more obligations under the contract must be impossible. Within this stance, a legal norm may cause impossibility of performance as well, *i.e.*, legal impossibility.[36]

Secondly, impossibility of the performance must be already present at the time of the conclusion of the contract.[37] If performance was possible during contract formation, but impossibility arises later on, the contract would not be subject to the Article 20/I OR—or Article 27/I TCO.[38] On the other hand, as accepted in the former BGB, if performance is objectively impossible at the time of contract formation, this is sufficient to cause voidness.[39]

---

[36] In one of its decisions, the Turkish Court of Appeals ruled that the construction agreement regarding establishment of a five storey building is void due to initial impossibility, since the relevant regulation, which was in effect on the date of contract formation, prohibited such construction. Yarg. 15. HD., 1981/331 E , 1981/1050 K., 7.5.1981. Also according to the Turkish Court of Appeals, if at the date of contract formation, the subject-matter land is a protected area, the construction agreement concerning such land is invalid due to legal impossibility. Yarg. 15. HD., 1993/1707 E., 1994/1232 K., 2.3.1994. For similar decisions, see Yarg. 15. HD., 1997/1995 E., 1997/2319 K., 1.5.1997; Yarg. 15. HD., 1999/1573 E., 1999/3113 K., 13.9.1999; Yarg. 15. HD., 2001/2101 E., 2001/4508 K., 11.10.2001.

[37] **Basler/Huguenin**, Art. 19–20, N. 46; **Gauch/Schluep**, Band II, Nr. 2525; **Koller**, § 13, Nr. 41; **Bucher**, p. 247; **Zürcher/Oser/Schönenberger**, Art. 20, N. 3; **CHK/Kut**, OR 19–20, Rdnr. 32; **Reisoğlu**, p. 105; **Oğuzman/Öz**, p. 78; **Eren**, p. 295; **Topuz/Canbolat**, AÜHFD 2008, 673, 681. "*Impossibility within the meaning of Article 20 OR is likely only if it has existed from the beginning; the promised performance must be definitely unperformable due to factual or legal reasons.*" BGE 96 II 18, 21.

[38] Oğuzman/Öz make a distinction between impossibility of the subject of the contract and impossibility of performance. The authors use the former for cases of initial impossibility and the latter for subsequent impossibility. **Oğuzman/Öz**, p. 78.

[39] If performance becomes somehow possible later on, the contract does not become valid. **Eren**, p. 298; **Oğuzman/Öz**, p. 78. However, it is also argued in the doctrine that if there is a time interval between the conclusion and performance of the contract, impossibility of performance must be evaluated by taking the time of performance into consideration. In other words, if initial impossibility of performance disappears on the date of performance, the contract would not be null and void due to initial impossibility. Similarly, it is argued that in conditional contracts, if performance which was impossible at the time of contract formation, becomes possible at the time of occurrence of the condition, the provision would not apply. **Tunçomağ**, p. 179. On the other hand, Oğuzman/Öz state that disappearance of initial impossibility prior to performance (*i.e.*, between contract formation and performance) eliminates voidness of the contract only if the parties have concluded the contract with an expectation that performance will be possible in the future. **Oğuzman/Öz**, p. 78.

Thirdly, impossibility must be objective in nature. Although this requirement is not explicit under the law, there is consensus in the jurisprudence and doctrine that only objective impossibility might lead to voidness due to initial impossibility.[40] Therefore, cases of subjective impossibility will not be dealt with under the relevant provision. In this respect, Swiss and Turkish laws are identical with the old German law—as the former § 306 BGB only addressed objective initial impossibility as well.

Fourthly impossibility must be permanent.[41] This means that temporary impossibility of performance does not lead to voidness of the contract.[42]

c) Legal Results of Initial Impossibility

aa) Voidness of the Contract

(1) Voidness of the Entire Contract

The result of initial impossibility is voidness of the contract. Such result is based on the idea that any illogical and irrational obligation is at the same time illegal.[43] In other words if, at the time of contract formation, an obligation was impossible, it is regarded as illogical and irrational. Therefore such contract creates no results before the law.

Voidness is a very heavy sanction that a might be imposed on a contract[44] because if a contract is null and void, it creates no legal results *ex tunc*.[45] Voidness

---

[40] **Guhl/Koller**, § 7, Nr. 18; **Berner/Becker**, Art. 20, N. 2; **Gauch/Schluep**, Band I, Nr. 634; **Basler/Huguenin**, Art. 19–20, N. 46; **Koller**, § 13, Nr. 28; **Schwarz**, p. 359; **Huguenin**, Nr. 570; **Bucher**, p. 248; **CHK/Kut**, OR 19–20, Rdnr. 32; **Topuz/Canbolat**, AÜHFD 2008, 673, 682; **İnan**, p. 194; **Eren**, p. 295; **Reisoğlu**, p. 105; **Akıntürk**, Borçlar, p. 137; **Uygur**, p. 1020; **Oğuzman/Öz**, p. 78. According to the Turkish Court of Appeals, "... *if it is found that performance impossibility occurred before the formation of the contract (as expropriation of the land, recognition of the land as green area or allocation to public service...), since the subject-matter of the contract would be 'objectively impossible' for everyone, such contract is void.*" Yarg. 15. HD., 2003/6203 E., 2004/3318 K., 14.6.2004.

[41] **Zürcher/Oser/Schönenberger**, Art. 20, N.3; **von Tuhr/Escher**, p. 96; **Guhl/Koller**, § 38, Nr. 35; **CHK/Kut**, OR 19–20, Rdnr. 32; **Schwenzer**, Obligationenrecht, Nr. 64.02; **Koller**, § 13, Nr. 28; **Eren**, p. 295; **Topuz/Canbolat**, AÜHFD 2008, 673, 682.

[42] In one of the cases resolved by the Turkish Court of Appeals: at the date of the sales contract, although the subject-matter immovables were registered under his name at the land registry, the seller could not perform the preliminary sales contract due to an engagement with the Ministry of Treasury in a lawsuit. The Court of Appeals ruled that due to the possibility of performance at the end of the lawsuit between the seller and the Ministry of Treasury, there is no impossibility and the preliminary sales contract is valid. Yarg. HGK., 2010/14-386 E., 2010/427 K., 29.9.2010.

[43] **Serozan**, § 14, Nr. 17.

[44] Theories of invalidity are separated into two groups as classical theory and modern theory. The classical theory accepts invalidity as a defect in the valid formation of legal transactions. On the other hand, according to the modern theory invalidity is a sanction (a legal result). Accordingly, the classical theory classifies invalidity as voidness and cancellation (voidability). However, the modern theory accepts that there are mid-categories of invalidity in between voidness and cancellation. **Eren**, p. 299. In the Turkish legal doctrine, the main types of invalidity are: non-existence, incompleteness, voidness and cancellation.

[45] BGE 97 II 108, 115.

of a contract is an automatic sanction, which does not require a notice, notification or initiation of an action by the parties of the contract or any third parties.[46] In case of a legal dispute, the judge must consider voidness *ex officio*.[47] Such illegality cannot be reversed by any transaction.[48]

As explained above, subjective initial impossibility does not cause the contract to be void.[49] Accordingly, there are two different opinions in the doctrine regarding the results of subjective initial impossibility. The first opinion in the doctrine equates subjective initial impossibility with subjective subsequent impossibility. Therefore according to this opinion, provisions of subjective subsequent impossibility would apply to the cases of subjective initial impossibility.[50] For instance, it makes no difference if the subject matter of the contract was already burnt (objective impossibility) or stolen (subjective impossibility) at the time of contract formation. The legal results would apply depending on the responsibility of the debtor on impossibility of the performance.

According to the second opinion,[51]—as in the former BGB—it must be accepted that in case of subjective initial impossibility the debtor is liable under a guarantee.[52] Serozan argues that the law has set forth some cases, where the debtor is liable under a guarantee for the cases of subjective initial impossibility. For instance, the principle of *genus non perit* is a typical example of such cases. Within this scope, regardless of his fault, the debtor is held responsible for his non-performance due to guarantee liability. The author proposes to apply such guarantee liability to all cases of subjective initial impossibility by analogy.[53] According to such opinion, prior to making a commitment, the debtor must consider if he is capable of performing such

[46] **Guhl/Koller**, § 7, Nr. 38; **Berner/Becker**, Art. 20, N. 11; **Olgaç**, p. 90; **Kocayusufpaşaoğlu**, § 43, Nr. 21. Voidness is an exceptional case that enables third parties to interfere with the relativity of the contract and claim invalidity of the contract. **Tekinay/Akman/Burcuoğlu/Altop**, p. 375.

[47] **Berner/Becker**, Art. 20, N. 11.

[48] **Berner/Becker**, Art. 20, N. 10; **Basler/Huguenin**, Art. 19–20, N. 53; **Huguenin**, Nr. 397; **Gauch/Schluep**, Band I, Nr. 681; **Eren** p. 301; **Tekinay/Akman/Burcuoğlu/Altop**, p. 376; **Topuz/Canbolat**, AÜHFD 2008, 673, 683; **Oğuzman/Barlas**, p. 167–168.

[49] **Gauch/Schluep**, Band I, Nr. 634; **Serozan**, § 14, Nr. 16 According to the Turkish Court of Appeals: "*. . .since the person who has sold the immovable may buy it from the owner and deliver to the buyer, the impossibility hereunder is not the absolute impossibility which is shown as a reason of voidness under the said article* (*Article 27 of TCO*)" Yarg. 13. HD., 1977/2466 E., 1977/2982 K., 24.5.1977.

[50] In this opinion, see **Schwenzer**, Obligationenrecht, Nr. 64.08; **Guhl/Koller**, § 7, Nr. 18.

[51] In this opinion, see **Serozan**, § 14, Nr. 26.

[52] Also, under the new BGB, one might argue that there will be (at least quite often) an implicit guarantee of the debtor that there is no subjective initial impossibility.

[53] The author assumes that there is a gap in Article 27 of TCO, which must be filled by analogy to the provisions of TCO, where a guarantee liability is set forth for specific cases of subjective initial impossibility. **Serozan**, § 14, Nr. 26.

obligation. The creditor is entitled to interpret a commitment of the debtor as an expression of capability.[54]

(2) Partial Voidness

Invalidity sanction applies to contracts which exceed the boundaries of the freedom of contract. However, it is probable that some parts of a contract exceeds such freedom, but the remaining provisions are in accordance with the law. In such cases, the principle of interpretation in favour of the contract (*favor contractus*) requires that a certain part of the contract be deemed invalid, but the remaining provisions survive.[55] Within this stance, partial voidness of a contract is dealt with under Article 20/II OR as follows[56]:

> However, where the defect pertains only to certain terms of a contract, those terms alone are void unless there is cause to assume that the contract would not have been concluded without them.[57]

The first condition required for partial voidness[58] of the contract is that the contract is divisible in its nature.[59] Moreover, only a part of the contract's content must be affected; the parties must not have concluded a voidness agreement[60]; and the presumed wills of the parties must be the preservation of the contract.[61] Finally,

---

[54] **Serozan**, § 14, Nr. 24–26. According to the author, only exception to such guarantee liability is atypical risks, *i.e., force majeure*. **Serozan**, § 14, Nr. 27.

[55] **Eren**, p. 303.

[56] In Turkish law, the same provision is regulated under Article 27/II of TCO.

[57] Such provision is opposite to § 139 BGB, titled as "*Partial invalidity*": "*If a part of a legal transaction is void, then the entire legal transaction is void, unless it is to be assumed that it would have been undertaken even without the void part.*"

[58] There are two types of partial voidness: modified partial voidness and extended partial voidness. The first refers to the cases, where the invalid provision is replaced by a provision of the law. On modified partial nullity, see **Koller**, § 13, Nr. 77 ff. **Gauch/Schluep**, Band I, Nr. 703 ff.; **Başpınar**, p. 152 ff. The extended partial voidness refers to the cases where the voidness of the provisions of a contract is extended to cover such contract's other provisions, which would be unacceptable by the parties due to the voidness of the former part. In other words, if any remaining part of the contract is unacceptable for the parties, such part would also be deemed as void. **Oğuzman/Barlas**, p. 170–171. Article 20/II OR refers to extended partial voidness.

[59] **Topuz/Canbolat**, AÜHFD 2008, 673, 684; **Eren**, p. 304; **Başpınar**, p. 57.

[60] In the doctrine it is accepted that the provision on partial nullity is not a mandatory provision. Therefore parties are entitled to make a voidness agreement regarding the results of the voidness of some provisions of their contract. Accordingly, they may choose to accept that partial voidness does not affect the remaining provisions or void provisions would be replaced by certain secondary provisions. **Gauch/Schluep**, Band I, Nr. 696; **Basler/Huguenin**, Art. 19–20, N. 68; **Eren**, p. 308–309.

[61] **Topuz/Canbolat**, AÜHFD 2008, 673, 684; **Başpınar**, p. 87. It is argued that assessment of the presumed wills of the parties must be made objectively. It must be considered, how the reasonable honest parties would react to conclude the contract provided that they were aware of the partial voidness at the time of contract formation. **Gauch/Schluep**, Band I, Nr. 700; **Basler/Huguenin**, Art. 19–20, N. 64; **Eren**, p. 308. This criterion actually refers to the exception in Article 20/II OR

excluding its invalid provisions, the remaining parts of the contract must still involve the minimum required content and elements of a contract. Otherwise the voidness affects the contract in its entirety.[62]

In case of partial voidness, the void part of the contract is not binding on the parties, but the parties are still bound by the remaining valid part of the contract. However, this principle applies "*unless there is cause to assume that the contract would not have been concluded without them.*" This provision enables to protect the party that will be disadvantaged due to partial voidness.[63] If such party proves that he would not conclude the contract with its new content, the entire contract would be deemed void. The status of the parties; evidence reflecting the importance they have given to the invalid provision while concluding the contract; the relationship between the invalid provision and the other provisions; and the entirety of the contract may be used to prove such case.[64]

bb) Counter-Obligation and Return of Already Performed Counter-Obligation

The practical result of voidness of the contract is that the parties will not be under any obligation to perform. In fact, neither the debtor nor the creditor is under an obligation to perform due to a null and void contract. Moreover, any obligation that has already been performed must be returned according to the principles of unjust enrichment.[65]

cc) Compensation Payment

Voidness of the contract takes place regardless of the existence of the debtor's fault in the occurrence of initial impossibility. However, as in German law, if the debtor was aware or should have been aware of the impossibility while concluding the contract, the creditor may ask for compensation from the debtor. Within this stance, it is accepted in Swiss and Turkish doctrines that such compensation covers the

---

and Article 27/II s. 2 TCO, which set forth that, when it is clearly understood that the contract would not be concluded without such provisions, the whole contract is void.

[62] **Tekinay/Akman/Burcuoğlu/Altop**, p. 379.

[63] **Tekinay/Akman/Burcuoğlu/Altop**, p. 379; **Eren**, p. 303.

[64] **Tekinay/Akman/Burcuoğlu/Altop**, p. 380.

[65] **Serozan**, § 14, Nr. 3; **Topuz/Canbolat**, AÜHFD 2008, 673, 683; **Tekinay/Akman/Burcuoğlu/Altop**, p. 376. "*Following a validly concluded immovable contract, if performance of the contract becomes impossible, the sales price that was paid to the seller may be claimed back at the market value on the date, when performance has become impossible.*" Yarg. 13. HD., 2009/5788 E., 2009/13309 K., 16.11.2009.

negative damages of the creditor.[66] This was also the principle accepted in the German law before the reform.

The legal ground of compensation in case of initial impossibility is *culpa in contrahendo*.[67] In fact, creditor's negative damages are basically the damages incurred due to the breach of the creditor's trust that there is a valid contract. In such cases the liability of the debtor arises not due to breach of a contractual obligation, but a breach of *behaviour obligation*. As a matter of fact, it cannot be argued that the debtor breached his contractual obligations because at the time of occurrence of the impossibility there was no contract. On the other hand, the debtor has failed to inform the creditor of impossibility and created a false trust that there is a valid contract.[68]

3) *Subsequent Impossibility of Performance*

a) In General

The main distinction in OR and TCO concerning the subsequent impossibility is based on the responsibility of the debtor with regard to impossibility. Accordingly, cases of (*i*) subsequent impossibility for which the debtor is not responsible; and (*ii*) subsequent impossibility for which the debtor is responsible are dealt with under different provisions of the law.

Impossibility of performance, which occurs after formation of the contract without the responsibility of the debtor is regulated under Article 119 OR—as well as Article 136 TCO. Such provision only regulates the cases of subsequent impossibility for which the debtor is not responsible. Since initial impossibility is regulated as a reason of voidness, it has been excluded from the scope of Article 119 OR, which reads as follows:

> An obligation is deemed extinguished where its performance is made impossible by circumstances not attributable to the obligor.
>
> In a bilateral contract, the obligor thus released is liable for the consideration already received pursuant to the provisions on unjust enrichment and loses his counter-claim to the extent it has not yet been satisfied.
>
> This does not apply to cases in which, by law or contractual agreement, the risk passes to the obligee prior to performance.[69]

---

[66] Yarg. 13. HD., 1984/2594 E., 1984/4113 K., 29.5.1984; **Serozan**, § 14, Nr. 21; **Tunçomağ**, p. 182; **Altunkaya**, p. 238.

[67] **Berner/Weber**, Art. 97, N. 109; **Schwenzer**, Obligationenrecht, Nr. 63.06; **Kramer**, Obligationenrecht, N. 218; **Bucher**, p. 249; **Huguenin**, Nr. 395; **Brieskorn**, p. 48; **Serozan**, § 14, Nr. 21; **Altunkaya**, p. 239; **Tekinay/Akman/Burcuoğlu/Altop**, p. 377; **Oğuzman/Öz**, p. 79.

[68] **Serozan**, § 14, Nr. 21.

[69] Such provision corresponds to Article 136 of the TCO, which is titled as "*Performance Impossibility*". During the reform of TCO, the lawmakers have amended the provision and

Subsequent impossibility for which the debtor is responsible is not regulated by a special provision in OR—as well as TCO. Therefore, such cases are dealt with under the general provision on non-performance, *i.e.*, Article 97 OR/Article 112 TCO.[70] Article 97/I OR, which is identical to Article 112 TCO reads as follows:

> An obligor who fails to discharge an obligation at all or as required must make amends for the resulting loss or damage unless he can prove that he was not at fault.

b) Elements of Subsequent Impossibility

Subsequent impossibility takes place if performance of the contract becomes impossible after the formation of the contract. Therefore, the first requirement of subsequent impossibility is that performance must be impossible. Second, such impossibility must occur after the formation of the contract.[71]

According to the classical and prevailing opinion in the doctrine, subsequent impossibility may either be objective or subjective in nature.[72] However, another opinion in the doctrine argues that in order to refer to subsequent impossibility, performance must be objectively impossible.[73] Under any circumstances, it is accepted that a legal norm may cause subsequent impossibility as well.[74]

---

added a final paragraph regarding the duty of notification. The amended paragraph reads as follows: "*If the debtor fails to immediately notify the creditor about the occurrence of performance impossibility and to take necessary precautions for prevention of increase of damages, the debtor is obliged to cover the loses arising therefrom.*"

[70] "*If . . . afterwards (the formation of the contract), performance of the obligation has become impossible with the fault of the debtor, Article 96 (former Article 112 TCO) should apply. . .*" Yarg. 15. HD., 2003/1513 E., 2003/2093 K., 21.4.2003. For a similar decision, see Yarg. 11. HD., 1988/9411 E., 1990/1087 K., 20.2.1990.

[71] If expropriation takes place after the formation of the lease agreement, there is impossibility of performance in accordance with Article 117 (former Article 136) of TCO. Yarg. 14. HD., 2008/520 E., 2008/1833 K., 18.2.2009.

[72] In this opinion, see **Schwenzer**, Obligationenrecht, Nr. 64.09; **von Tuhr/Escher**, p. 94; **Berner/Weber**, Art. 97, N. 121; **Basler/Wiegand**, Art. 97, N. 13; **Tunçomağ**, p. 482; **Serozan**, § 15, Nr. 1.

[73] In this opinion, see **Gauch/Schluep**, Band II, N. 2533 and N. 2575; **Zürcher/Aepli**, Art. 119, N. 47; **Eren**, p. 1249; **Dural**, Sonraki İmkansızlık, p. 89.

[74] For instance, if construction is prevented as a result of the amendments to relevant zoning legislation after the formation of the contract, this would cause extinguishment of the obligation under Article 117 (former Article 136) of TCO. Yarg. 15. HD., 2001/5744 E., 2002/2065 K., 25.4.2002; Yarg. 15. HD., 2004/1009 E., 2004/5441 K., 27.10.2004; Yarg. 16. HD., 2001/4839 E., 2001/4786 K., 24.10.2001. "*Due to their private laws, state enterprises must take permission of the Ministry prior to the sale of immovables. Therefore, it must be accepted that there is impossibility under Article 117 (former Article 136) since the sale of the immovables have been halted by the order of the Ministry, despite the obligation of sale under the protocol.*" Yarg. HGK., 1987/11-539 E., 1989/320 K., 6.4.1988.

Moreover, subsequent impossibility must be permanent in nature.[75] In other words, temporary impossibility would not be regarded as impossibility of performance under Article 119 OR or Article 136 TCO. However, it must be noted that as in German law, in some cases temporary impossibility may be deemed as permanent impossibility.

Finally, similar to German law, it is also accepted in Swiss and Turkish laws that impossibility does not occur regarding debt in kind[76] and monetary obligations.[77]

c) Interference with the Basis of the Contract

In Swiss and Turkish laws, interference with the basis of the contract is not covered by the rules on impossibility of performance.[78] More specifically, in such cases the obligation of the debtor would not be extinguished *ipso iure*, even if the debtor is not responsible for the change of circumstances. On the other hand, there is no express provision in the OR regarding the legal results of interference with the basis

[75] **Guhl/Koller**, § 31, Nr. 3; **Kälin**, recht 2004, 246, 248; **Zürcher/Aepli**, Art. 119, N. 44; **Eren**, p. 1250.

[76] However, as in German law, objective impossibility may occur regarding limited debt in kind. **Berner/Weber**, Art. 97, N.115; **Zürcher/Aepli**, Art. 119, N. 50.

[77] **Gauch/Schluep**, Band II, Nr. 2572.

[78] "*If performance has become impossible without the debtor's fault after the formation of the obligatory relationship, in such case the obligation is extinguished (TCO Article 117 (former Article 136)). However, if the performance of the obligation becomes excessively difficult for the debtor, this lies outside the scope of Article 117. Excessive difficulty must not be confused with impossibility of performance.*" Yarg. 13. HD., 1990/5697 E., 1990/8708 K., 14.12.1990. In a decision, where the claimant argued performance impossibility due to devaluation, the Turkish Court of Appeals ruled that during the said years the Turkish press was frequently publishing articles on the loss of value of Turkish liras. Therefore, the claimant cannot argue that he could not expect devaluation. Yarg. HGK., 1978/11-773 E., 1980/2310 K., 17.10.1980. In another decision, where the claimant argued that the foreign exchange bottle-neck caused impossibility, the court ruled that the foreign exchange bottle-neck was a known reality in Turkey; therefore there is no impossibility. Yarg. 13. HD, 1981/2749 E., 1981/3786 K., 14.5.1981. For a similar decision, see Yarg. HGK., 1982/13-264 E., 1984/501 K., 2.5.1984. In another decision, where the claimant argued that devaluation caused impossibility, the court ruled that "*It (impossibility) does not enable adaptation of the contract to the new circumstances. Therefore the case at hand should not be dealt with under impossibility, but excessive difficulty.*" Yarg. 13. HD., 1996/3653 E., 1996/3920 K., 16.4.1996. "*The respondent Soil Products Office, who knows the Turkish import regime and the authorities of the Ministry of Finance with regard to allocation of foreign exchange could have taken the necessary precautions; it could have made the foreign exchange allocation beforehand as in the former contracts or at least, as it did in the former contract, it could bind the import to the requirement of foreign exchange allocation by the competent authority. It cannot be accepted that the party, who incurs debt without taking necessary precautions, relies on an event of impossibility that could be prevented by taking such precautions.*" Yarg. HGK., 1984/11-139 E., 1984/426 K., 18.4.1984.

of the contract. Within this stance, in Switzerland, the doctrine of the interference with the basis of the contract is developed by the jurisprudence.[79]

According to the jurisprudence of the Swiss Federal Court, interference with the basis of the contract requires that the circumstances at the time of contract formation have changed unforeseeably[80] and such change in circumstances has seriously damaged the balance between the obligation and counter-obligation causing gross disproportionality.[81] In any case, the risk regarding change of circumstances must not have been assumed by either of the parties in accordance with the contract or the law.[82] When the above stated requirements exist, the court has the discretion to adapt the contract to the changed circumstances or terminate the contract.[83] Within this stance, the court considers the hypothetical wills of the parties and the requirement of good faith.[84]

Until the reform of TCO, interference with the basis of the contract was handled by Turkish courts in accordance with the above explained application in Switzerland. During the reform, Turkish lawmakers regulated excessive performance difficulty as an explicit provision under Article 138 of TCO.[85] However, such provision is merely a restatement of the common principle already accepted by Swiss and Turkish courts and doctrines.[86]

---

[79] For adaptation of the contract under Swiss law, see **Kälin**, recht 2004, 246, 251 ff.

[80] BGE 101 II, 17, 21.

[81] "*A judicial intervention at the request of the debtor, based on Article 2 of the ZGB is permitted only if the relationship between the obligation and counter-obligation is disturbed because of exceptional change in circumstances such that the insistence of the creditor on his contractual claim is simply an excessive exploitation of the disproportion so that it constitutes a manifest abuse of right, which finds no legal protection under Article 2, paragraph 2 of the ZGB (BGE 93-II-188, 68-II-173, 67-I-300, 62-II-45, 59-II-378/9).*" BGE 107 II 343, 348.

[82] **Schwenzer**, Obligationenrecht, Nr. 35 07.

[83] **Schwenzer**, Obligationenrecht, Nr. 35 10.

[84] "*Is there lack of such a contractual or statutory rule, for the adaptation of the contract by the judge the hypothetical wills of the parties must be taken into account... The court must determine, therefore, what the parties would have agreed in accordance with the principle of good faith, if they had taken into consideration the ordinary course of events.*" BGE 127 III, 300, 307.

[85] The provision reads as follows: "*If a condition, which at the time of the conclusion of the contract could not be foreseen by the parties and it cannot also be expected that the parties should have foreseen it, arises with a reason not originating from the debtor and changes the facts present at the time of the conclusion of the contract against the debtor in such a way that demanding performance from him results against the principles of good faith, and if the debtor has not performed yet or he has performed by reserving his/her rights arising from the excessive difficulty of performance, the debtor has the right to demand from the judge adaptation of the contract to the new conditions, or if this is not possible, he has the right to avoid the contract. In long-term contracts, in principle, the debtor uses a right of termination rather than avoidance.*"

[86] If the balance between the obligations of the parties is excessively damaged after contract formation, the modern legal systems—including Swiss and Turkish laws—require either the adaptation of the contract by the judge, or termination of the contract. For a detailed study on adaptation of the contract in Turkish law, see **Baysal** p. 1 ff. For detailed information and an

d) Responsibility of the Debtor for the Occurrence of Subsequent Impossibility

Similar to German law, under Swiss and Turkish laws, if the debtor is responsible for the occurrence of subsequent impossibility, he must compensate the damages of the creditor. Within this stance, Article 99/I OR (Art. 114/I s. 1 TCO) sets forth that the debtor is responsible for any kind of his fault.[87] Therefore, if the debtor has caused impossibility intentionally or negligently, he would be responsible.

As set forth under § 276 BGB, the parties are entitled to make designations in the contract that restrict or extend the scope of the debtor's responsibility. For instance, the parties may decide that the debtor will be responsible for impossibility, which will be caused by *force majeure*. Similarly, the parties may accept that the debtor will not be responsible for impossibility caused by his light negligence.[88]

According to Article 99/II OR, "*The scope of such liability is determined by the particular nature of the transaction and in particular is judged more leniently where the obligor does not stand to gain from the transaction.*"[89] Moreover, it must be emphasized that the debtor's responsibility for impossibility is not identical to his fault. To be more precise, there might be situations, where the law accepts the debtor's responsibility even if he has no fault in occurrence of impossibility.[90]

Similar to § 280 I s. 1 BGB, in case of non-performance of the obligation, there is a presumption in the Swiss and Turkish laws that non-performance is caused due to the fault of the debtor.[91] However, as in the German law, such presumption can be challenged by the debtor, who is entitled to prove that there is no fault on his part.

---

analysis of the concept of economic impossibility from the perspective of law and economics, see **Aksoy/Schäfer**, EJLE 2012, 105, 105 ff.

[87] Unless there is a specific provision in law or in the contract, the level of care to be followed by the debtor would be determined by considering the concepts and perspectives in trade and also the principle of good-faith. **Tunçomağ**, p. 494; **Oğuzman/Öz**, p. 343. Therefore the criterion to be used when evaluating the existence of the debtor's fault is an objective one. The debtor would be deemed to be careful only if he has acted like any careful person from such community would act under the same circumstances. **Tunçomağ**, p. 494.

[88] According to Article 100 OR (and similarly in Article 115 TCO), "*Any agreement purporting to exclude liability for unlawful intent or gross negligence in advance is void.*" Moreover in some cases regulated under the proceeding paragraphs, the law has even prevented exclusion of liability for light negligence.

[89] The provision corresponds to Article 114/I s. 2 and s. 3 TCO.

[90] There are other provisions, which rule that the debtor is liable for impossibility regardless of his fault. For instance, according to Article 101 OR (Article 116 TCO), debtor is strictly liable for impossibility caused by his assistants in performance of the obligation. Similarly, Article 103 OR (Article 119 TCO) rules that in case of his default, the debtor is also liable for damage and loss (impossibility) caused by accident.

[91] **Gauch/Schluep**, Band II, N. 2612; **Topuz/Canbolat**, AÜHFD 2008, 673, 687; **Oğuzman/Öz**, p. 342.

The most common cases where the debtor is not responsible for impossibility are the fault of the creditor[92] or a third party,[93] accident,[94] or *force majeure*,[95] because in such cases no fault can be attributed to the debtor.[96]

Despite the express provision in German Law, there is no provision in the Swiss—or Turkish—legislation regarding impossibility caused by the creditor. However, in the doctrine it is argued that when the impossibility is caused by the creditor, it would be unfair to accept that the counter-obligation of the creditor would be extinguished. In other words, as accepted under § 326 II BGB, when the creditor is responsible for impossibility, the debtor who cannot perform must still be able to claim the counter-obligation.[97]

In cases where the creditor is responsible for impossibility, the reason why he still performs the counter-obligation is to maintain that the debtor reaches the economic status as if the impossibility was not caused by the creditor. However, there is no aim to cause unjust enrichment of the debtor. Therefore, as regulated under § 326 II BGB, as a result of being released of his obligation to perform, if the debtor has gained some financial benefits, such amounts should be deducted from the counter obligation of the creditor.[98]

Finally, similar to § 278 BGB, Article 101/I OR[99]—likewise Article 116/I TCO—sets forth that the debtor is responsible also for the losses given by the behaviours of his assistants.[100] However, unlike German law, the responsibility of

---

[92] For a study on impossibility for which the creditor is responsible see **Giger**, p. 1 ff.

[93] In one of its decisions, the Turkish Court of Appeals ruled that in cases, where impossibility is caused by the fault of the creditor, provisions of Article 117 (former version of Article 119) would not apply. Yarg. HGK, 1984/11-139 E., 1984/426 K., 18.4.1984.

[94] "*As it has been determined . . . that the immovable, which is subject matter to the lawsuit burned down as a result of a fire, which broke out when the immovable was at the use of the claimant and the immovable has become unusable, the lease agreement is extinguished due to TCO Article 117 (former Article 136).*" Yarg. HGK., 1982/11-553 E., 1984/830 K., 19 10.1984.

[95] **Oğuzman/Öz**, p. 345; **Topuz/Canbolat**, AÜHFD 2008, 673, 687. "*As a result of an earthquake, the collapse of the building, which is the subject-matter to the lease agreement constitutes force majeure and it must be accepted that the contract is extinguished.*" Yarg. 19. HD., 2002/10423 E., 2003/7437 K., 4.7.2003. Also see, Yarg. 19. HD., 1996/8299 E., 1997/2559 K., 13.3.1997.

[96] **Topuz/Canbolat**, AÜHFD 2008, 673, 687.

[97] **Huguenin**, Nr. 580; **Schwenzer**, Obligationenrecht, Nr. 64.29; **Dural**, Sonraki İmkansızlık, p. 170; **Serozan**, § 15, Nr. 11; **Oğuzman/Öz**, p. 282; **Akıntürk**, p. 55. In such cases, the debtor must prove that impossibility is caused by the creditor. **Barth**, p. 124. **Akıntürk**, p. 54.

[98] **Basler/Wiegand**, Art. 97, N.23; **Zürcher/Aepli**, Art. 119, N. 152; **Schwenzer**, Obligationenrecht, Nr. 64.29; **Oğuzman/Öz**, p. 282; **Dural**, Sonraki İmkansızlık, p. 173–174.

[99] Article 101 OR: "*A person who delegates the performance of an obligation or the exercise of a right arising from a contractual obligation to an associate, such as a member of his household or an employee is liable to the other party for any loss or damage the associate causes in carrying out such tasks, even if their delegation was entirely authorised.*"

[100] Although the assistants of debtor are listed under Article 101/I OR as "*his member of his household or an employee*", in the doctrine it is accepted that such list is not exhaustive but exemplary. **Zürcher/Oser/Schönenberger**, Art. 101 N. 5; **Akıntürk**, p. 45; **Oğuzman/Öz**, p. 352. Therefore the assistants of the debtor are all people who conduct actions under knowledge and

the debtor under the provision does not require the existence of the debtor's or his assistant's fault in occurrence of the performance impossibility.[101] However, according to the prevailing opinion in the doctrine, responsibility of the debtor under the provision requires that the debtor would be responsible if he himself conducted the same behavior of the assistant (hypothetische Vorwerfbarkeit).[102] However, the burden of proof that the debtor would not be held responsible if he conducted the same behavior, *i.e.*, he would not be able to prevent the accident, lies on the debtor.[103] In principle, by an agreement the parties may limit or exclude the debtor's liability for the losses given by his assistants.[104]

e) Legal Results of Subsequent Impossibility

Legal results of subsequent impossibility are dealt with separately considering the existence of the debtor's responsibility for impossibility. Article 119/I OR—as well as Article 136/I TCO—deals with the cases, where subsequent impossibility occurs without the debtor's responsibility. Accordingly, in cases where the performance of an obligation becomes impossible without the debtor's fault, the obligation is extinguished. On the other hand, there is no specific provision for the cases of subsequent impossibility for which the debtor is responsible. Therefore, subsequent impossibility for which the debtor is responsible is dealt with under the provisions regarding non-performance in general.[105]

---

consent of the debtor for the performance of his obligation. **Schwenzer**, Obligationenrecht, Nr. 23.04; **Zürcher/Oser/Schönenberger**, Art. 101 N. 5; **Koller**, § 54, Nr. 92; **Akıntürk**, p. 45; **Oğuzman/Öz**, p. 353. Moreover, there is no requirement that the assistants of debtor be dependent on the debtor. **Koller**, § 54, Nr. 94; **Schwenzer**, Obligationenrecht, Nr. 23.04; **Akıntürk**, p. 46; **Oğuzman/Öz**, p. 352.

[101] **Schwenzer**, Obligationenrecht, Nr. 23.10; **Oğuzman/Öz**, p. 358. In cases, where the assistant of the debtor is at fault in occurrence of the impossibility of performance, the debtor would be responsible at all times. **von Tuhr/Escher**, p. 128; **Oğuzman/Öz**, p. 359.

[102] **Zürcher/Oser/Schönenberger**, Art. 101, N. 12; **Oğuzman/Öz**, p. 359; **Akıntürk**, p. 48.

[103] **Oğuzman/Öz**, p. 358.

[104] According to Article 101/II OR (and Article 116/II OR), in principle, such liability may be restricted or excluded by prior agreement. The exception to such principle may be found under Article 101/III OR (and Article 116/III TCO with some changes).

[105] Article 97 OR reads as follows: "*An obligor who fails to discharge an obligation at all or as required must make amends for the resulting loss or damage unless he can prove that he was not at fault.*" The provision corresponds to Article 112 TCO.

aa) Legal Results of Impossibility for Which the Debtor Is Not Responsible

(1) Extinguishment of the Obligation

The first result of extinguishment of the debtor's obligation is that the debtor will no longer have to perform.[106] In such cases, the debtor is released from his obligation *ipso iure*.[107] Although this is similar to the legal result set forth under § 275 BGB, it is not entirely the same. More specifically, § 275 BGB rules for the extinguishment of the primary obligation. However, under Article 119/I OR—as well as Article 136/I TCO—the compensation claim is extinguished as well. As a matter of fact, the provision applies only if the debtor is not responsible for the occurrence of impossibility.[108]

It is arguable that under Article 119/I OR—as well as Article 136/I TCO—not only the obligation to perform, but also the whole contractual relationship between the parties is extinguished.[109] However, such opinion cannot be accepted[110] because a contractual relationship is a living organism, which creates various obligations. The debtor's obligation to perform is only one of the obligations created by the contractual relationship.[111] Therefore, it must be accepted that under Article 119/I OR—as well as Article 136/I TCO—only the primary claim and the compensation claims are eliminated.

(2) Counter-Obligation and Return of Already Performed Counter-Obligation

Article 119/I OR—as Article 136/I TCO—does not contain any explanation regarding the effects of impossibility on the counter-obligation of the creditor in reciprocal contracts. However, this does not mean to construe that in reciprocal contracts, the counter obligation of the creditor must still be performed.

The status of counter-obligations in reciprocal contracts is dealt with under Article 119/II OR—which corresponds to Article 136/II TCO. According to the said provision, in case of reciprocal contracts, the debtor who is released from obligation due to impossibility also loses his right to claim counter-performance. This is not different from the rule set forth under § 326 I s. 1 BGB. Also in similarity with § 326 I BGB, Article 119/II OR—likewise Article 136/II TCO—applies only

[106] In other words, the risk of investment which includes the expenses to be made by the debtor, would be born by the debtor. This is regarded as the amount of the profit that the debtor would incur, if he could perform. **Serozan**, § 15, Nr. 7a.

[107] **CHK/Killias/Wiget**, OR 119, Rdnr. 35; **Zürcher/Aepli**, Art. 119, N. 62; **Dural**, Sonraki İmkansızlık, p. 126.

[108] It cannot be argued that the provision eliminates the secondary claims in its entirety. For instance, it will be explained below that similar to German law, in Swiss and Turkish laws the creditor is entitled to demand substitutes from the debtor, if any.

[109] **von Büren**, p. 386; **Tunçomağ**, p. 485; **Dural**, Sonraki İmkansızlık, p. 125–126.

[110] In the same opinion, see **Basler/Wiegand**, Art. 119, N. 4; **Kälin**, recht 2004, 246, 246.

[111] **Serozan**, § 15, Nr. 9.

in perfect reciprocal contracts (vollkommen zweiseitiger Vertrag), where there is a synallagma between the existence and performance of the obligations of the parties.[112]

As regulated under § 326 IV BGB, if the debtor has previously obtained the counter-performance from the creditor, the debtor is obliged to return the performance. Under the provision it is stated that such return would take place in accordance with the provisions of unjust enrichment,[113] because in such cases, *causa* of acquiring the counter-performance has disappeared.[114]

Article 119/II OR—as Article 136/II TCO—makes a distribution of loss between the parties of reciprocal contracts.[115] However, the distribution of loss set forth under the provision is not mandatory. It is clearly explained in the last sentence of Article 119/II OR—as well as Article 136/II TCO—that a different distribution of loss may be accepted by the parties or the law. Therefore, in cases where the contract or the law passes the risk to the creditor, the creditor who cannot receive the performance of the debtor must still perform, *i.e.*, bear the loss.

Unlike German law, there is no consensus in Swiss and Turkish doctrines if the cases of accomplishment and destruction of purpose are regarded as impossibility under Article 119 OR—as well as Article 136 OR.[116] Within this stance, there is a gap in the law, which must be filled by the judge. When such cases are regarded as impossibility, the matter of extinguishment of the counter-obligation deserves an evaluation under such cases as well. Within this stance, Gauch/Schluep argue that the debtor is entitled to the counter-obligation, but the debtor's savings and other benefits gained must be deducted.[117] Similarly, according to Serozan, it cannot be expected from the creditor to provide the debtor with the counter-obligation. However, it would also be unfair to expect the debtor to bear the risk entirely, since impossibility has occurred in the creditor's sphere. The author argues that the

[112] **Zürcher/Aepli**, Art. 119, N. 69; **Basler/Wiegand**, Art. 119, N. 9; **Tunçomağ**, p. 486.

[113] In the doctrine it is argued that the obligation of the debtor to return the counter-obligation that has already been performed is not based on unjust enrichment in technical terms. This is actually an obligation to return, which arises from the law. The reason why the law makes reference to unjust enrichment is that provisions regarding unjust enrichment and the method of return would apply by analogy to the debtor's obligation to return the counter-obligation in case of subsequent impossibility. **Kramer**, Obligationenrecht, N. 486; **Oğuzman/Öz**, p. 430; **Dural**, Sonraki İmkansızlık, p. 163; **Serozan**, § 15, Nr. 9.

[114] **Basler/Wiegand**, Art. 119, N. 18; **Topuz/Canbolat**, AÜHFD 2008, 673, 688; **Eren**, p. 1253; **Dural**, Sonraki İmkansızlık, p. 164.

[115] Accordingly, subsequent impossibility for which the debtor is not responsible will cause extinguishment of the obligations of both parties. This means that the creditor will not receive the performance by the debtor, but also the debtor will not receive the counter-performance. Since none of the parties will compensate the other, each will bear his own loss.

[116] According to Aepli, accomplishment and destruction of purpose are not impossibility under Article 119 OR. **Zürcher/Aepli**, Art. 119, N. 51. In the same opinion, see **Basler/Wiegand**, Art. 119, N. 6. Similar to German law, cases of an impossibility of use are not regarded as impossibility under Article 119 OR. **Zürcher/Aepli**, Art. 119, N. 31.

[117] **Gauch/Schluep**, Band II, Nr. 2561.

risk of counter-obligation must be fairly distributed between the creditor and the debtor.[118]

(3) Substitutes

Despite the explicit provisions regarding the issue in BGB, there is no provision in OR and TCO regarding acquisition of substitutes in case of impossibility. However, the Swiss and Turkish doctrines accept a solution, which is parallel to the provisions in German law.[119] Within this stance, if there are any substitutes, which replace the obligation, which has become impossible, impossibility would not cause extinguishment of the obligation of the debtor.[120] Accordingly, in case of impossibility for which the debtor is not responsible, if the debtor receives a substitute replacing the performance, the contractual relationship would not be extinguished, but it would continue with a new subject, *i.e.*, the substitute.[121] This is due to the fact that the legal provision, which regulates the extinguishment of the obligation, aims to protect the debtor by not putting an unfair burden on him. However, if the debtor receives substitutes, there would be no such result.[122]

Similar to German law, the creditor is entitled to request the substitutes or not.[123] However, if the creditor does not want to receive the substitute, it must be accepted that performance impossibility has occurred and the provisions of Article 119 OR—

---

[118] **Serozan**, § 13, Nr. 7–12.

[119] **Berner/Becker**, Art. 119, N. 1; **Basler/Wiegand**, Art. 119, N. 15; **Zürcher/Aepli**, Art. 119, N. 125 ff. **Schwenzer**, Obligationenrecht, Nr. 64.14; **von Tuhr/Escher**, p. 131; **Koller**, § 54, Nr. 14; **Guhl/Koller**, § 38, Nr. 38; **Serozan**, § 15, Nr. 7; **Arık**, p. 215; **Reisoğlu**, p. 325; **İnan**, Bankacılar, p. 148; **Olgaç**, p. 905; **Dural**. Sonraki İmkansızlık, p. 185; **Eren**, p. 1254; **Arsebük**, p. 802; **Akıntürk**, Borçlar, p. 139.

[120] **Gauch/Schluep**, Band II, N. 2598; **Basler/Wiegand**, Art. 119, N 15; **Schwenzer**, Obligationenrecht, Nr. 64.14; **Serozan**, § 15, Nr. 6; **Topuz/Canbolat**, AÜHFD 2008, 673, 687; **Arık**, p. 215; **Akıntürk**, Borçlar, p. 139.

[121] *"Although Art. 119 OR has not expressly adopted the common law claim of substitute benefits, it emerges from the meaning of the provision. (BGE 51 II 175 E. 3: claim for the insurance sum in case of destruction of the purchase object by fire; BGE 43 II 233 E. 5: claim of compensation acquired from the military authorities for the confiscation of the purchase object, but BGE 46 II 436 E. 2, where a claim of the profit of the seller as a result of otherwise disposal of the vacant purchase object was rejected."* BGE 112 II 235, 239. *"If the debtor has obtained a substitute, which replaces the performance, which has become impossible without the responsibility of the debtor, in other words, if a surrogate benefit has replaced the performance, the obligatory relationship is not extinguished and it continues with a change of its subject. In the case at hand, instead of the immovable, which was promised for sale, the expropriation price, in other words the value that replaces it, would come."* Yarg.13. HD, 1986/4826 E., 1986/5536 K., 17.11.1986. In a similar decision, the Court has also ruled that the creditor is entitled to ask for the payment of such substitute to him. Yarg. 13. HD., 1991/8883 E., 1991/11265 K., 10.12.1991.

[122] **Serozan**, § 15, Nr. 15.

[123] **von Tuhr/Escher**, p. 133; **Bucher**, p. 425; **Zürcher/Aepli**, Art. 119, N. 133; **Gauch/Schluep**, Band II, Nr. 2598; **Basler/Wiegand**, Art. 119, N. 15; **Dural**, Sonraki İmkansızlık, p. 183; **Serozan**, § 15, Nr. 7.

Article 136 TCO—would apply. In fact, substitutes may only be acquired by the creditor upon his request and following the transfer of the substitutes to the creditor by the debtor.[124]

If the creditor requests the substitutes from the debtor, he must perform his counter-obligation arising from the contract as well.[125] This is not different from the principle accepted in German law. In fact, in such case, the substitutes will replace the obligation of the debtor and *synallagma* requires that the obligation of the creditor be performed as well.

As in the German law, if the value of the substitute is less than the value of the original performance, the counter-obligation of the creditor would be proportionally reduced.[126] On the other hand, if the value of the substitute exceeds the value of the original performance, the entire substitute must be given to the creditor in return of the creditor's contractually agreed counter-obligation.[127] As a matter of fact, the debtor must not be better-off than the case if he had performed.

Finally, delivery of the substitutes to the creditor is not a method of compensation because when the debtor delivers the substitutes, he performs his obligation. Therefore the creditor, who asks for substitutes, does not ask for compensation, but performance of the debtor's obligation. Therefore the creditor does not have to prove his damages to ask for the substitutes.[128] However, the creditor has to prove that substitutes have replaced the performance, which has become impossible.[129]

bb) Legal Results of Impossibility for Which the Debtor Is Responsible

(1) Compensation Payment

In case of performance impossibility for which the debtor is responsible, the first legal result is the compensation of the damages of the creditor. However, as explained above, OR and TCO do not contain any specific provision for such

[124] **Eren**, p. 1255; **Dural**, Sonraki İmkansızlık, p. 196.

[125] **Huguenin**, Nr. 579; **Oğuzman/Öz**, p. 432; **Eren**, p. 1255; **Arık**, p. 215; **Serozan**, § 15, Nr. 15; **Dural**, Sonraki İmkansızlık, p. 197; **Arsebük**, p. 805.

[126] **Gauch/Schluep**, Band II, Nr. 2602; **Basler/Wiegand**, Art. 119, N. 16; **CHK/Killias/Wiget**, OR 119, Rdnr. 29.

[127] **CHK/Killias/Wiget**, OR 119, Rdnr. 29; **Gauch/Schluep**, Band II, Nr. 2603; **Basler/Wiegand**, Art. 119, N. 16; **Serozan**, § 15, Nr. 15. According to Eren, if the value of the substitutes is higher than the counter-obligation, the creditor may only request as much amount of the substitute as his counter-obligation. On the other hand, if the value of the substitutes is less than the value of the counter obligation, the creditor may not request more than what the debtor has received as substitute. **Eren**, p. 1255.

[128] **Basler/Wiegand**, Art. 119, N. 15; **Dural**, Sonraki İmkansızlık, p. 184.

[129] **Dural**, Sonraki İmkansızlık, p. 187.

cases, but such type of impossibility is dealt with under Article 97 OR—and Article 112 of TCO—which regulates non-performance of the obligation in general.[130]

When the debtor is responsible for impossibility, the obligations of the parties are not extinguished.[131] In other words, following the occurrence of impossibility, the obligation of the debtor transforms into and survives as compensation.[132] Therefore the debtor who cannot provide the creditor with the performance agreed in the contract, provides the debtor with compensation instead. Since the contractual obligations of the parties survive and the debtor performs his obligation in the form of compensation, the creditor must also perform his obligation in return.[133]

Despite the fact that the law places the burden of proof regarding the lack of fault on the debtor, the creditor must still prove the occurrence of impossibility and (the amount of) his damages.[134] The damages to be recovered under the provision are positive damages of the creditor.[135] In other words, these are the damages, which are caused as a result of non-performance of the obligation.[136]

(2) Counter-Obligation and Return of Already Performed Counter-Obligation

In cases, where the debtor compensates the damages of the creditor, the faith of the counter-obligation depends on the application of the exchange theory or difference theory. In fact this is the same as the principle in German law.[137] Similarly, if the creditor has already performed his counter-obligation, the question of its return

---

[130] The provision covers non-performance of the obligation in the broadest sense. Default of the debtor, defective performance, positive breach of contract and finally non-performance due to impossibility are all covered by the provision.

[131] In this opinion, see **Schwenzer**, Obligationenrecht, Nr. 64.20; **Basler/Wiegand**, Art. 97, N. 47; **Serozan**, § 16, Nr. 3; **Tekinay**, p. 639. Oğuzman/Öz are against the prevailing opinion in the doctrine. The authors argue that without a distinction of culpability, in cases of subsequent impossibility the obligations of the parties are extinguished because it would be illogical to expect someone to perform something impossible. Therefore the creditor would not perform his obligation in return of compensation. If the creditor has already performed his obligation prior to impossibility, his obligation would be returned in accordance with the regime in Article 136 TCO—Article 119 OR. According to this view, the creditor's compensation claim is a new obligation arising from the law. Therefore, the creditor is entitled to claim compensation prior to the due date of the obligation contemplated in the contract. **Oğuzman/Öz**, p. 301–304. Also against the prevailing opinion, see **Eren** p. 311.

[132] BGE 117 II 273, 278; **Basler/Wiegand**, Art. 97, N. 47; **Schwenzer**, Obligationenrecht, Nr. 64.20.

[133] **Oğuzman/Öz**, p. 301.

[134] **Tunçomağ**, p. 498.

[135] **Schwenzer**, Obligationenrecht, Nr. 64.22.

[136] **Schwenzer**, Obligationenrecht, Nr. 64.22; **Tekinay**, p. 540; **Serozan**, § 16, Nr. 3.

[137] As explained above, according to the exchange theory, when claming compensation from the debtor, the creditor must also perform the counter-obligation. On the other hand, the difference theory which is the modern opinion, argues that the creditor does not have to perform the counter-obligation. However, the value of the creditor's counter-obligation must be deducted from the compensation that he would receive from the debtor.

would be settled according to these theories as well. More specifically, if the difference theory applies, the counter-claim must be returned. However, if the exchange theory applies, the debtor must be entitled to reserve the counter-obligation. The most appropriate solution would be to entitle the creditor to choose between either of the methods.[138]

(3) Substitutes

As in the case of impossibility for which the debtor is not responsible, if there are substitutes, which replace the debtor's obligation, the creditor is entitled to make a choice between compensation and the substitutes.[139] If the value of the substitute is below the value of the compensation, the creditor, who asks for the substitutes, would also be entitled to claim his damages exceeding the value of the substitute.[140] On the other hand, if the value of the substitute exceeds his damages (the value of the compensation), the creditor would be entitled to claim the entire substitute.[141]

(4) Creditor's Right to Revocation

Unlike German law, the creditor's right to revoke the contract in case of impossibility has not been regulated in the Swiss or Turkish laws. However, in the doctrine it is argued that the creditor must be entitled to revoke the contract, in cases where the debtor is responsible for impossibility.[142] It is rightfully argued that considering that the law entitles the creditor to revoke the contract in case of default, such right must be *a fortiori* available in case of performance impossibility for which the debtor is responsible.[143] More specifically, in case of default the creditor is given the chance to reverse the contractual relationship, just because the purpose/performance of the contract has been threatened. However, let alone threat, in case of impossibility the balance of the contract is destroyed in a way that there is not even the chance of performance. Therefore the creditor must be entitled to revoke the contract and return to the *status quo ante*.[144]

---

[138] In the same opinion, see **Gauch/Schluep**, Band II, N. 2590; **Schwenzer**, Obligationenrecht, Nr. 64.26.

[139] **Basler/Wiegand**, Art. 119, N. 15; **Schwenzer**, Obligationenrecht, Nr. 64.23.

[140] **Serozan**, § 16, Nr. 16.

[141] **Serozan**, § 16, Nr. 16.

[142] **Berner/Weber**, Art. 97, N.118; **Gauch/Schluep**, Band II, N. 2587 ff.; **Basler/Wiegand**, Art. 97, N. 58; **Bucher**, p. 339 ff.; **Schwenzer**, Obligationenrecht, Nr. 64.27; **Serozan**, Dönme, p. 292.

[143] **Schwenzer**, Obligationenrecht, Nr. 64.27; **Serozan**, Dönme, p. 292.

[144] **Serozan**, Dönme, p. 292.

cc) Duty of Notification

The duty of notification is neither explicitly regulated in the OR nor it was found in the former TCO. However, Article 136/III of the new TCO obliges the debtor to immediately notify the creditor about the occurrence of impossibility and to take necessary precautions for prevention of increase in damages.[145] Otherwise the debtor must cover the damages arising therefrom.

Since the impossibility regime of the former code of obligations was followed in the TCO of 2012 as well, Article 136/III is one of the most significant amendments brought by the Turkish Code of Obligations with regard to impossibility. However, it is not a significant amendment as the obligations of notification and precaution arise from the principle of good faith.[146] Even if there were no provisions in the law, it would be expected from the debtor to notify the debtor of impossibility and to take necessary precautions to prevent the increase in damages.[147] Therefore despite the lack of an express provision in the OR, the duty of notification exists in the Swiss law as well.[148] As a result, the new TCO only expressly acknowledged the principle that was already accepted in Swiss and Turkish legal systems.

The liability of the debtor who fails to behave as required by the provision is limited to the losses arising from such failure. In other words, the debtor, who fails to notify or take precautions, would cover only the damages that the creditor suffers because of not being notified of impossibility on time, or the amount of damages that would not occur if the debtor had taken necessary precautions.[149]

4) Special Provisions Regarding Partial Impossibility of Performance

Similar to duty of notification, there is no explicit provision in the OR regarding partial impossibility. Therefore this was not also regulated in the former TCO. However, the matter of partial impossibility of performance and its results are regulated in Article 137 of TCO.[150] Nevertheless, it must be underlined that Article

---

[145] This being the rule, if the creditor was already aware or could have been aware of impossibility, the debtor is not under the obligation to notify. **Zürcher/Aepli**, Art. 119, N.107; **Barth**, p. 57; **Dural**, Sonraki İmkansızlık, p. 131.

[146] **Zürcher/Aepli**, Art. 119, N. 104; **Oğuzman/Öz**, p. 431; **Tunçomağ**, p. 488; **Dural**, Sonraki İmkansızlık, p. 131.

[147] **Bucher**, p. 423; **Zürcher/Aepli**, Art. 119, N. 104; **Tunçomağ**, p. 488; **Serozan**, § 15, Nr. 6.

[148] **Berner/Becker**, Art. 119, N. 10; **Zürcher/Aepli**, Art. 119, N. 104 **Bucher**, p. 423.

[149] **Zürcher/Aepli**, Art. 119, N. 108; **Berner/Becker**, Art. 119, N. 10; **Oğuzman/Öz**, p. 488; **Dural**, Sonraki İmkansızlık, p. 132.

[150] Art. 137 TCO: "*If performance of the obligation becomes partially impossible due to reasons the debtor cannot be made responsible, the debtor is released only from that part of the obligation, which has become impossible. However, when it is clearly understood that the parties would not*

137 TCO is mainly a restatement of the prevailing opinion in the doctrine regarding partial impossibility of performance.[151]

Article 137/I TCO regulates partial impossibility with no difference from BGB. Accordingly, in case of partial impossibility, obligation of the debtor is extinguished partially as well. In other words, the debtor is not released from his obligation to deliver the unaffected part of his obligation. However, in some cases partial performance may not be enough to satisfy the creditor. Considering this possibility, the last sentence of Article 137/I states that "*when it is clearly understood that the parties would not have concluded such contract, if they could foresee such partial performance impossibility, the obligation is extinguished in full.*"

According to the provision, the creditor is not obliged to accept partial performance. However, as in German law, if he accepts partial performance, the counter-obligation of the creditor would be reduced in the same ratio. If the creditor does not accept partial performance or in cases where the counter-obligation of the creditor is indivisible by nature, provisions of full impossibility would apply. In other words, in such cases the obligation of the debtor will be extinguished in full.

5) A Closer Look to the Legal Results: Voidness and Validity of the Contract

a) Negative Results of Voidness

At a first glance, the difference between the legal results of initial impossibility and subsequent impossibility may be difficult to realize. As explained above, as long as the debtor is not responsible for impossibility, initial impossibility causes voidness of the contract and subsequent impossibility causes extinguishment of the obligation. As a matter of fact in both of the cases neither of the parties performs. Moreover the debtor is not entitled to counter-obligation and if the creditor has already performed, the counter-obligation must be returned. Additionally, in principle, partial subsequent impossibility leads to partial extinguishment of the obligation and partial initial impossibility leads to partial voidness of the contract. Similarly, if the debtor is responsible, he must compensate the damages of the creditor both in case of initial impossibility and subsequent impossibility.

---

have concluded such contract, if they could foresee such partial performance impossibility, the obligation is extinguished in full.

In case of reciprocal contracts, if obligation of either party becomes partially impossible and the creditor accepts partial performance, the counter-obligation would be performed in the same ratio. If the creditor does not accept such performance or the counter-obligation is indivisible by nature, provisions of full impossibility would apply."

[151] See, **Berner/Weber**, Art. 97, N. 141; **Bucher**, p. 420; **Zürcher/Aepli**, Art. 119, N. 111 ff.; **Berner/Becker**, Art. 119, N. 13; **Schwenzer**, Obligationenrecht, Nr. 64.31.

Despite the above indicated similarities, there are major theoretical and practical differences between voidness and validity of the contract, which is impossible to perform. The theoretical difference between the two sanctions is that void contracts do not create any legal results. However, in case of subsequent impossibility, even when the debtor is not responsible for impossibility, the obligation arises at the time of contract formation and it is extinguished following the occurrence of impossibility.

There are also some practical differences between voidness of the contract and its validity in case of impossibility. Such differences are with regard to return of substitutes and restitution regimes attached to each result. First of all, as it has been explained above, in the doctrine it is accepted that in case of subsequent impossibility, the creditor is entitled to substitutes, if any. However, there is no consensus whether substitutes obtained due to initial impossibility may be requested by the creditor.[152]

The second practical difference between the two legal results is the difference in restitution regimes. Restitution of the contract generally refers to the method and scope of the return of already performed obligations. In case of voidness, restitution of the contract takes place in accordance with the provisions of unjust enrichment (*condictio indebiti*). On the other hand, in case of extinguishment of the obligation (when the debtor is not responsible for impossibility) restitution takes place in accordance with the contractual provisions.[153]

Restitution of the contract in accordance with the contractual provisions is preferable to restitution in accordance with unjust enrichment due to several reasons.[154] Firstly, in case of restitution in accordance with contractual provisions, the party to return is not entitled to claim that the enrichment has decreased.[155] Secondly, in case of restitution in accordance with contractual provisions, the enrichment of the party to return is not limited to his objective enrichment. In other words, the amount to be returned would be calculated in accordance with the subjective contractual value of the performance and the return of the solely objective market value of the performance would not be enough. Finally, in case of restitution in accordance with the contractual provisions, the contractual prescription of 10 years would apply.[156] However, according to Article 67 OR, the prescription period for claims based on unjust enrichment is 1 year from the date, when the party to claim return becomes aware of the right to return (and 10 years from the date of enrichment).[157] There is no doubt that 10 years of prescription

[152] **Serozan**, § 15, Nr. 7.

[153] **Serozan**, § 15, Nr. 3.

[154] See **Serozan**, § 14, Nr. 17.

[155] In case of unjust enrichment, the party, who is bound to return may argue that the enrichment has decreased. In other words, his obligation to return may be limited to what remains from the enrichment.

[156] Article 127 OR as well as Article 146 TCO sets forth that the prescription period based on contractual claims is, in principle, ten years from the date that the receivable is due.

[157] After the reform of TCO, Article 82 TCO has increased the prescription period for claims based on unjust enrichment (from one year) to two years from the date that the party to claim return becomes aware of the right to return.

period favors the party to claim return. As the debtor cannot perform his obligation, it is equitable that the creditor who has already performed is favored with a longer prescription period to claim return.

Finally, voidness of the contract is not favourable also in cases, where the debtor is under the obligation to compensate damages of the creditor. More specifically, in case of subsequent impossibility for which the debtor is responsible, the debtor would pay full compensation, which covers the positive damages of the creditor. On the other hand, in case of initial impossibility for which the debtor is responsible, the debtor would compensate negative damages of the creditor based on *culpa in contrahendo*.[158] Therefore, the creditor is in a less favourable position when the contract is void due to initial impossibility.

b) Overcoming the Negative Results of Voidness

Despite the express provisions of the OR and TCO regarding the effects of initial impossibility, there has been an attempt in the doctrine to overcome the negative results of voidness.[159]

The first proposal for overcoming the voidness sanction of Article 20 OR—Article 27 TCO—for initial impossibility is the application of provisions regarding subsequent impossibility to initially impossible performances. Accordingly, it might be accepted that the voidness sanction of Article 20 OR—Article 27 TCO—exceeds its purpose; hence there is a gap in law. Through teleological reduction[160] of the provision, this gap may be filled in accordance with the law's provisions on subsequent impossibility.

[158] **Serozan**, § 14, Nr. 21; **Schwenzer**, Obligationenrecht, Nr. 63.06; **Kramer**, Obligationenrecht, N. 218; **Bucher**, p. 249; **Huguenin**, Nr. 395.

[159] See **Serozan**, § 14.

[160] The scope of a legal norm may be too wide, as it fails to consider an atypical condition that requires a restrictive exception to such provision. In such cases, that norm needs to be restricted in accordance with its own purpose and the principle of justice because the expression of the norm does not fit into the exceptional characteristics of the case and an application of such provision creates unfair results. Despite such necessity of restriction, a narrow interpretation of the norm may not be sufficient to restrict its wide expression. Then it is accepted that there is hidden gap in the law. **Kırca**, AÜHFD 2001, 91, 96; **Serozan**, Medeni Hukuk, p. 116–117. According to Article 1 of the ZGB—as well as TCC—, the hidden gap in the law must be filled by the judge. Since hidden gap refers to a wide legal norm, which fails to cover the exceptional features of the case, if such norm's clear expression clearly contradicts with its own purpose, the gap must be filled through restriction of the norm in accordance with its purpose (*ratio legis*). As a result, restriction in accordance with the purpose of the norm (teleologische Reduktion or teleologische Restriktion) refers to a restriction of the clear expression of the law (which is very wide and fails to cover the features of the exceptional case) in accordance with its purpose to be determined following an interpretation of the provision. The said purpose (teleology), may be (*i*) the enactment of such legal norm in the first place, (*ii*) the principal purpose of another law, which cannot be maintained by any other means, (*iii*) the nature of things (Natur der Sache), or (*iv*) a fundamental principle of

According to a similar opinion in the doctrine, the scope of Article 20 OR—Article 27 TCO—may be restricted by narrow interpretation of the provision. Accordingly, the provision must be interpreted in a way to cover only legal impossibility and cases, where *factual nonsensical impossibility*—such as an obligation to construct a time machine—occurs. This would enable the creditor be entitled to positive interest in the remaining cases.[161] As a result, the creditor would not be restricted to claim only his negative damages due to *culpa in contrahendo*.

In some exceptional cases, the lawmakers have acknowledged that initial impossibility of performance would not lead to voidness of the contract but the debtor is liable under a guarantee.[162] In the remaining cases, where no legal guarantee liability has been acknowledged by the law, the voidness sanction of Article 20 OR—Article 27 TCO—may be overcome through assumption of a contractual guarantee liability. In other words, depending on the circumstances of the case, the debtor might be deemed to have given contractual guarantee regarding the performance of his obligation.[163] Such assumption requires a case-by-case analysis, but it may be useful in terms of overcoming the results of voidness.

Another way of overcoming the negative results of voidness of the contract due to initial impossibility is granting the creditor with the claim of substitutes. Despite the consensus in the doctrine that the creditor is entitled to substitutes, which replace the subsequently impossible performance, it is debated if the substitutes, which have been obtained due to initial impossibility may be requested by the creditor.[164] Within this stance, through teleological reduction of Article 20 OR—Article 27 TCO—the creditor must be entitled to substitutes in case of initial impossibility, so that the negative results of voidness may be overcome to some extent.[165]

References

Aepli, Viktor: Kommentar zum schweizerischen Zivilrecht (Zürcher Kommentar), Band. V/1h/1, Das Erlöschen der Obligationen, Art. 114 - 126 OR, Schulthess, Zürich 1991. (Cited as: Zürcher/Aepli)

Akıntürk, Turgut: Satım Akdinde Hasarın İntikali, Sevinç, Ankara 1956.

law. **Larenz**, Methodenlehre, p. 392. For discussions on the teleological reduction of Article 20 OR (equivalent to Article 27 TCO), see **Ziegler**, p. 14 ff.

[161] **Ergüne**, p. 238. Such opinion arises from the application of the Austrian law.

[162] In such cases, "risk liability" independent from the fault of the debtor has been contemplated. For instance, according to Article 171 OR—as well as Article 191 TCO—, in case of sale of receivables, the seller is liable under a guarantee to the buyer regarding the existence of the subject matter receivable at the time of assignment. **Serozan**, § 14, Nr. 18.

[163] **Serozan**, § 14, Nr. 3; **Ergüne**, p. 238.

[164] **Serozan**, § 15, Nr. 7.

[165] **Serozan**, § 14, Nr. 19.

Akıntürk, Turgut: Borçlar Hukuku – Genel Hükümler – Özel Borç İlişkileri, Sevinç, Ankara 1986. (Cited as: Akıntürk, Borçlar)

Aksoy, Hüseyin Can/Schäfer, Hans-Bernd: Economic impossibility in Turkish contract law from the perspective of law and economics, EJLE, Vol. 34, No.1, 2012, pp.105 - 126.

Altunkaya, Mehmet: Edimin Başlangıçtaki İmkansızlığı, Yetkin, Ankara 2005.

Arık, Kemal Fikret: Borçlar Hukuku I, Genel Hükümler, Balkanoğlu, Ankara 1964.

Arsebük, Esat: Borçlar Hukuku, Güney, Ankara 1950.

Barth, Hans Rudolf: Schadenersatz bei nachträglicher Unmöglichkeit der Erfüllung, Verlag H.R. Sauerländer and Co., Aarau 1958.

Başpınar, Veysel: Borç Sözleşmelerinin Kısmı Butlanı, Batıder, Ankara 1998.

Baysal, Başak: Sözleşmenin Uyarlanması, XII Levha, İstanbul 2009.

Becker, Hermann: Berner Kommentar, Kommentar zum Schweizerisches Zivilgesetzbuch, Band VI, Obligationenrecht, 1. Abteilung, Allgemeine Bestimmungen, Art. 1 - 183 OR, Stämpfli and Cie, Bern 1945. (Cited as: Berner/Becker)

Brieskorn, Konstanze: Vertragshaftung und responsabilité contractuelle, Mohr Siebeck, Tübingen 2010.

Brunner, Christoph: Force majeure and Hardship Excuse Under General Contract Principles, Wolters Kluwer, Alphen aan den Rijn 2009.

Bucher, Eugene: Schweizerisches Obligationenrecht, Allgemeiner Teil, Schulthess, Zürich 1988. (Cited as: Bucher)

Dural, Mustafa: Borçlunun Sorumlu Olmadığı Sonraki İmkansızlık (BK. 117), Fakülteler Matbaası, İstanbul 1976. (Cited as: Dural, Sonraki İmkansızlık)

Emmert, Jochen: Auf der Suche nach den Grenzen vertraglicher Leistungspflichten, Mohr Siebeck, Tübingen 2001.

Eren, Fikret: Borçlar Hukuku Genel Hükümler, Beta, İstanbul 2006.

Ergüne, Mehmet Serkan: Olumsuz Zarar, Beta, İstanbul 2008.

Esser, Josef/Schmidt, Eike: Schuldrechts, Band I, Allgemeiner Teil, C.F. Müller, Heidelberg 1984.

Furrer, Andreas/Schnyder, Anton K.: Handkommenar zum Schweizer Privatrecht, Obligationenrecht Allgemeine Bestimmungen, Schulthess, Zürich 2012. (Cited as: CHK/Author)

Gauch, Peter/Schluep, Walter R.: Schweizerisches Obligationenrecht, Allgemeiner Teil, Band I, Schulthess, Zürich/Basel/Genf 2008. (Cited as: Gauch/Schluep, Band I)

Gauch, Peter/Schluep, Walter R.: Schweizerisches Obligationenrecht, Allgemeiner Teil, Band II, Schulthess, Zürich/Basel/Genf 2008. (Cited as: Gauch/Schluep, Band II)

Giger, Marcel: Die vom Gläubiger verschuldete Leistungsunmöglichkeit, Haupt, Bern 1992.

Guhl, Theo: Das Schweizerische Obligationenrecht, Schulthess, Zürich 2000. (Cited as: Guhl/ Author)

Honsell, Heinrich: 100 Jahre Schweizerisches Obligationenrecht, ZSR 2011 II, pp. 5 - 115.

Honsell, Heinrich/Vogt, Nedim Peter/Wiegand, Wolfgang: Basler Kommentar zum Schweizerischen Privatrecht, Obligationenrecht I, Art. 1 - 529 OR, Helbing and Lichtenhahn, Basel/Genf/München 2003. (Cited as: Basler/Author)

Huber, Ulrich: Handbuch des Schuldrechts, Leistungsstörungen, Band I, Die allgemeinen Grundlagen; Der Tatbestand des Schuldnersverzug; Die vom Schuldner zu vertretenden Umstände, Mohr Siebeck, Tübingen 1999. (Cited as: Huber, Leistungsstörungen I)

Huguenin, Claire: Obligationenrecht, Allgemeiner Teil, Schulthess, Zürich/Basel/Genf 2006.

Immenhauser, Martin: Das Dogma von Vertrag und Delikt, Böhlau, Köln 2006.

İnan, Ali Naim: Borçlar Hukuku, Genel Hükümler, Birinci Kitap, Ankara Üniversitesi Hukuk Fakültesi Yayınları, Ankara 1971. (Cited as: İnan)

İnan, Ali Naim: Bankacılar İçin Borçlar Hukuku Bilgisi, Banka ve Ticaret Hukuku Araştırma Enstitüsü, Ankara 1997. (Cited as: İnan, Bankacılar)

Kälin, Oliver: Unmöglichkeit der Leistung nach Art. 119 OR und clausula rebus sic stantibus, recht 2004, pp. 246 - 256.

Keller, Max/Schöbi, Christian: Allgemeine Lehren des Vertragsrecht, Band I, Helbing and Lichtenhahn, Basel/Frankfurt am Main 1982.

Kırca, Çiğdem: Örtülü (Gizli) Boşluk ve Bu Boşluğun Doldurulması Yöntemi Olarak Amaca Uygun Sınırlama (Teleologische Reduktion), AÜHFD, Vol. 50, No. 1, 2001, pp. 91 - 120.

Kocayusufpaşaoğlu, Necip: Borçlar Hukukuna Giriş, Hukuki İşlem, Sözleşme, Filiz, İstanbul 2008.
Koller, Alfred: Schweizerisches Obligationenrecht, Allgemeiner Teil. Handbuch des allgemeinen Schuldrechts, Stämpfli, Bern 2009. (Cited as: Koller)
Kramer, Ernst A.: Obligationenrecht Allgemeiner Teil, Helbing Lichtenhahn Verlag, Basel 2009. (Cited as: Kramer, Obligationenrecht)
Larenz, Karl: Methodenlehre der Rechtswissenschaft, Springer, Berlin 1991. (Cited as: Larenz, Methodenlehre)
Mommsen, Friedrich: Die Unmöglichkeit der Leistung in ihrem Einfluss auf obligatorische Verhältnisse, Schwetschke, Braunschweig 1853.
Oğuz, Arzu: Türk Medeni Hukuku'nun Gelişim Çizgisi ve Karşılaştırmalı Hukukun Rolü, AÜHFD, Vol. 55, No. 1, 2006, pp. 195 - 206.
Oğuzman, Kemal/Barlas, Nami: Medeni Hukuk, Beta, İstanbul 2007.
Oğuzman, Kemal/Öz, Turgut: Borçlar Hukuku Genel Hükümler, Filiz, İstanbul 2000.
Olgaç, Senai: Kazai ve İlmi İçtihatlarla Türk Borçlar Kanunu Genel Hükümler, İsmail Akgün Matbaası, İstanbul 1970.
Oser, Hugo/Schönenberger, Wilhelm: Kommentar zum Schweizerischen Zivilgesetzbuch, Das Obligationenrecht, Erster Halbband: Art. 1 - 183, Schulthess, Zürich 1929. (Cited as: Zürcher/Oser/Schönenberger)
Poszewiecki, Adam: Perspective of Unification of Obligation Law in Aspect of Impossibility of Performance, <http://www.law.muni.cz/sborniky/ccfola2008/files/pdf/mps/poszewiecki_adam.pdf>.
Reisoğlu, Safa: Borçlar Hukuku Genel Hükümler, Beta, İstanbul 1998.
Schwarz, Andreas B.: Borçlar Hukuku Dersleri, I. Cilt, Kardeşler Basımevi, İstanbul 1948.
Schwenzer, Ingeborg: Schweizerisches Obligationenrecht Allgemeiner Teil, Stämpfli, Bern 2006. (Cited as: Schwenzer, Obligationenrecht)
Serozan, Rona: Sözleşmeden Dönme, İstanbul Üniversitesi Hukuk Fakültesi, İstanbul 1975. (Cited as: Serozan, Dönme)
Serozan, Rona: Medeni Hukuk Genel Bölüm, Vedat, İstanbul 2004. (Cited as: Serozan, Medeni Hukuk)
Serozan, Rona: Borçlar Hukuku Genel Bölüm Üçüncü Cilt - İfa, İfa Engelleri, Haksız Zenginleşme, Filiz, İstanbul 2006. (Cited as: Serozan)
Sutschet, Holger: Garantiehaftung und Verschuldenshaftung im gegenseitigen Vertrag, Mohr Siebeck, Tübingen 2006. (Cited as: Sutschet, Garantiehaftung)
Tekinay, Sulhi Selahattin: Borçlar Hukuku, Fakülteler Matbaası, İstanbul 1973.
Tekinay, Sulhi Selahattin/Akman, Sermet/Burcuoğlu, Haluk/Altop, Atilla: Borçlar Hukuku Genel Hükümler, Filiz, İstanbul 1993.
Topuz, Seçkin/Canbolat, Ferhat: Türk - İsviçre ve Alman Borçlar Hukukunda İmkansızlığın Düzenlenişi, AÜHFD, Vol. 57, No. 3, 2008, pp. 673 - 718.
Tunçomağ, Kenan: Borçlar Hukuku, I. Cild, Genel Hükümler, Fakülteler Matbaası, İstanbul 1972.
Uygur, Turgut: Açıklamalı – İçtihatlı Borçlar Kanunu, Sorumluluk ve Tazminat Hukuku, Giriş ve Madde 1 - 40, Cilt I, Seçkin, Ankara 2003.
von Büren, Bruno: Schweizerisches Obligationenrecht, Allgemeiner Teil, Schulthess, Zürich 1964.
von Tuhr, Andreas/Escher, Arnold: Allgemeiner Teil des Schweizerischen Obligationenrechts, Band II, Schulthess Polygraphischer Verlag AG, Zürich 1974.
Weber, Rolf H.: Berner Kommentar, Kommentar zum schweizerischen Privatrecht, Band VI: Das Obligationenrecht, 1. Abteilung: Allgemeine Bestimmungen, 5. Teilband: Die Folgen der Nichterfüllung (Art. 97 - 109 OR), Stämpfli, Bern 2000. (Cited as: Berner/Weber)
Wollschläger, Christian: Die Entstehung der Unmöglichkeitslehre, Böhlau, Köln, Wien 1970.
Ziegler, Antje: Die anfängliche Unmöglichkeit der Leistung in der schweizerischen Lehre, Paul Haupt, Bern 1992.
Zimmermann, Reinhard: Law of Obligations: Roman foundations of the civilian tradition, Oxford University Press, Oxford 1996. (Cited as: Zimmermann, Law of Obligations)

4) Treatment of Impossibility in CISG and Other Unification Instruments

I) Unification Instruments in General

Unification of law, especially the contract law, is a result of the necessities of international trade. Following the elimination of national borders, globalization has increased the importance of cross-border trade. This being the fact, every contractual relationship embodies certain amount of risks, which the parties want to analyze while deciding whether to conclude a contract or not. Such risks become more difficult to analyze in case of cross-border trade.

Risks of a contract are mainly shaped by the applicable law in case of disputes. However, in practice, often the stronger party imposes its national law to the other party, or the parties do not agree on the choice of law at all. In such cases of no choice of law in the contract, the conflict of law rules determine the applicable law, which can be an unknown law at least for the weaker party.[1] If the parties are not familiar with the applicable law, they cannot calculate risks and this affects their choice of concluding the contract. Unification Instruments are a result of harmonization of private law in order to eliminate this legal barrier to international trade—especially in the field of contract law.[2]

Despite the advantages of a uniform law, there are some obstacles in front of unification of law. One of such obstacles is that the countries participating in the preparation of Unification Instruments come from mainly two different legal systems: civil law and common law. This fact both maintains substantiality to Unification Instruments and at the same time makes it harder to reach a consensus. As a result, each Unification Instrument appears as a compromise between the two legal systems.

Despite their similar purposes, Unification Instruments mainly differ from each other in terms of their (*i*) binding—non-binding nature, (*ii*) material scope of application; and (*iii*) geographical scope of application.

---

[1] **Baumgartner**, p. 3.

[2] **Felemegas**, p. 37. Also see, **Zeller**, p. 1 ff.

H.C. Aksoy, *Impossibility in Modern Private Law*, DOI 10.1007/978-3-319-01704-4_4,

1) CISG

CISG was adopted in Vienna during a Diplomatic Conference in 1980. CISG is based on the preceding Uniform Law on the International Sale of Goods (ULIS) and the Uniform Law on the Formation of Contracts for the International Sale of Goods (ULF) dated 1964. However, ULIS and ULF could not reach the expected success, and they were ratified by nine states only.[3] As a result, the General Assembly tasked the United Nations Commission on International Trade Law (UNCITRAL), which is the core legal body within the UN system in the field of international trade law, to improve ULIS and ULF and come up with a more successful product to uniform international trade law.[4]

The scope of the CISG is only limited to the contracts for international sale of goods, but it does not cover consumer transactions.[5] As a convention, CISG is binding for all contracting states and in such states, the provisions of the CISG become domestic law. As of 5 March 2013, 79 states, including Germany, Switzerland, and Turkey as well as the US, and many of the European States have adopted the CISG and replaced their domestic law provisions with the CISG. Despite its binding character on the contracting states, parties of a contract, which are subject to the CISG may opt-out of its application. However, the main principle is the application of the CISG unless the parties have opted out of it.[6] This is a distinctive feature of the CISG in comparison to other soft law Unification Instruments.

2) PICC

PICC is a non-binding, soft-law codification of the law of international commercial contracts.[7] Under the roof of the International Institute for the Unification of Private Law (UNIDROIT), PICC has been prepared by a group of independent researchers and experts from different major legal systems and geopolitical areas of the world. Being originally published in 1994, the Governing Council of UNIDROIT adopted the new edition of the PICC in 2004.[8]

---

[3] **Brunner**, p. 17; **Lookofsky**, p. 4; **Lando**, AJCL 2005, 379, 379; **Saidov**, p. 2–3; **Baumgartner**, p. 8–9.

[4] **Liu**, p. 1 ff.; **Baumgartner**, p. 8–9.

[5] Article 1 CISG. See Article 4 CISG for matters not governed by the Convention.

[6] Article 6 CISG.

[7] **Saidov**, p. 5; **Baumgartner**, p. 12; **Viscasillas**, p. 288.

[8] As compared to the first edition published in 1994, the second edition contains 5 additional chapters as well as an expanded preamble and new provisions on inconsistent behaviour and on release by agreement. Moreover wherever appropriate the 1994 edition of the Principles has been adapted to meet the needs of electronic contracting. For the full text of the PICC see <http://www.unidroit.org/english/principles/contracts/main.htm>.

The provisions of the PICC do not have the force of law and apart from their wider scope, the only difference between PICC and many other international soft law instruments (such as the INCOTERMS or the Uniform Customs and Practices relating to Documentary Credits, which are issued by the International Chamber of Commerce) is that the PICC has been prepared under the supervision of and also adopted by an intergovernmental organization.[9]

CISG was a point of reference to PICC. Therefore PICC includes various provisions derived from the Convention.[10] Similar to CISG, PICC has an international and universal character and it does not cover consumer transactions either. However, it is accepted that the scope of the PICC is broader than that of the CISG, as they are not confined to any single one of commercial contracts, such as sales contract.[11] Despite the lack of any express definition, it is assumed that the concept of *commercial* contracts should be understood "*in the broadest possible sense, so as to include not only trade transactions for the supply or exchange of goods or services, but also other types of economic transactions, such as investment and/or concession agreements, contracts for professional services, etc.*"[12] Due to the soft law feature of the PICC, its provisions are in general applicable if the parties to a contract have agreed that their contract be governed by the PICC.[13]

3) PECL

PECL is the European initiative to unify contract law in European states. In fact, the European Communities was initially formed with the central objective to establish a common market in Europe.[14] However, different domestic laws of European states constituted a barrier in front of the common-market and cross-border trade. Therefore the studies of formation of a uniform contract law for Europe began in 1982 following the formation of the Commission on European Contract Law (also known as Lando-Commission after its Chairman Ole Lando).[15] As a result, PECL was published in three parts in 1995, 1999 and 2003 respectively.

Similar to PICC, PECL is a non-binding soft-law codification.[16] Therefore it applies "*when the parties have agreed to incorporate them into their contract or that their contract is to be governed by them*".[17] One of the significant features that

[9] **Bonell**, ULR 2007, 233, 233.

[10] **Brunner**, p. 18; **Bonell**, ULR 2007, 233, 234.

[11] **Saidov**, p. 6; **Viscasillas**, p. 288; **Guillemard**, p. 111.

[12] PICC Commentary, p. 2–3.

[13] Preamble of the PICC.

[14] **Kallweit**, VUWLR 2004, 269, 269.

[15] Lando Commission carried its studies with funding from the European Community and its work was specifically endorsed by the European Parliament in a resolution in 1994; **Liu**, p. 1 ff.

[16] **Saidov**, p. 7; **Viscasillas**, p. 288.

[17] Article 1:101 of PECL.

differentiate PECL from CISG and PICC is that it is intended to create a uniform contract law regime specifically restricted to Europe.[18] Moreover, despite lacking an international character, PECL has a wider scope than CISG and PICC as they apply to contracts in general whether domestic or international, commercial or non-commercial.[19] Within this stance, PECL covers not only contract of sales or commercial transactions but also other types of contracts.[20]

4) DCFR

DCFR is an academic initiative of distinguished private law scholars across Europe as a step for creating "*a 'political' Common Frame of Reference (CFR) which was called for by the European Commission's 'Action Plan on A More Coherent European Contract Law' of January 2003*".[21] DCFR has been prepared as a result of the collaboration of two separate bodies: the Study Group on a European Civil Code (the so-called Study Group) and the Research Group on EC Private Law (the so-called Acquis Group).[22] The interim DCFR was published in 2008, and the extended final version of the DCFR was published in 2009.

DCFR is a follow-up to the PECL but it has a more extensive scope. Accordingly, in addition to covering the matters within the scope of the PECL, the DCFR involves existing European legislation *acquis* with a consumer protection nature.[23] Moreover, contracts between businesses, contracts between businesses and consumers and contracts between persons neither of whom is acting in the course of a business are all within the scope of DCFR.[24] The DCFR also covers non-contractual obligations to a far greater extent than the PECL. Accordingly, rights and obligations arising from unjust enrichment, tortuous act and benevolent intervention in another's affairs are all covered by DCFR. As an academic piece of work, DCFR has a non-binding nature as well.

5) CESL

DCFR was seen as a step to formation of a Common Frame of Reference. However, when the DCFR was completed, it was argued that the entire plan was a failure.[25] In

[18] **Saidov**, p. 7.

[19] **Guillemard**, p. 111; **Saidov**, p. 8; **Bonell**, A New Approach, p. 5.

[20] PECL has neither excluded consumer contracts from its scope, nor provided special protective measures for consumers.

[21] DCFR, Introduction, p. 1.

[22] **Macgregor**, p. 1; **Whittaker**, p. 3.

[23] **Macgregor**, p. 1; **Whittaker**, p. 3.

[24] **Whittaker**, p. 66.

[25] **Hondius**, ERPL 2011, 709, 710.

the meantime, it came into question to simplify and narrow the subject matter of DCFR. This led to the formation of a Committee of Experts, which published a feasibility study on 3 May 2011 for the unification of sales law in the EU. Following the revisions of such feasibility study, on 11 October 2011, the European Commission published the Proposal for the Regulation of the European Parliament and of the Council on a Common European Sales Law.[26]

CESL aims the unification of the sales law within the EU. It is applicable to contracts for cross-border sale of goods, digital content and related services. It is designated as a *second national regime* for EU member states. Therefore, unlike PICC, PECL and DCFR, the CESL is designated as a binding legal instrument. However, it applies only if the parties of such contract expressly *opt-in*.

The scope of the CESL covers both business-to-business contracts and business-to-consumer contracts. However, its scope of application is limited to cross-border trade within the EU.

II) An Overview of the Relevant Rules

Under Unification Instruments, the cases of impossibility are dealt with under the "*force majeure*" or "exemption from liability" provisions.[27] Within this stance, there are some court decisions, which restrict the scopes of such clauses to cases of impossibility and show that courts seek impossibility of performance in order to apply exemption provisions. On the other hand, some courts have accepted that the scopes of exemption clauses exceed impossibility and include cases of hardship as well.[28]

Unification Instruments set forth that impediment beyond control of the debtor (also referred as "promisor") might lead to the debtor's exemption from liability. Within this stance, it must be noted that Unification Instruments accept the strict-liability regime of the common law systems.[29] Therefore, unlike BGB, OR or TCO,

---

[26] **Hondius**, ERPL 2011, 709, 710. For a historical background of the CESL also see, **Eidenmüller**, JZ 2012, 269, 269 ff.; **Staudenmayer**, NJW 2011, 3491, 3493 ff. Proposal for the Regulation of the European Parliament and of the Council on a Common European Sales Law is available at <http://eur-lex.europa.eu/LexUriServ/LexUriServ do?uri=COM:2011:0635:FIN:EN:PDF>.

[27] **Hudson**, p. 267; **Tallon**, in: Bianca/Bonell, Art. 79, Nr. 2.1; **Nicholas**, LQR 1989, 201, 235. *"The drafters of the CISG chose the broad term "Exemptions", rather than something more specific, in order to avoid any association with a national legal system."* **Mazzacano**, NJCL 2011, 1, 50. In fact, it was argued that term *force majeure* could "*cause problems for lawyers familiar with the types of events which bring the English doctrine of discharge by impossibility of performance into play.*" **Hudson**, p. 276.

[28] For the court decisions, see fn. 582.

[29] Germany 5 March 2008 Appellate Court München (Stolen car case) (http://cisgw3.law.pace.edu/cases/080305g1.html); Austria 29 June 1999 Supreme Court (Dividing wall panels case) (http://cisgw3.law.pace.edu/cases/990629a3.html); Greece 2009 Decision 4505/2009 of the Multi-Member Court of First Instance of Athens (Bullet-proof vest case) (http://cisgw3.law.pace.edu/cases/094505gr.html).

the exemption clauses make no distinction considering the fault of the debtor. In case of non-performance, the debtor is strictly liable to compensate damages of the creditor (also referred as "promisee"). However, the occurrence of an impediment may result in the exemption of the debtor and this serves as an exception to the strict liability principle.[30] In fact, the debtor is held to be liable, unless he can establish reasons for exemption.[31] If the debtor is not exempt under the exemption provision, he must compensate the damages of the creditor.

In general, the relevant clauses of Unification Instruments set forth that in order to be exempt from liability, the promisor should prove that (*i*) the failure was due to an impediment beyond his control, (*ii*) he could not reasonably be expected to have taken the impediment into account at the time of the conclusion of the contract, and (*iii*) he could not reasonably be expected to have avoided or overcome the impediment or its consequences.

The *force majeure* excuse is regulated in substantially similar terms in Article 79 of the CISG, Article 7.1.7 of the PICC, Article 8:108 of the PECL, Article III-3:104 of the DCFR and Article 88 of the CESL:

CISG – Section IV. Exemptions – Article 79

(1) A party is not liable for a failure to perform any of his obligations if he proves that the failure was due to an impediment beyond his control and that he could not reasonably be expected to have taken the impediment into account at the time of the conclusion of the contract or to have avoided or overcome it or its consequences.
(2) If the party's failure is due to the failure by a third person whom he has engaged to perform the whole or a part of the contract, that party is exempt from liability only if:

    (a) he is exempt under the preceding paragraph; and
    (b) the person whom he has so engaged would be so exempt if the provisions of that paragraph were applied to him.

(3) The exemption provided by this article has effect for the period during which the impediment exists.
(4) The party who fails to perform must give notice to the other party of the impediment and its effect on his ability to perform. If the notice is not received by the other party within a reasonable time after the party who fails to perform knew or ought to have known of the impediment, he is liable for damages resulting from such non-receipt.
(5) Nothing in this article prevents either party from exercising any right other than to claim damages under this Convention.

[30] "*Liability for damages from breach of contract —pursuant to the CISG— does not require fault of the party in breach. Rather, the CISG features a system of strict liability from which the debtor can, however, exempt itself from liability to a certain extent.*" Austria 21 April 2004 (Oberster Gerichtshof) [Supreme Court] (Omnibus case) (http://cisgw3.law.pace.edu/cases/040421a3.html). Similarly, "*. . .if the debtor fails to fulfill an obligation he is liable under Art. 74 CISG regardless of his misconduct or fault* [*Garantiehaftung*]. *This liability, which in principle is not dependent on fault, is limited by the liability exemption under Art. 79 CISG, which must be proved by the debtor.*" Austria 29 June 1999 Supreme Court (Dividing wall panels case) (http://cisgw3.law.pace.edu/cases/990629a3.html).

[31] **Maskow**, AJCL 1992, 657, 664.

PICC – Article 7.1.7 – (Force majeure)

(1) Non-performance by a party is excused if that party proves that the nonperformance was due to an impediment beyond its control and that it could not reasonably be expected to have taken the impediment into account at the time of the conclusion of the contract or to have avoided or overcome it or its consequences.
(2) When the impediment is only temporary, the excuse shall have effect for such period as is reasonable having regard to the effect of the impediment on the performance of the contract.
(3) The party who fails to perform must give notice to the other party of the impediment and its effect on its ability to perform. If the notice is not received by the other party within a reasonable time after the party who fails to perform knew or ought to have known of the impediment, it is liable for damages resulting from such non-receipt.
(4) Nothing in this article prevents a party from exercising a right to terminate the contract or to withhold performance or request interest on money due.

PECL – Article 8:108: Excuse Due to an Impediment

(1) A party's non-performance is excused if it proves that it is due to an impediment beyond its control and that it could not reasonably have been expected to take the impediment into account at the time of the conclusion of the contract, or to have avoided or overcome the impediment or its consequences.
(2) Where the impediment is only temporary the excuse provided by this Article has effect for the period during which the impediment exists. However, if the delay amounts to a fundamental non-performance, the creditor may treat it as such.
(3) The non-performing party must ensure that notice of the impediment and of its effect on its ability to perform is received by the other party within a reasonable time after the non-performing party knew or ought to have known of these circumstances. The other party is entitled to damages for any loss resulting from the non-receipt of such notice.

DCFR – III.–3:104: Excuse due to an impediment

(1) A debtor's non-performance of an obligation is excused if it is due to an impediment beyond the debtor's control and if the debtor could not reasonably be expected to have avoided or overcome the impediment or its consequences.
(2) Where the obligation arose out of a contract or other juridical act, non-performance is not excused if the debtor could reasonably be expected to have taken the impediment into account at the time when the obligation was incurred.
(3) Where the excusing impediment is only temporary the excuse has effect for the period during which the impediment exists. However, if the delay amounts to a fundamental non-performance, the creditor may treat it as such.
(4) Where the excusing impediment is permanent the obligation is extinguished. Any reciprocal obligation is also extinguished. In the case of contractual obligations any restitutionary effects of extinction are regulated by the rules in Chapter 3, Section 5, Sub-section 4 (Restitution) with appropriate adaptations.
(5) The debtor must ensure that notice of the impediment and of its effect on the ability to perform reaches the creditor within a reasonable time after the debtor knew or could reasonably be expected to have known of these circumstances. The creditor is entitled to damages for any loss resulting from the non-receipt of such notice.

CESL – Article 88: Excused non-performance

(1) A party's non-performance of an obligation is excused if it is due to an impediment beyond that party's control and if that party could not be expected to have taken the

impediment into account at the time of the conclusion of the contract, or to have avoided or overcome the impediment or its consequences.

(2) Where the impediment is only temporary the non-performance is excused for the period during which the impediment exists. However, if the delay amounts to a fundamental non-performance, the other party may treat it as such.

(3) The party who is unable to perform has a duty to ensure that notice of the impediment and of its effect on the ability to perform reaches the other party without undue delay after the first party becomes, or could be expected to have become, aware of these circumstances. The other party is entitled to damages for any loss resulting from the breach of this duty.

III) Conditions for Exemption from Liability

1) Impediment Beyond Control

The first condition for the promisor's exemption from liability is that non-performance is caused by an impediment beyond the promisor's control. Impediment is not defined under Unification Instruments. However, the legislative history of the CISG shows that the term "impediment" has been chosen by the drafters of the Convention against the terms "obstacle" and "circumstances". Thus, UNCITRAL Working Group's introduction of the notion of impediment in Article 79 intended to ensure a narrow and objective interpretation of the provision.[32]

[32] Article 79 CISG is a revised version of Article 74 ULIS. Article 74 (1) sets forth that "*Where one of the parties has not performed one of his obligations, he shall not be liable for such non-performance if he can prove that it was due to circumstances which, according to the intention of the parties at the time of the conclusion of the contract, he was not bound to take into account or to avoid or to overcome; in the absence of any expression of the intention of the parties, regard shall be had to what reasonable persons in the same situation would have intended.*" This provision was heavily criticized for excusing non-performance too readily and also unjustifiably facilitating the promisor's excuse for performance. **Flambouras**, PILR 2001, 261, 265; **Flambouras**, Exemption, p. 501; **Rimke**, p. 211. For a comparative analysis of CISG Article 79 and ULIS Article 74 see **Nicholas**, AJCL 1979, 231, 232 ff.; **Tallon**, in: Bianca/Bonell, Art. 79, Nr. 1.3 ff. For full text of ULIS see <http://www.unidroit.org/english/conventions/c-ulip.htm>. On the other hand, during the drafting of ULIS, the term "circumstances" was preferred over the term "obstacles", in order to avoid an overly narrow restriction on excuse. It was feared that the term "obstacles" might refer only to supervening and external events, but not the more personal issues as to the seller's due care or faults, and it might bar excuse based on an extreme and onerous change in economic circumstances. **Weitzmann**, JLC 1997, 265, 284; **Honnold**, p. 617. In the CISG, the term "impediment" was chosen against "circumstance" to eliminate the risk that the absence of fault be regarded as a reason of exemption. **Honnold**, Documentary History, p. 631. However, according to Nicholas "*The words 'due to an impediment' are obviously very elastic and elasticity is particularly undesirable in an area such as this in which national systems differ very widely in the scope which they allow to doctrines variously labeled as impossibility, impracticability, force majeure, etc.*" **Nicholas**, LQR 1989, 201, 235.

Among the circumstances which prevent performance, only those which are objective[33] in nature and external to the promisor might be considered as impediments.[34] In other words, impediments, which excuse non-performance might be external circumstances or exogenous causes.[35] If the impediment is not extraneous to the activity of the promisor, *i.e.*, if it is under his control, it produces no exempting effect.[36] For instance, natural catastrophes, war, measures taken by a government such as import and export bans, boycotts, closing of traffic routes, embargoes or exchange controls, major accidents and epidemics are examples of events falling outside the promisor's sphere of control.[37]

The exemption notion is based on the correct assumption that the promisor has his sphere of control for which he is basically responsible.[38] In his sphere of control, it is objectively possible for, and can be expected of the promisor to take measures of organization and appropriate controls to secure the performance of the contract. Exceptionally, some circumstances, originating from the promisor's sphere of control might be beyond the promisor's control. For instance, an act of sabotage in the seller's plant might be deemed beyond his control.[39]

The promisor's sphere of control includes business failures, personal incapability,[40] restitution or bankruptcy,[41] failure of production or accounting systems, failure of data processing equipments, failure to maintain the necessary personnel, illness or arrest of the promisor, incapability of the promisor's supplier to provide

---

[33] "*Impediments can only be objective circumstances that hinder the performance. The contrast to that are personal circumstances that constitute an incapacity to perform.*" Switzerland 12 March 2004 County Court Willisau (Wood case) (http://cisgw3.law.pace.edu/cases/040312s1.html).

[34] **Stoll/Gruber**, in: Schlechtriem/Schwenzer, Art. 79, Nr. 11.

[35] **Stoll/Gruber**, in: Schlechtriem/Schwenzer, Art. 79, Nr. 11.

[36] **Tallon**, in: Bianca/Bonell, Art. 79, Nr. 2.6.2.

[37] **Stoll/Gruber**, in: Schlechtriem/Schwenzer, Art. 79, Nr. 14. "*... in cases where the contract provided for the list of force majeure circumstances, the ICAC did not recognise the events which were not included in the list as grounds for exemption from liability. The Tribunal seems to have taken the view that where the parties provide for a list of 'force majeure' events, such a list must be deemed as exhaustive.*" **Saidov**, VJ 2003, 1, 55 ff. For the concerning case see, Russia 17 October 1995 Arbitration proceeding 123/1992 (http://cisgw3.law.pace.edu/cases/951017r1.html).

[38] **Stoll/Gruber**, in: Schlechtriem/Schwenzer, Art. 79, Nr. 14; **Southerington**, p. 24; **Schlechtriem/Butler**, Nr. 289.

[39] **Stoll/Gruber**, in: Schlechtriem/Schwenzer, Art. 79, Nr. 14.

[40] "*Although a party is not liable for a failure to perform any of its obligations if* [seller] *proves that the failure was due to an impediment beyond its control and ability to influence and that it could not reasonably be expected to have taken the impediment into account at the time of the conclusion of the sales contract or to have avoided or overcome it or its consequences* (*Art. 79 CISG*), *mere lack of financial wherewithal and capital is generally irrelevant; this general rule is even more applicable if the lack of financial ability is based on mismanagement.*" Switzerland 3 December 2002 Commercial Court St. Gallen (Sizing machine case) (http://cisgw3.law.pace.edu/cases/021203s1.html).

[41] In Russia 6 October 1998 Arbitration proceeding 269/1997(http://cisgw3.law.pace.edu/cases/981006r1.html) it was emphasized that "*...bankruptcy is not a ground relieving a party from his liability under Article 79 CISG.*"

him with raw material, excessive increase in the price of raw material,[42] and strike constituting internal confrontation at a factory.[43] On the other hand, state interventions such as quotas or export or import bans, rationing of goods or exchange controls, or trade bans, which prevent performance are generally outside the sphere of control of the parties. Therefore they would be considered as impediments.[44]

If the non-performance of the promisor is prevented by a labor dispute, it is debatable whether this might be accepted as an impediment. In fact, a strike or lock-out solely within the promisor's business is part of the general personnel and business risk that the promisor should bear. However, depending on the case, general strikes with political nature, which also involve the promisor's business, may relieve the promisor. Yet the promisor cannot be expected to prevent a general strike.[45]

According to the exemption/*force majeure* provisions of the CISG, PICC and PECL the burden of proof regarding the existence of an impediment beyond control

---

[42] In Germany 28 February 1997 Appellate Court Hamburg (Iron molybdenum case) (http://cisgw3.law.pace.edu/cases/970228g1.html) it was ruled that "*The Seller is also not exempted by the fact that acquiring the goods elsewhere would have led to considerable financial loss because it would have had to pay a higher price. The Seller generally bears the risk of considerable extra expenses in connection with acquiring the goods elsewhere, even the loss of transactions, as it has accepted the risk of acquiring the goods and the risk that they cannot be acquired at a certain price.*"

[43] **Flambouras**, PILR 2001, 261, 267 ff. In Germany 22 August 2002 District Court Freiburg (Automobile case) (http://cisgw3.law.pace.edu/cases/020822g1.html) case it was ruled that: "*The* [*seller*] *cannot rely on exceptions from its duty to perform under Art. 79(1) CISG.* [*Seller*]*'s failure to transfer the property is not due to an impediment beyond its control. On the contrary, it was the responsibility of the* [*seller*] *to inquire into the background of the car. If it did, the* [*seller*] *should have found out that the car had actually been stolen, and thus should have refrained from selling it. In this respect, the* [*seller*]*'s inquiry at the relevant German agency (the Kraftfahrtbundesamt) was insufficient. A report of the Kraftfahrtbundesamt only refers to events that happen within the Federal Republic of Germany, and only to those which had been recorded either by the Bundeskriminalamt (Federal crime agency) or by the Kraftfahrtbundesamt itself. The agency's response to the* [*seller*] *made clear that it is not equivalent to a record of ownership. The record of ownership, which the* [*seller*] *was provided with by its retailer is insufficient because it did not have any signature and it deviated from the registration documents in terms of the identity of the producer ("VM" instead of "VW") of product identification ("SGFM52JO24M4" instead of "SGFM52OO24M4") and in terms of the chassis identification number ("1 JZ" instead of "1 OZ").*"

[44] **Stoll/Gruber**, in: Schlechtriem/Schwenzer, Art. 79, Nr. 37. However, in China 17 September 2003 CIETAC Arbitration proceeding (Australia cotton case) (http://cisgw3.law.pace.edu/cases/030917c1.html) case "*the Arbitration Tribunal notes that for an international sales contract, unless it was clearly indicated that a quota and import permission can be one kind of force majeure, or that they are preconditions for the performance of the contract, generally, they cannot be the reason to exempt the non-performing party from bearing liability.*"

[45] **Stoll/Gruber**, in: Schlechtriem/Schwenzer, Art. 79, Nr. 35; **Schlechtriem/Butler**, Nr. 293; **Brunner**, p. 169.

is on the promisor.[46] Although there is no explicit reference in DCFR Article III-3:104 to burden of proof, according to the DCFR Commentary, it is for the party who invokes the provision to show that the requirements are satisfied.[47] A similar approach would be appropriate for CESL as well.

2) *Unforeseeability*

The second condition for the promisor's exemption from liability is the unforeseeability of the impediment. Unforeseeability means that in case of an impediment beyond his control, the promisor could not reasonably be expected to have taken the impediment into account at the time of the conclusion of the contract.[48] In other words, the promisor is responsible even for impediments, which are outside his sphere of control, if he could foresee them.[49]

According to the foreseeability criterion, it should be investigated on a case-by-case analysis, whether, under the actual circumstances at the time of the conclusion of the contract and taking into account the trade practice,[50] the promisor should have foreseen the existence or the subsequent existence of the impediment.[51] During this investigation, the reference point should neither be an excessively concerned "*pessimist who foresees all sorts of disasters*" nor a "*resolute optimist*

[46] The issue of burden of proof is expressly regulated under the CISG only in Article 79. For the discussion, if burden of proof is a matter governed by the CISG see Switzerland 11 February 2004 Appellate Court Bern (Wire and cable case) (http://cisgw3.law.pace.edu/cases/040211s1.html).

[47] Comments on DCFR, p. 358.

[48] **Stoll/Gruber**, in: Schlechtriem/Schwenzer, Art. 79, Nr. 22. In Bulgaria 24 April 1996 Arbitration Case 56/1995 (Coal case) (http://cisgw3.law.pace.edu/cases/960424bu.html) it was ruled that "*The Governmental prohibition for coal export and the Decrees of the Ukraine Government for export restrictions of coal on which the* [*buyer*] *relies in his letter of 22 February 1996 do not correspond either with the requirements of the CISG for the existence of force majeure nor with the clauses of the contract. They have occurred before the conclusion of the contract.*"

[49] In Russia 24 November 1998 Arbitration proceeding 96/1998 (http://cisgw3.law.pace.edu/cases/981124r1.html) case: "[*T*]*he* [*buyer*] *argued that it should have been exempt from liability because it did not have the official licence of the Bank of Russia. The Tribunal rejected this argument by stating that the* [*buyer*] *ought to have foreseen that it would need such a license in order to perform the contract.*"

[50] "*According to the contract and international trade custom,* [*Buyer*] *shall be liable and take the risk for getting the import approval. (...) Moreover, failure to get the import approval can be foreseen and is not force majeure, so* [*Buyer*]*'s cannot be exempted from damages for that.*" China 7 August 1993 CIETAC Arbitration proceeding (Semi-automatic weapons case) (http://cisgw3.law.pace.edu/cases/930807c1.html).

[51] **Stoll/Gruber**, in: Schlechtriem/Schwenzer, Art. 79, Nr. 22; **Flambouras**, PILR 2001, 261, 270; **Schlechtriem/Butler**, Nr. 289; **Zeller**, Damages, p. 181. Foreseeability of an impediment is left to the judge or the arbitrator to decide by considering the circumstances of each case. **Tallon**, in: Bianca/Bonell, Art. 79, Nr. 2.6.3.

who never anticipates the least misfortune".[52] As a result, the promisor, who made no reservation regarding a foreseeable risk should be accepted to have assumed the risk that might arise from the impediment.[53] Within this stance, in case of a foreseeable risk, in the civil law systems—including Germany, Switzerland and Turkey—the debtor would be held liable due to assumption of the risk as well.

DCFR has limited the unforeseeability requirement to the cases "*Where the obligation arose out of a contract or other juridical act*". This condition excludes the obligations which arise by operation of law. More specifically, unforeseeability requirement will not be sought for exemption from an obligation arising by operation of law.[54] This approach is functional as it cannot be argued that the promisor took the risk of a foreseeable impediment, when the obligation arises by operation of law. In other words, in such cases, the promisor has no choice to reject being committed to such obligation.

3) Unavoidability

The promisor's exemption from liability also requires that the promisor could not reasonably be expected to have avoided or overcome the impediment or its consequences. In other words, Article 79 requires the debtor to counteract the impediment.[55] To "avoid" means taking all the necessary steps to prevent the occurrence of the impediment. To "overcome", on the other hand, means to take the necessary steps to preclude the consequences of the impediment.[56]

If the impediment is not beyond the control of the debtor, and it originates from the debtor's sphere of control, it would certainly be accepted that it is avoidable by the debtor. However, the unavoidability criterion bears significant importance if the impediment is outside the sphere of control of the debtor. In fact, in such cases, the

---

[52] **Flambouras**, PILR 2001, 261, 270; **Tallon**, in: Bianca/Bonell, Art. 79, Nr. 2.6.3. According to Zeller, such investigation of foreseeability has no commercial value. In practice judges and arbitrators should use the *reasonableness* criterion of the CISG and decide if a reasonable person under the same circumstances could foresee the impediment. **Zeller**, Damages, p. 181.

[53] **Stoll/Gruber**, in: Schlechtriem/Schwenzer, Art. 79, Nr. 22; **Flambouras**, PILR 2001, 261, 270; **Rimke**, p. 215; **Schwenzer**, VUWLR 2008, 709, 719; **Southerington**, p. 25; **Schlectriem/Hachem/Kee**, Nr. 45.43; **Brunner**, p. 158; **Liu**, *Force majeure*, p. 1 ff. "*...despite the change in the terms of purchase for the buyer, the latter should, as a professional well-versed in international commercial practice, had stipulated that the contract should contain guarantee or review mechanisms. ... failing such provisions, the buyer should have assumed the risk of non-performance and could therefore not invoke CISG article 79.*" France 30 June 2004 Supreme Court (Société Romay AG v. SARL Behr France) (http://cisgw3.law.pace.edu/cases/040630f1.html).

[54] Comments on DCFR, p. 359.

[55] **Enderlein/Maskow**, Art. 79, Nr. 6.1.

[56] **Tallon**, in: Bianca/Bonell, Art. 79, Nr. 2.6.4.

debtor's exemption may still be prevented if the debtor may reasonably be expected to have avoided or overcome the impediment or its consequences.

The promisor's duty to overcome the impediment includes the promisor's obligation to take reasonable steps to affect performance by alternative means or to find an agreeable substitute.[57] Similar to the principle in German and Turkish laws, in debt in kind, the seller will bear the procurement risk. Hence he cannot claim exemption.[58] Such principle applies unless there is a limited debt in kind.[59] From this perspective, the promisor must generally avoid and/or overcome the impediment even when he would have to incur additional costs or suffer a substantial loss.[60]

The unavoidability criterion arises from the necessity that any person must do all in his power to fulfill his obligation before relying on the occurrence of the impediment in order to justify his non-performance.[61] In other words, before expecting his exemption from liability, the promisor must do all in his power to avoid the impediment.[62] However, when analyzing the avoidability of an impediment, reasonable economic boundaries should be taken into consideration because some impediments that can be overcome might not be economically viable.[63] In other words, although it is indicated in the Secretariat Commentary that the promisor must do all in his power to carry out his obligation, the promisor should not be expected to risk his own existence by performing his obligations at all costs.[64] Similar to the assessment of foreseeability, here the reference should be made to the reasonable person with a case-by-case analysis as well.[65]

The avoidability criterion of Unification Instruments—together with the beyond control criterion—to some extent corresponds to the fault requirement of the civil law systems. In fact, under the civil law countries—including Germany, Switzerland and Turkey—if the debtor fails to avoid an impediment that he could

---

[57] **Brunner**, p. 321. In Switzerland 12 March 2004 County Court Willisau (Wood case) (http://cisgw3.law.pace.edu/cases/040312s1.html) the court ruled that "*a strict standard has to be applied*" in the assessment whether the impediment can be overcome or not.

[58] "*... an impediment can be overcome by the seller as long as there are replacement goods available on the market.*" Germany 28 February 1997 Appellate Court Hamburg (Iron molybdenum case), (http://cisgw3.law.pace.edu/cases/970228g1.html). Also see Germany 4 July 1997 Appellate Court Hamburg (Tomato concentrate case) (http://cisgw3.law.pace.edu/cases/970704g1.html); Germany 28 February 1997 Appellate Court Hamburg (Iron molybdenum case) (http://cisgw3.law.pace.edu/cases/970228g1.html).

[59] **Schlectriem/Hachem/Kee**, Nr. 45.51.

[60] **Brunner**, p. 322.

[61] Secretariat Commentary, Art. 65, Nr. 7.

[62] "*This rule reflects the policy that a party who is under an obligation to act must do all in his power to carry out his obligation and may not await events which might later justify his non-performance.*" Secretariat Commentary, Art. 65, Nr. 7.

[63] **Zeller**, Damages, p. 182.

[64] **Southerington**, p. 25; **Liu**, *Force majeure*, p. 1 ff.

[65] **Flambouras**, PILR 2001, 261, 272; **Tallon**, in: Bianca/Bonell, Art. 79, Nr. 2.6.4; **Zeller**, Damages, p. 182; **Liu**, *Force majeure*, p. 1 ff.

avoid, this would be deemed as negligence. Moreover, the good-faith principle would to some extent require the debtor to mitigate damages.

4) Causation

Another condition of exemption from the promisor's liability is the causal link between the impediment and the non-performance. This requirement is expressed in *force majeure* clauses of all of Unification Instruments as they require the non-performance be *due to* the impediment.

An impediment may result in the promisor's exemption from liability, only if such impediment is the sole reason of the promisor's non-performance.[66] From this perspective, the promisor would not be exempt from liability if: (*i*) the breach of the contract is a concurrent cause of the failure to perform; or (*ii*) the failure to perform is the result of the conjunction of several events, at least one of which could have been foreseen or avoided by the promisor. Similarly, as accepted under BGB, OR and TCO, the promisor would not be exempt in case of a delayed delivery, if the impediment would not have had any effect had the delivery been made on time. In such cases, in principle, it is assumed that the damage would not occur if the promisor had performed his obligation on time. However, the promisor may prove that the damage would have occurred even if the performance had been made on time.[67]

5) Notice

Each of Unification Instruments requires that the party who fails to perform gives notice to the other party about the impediment and its effect on his ability to perform.[68]

The notice requirement is a manifestation of the principle of good faith.[69] The rationale behind the duty to give notice is to prevent unpleasant surprises and to provide the promisee with an opportunity to avoid and overcome the consequences

[66] **Stoll/Gruber**, in: Schlechtriem/Schwenzer, Art. 79, Nr. 24; **Flambouras**, PILR 2001, 261, 273; **Tallon**, in: Bianca/Bonell, Art. 79, Nr. 2.6.6; **Brunner**, p. 340.

[67] **Brunner**, p. 341; **Stoll/Gruber**, in: Schlechtriem/Schwenzer, Art. 79, Nr. 24.

[68] The notice requirement is a divergence from the common law systems, where there is no requirement of notice in cases of frustration as the contract is avoided *ipso facto*. **Schlectriem/Hachem/Kee**, Nr. 45.73.

[69] **Brunner**, p. 342. Therefore such requirement may be inferred from a general obligation of good faith in German and Turkish laws as well.

of the impediment.[70] Therefore, the notice should be detailed enough to reflect the nature, gravity and duration of the impediment, so that the promisee can decide on his future action.[71] More specifically, the promisor must inform whether the impediment excludes the performance permanently or temporarily, and how long it is likely to last.[72] Moreover, depending on the circumstances, if the effects of the circumstances on the performance vary, good faith may require that two successive notices be given.[73]

If the notice is not received by the promisee within a reasonable time after the promisor knew or ought to have known the impediment, the promisor is liable for damages resulting from such non-receipt. Therefore, the promisor bears the risk of notice not reaching the promisee at all or reaching him after the lapse of a *reasonable* period of time.[74] Whether the promisor has given the notice in a reasonable time or not depends on the circumstances of each specific case. Within this stance, it should especially be taken into consideration if the time is of the essence for the promisee to avoid and overcome the consequences of the impediment or to minimize his loss.[75]

If the notice requirement is not fulfilled, the damage to be covered by the promisor for non-receipt of the notice is the promisee's negative interest.[76] In other words, notice is not one of the conditions of exemption[77] and the failure to give notice does not affect the promisor's exemption itself.[78] Hence the promisee can only claim to be placed in the position in which he would have been if the notice had been served on time, but the promisee cannot claim his positive interest.[79] Similarly, the promisee cannot claim damages if it can be proven that he was aware of the impediment.[80]

---

[70] **Zeller**, Damages, p. 186; **Brunner**, p. 342.

[71] **Stoll/Gruber**, in: Schlechtriem/Schwenzer, Art. 79, Nr. 49.

[72] **Stoll/Gruber**, in: Schlechtriem/Schwenzer, Art. 79, Nr. 49; **Tallon**, in: Bianca/Bonell, Art. 79, Nr. 2.8.

[73] **Philippe**, p. 48.

[74] **Stoll/Gruber**, in: Schlechtriem/Schwenzer, Art. 79, Nr. 50; **Tallon**, in: Bianca/Bonell, Art. 79, Nr. 2.8; Secretariat Commentary, Art. 65, Nr. 16; **Brunner**, p. 343.

[75] **Brunner**, p. 343.

[76] **Flambouras**, PILR 2001, 261, 274.

[77] **Saenger**, in: Ferrari/Kieninger/Mankowski/Otte/Saenger/Schulze/Staudinger, Art. 79, Nr. 10.

[78] **Stoll/Gruber**, in: Schlechtriem/Schwenzer, Art. 79, Nr. 50; **Brunner**, p. 343.

[79] **Stoll/Gruber**, in: Schlechtriem/Schwenzer, Art. 79, Nr. 50; **Tallon**, in: Bianca/Bonell, Art. 79, Nr. 2.8; Secretariat Commentary, Art. 65, Nr. 15.

[80] **Stoll/Gruber**, in: Schlechtriem/Schwenzer, Art. 79, Nr. 50. The promisor may exempt himself even from such damage claim by proving that the fulfillment of the notification requirement was also prevented by an impediment beyond his control. **Stoll/Gruber**, in: Schlechtriem/Schwenzer, Art. 79, Nr. 50.

IV) Scopes of Exemption Provisions

Exemption clauses are applicable in any case where one of the parties to the contract has improperly performed one of his contractual duties or has not performed at all. Accordingly, the different types of non-performance, *i.e.*, failure to perform due to impossibility, delay or defective performance may be subject to exemption provisions.[81] Similarly cases of partial non-performance and also obligations arising from the restitution of the contract following avoidance might be subject to exemption.[82]

1) Hardship (Interference with the Basis of the Transaction/ Excessive Performance Difficulty)

In order to refer to the cases, which BGB names "interference with the basis of the transaction", or TCO regulates under "excessive performance difficulty", Unification Instruments refer to the notion of "hardship". Within this stance, hardship refers to the cases where the performance of the contract becomes considerably more burdensome albeit possible. There are specific provisions in PICC, PECL, DCFR[83] and CESL regarding cases of hardship.[84] Therefore in relation to PICC, PECL, DCFR and CESL, it is evident that cases of hardship are not subject to *force majeure*/exemption clauses. However, there is no provision in the CISG with regard to hardship. Therefore it is debated in the doctrine, whether Article 79 (1) covers cases of hardship.[85]

The main argument of the authors, who are in favour of the application of Article 79 to hardship is that if hardship is not covered under Article 79, the courts and tribunals would recourse to domestic law and invoke national concepts, such as imprevision, Wegfall der Geschäftsgrundlage, frustration, *clausula rebus sic stantibus*, etc., and this would result in diverging interpretations of the CISG. "*Such a result would undermine the purposes of the CISG to create a uniform sales law that is able to transcend national borders.*"[86] However, such intention is not adequate to argue that Article 79 covers the cases of hardship. More

[81] **Stoll/Gruber**, in: Schlechtriem/Schwenzer, Art. 79, Nr. 5; **Tallon**, in: Bianca/Bonell, Art. 79, Nr. 2.4.1.

[82] **Stoll/Gruber**, in: Schlechtriem/Schwenzer, Art. 79, Nr. 5.

[83] For a case-based assessment of hardship, *force majeure* and change of circumstances in aleatory contract under the DCFR, see **Bineva**, p. 77 ff.

[84] See Art. 6.2.1 ff. PICC, Art. 6:111 PECL, III-1:110 DCFR, Art. 89 CESL.

[85] For a discussion of applicability of hardship rules of the PICC to supplement the CISG, see **Veneziano**, ULR 2010, 137, 137 ff.

[86] **Mazzacano**, NJCL 2011, 1, 48. Also in the same opinion, see **Tallon**, in: Bianca/Bonell, Art. 79, Nr. 3.1.2; **Atamer**, Satıcının Yükümlülükleri, p. 465; **Lindström**, NJCL 2006, 1, 25.

specifically, in case of change of economic circumstances, many legal systems may entail the avoidance or revision of the contract (adaptation of the contract to the changed circumstances) by the judge. However, revision of the contract is not a remedy expressly set forth under the CISG. Therefore it is not applicable to change of economic circumstances.[87] Thus, in such cases only available remedy under CISG might be avoidance.[88] As a result, despite the prevailing opinion in the doctrine, Article 79 (1) is not appropriate for the cases of hardship, where performance is still possible despite being more difficult for the promisor.[89] Court decisions regarding the issue vary.[90]

---

[87] **Stoll/Gruber**, in: Schlechtriem/Schwenzer, Art. 79, Nr. 30.

[88] **Tallon**, in: Bianca/Bonell, Art. 79, Nr. 3.1.

[89] According to Rimke, even if CISG refers to a more flexible standard than that of traditional *force majeure*, it is undoubtedly stricter than frustration or hardship/impracticability. **Rimke**, p. 223. Also in the opinion that hardship cannot be dealt with under Article 79, see **Philippe**, p. 46. In the contrary opinion, see **Enderlein/Maskow**, Art. 79, Nr. 6.3; **Schwenzer**, VUWLR 2008, 709, 715; **Schlechtriem/Butler**, Nr. 291; **Magnus**, p. 304; **Stoll/Gruber**, in: Schlechtriem/Schwenzer, Art. 79, Nr. 32; **Schlectriem/Hachem/Kee**, Nr. 45.14. Similarly, in the CISG Advisory Council Opinion No. 7, it has been stated that the term impediment in Article 79 is not equated with an event that makes performance absolutely impossible. Therefore, an exemption claim under Article 79 may be made based on hardship. CISG Advisory Council Opinion No. 7, comment 3.1. According to the CISG Advisory Council, CISG Article 79 (5) may be relied upon by a court or arbitral tribunal to adapt the terms of the contract to the changed circumstances. Advisory Council also sets forth that, based upon Article 7 (1) of the CISG, the obligation to interpret the CISG in good faith imposes a duty upon the parties to deal in good faith with each other and renegotiate the terms of the contract with a view to restore a balance of the performances. CISG Advisory Council Opinion No. 7, Nr. 40. Stoll and Gruber argue that despite the lack of express provision in CISG, in case of a change in economic circumstances there must be a limit of sacrifice beyond which the promisor cannot be expected to perform. Following the application of a very strict test, if the hardship is found to impose unreasonable obligations on the promisor, the promisee should be obliged to renegotiate and adapt the contract or release the promisor from his obligation. This might be based on the principle of good faith prescribed under Article 7 (1) or on a "reasonable interpretation" of the contract by considering the contractual allocation of risk. **Stoll/Gruber**, in: Schlechtriem/Schwenzer, Art. 79, Nr. 32. Moreover it is argued that the duty to mitigate damages pursuant to Article 77 may require the aggrieved party strike a deal even with the contract breaching party and renegotiate the terms of the contract. **Schwenzer**, VUWLR 2008, 709, 725. It is a fact that in many countries including Germany, Switzerland and Turkey, collapse of the basis of the transaction is regulated departing from the general notion of good faith. Accordingly, it could be argued that cases of hardship may also be decided under Article 7 (1) on good faith. However, even then, such cases would not be covered by Article 79.

[90] For instance, a German court ruled that there was no ground for exemption within the meaning of Article 79 CISG because "*The owed class of goods was undoubtedly not exhausted.*" Germany 4 July 1997 Appellate Court Hamburg (Tomato concentrate case) (http://http://cisgw3.law.pace.edu/cases/970704g1.html). Similarly, another German court ruled that "*Only if goods of an equal or similar quality were no longer available on the market would the seller be exempted from liability.*" Germany 28 February 1997 Appellate Court Hamburg (Iron molybdenum case) (http://cisgw3.law.pace.edu/cases/970228g1.html). In the case, Nuova Fucinati v. Fondmetall International it was ruled that Article 79 does not lead to exemption from liability unless the performance becomes impossible. In one of its decisions, an Italian court even rejected the availability of avoidance as a remedy: "*Article 79 of the Vienna Convention provides for release from an*

The historical background of Article 79 also shows that change of economic circumstances does not exempt the promisor from liability under Article 79. While narrowing the scope of Article 79 in comparison with Article 74 of ULIS, the UNCITRAL Working Group intended to prevent the promisor from escaping to fulfill his obligations based on claims of economic difficulty.[91] Parallel to this stance, at the Vienna Conference, a proposal made by the Norwegian delegation that "*the party who fails to perform is permanently exempted to the extend that, after the impediment is removed, the circumstances are so radically changed that it would be manifestly unreasonable to hold him liable*" was rejected.[92] Finally, it has been stated in the Secretariat Commentary that:

> Neither [Article 79] nor any other provision of this Convention would release the seller from the obligation to deliver the goods on the grounds that there had been such a major change in the circumstances that the contract was no longer that originally agreed upon. The parties could, of course, include such a provision in their contract.

As a result, the aim of preventing recourse to domestic law is not solely sufficient to accept that Article 79 covers the cases of hardship. Article 79 of the CISG exempts the debtor from compensating the damages of the creditor. Within this stance, there is no option of adaptation of the contract. However, in cases of hardship, adaptation is the primary and appropriate remedy, which balances the interests of both parties. If it is accepted that the debtor may rely on Article 79 in

---

obligation made impossible by a supervening impediment not attributable to a party according to a rule similar to article 1463 et seq. of the Civil Code, but it does not seem to contemplate the remedy of dissolution for supervening excessive onerousness of a performance as provided for in article 1467 of the Civil Code for contracts involving performance over time or deferred performance." Italy 14 January 1993 District Court Monza (Nuova Fucinati v. Fondmetall International) (http://cisgw3.law.pace.edu/cases/930114i3.html). Similarly in another decision, a Greek court followed "*the view that the CISG does not release the promisor from his liability in case of change of the economic background on which the parties relied on, upon conclusion of the contract, neither does it grant him the right to renegotiate the terms of the contract in case of change of the actual facts or in case of economic inability*" see Greece 2006 Decision 63/2006 of the Court of Appeals of Lamia (Sunflower seed case) (http://cisgw3.law.pace.edu/cases/060001gr.html). In a decision, a Belgian court ruled that price increase cannot be regarded as *force majeure* and coincidence, "*because the circumstances that are relied on do not make the performance of the obligation impossible.*" Belgium 25 January 2005 Commercial Court Tongeren (Scafom International BV & Orion Metal BVBA v. Exma CPI SA) (http://cisgw3.law.pace.edu/cases/050125b1.html). However, this decision was subsequently overturned by the Supreme Court, which ruled that: "*Changed circumstances that were not reasonably foreseeable at the time of the conclusion of the contract and that are unequivocally of a nature to increase the burden of performance of the contract in a disproportionate manner, can, under circumstances, form an impediment in the sense of this provision of the Convention.*" Belgium 19 June 2009 Court of Cassation [Supreme Court] (Scafom International BV v. Lorraine Tubes S.A.S.) (http://cisgw3.law.pace.edu/cases/090619b1.html).

[91] **Stoll/Gruber**, in: Schlechtriem/Schwenzer, Art. 79, Nr. 30; **Flambouras**, Guide to Article 79, p. 1 ff.

[92] Norwegian proposal (A/CONF.97/C.1/L.191/Rev.1) in United Nations Conference on Contracts for the International Sale of Goods, Vienna, 10 March - 11 April 1980 (Official Records, New York, 1981) p. 381; See Legislative History 1980 Vienna Conference, available at <http://www.cisg.law.pace.edu/cisg/1stcommittee/summaries79,80.html>.

case of hardship, this would over-protect the debtor. Moreover, when the historical background and Secretariat Commentary on Article 79 is taken into consideration, it is clear that the provision does not cover cases of hardship.

2) *Non-conformity of the Goods with the Contract*

Unification Instruments do not contain any provisions which explain if *force majeure* provisions would apply to goods that are non-conforming with the contract. For instance, it is not clear if the seller could be exempt from liability if the goods (oranges, milk, pharmaceuticals etc.), which have been sent to the buyer for delivery, have been poisoned by terrorists prior to the passing of the risk to the buyer.[93] This issue is to be resolved by the doctrine, courts and tribunals. However, currently there is only one decision rendered by a French court, where it is answered that the promisor may rely on the *force majeure* provision of the relevant Unification Instrument and ask to be exempt from his liability arising from non-conformity of the goods.[94]

With regard to the CISG, the prevailing opinion is that Article 79 is applicable to any kind of breach by the seller because Article 79 refers to the promisor's "*failure to perform any of his obligations*"—which includes the delivery of conforming goods.[95] In fact, non-conformity of the goods with the contract is included in the concept of breach under Article 45 (1).[96] Within this stance, Stoll/Gruber argue that in case of sale of specific goods in the seller's possession, if the defect was hidden and could not have been discovered by methods which a reasonable person in the seller's position could reasonably have been expected to discover, the seller might

---

[93] **Magnus**, p. 304.

[94] In a well-known German case regarding the issue, where it was ruled that the seller was liable for non-performance, the court did not decide whether Article 79 was applicable or not. The court stated that even if Article 79 were applicable to the case, it would not exempt the seller from liability since the defect in the good was not an impediment beyond the seller's control. See, Germany 24 March 1999 Supreme Court (Vine wax case) (http://cisgw3.law.pace.edu/cases/990324g1.html). However, in another decision, the court applied an exemption provided under Article 79 to a seller that delivered non-conforming goods: "*Whereas nonetheless, on the one hand, [buyer] does not produce proof that the entire quantity of the goods had posed a problem, and that he also derived a profit from part of the delivered goods; on the other hand, that [seller] finding itself in the position of a seller of a product whose manufacture and notably whose elaboration of the fabrics are beyond [seller]'s control, it is proper, in the absence of a showing of bad faith on [seller]'s part, to allow [seller] the benefit of Article 79 CISG.*" See France 19 January 1998 District Court Besançon (Flippe Christian v. Douet Sport Collections) (http://cisgw3.law.pace.edu/cases/980119f1.html).

[95] **Huber/Mullis**, p. 258; **Flambouras**, PILR 2001, 261, 275; **Brunner**, p. 111; **Atamer**, Satıcının Yükümlülükleri, p. 455; **Schlectriem/Hachem/Kee**, Nr. 45.55.

[96] **Huber/Mullis**, p. 258.

be exempt from liability. However, if the seller manufactures the goods himself, exemption is possible only if it can be shown that an insuperable event such as a natural catastrophe caused the event. Similar to the opinion in German, Swiss and Turkish laws, in cases of debt in kind, it can be accepted that the seller is obliged to deliver goods free of defects. However, it is argued that even in such cases, the seller should be exempted from liability if he received the goods from a reliable supplier and the defect could not have been discovered using methods which could reasonably be expected of a reasonable person in the seller's position and was therefore unavoidable.[97]

Unlike Article 79, which makes reference to the promisor's "*failure to perform any of his obligations*", PICC, PECL, DCFR and CESL refer to *non-performance* in general. It should be noted that non-performance also includes the cases of defective performance.[98] In the end, the purpose of *force majeure* clauses is to restrict the liability of the promisor if he cannot perform his obligation arising from the contract due to an *unforeseeable* and *unavoidable* external event *beyond control*. When the essence of *force majeure* provisions are considered, it makes no difference whether the external event causes impossibility of performance permanently, temporarily or partially. Similarly, the same external event may cause non-conformity, rather than destroying the subject matter of the contract. In the end the promisor must prove that the requirements of *force majeure* provisions are met. Even in such cases, the promisor's liability to pay damages is eliminated but the promisee may still seek other remedies for delivery of non-conforming goods. This is a balance between the interests of both parties. Any narrow interpretation of Unification Instruments, which excludes the delivery of non-conforming goods from the scope of *force majeure* provisions, is an alienation to the purpose of *force majeure* provisions.

3) Temporary Impediments to Performance

Unification Instruments have explicit provisions regarding the effects of temporary impediments to performance. CISG Article 79 (3) anticipates that "*The exemption provided by this article has effect for the period during which the impediment exists.*"[99] In other words, a temporary impediment exempts the promisor from liability only for the length of its duration.[100]

[97] **Stoll/Gruber**, in: Schlechtriem/Schwenzer, Art. 79, Nr. 39–40.

[98] See PICC Article 7.1.1, PECL 1:301 (4) and DCFR III-I:101 (3).

[99] This is an apparent divergence from the common law system, where temporary impediments are not recognized. **Schlectriem/Hachem/Kee**, Nr. 45.57.

[100] During the time of the original impediment, other impediments may occur and such new impediments might cause permanent exemption of the promisor in accordance with Article 79 (1). **Schlechtriem/Butler**, Nr. 295.

In the event of a temporary impediment, the effects of the impediment might last longer than the existence of the impediment itself. In such cases, it is clear that the promisor cannot perform his obligation as soon as the impediment disappears. A very good illustration of such cases is found in the PICC Commentary:

> A contracts to lay a natural gas pipeline across country X. Climatic conditions are such that it is normally impossible to work between 1 November and 31 March. The contract is timed to finish on 31 October but the start of work is delayed for a month by a civil war in a neighbouring country which makes it impossible to bring in all the piping on time. If the consequence is reasonably to prevent the completion of the work until its resumption in the following spring, A may be entitled to an extension of five months even though the delay was itself of one month only.[101]

The relevant provisions of PICC, PECL, DCFR and CESL reflect the above-stated concern. Accordingly, PICC Article 7.1.7 contemplates that the effect of excuse is "*for such period as is reasonable having regard to the effect of the impediment on the performance*".[102] This criterion explicitly considers not the term of the impediment itself, but the term of the effect of the impediment on the performance. Based on the same concern, it is accepted under PECL and DCFR that if the consequences which follow the obstacle last longer than the obstacle itself, the excuse covers the whole period during which the promisor is unable to perform.[103] A similar approach would be appropriate for CESL as well.

In case of temporary impediments to performance, an exemption only relieves the promisor from paying damages caused by late performance.[104] In other words, exemption does not change the fact that the delay in performance constitutes a breach of contract. Therefore the promisee, who cannot ask for compensation, still has the option to avoid the contract if the breach is fundamental and the late performance will be of no use to him.[105] In contrast to CISG and PICC, such right has been explicitly set forth in PECL, DCFR and CESL. In any case, if the contract is not avoided by the promisee, disappearance of the temporary impediment reinstates the obligations of both parties under the contract.[106]

---

[101] PICC Commentary, Art. 7.1.7, Comment 2.

[102] "*In some cases the impediment will prevent any performance at all but in many others it will simply delay performance and the effect of the article will be to give extra time for performance.*" PICC Commentary, Article 7.1.7, Comment 2.

[103] PECL Commentary, Art. 8:108, Comment E; DCFR Commentary, III-3:104, Comment D.

[104] **Tallon**, in: Bianca/Bonell, Art. 79, Nr. 2.10.4.

[105] **Stoll/Gruber**, in: Schlechtriem/Schwenzer, Art. 79, Nr. 41; **Flambouras**, PILR 2001, 261, 274.

[106] Secretariat Commentary, Art. 65, Nr. 14.

4) Partial Impediments to Performance

Unification Instruments do not contain any express provision regarding the effects of partial impediment to performance. However, considering the provisions regarding temporary impediments, it may be inferred that an impediment may in principle excuse non-performance to the extent that it really exists. Therefore, it is argued that if the impediment impairs only part of the agreed performance, for such part, the promisor may rely on the *force majeure* provision of the relevant Unification Instrument.[107]

5) Liability for Third Persons

Liability of the promisor for conduct of third persons is specifically regulated under CISG, PECL, DCFR and CESL. Under Article 79 (2) of the CISG, the promisor is liable for the conduct of third persons who are engaged to perform the whole or part of the contract on behalf of the promisor. However, it is a middle ground taken by the CISG that under the specific conditions indicated in Article 79 (2), the promisor might be exempt from such liability.[108]

Article 79 (2) rules that if the promisor has engaged third persons to perform the whole or part of the contract, the impediment must exempt both the promisor and the third person from liability.[109] In other words, for being exempt from liability, the promisor must prove that the conditions of Article 79 (1) are fulfilled not only in relation to himself, but also in relation to the third person.[110] As a result, even if the third party's failure to perform is excused, the promisor is still bound to avoid or overcome such impediment in order to claim exemption.[111]

---

[107] **Brunner**, p. 260–261.

[108] **Zeller**, Damages, p. 183.

[109] In Russia 30 July 2001 Arbitration proceeding 198/2000 (http://cisgw3.law.pace.edu/cases/010730r1.html) the tribunal's ruling deserves attention: "*In this connection, the Tribunal cannot take into consideration the [Buyer]'s argument that he instructed his bank in Russia to make a transfer on 6 October 1998 because the money was not deposited to the [Seller]'s account due to the instructions issued by the Russian Federation Central Bank. The [Buyer]'s reference to the impediments that prevented him from fulfilling his obligations, i.e., the said instruction of the Central Bank, is not grounded in Article 79 CISG. In addition, the Tribunal cannot take such argument into account because [Buyer]'s failure to fulfill his obligations resulted from a third party actions, i.e., the Russian bank, which was necessary for the performance of the contract. It was not established that such third party was relieved from liability.*"

[110] **Flambouras**, PILR 2001, 261, 274; **Tallon**, in: Bianca/Bonell, Art. 79, Nr. 5.7.2; **Brunner**, p. 187. According to Morrissey/Graves, the "inability of the third party to perform" constitutes the impediment beyond control for the debtor. **Morrissey/Graves**, p. 294.

[111] **Garro**, p. 239. In Switzerland 22 November 2010 Commercial Court Zurich (Clothing case) where the defendant argued that his non-delivery was caused by the delivery delays of the Chinese producers, the court ruled that the buyer cannot rely on Article 79. Accordingly, the delivery

The concept of third person under Article 79 (2) only covers people who are acting independently and are neither within the promisor's organizational sphere nor under his responsibility.[112] These people are not only separate real or legal persons, but also economically and functionally independent from the promisor.[113] The principle under Article 79 (2) applies even if the third person is not involved in the dispute between the promisor and the promisee.[114] On the other hand, the promisor cannot request exemption from liability for the acts of those people, who only enable, assist or create the preconditions for the seller's delivery of conforming goods.[115]

The principle underlying Article 79 (2) is that the promisor ought not to benefit from a third person's assumption of performance. Therefore it is irrelevant whether the third person was carefully selected or supervised or the involvement of the third person was unavoidable for the promisor.[116] In any case, the third person must be aware that his action is a means of performing the main contract and he is fully or partially fulfilling an obligation of the promisor on his behalf.[117] However, Article

---

problems regarding textiles from far East were known and not uncommon. Therefore, such impediments were foreseeable and the buyer and his supplier had to take the necessary measures to prevent such impediments. As a result, the buyer cannot rely on Article 79, since the conditions of Article 79 (1) and (2) are not met. For the text of the decision in German language see http://globalsaleslaw.com/content/api/cisg/urteile/2160.pdf.

[112] **Flambouras**, PILR 2001, 261, 274; **Stoll/Gruber**, in: Schlechtriem/Schwenzer, Art. 79, Nr. 25; CISG Advisory Council Opinion No.7, Nr. 19; **Garro**, p. 238. In Switzerland 10 February 1999 Commercial Court Zürich (Art books case) (http://cisgw3.law.pace.edu/cases/990210s1.html) case it was ruled that the person (the carrier) that the seller hands over the goods for transmission to the buyer is not a third party under Article 79 (2).

[113] CISG Advisory Council Opinion No.7, Nr. 19. On the other hand, PECL Commentary does not require the third person be independent: "*The internal relationship between the debtor and the third person is irrelevant in this context The third person may be subject to instructions of the debtor, such as an employee or an agent; or may be an independent subcontractor.*" PECL Commentary, Article 8:107, Comment B.

[114] UNCITRAL, Digest of Article 79 case law, Nr. 21.

[115] CISG Advisory Council Opinion No.7, p. 18. Article 79 (2) was incorporated into the provision as a response to the increasing development of sub-contracting. **Tallon**, in: Bianca/Bonell, Art. 79, Nr. 2.7; **Brunner**, p. 186; **Magnus**, in: Honsell, Art. 79, Nr. 18. According to Achilles, the following may be regarded as third parties under Article 79 (2): "*subcontractors, to whom the buyer entrusts the independent performance production, instruction and maintenance operations that the buyer owes himself; or service providers such as banks or forwarding agents, over which the buyer handles the contractually owed payments and transport processes.*" **Achilles**, Art. 79, Nr. 9. According to the prevailing doctrine, suppliers of the goods or raw materials are not third parties under Article 79 (2). Secretariat Commentary, Art. 65, Nr. 12; **Salger**, in: Witz/Salger/Lorenz, Art. 79, Nr. 9; **Magnus**, in: Honsell, Art. 79, Nr. 19. For the ongoing discussion in the doctrine, whether the suppliers of the promisor are third persons within the meaning of Article 79, also see **Zeller**, Damages, p. 184.

[116] **Stoll/Gruber**, in: Schlechtriem/Schwenzer, Art. 79, Nr. 27.

[117] **Tallon**: in Bianca/Bonell, Art. 79, Nr. 2.7.1; **Stoll/Gruber**, in: Schlechtriem/Schwenzer, Art. 79, Nr. 26; **Soergel-CISG/Lüderitz/Dettmeier**, Art. 79, Nr. 22.

79 (2) does not require that the third person engages in direct contact with the promisee.[118]

Regulations of PECL, DCFR and CESL regarding the liability of the promisor for conduct of third persons is merely clarification of the lack of a provision corresponding to Article 79 (2) of the CISG. For instance, Article 8:107 of PECL states that "*A party who entrusts performance of the contract to another person remains responsible for performance.*"[119] This means that there is no separate exemption regime that the promisor may rely on in case of conduct of third persons. Within this stance, under PECL, DCFR, CESL and also PICC, issues dealt with under CISG Article 79 (2) would be handled by the general *force majeure* provisions. Therefore, non-inclusion of a provision corresponding to CISG Article 79 (2) should not be interpreted in a way that the promisor cannot ask for exemption from liability if he has entrusted performance to another person. In fact, the term impediment covers every sort of event including the acts of third parties.[120]

6) Exemption due to Interference by the Other Party

Force majeure excuse under Unification Instruments has to be distinguished from the cases where the performance is prevented by an action or omission of the other party to the contract, *i.e.*, the promisee. In fact, in such cases performance of the contract by the promisor is not prevented by an impediment, which is external to both of the parties, but because of conduct attributable to the promisee.[121]

Exemption due to interference by the other party is specifically regulated under each of Unification Instruments. For instance, it is stated under Article 80 of the CISG that "*A party may not rely on a failure of the other party to perform, to the extent that such failure was caused by the first party's act or omission.*"[122] Similarly, Article 7.4.7 of the PICC further states that "*Where the harm is due in part to an act or omission of the aggrieved party or to another event as to which that party bears the risk, the amount of damages shall be reduced to the extent that these*

[118] **Stoll/Gruber**, in: Schlechtriem/Schwenzer, Art. 79, Nr. 26.

[119] Similarly, DCFR III-2:106 reads as follows: "*A debtor who entrusts performance of an obligation to another person remains responsible for performance.*"

[120] PECL Commentary, Article 8:108, Comment B; **Garro**, p. 239.

[121] **Brunner**, p. 113.

[122] In the international level, it is debated if Article 80 also covers the cases, where both parties contributed to non-performance. According to the prevailing opinion, the provision applies to joint responsibility as well. **Schwenzer/Hachem/Kee**, Nr. 45.127. For the approaches at the international level to the method of application of Article 79 when both parties contribute to the breach, see **Schwenzer/Hachem/Kee**, Nr. 45.128 ff.

factors have contributed to the harm, having regard to the conduct of each of the parties."[123]

As a result, if the performance of the promisor is prevented by the conduct of the promisee, the promisee cannot rely on such non-performance. In other words, to the extent that the creditor has contributed to the damages, he may not claim compensation.[124] This principle must be read in conjunction with another principle recognized by Unification Instruments: mitigation of harm.[125] In fact under Unification Instruments, the aggrieved party is under the obligation to mitigate the damages resulting from the breach.[126] More specifically, the creditor must take reasonable steps to reduce the harm, which certainly includes preventing the increase of the amount of damages. However, the creditor is entitled to his expenses incurred for the mitigation of damages.[127]

7) *Initial Impossibility*

The distinction of initial impossibility and subsequent impossibility is regulated quite differently under Unification Instruments. Within this scope, the distinction of initial and subsequent impossibility must be analyzed for each of Unification Instruments separately. Moreover, it must be answered if the cases of initial impossibility would be covered by the *force majeure* provisions of Unification Instruments.

a) CISG

The CISG contains no provision regarding the time of the impediment's occurrence and its effects to the promisor's exemption from liability. Within this scope, the major discussion is about the effect of initial impossibility on performance because in cases of initial impossibility it is comparatively difficult to argue that the conditions set forth in Article 79 (1) for exemption are met. Especially it is hard to prove that the promisor "*could not reasonably be expected to have taken the*

[123] Within this stance, Articles 7.1.2 and 7.4.7 of the PICC, Articles 8:101 (3) and 9:505 of the PECL, Articles III.–3:101 (3) and III-3:704 of the DCFR and Articles 106 (5) and 131 (3) of the CESL have similar scopes.

[124] Art. 80 CISG, Art. 7.4.7 PICC, Art. 9:504 PECL, III.-3:704 DCFR, Article 162.

[125] "*While the present article is concerned with the conduct of the aggrieved party in regard to the cause of the initial harm, Art. 7.4.8* [*on mitigation of harm*] *relates to that party's conduct subsequent thereto.*" PICC Commentary, Art. 7.4.7, Comment 4.

[126] See CISG, Art. 77, Art. 7.4.8 PICC, Art. 9:505 PECL, III-3:705 DCFR, Art. 163 CESL.

[127] See Art. 7.4.8 (2) PICC, Art. 9:505 (2) PECL, III-3:705 (2) DCFR, Art. 163 (2) CESL. Despite the lack of a similar provision in the CISG, such principle is implicit in Article 77. **Brunner**, p. 357, fn. 1795.

impediment into account at the time of the conclusion of the contract".[128] In fact, even if it is accepted that initial impossibility lies within the scope of Article 79, in order to be exempt from liability, the seller must be unaware of the initial impossibility and must have been reasonable in not expecting to take it into account at the time of the conclusion of the contract.[129]

Although there is no express provision in the Convention, the Secretariat Commentary contains an answer to such ambiguity. Within this stance, the Secretariat Commentary provides that the impediment may have existed at the time of the conclusion of the contract.[130] In other words, in the Commentary it has been accepted that if the conditions indicated under Article 79 are met, initial impossibility might lead to exemption of the promisor.

Despite the Secretariat Commentary, the authors in the doctrine still discuss if initial impossibility might cause exemption from liability under the CISG. As explained under the examples of Switzerland, Turkey and Germany prior to the reform, in some legal systems which follow the *impossibilium nulla obligation est* principle, the absence of the subject matter at the time of the conclusion of the contract (*i.e.*, initial impossibility) raises a problem of validity. However, validity issues are not governed by the CISG (Art. 4 (a)).[131]

Article 4 (a) of the CISG excludes validity issues from the scope of the CISG.[132] In Article 4 it has been stated that the CISG governs only (*i*) the formation of the contract of sale, and (*ii*) the rights and obligations of the seller and the buyer arising from such contract. It has been specifically indicated that, except as otherwise expressly provided in the CISG, it is not concerned with the validity of the contract or of any of its provisions or of any usage. Therefore, this stance asserts that in countries, where initial impossibility causes invalidity of contracts, the CISG (including Article 79 on exemption from liability) would not apply. Therefore the judge/arbitrator should make reference to the domestic law to be determined by the conflict of laws rules of the forum.[133]

This view arises from the perspective that there is an external gap in the CISG. Accordingly, there is no provision in the CISG, which sets forth whether or not cases of initial impossibility lie within the scope of the Convention. Therefore, it is arguable that initial impossibility is one of the validity matters mentioned under Article 4 (a) of the Convention. To understand the legal background of such perspective it is necessary to examine the concept of external gap.

---

[128] **Marcantonio**, HICLR 1984, 41, 58.

[129] CISG Advisory Council Opinion No. 7, Nr. 8. If the promisor guaranteed the existence of a certain fact or otherwise assumed the risk of an initial impediment, he may not also claim exemption under Article 79. **Brunner**, p. 234.

[130] Secretariat Commentary, Art. 65, Nr. 4.

[131] **Flambouras**, PILR 2001, 261, 269; **Tallon**, in: Bianca/Bonell, Art. 79, Nr. 2.4.3.

[132] According to Zeller, Article 4 *(a) "reflects the compromise between the political ambitions of sovereign states and the need for international commerce."* **Zeller**, CISG, p. 68.

[133] **Flambouras**, PILR 2001, 261, 269–270; **Rimke**, p. 213–214; **Tallon**, in: Bianca/Bonell, Art. 79, Nr. 2.4.3.

Gaps are divided into two as external gaps and internal gaps.[134] Any matter that is outside the scope of the CISG is regarded as an external gap.[135] If the Convention accepts initial impossibility as a matter of validity. there exists an external gap in the Convention, since it is clear that validity issues are left outside of the scope of the CISG (Article 4 (a)). In case of external gap, domestic law to be determined by the conflict of laws rules of the forum needs to be applied without any recourse to the CISG, therefore without any interpretation or gap filling activity.[136] On the other hand internal gaps are gaps where a discoverable general principle will supply the answer that is unanswered in the Convention. These are the matters that require interpretation and gap filling.[137]

Although external gaps are not to be filled in through interpretation, the provisions of the Convention must still be interpreted to find out if there is an external gap with regard to any matter. Interpretation of the provisions of the CISG is dealt with under Article 7 (1) of the Convention. Accordingly, the provision rules that when interpreting the provisions of the CISG, three things must be considered: (*i*) international character of the Convention, (*ii*) the need to promote uniformity in its application, and (*iii*) the observance of good faith in international trade. Therefore the provisions of the Convention must be interpreted in accordance with the above-stated principles in order to find out if initial impossibility is not governed by the Convention.

It must be accepted that there is no external gap in the CISG with regard to initial impossibility.[138] Therefore it cannot be claimed that cases of initial impossibility fall under validity issues that are ungoverned by the Convention. In other words, even when the domestic law to be determined by the conflict of laws rules of the forum regards initial impossibility as a reason of invalidity, contracts, which cannot be performed due to initial impossibility, would still be subject to the CISG and Article 79. This opinion is based on four reasons, which would be explained below.

Firstly, initial impossibility is actually regulated under the Convention. As rightfully argued by Schlechtriem, impossibility is an impediment to the performance of the debtor and it leads to non-performance. In other words, it is evident that non-performance of contractual obligations is an issue, which is regulated and governed by the Convention; and cases of impossibility fall under the CISG's provisions regarding non-performance. From this perspective, it cannot be argued

[134] **Janssen/Kiene**, p. 264; **Zeller**, Damages, p. 28. Synonyms for internal gap are "*lacuna praeter legem*", "concealed gap" and "hidden gap". **Janssen/Kiene**, p. 264.

[135] Synonyms for external gap are "*lacuna intra legem*", "apparent gap" and "obvious gap". **Janssen/Kiene**, p. 264.

[136] **Janssen/Kiene**, p. 264; **Zeller**, Damages, p. 29.

[137] **Zeller**, Damages, p. 28.

[138] In the opinion that the term impediment is flexible enough to cover cases of initial impossibility and there is no gap in the CISG, see **Düchs**, p. 349.

that initial impossibility is not governed by the CISG.[139] Moreover, under the Convention there is no distinction of initial and subsequent impossibility. The CISG recognizes impossibility as a whole. Considering that the Convention does not make a distinction between different types of impossibility, there is no rationale in arguing that initial impossibility must be subject to different legal results than subsequent impossibility.

Secondly, Article 68 of the CISG,[140] which deals with the passing of risk in respect of goods sold in transit points to the same direction. According to the last sentence of the provision "*if at the time of the conclusion of the contract of sale the seller knew or ought to have known that the goods had been lost or damaged*" this would cause the liability of the seller. This shows that the CISG has regulated initial impossibility, which prevents the recourse to domestic laws, which deem initial impossibility as a reason of voidness.[141]

Thirdly, in matters regarding interpretation and application of the provisions of the Convention, the intentions of the parties must be taken into consideration. To be more specific, in cases where the contract falls under the scope of application of the CISG, domestic rules should only be regarded as dispositive rules of interpretation. Accordingly, when the domestic law to be determined by the conflict of laws rules of the forum regards the contract void due to initial impossibility, the provisions of the CISG regarding the intentions of the parties should prevail over domestic rules.[142] Within this scope, the judge or the arbitrator should determine whether the parties would wish their contract be regarded as void if the subject matter did not exist at the time of the conclusion of the contract. Moreover, even when there is an internal gap, Article 7 (2)[143] sets forth that gaps should be filled in conformity with the general principles on which the Convention is based. Within this stance, the general principle of *pacta sunt servanda* also requires upholding the intentions

[139] **Schlechtriem,** in: Schlechtriem/Schwenzer, Art. 4, Nr. 13.

[140] Article 68 of the CISG read as follows: "*The risk in respect of goods sold in transit passes to the buyer from the time of the conclusion of the contract. However, if the circumstances so indicate, the risk is assumed by the buyer from the time the goods were handed over to the carrier who issued the documents embodying the contract of carriage. Nevertheless, if at the time of the conclusion of the contract of sale the seller knew or ought to have known that the goods had been lost or damaged and did not disclose this to the buyer, the loss or damage is at the risk of the seller.*"

[141] **Hager**, in: Schlechtriem/Schwenzer, Art. 68, Nr. 2.

[142] **Stoll/Gruber**, in: Schlechtriem/Schwenzer, Art. 79, Nr. 13; **Flambouras**, PILR 2001, 261, 270; **Schwenzer**, VUWLR 2008, 709, 718. Accepting that an extensive interpretation is preferable as it creates uniformity, Tallon asserts that when the existence of the subject matter is accepted as a preemptory rule by the domestic law, in order to prevent any conflict with mandatory provisions of domestic law, domestic law must prevail over Article 79 by the virtue of Article 4 (a). **Tallon**, in: Bianca/Bonell, Art. 79, Nr. 2.4.3.

[143] "*Questions concerning matters governed by this Convention which are not expressly settled in it are to be settled in conformity with the general principles on which it is based or, in the absence of such principles, in conformity with the law applicable by virtue of the rules of private international law.*"

of the parties. For instance, if the debtor has provided an express or implied undertaking or guarantee regarding the existence of the subject matter, the domestic law which deems the contract void would not apply.[144] In fact, such guarantee reflects the intention of the parties that their contract be valid even if its subject matter does not exist at the time of the conclusion of the contract. Such approach would also be more appropriate to maintain a balance of interests of both parties to the contract.[145]

Fourthly, one of the major purposes of the CISG is to promote uniformity of application in several contracting states which follow different legal systems. Therefore there is too little reference to domestic law and resort to domestic law is accepted as a last resort. This is also why terms under the CISG must be interpreted autonomously.[146] If it is accepted that domestic law would apply to the claims of invalidity due to initial impossibility, this would damage the uniformity of the Convention's application. Therefore, the purpose of promoting uniformity of application also points to an interpretation that Article 4 (a) of the Convention does not cover initial impossibility.

As a result, it must be accepted that there is no external gap in the CISG regarding initial impossibility. Although it is difficult in specific cases to prove that the conditions of Article 79 are met, it is still theoretically possible that an impediment reasonably unknown to both parties at the time of the conclusion of the contract is revealed at a later date. In other words, requirements of Article 79 may be met even in case of initial impossibility.[147]

---

[144] **Flambouras**, PILR 2001, 261, 270.

[145] It cannot be argued that in case of initial impossibility, the promisor has implicitly guaranteed his ability to perform. Such assumption is not *ipso facto* enough to prevent the promisor's exemption from liability because in the absence of an explicit and specific guarantee by the promisor, the promisee cannot assume that the promisor always and absolutely intends to accept the responsibility for initial ability to perform. Therefore, in case of doubt regarding such guarantee by the promisor, it should be assessed if the promisor could reasonably have been aware of an insuperable impediment. In fact, the conditions in Article 79 (1) would not have been met if the promisor *could reasonably be expected to have taken the impediment into account at the time of the conclusion of the contract.*

Notwithstanding such principle, at the time of the conclusion of the contract, if the parties were aware of the existence of the impediment, the promisor's unqualified promise to perform would be accepted as a guarantee. **Stoll/Gruber**, in: Schlechtriem/Schwenzer Art. 79, Nr. 12; **Soergel-CISG/Lüderitz/Dettmeier**, Art. 79, Nr. 20.

[146] **Schlechtriem,** in: Schlechtriem/Schwenzer, Art. 4 Nr. 7; **Huber/Mullis**, p. 21.

[147] In the same opinion, see **Grunewald**, JZ 2001, 433, 434; **Atamer**, Satıcının Yükümlülükleri, p. 459. For a similar opinion that Article 79 CISG makes no distinction between initial and subsequent impossibility, see **Cerutti**, Nr. 487; **Saenger**, in: Ferrari/Kieninger/Mankowski/Otte/Saenger/Schulze/Staudinger, Art. 79, Nr. 3.

b) PICC

Unlike the CISG, the PICC has a provision with regard to the effects of initial impossibility on validity of contracts. Accordingly, Article 3.1 of the PICC lists the matters not covered by the PICC as "*invalidity arising from (a) lack of capacity; (b) immorality or illegality*". In order to eliminate the controversy if initial impossibility is a reason for invalidity, the first paragraph of Article 3.3 of the PICC explicitly sets forth that "*The mere fact that at the time of the conclusion of the contract the performance of the obligation assumed was impossible does not affect the validity of the contract.*"[148] Similarly, the second paragraph of Article 3.3 of the PICC sets forth that "*The mere fact that at the time of the conclusion of the contract a party was not entitled to dispose of the assets to which the contract relates does not affect the validity of the contract.*" In other words, in addition to initial objective impossibility, initial subjective impossibility does not cause the contract to be void either.

When Articles 3.1 and 3.3 of the PICC are interpreted together, it is irrelevant whether or not the applicable domestic law regards the contract as invalid due to initial impossibility. In other words, even if the domestic law provides that initial impossibility is a cause of invalidity, the contract will lie within the scope of the PICC,[149] because regardless of the definition of the domestic law, PICC accepts that initial impossibility is not a reason of invalidity—which is excluded from the scope of the PICC.

If performance is both initially impossible and at the same time illegal, special emphasis needs to be made on the word "*merely*". In fact, such cases will be excluded from the scope of the PICC not due to initial impossibility, but due to invalidity arising from illegality of the performance. Accordingly, if initial impossibility of performance arises from a legal prohibition of the domestic law, such as an export ban or an import embargo, the purpose of the law, which enacts the prohibition must be assessed. More specifically it must be assessed, whether such law intends to invalidate the contract or merely to prohibit its performance.[150] From this stance, if the legal prohibition of the domestic law aims at invalidating the contract, the case will generally fall under Article 3.1 (b) and the domestic prohibition would apply. On the other hand, if the legal prohibition of the domestic law simply prohibits the performance without invalidating the contract, the case will lie within the scope of the PICC and Article 3.3 would apply.[151]

The provision of the first paragraph of Article 3.3 of the PICC equates the cases of initial impossibility with subsequent impossibility. In other words, regardless of the time of occurrence of the impossibility, the same legal result would apply, *i.e.*,

---

[148] According to Article 3.19 of the PICC, this rule is not mandatory. Therefore the parties to a contract may agree that their contract will be invalid in case of initial impossibility.

[149] **Huber**, in: Vogenauer/Kleinheisterkamp, Art. 3.3, Nr. 6.

[150] PICC Commentary, Article 3.3, Comment 1.

[151] **Huber**, in: Vogenauer/Kleinheisterkamp, Art. 3.3, Nr. 10–12.

the rules of non-performance.[152] Although it is clear that in case of initial impossibility the contract would be deemed subject to the PICC, it should be answered whether *force majeure* provision of the PICC may apply to the cases of initial impossibility as well. Although there is no express provision in the PICC with regard to this matter, it is argued that Article 7.1.7 of the PICC covers the cases of initial impediments which render performance impossible.[153] Within this stance, in case of initial impossibility, the promisor might claim exemption from liability if he can prove that the conditions for *force majeure* have been met.

On the other hand, Huber states that in case of initial impossibility, the contract may be revoked due to mistake under Articles 3.4 and 3.5. Therefore, the debtor can be released from his obligation to perform only through revocation.[154] In other words, according to the author, initial impossibility cannot be deemed as *force majeure* under Article 7.1.7 and there is no room for applying Article 7.1.7 to the cases of initial impossibility.[155]

c) PECL AND DCFR

The PECL and the DCFR have diverging provisions regarding the ungoverned matters, but neither of them has listed initial impossibility as an ungoverned matter.[156] The effect of initial impossibility on contracts is explicitly regulated in both PECL and DCFR and any related controversy has been prevented.

The provisions of PECL and DCFR with regard to cases of initial impossibility are almost identical. According to Article II-7:102 of the posterior DCFR: "*A contract is not invalid, in whole or in part, merely because at the time it is concluded performance of any obligation assumed is impossible, or because a party is not entitled to dispose of any assets to which the contract relates.*"[157]

---

[152] Under these rules, special consideration can be given to the fact that one or both of the parties already knew of the impossibility of performance at the time of contracting. PICC Commentary, Article 3.3, Comment 1.

[153] **Kleinheisterkamp**, in: Vogenauer/Kleinheisterkamp, Art. 7.1.7, Nr. 5.

[154] On the other hand, it is also arguable that the PICC sets forth that the validity of the contract is not affected by initial impossibility and "*this implies that they are also removed from the scope of the provisions on mistake. A party cannot, therefore, claim avoidance on the grounds that he was mistaken as to the ability of either party to perform.*" **Leyens**, p. 1 ff.

[155] **Huber**, Leistungsstörungen I, § 4 III 2, p. 116. In the same opinion, see **Fischer**, p. 268. Within this stance, Huber argues that the debtor is liable under a guarantee regarding possibility of performance at the time of contract formation. **Huber**, Leistungsstörungen I, § 4 IV 2, p. 122.

[156] Article 4:101 of the PECL lists the matters not governed as "*invalidity arising from illegality, immorality or lack of capacity*". On the other hand, Article II-7:101 of the DCFR does not exclude cases of illegality and immorality (which it refers as "*infringement of fundamental principles or mandatory rules*") from its scope.

[157] This Article corresponds to Article 4:102 of the PECL, which reads as follows: "*A contract is not invalid merely because at the time it was concluded performance of the obligation assumed was impossible, or because a party was not entitled to dispose of the assets to which the contract*

Similar to PICC, there is no express provision in PECL or DCFR, which answers if cases of initial impossibility are covered by the relevant *force majeure* provisions. However, it is argued that under the PECL and DCFR the cases of initial impossibility are not accepted to be covered by the relevant *force majeure* provisions. Accordingly, it is asserted that if an impediment exists at the time when the contract is concluded, and without the parties knowing it, such contract might be avoided under the rules on mistake.[158]

According to Article 4:117 (1) of the PECL, the party who avoids the contract due to mistake "*may recover from the other party damages* (. . .), *provided that the other party knew or ought to have known of the mistake*".[159] Accordingly, if the debtor does not know or ought to have known the initial impossibility of performance, through avoidance of the contract, such party is released from his liability to compensate the damages of the mistaken creditor.[160] Similarly, *force majeure* provisions require that the promisor "*could not reasonably be expected to have taken the impediment into account at the time of the conclusion of the contract*". However, unlike avoidance due to mistake, in order to be exempt from liability, it is also required that the debtor is not responsible for the *occurrence* of initial impossibility. This is clear as the impediment must be beyond control of the debtor. Within this stance, it is more difficult for the debtor to be released from his compensation liability under exemption clauses and this provides a comparatively higher protection of the interest of the creditor. As a result, it can be said that, by closing the option of exemption in case of initial impossibility, the strict liability principle of PECL and DCFR would be actually softened by the right of avoidance due to mistake.[161]

d) CESL

Unlike PICC, PECL and DCFR, CESL does not contemplate any explicit article regarding the effects of initial impossibility on the validity of the contract. Preamble

relates." The main difference between the two provisions is that DCFR has further emphasized that initial impossibility does not invalidate the contract "*in whole or in part*".

[158] PECL Commentary, Article 8:108, Comment B; DCFR Commentary, Article III-3:104, Comment B. According to Brunner, rules on mistake and *force majeure*/hardship exemptions are in principle alternatively applicable to the cases of initial impossibility. **Brunner**, p. 235.

[159] It must be noted that both under the PECL and the DCFR the damages, which are recoverable after avoidance are the negative damages of the creditor. See PECL Commentary, Article 4:117, Comment B; DCFR Commentary, Article II-7:214, Comment B.

[160] Similarly, Article II.-7:214 (1) of the DCFR sets forth that "*A party who has the right to avoid a contract under this Section* (*or who had such a right before it was lost by the effect of time limits or confirmation*) *is entitled, whether or not the contract is avoided, to damages from the other party for any loss suffered as a result of the mistake, fraud, coercion, threats or unfair exploitation, provided that the other party knew or could reasonably be expected to have known of the ground for avoidance*."

[161] **Mitzkait**, p. 218.

No. 27 of CESL states that "*the invalidity of a contract arising from lack of capacity, illegality or immorality*" would be governed by the relevant national law.[162] However, similar to CISG, it is not clear whether cases of initial impossibility would be accepted as a reason of invalidity which is excluded from the scope of the CESL.

The above given explanations regarding CISG would apply to CESL as well.[163] Accordingly, initial impossibility cannot be deemed as a matter, which is excluded from the scope of the CESL. Since, Preamble No. 27 makes reference to invalidity of a contract arising from (*i*) lack of capacity, (*ii*) illegality, or (*iii*) immorality, this shows that during the drafting of the CESL, initial impossibility was not regarded as a matter of invalidity.

V) Legal Results of Exemption from Liability

The legal effects of *force majeure* have been contemplated differently in each of Unification Instruments. However, such difference is mainly as to the structure and wording of each relevant provision. Indeed, CISG, PECL, DCFR and CESL have listed the remedies unavailable to the aggrieved party in case of exemption. On the other hand, PICC has listed the remedies unaffected by *force majeure*. In the end, it might be argued that despite such different structures, the effects of *force majeure* are quite similar.

---

[162] "*All the matters of a contractual or non-contractual nature that are not addressed in the Common European Sales Law are governed by the pre-existing rules of the national law outside the Common European Sales Law that is applicable under Regulations (EC) No 593/2008 and (EC) No 864/2007 or any other relevant conflict of law rule. These issues include legal personality, the invalidity of a contract arising from lack of capacity, illegality or immorality, the determination of the language of the contract, matters of non-discrimination, representation, plurality of debtors and creditors, change of parties including assignment, set-off and merger, property law including the transfer of ownership, intellectual property law and the law of torts. Furthermore, the issue of whether concurrent contractual and non-contractual liability claims can be pursued together falls outside the scope of the Common European Sales Law*"

[163] Preamble No. 29 of the CESL enables a similar approach between the CESL and the CISG. The provision reads as follows: "*Once there is a valid agreement to use the Common European Sales Law, only the Common European Sales Law should govern the matters falling within its scope. The rules of the Common European Sales Law should be interpreted autonomously in accordance with the well-established principles on the interpretation of Union legislation. Questions concerning matters falling within the scope of the Common European Sales Law which are not expressly settled by it should be resolved only by interpretation of its rules without recourse to any other law. The rules of the Common European Sales Law should be interpreted on the basis of the underlying principles and objectives and all its provisions.*"

1) CISG

The legal effect of the exemption under CISG is dealt with under Article 79 (5). Accordingly, exemption from liability only prevents the promisee's right to claim damages. In other words, Article 79 (5) reserves all remedies arising from non-performance, except for damages.[164] Within this stance, the remedies available to the promisee include the right to price reduction (Article 50), the right to compel performance (Articles 46 and 62) and the right to avoid the contract (Articles 49 and 64).[165] As in BGB, OR and TCO, in cases, where the contract is avoided, the parties are also entitled to claim restitution, in case they have already supplied or paid under the contract.

Article 79 (5) leaves the promisee's right to specific performance unaffected in case of exemption from liability.[166] This is sensible in some cases. For instance, in case of a temporary impediment, the promisee might ask for delayed specific performance when the impediment disappears. In cases where a temporary impediment results in a partial non-performance or a delayed performance, the existence of the right to claim specific performance may encourage the parties to invest in efforts to overcome the impediment.[167] Therefore, it might be useful and logical not to eliminate the promisee's right to specific performance. However, in cases of objective impossibility, specific performance cannot be sought or obtained, and this constitutes a reasonable limitation to the provision of Article 79 (5).[168]

---

[164] Some authors think that there is a contradiction between the general formula of Article 79 (1) and the restrictive provision of Article 79 (5). Accordingly, under paragraph (1), the defaulting party is not liable for failure to perform. If this is the case, the other party cannot claim any kind of remedies at all. See **Tallon**, in: Bianca/Bonell, Art. 79, Nr. 2.9 ff. **Brunner**, p. 361.

[165] **Rimke**, p. 217; **Flambouras**, Exemption, p. 501; **Reinhart**, Art. 79, Nr. 11; **Stoll/Gruber**, in: Schlechtriem/Schwenzer, Art. 79, Nr. 45; **Zeller**, Damages, p. 187. These rights may be used only if the conditions required for their use under the CISG have been met. For instance, the contract can be avoided only if the non-performance amounts to a fundamental breach. Under the CISG, there is no automatic discharge of the contract but the creditor is entitled to avoid the contract due to insurmountable impediment. This is especially important in cases of temporary impossibility, where the creditor may prefer to wait for the impediment to pass. Similarly, in case of defective delivery, the creditor may choose price reduction, repair or replacement. **Atamer**, in: Kröll/Mistelis/Viscasillas, Art. 79, Nr. 40.

[166] For the contrary opinion see **Jenkins**, TLR 1998, 2015, 2027; **Salger**, in: Witz/Salger/Lorenz, Art. 79, Nr. 12. For a discussion on the court's power to order or deny specific performance considering the domestic law, see **Southerington**, p. 26–28. For an analysis of the availability of specific performance as a remedy under Article 79, see **Atamer**, p. 84 ff.

[167] **Garro**, p. 241.

[168] **Flambouras**, Guide to Article 79, p. 1 ff.; **Stoll/Gruber**, in: Schlechtriem/Schwenzer, Art. 79, Nr. 48. In the Vienna Conference, it was argued that in cases where it is physically impossible to fulfill obligations, the domestic legal doctrine of *impossibilium nulla obligatio est* (which is applicable according to Article 28) would generally prevent claim of specific performance anyway. **Rimke**, p. 217; **Schlechtriem**, Uniform Sales Law, p. 102; **Flambouras**, Exemption, p. 501; **Schwenzer**, VUWLR 2008, 709, 720; **Flambouras**, Guide to Article 79, p. 1 ff.

Consequently, it is suggested that in such cases, by adopting a teleological interpretation, a *limit of sacrifice* must be accepted, beyond which the promisor cannot reasonably be expected to perform his obligations.[169] Thus, in case of objective impossibility specific performance cannot be demanded.[170] Although there is no express provision in the CISG, if the seller is exempt from liability and specific performance, the synallagma between the obligations of the parties would require to accept that the debtor cannot claim the counter-performance from the creditor as well.[171]

According to Article 28 of the CISG a court is entitled to reject the claim of specific performance if the enforced performance would be contrary to the domestic rules of the forum.[172] In other words, courts are not bound to rule on specific performance, if they would not do so under their domestic laws.[173] Therefore it might be argued that as many domestic legal systems prevent specific performance claims in case of impossibility of performance, the remedy of specific performance is thus automatically excluded in such cases.[174]

The promisor, who is exempted from liability, may have acquired substitutes in the place of his performance.[175] In any of Unification Instruments—including the CISG—the claim of surrogate benefits is not regulated as a right of the parties in case of exemption from liability.[176] Therefore, in such cases, it must be determined whether the promisee is entitled to claim such acquisition, *i.e.*, surrogate benefit, which replaces the performance of the promisor. Within this stance, it is argued that

[169] **Flambouras**, PILR 2001, 261, 275; **Flambouras**, Guide to Article 79, p. 1 ff. According to Atamer, "*it is not Art. 79 where the limits to the specific performance claim should be sought for.*" Regardless of the debtor being exempt or not, if specific goods perish, specific performance cannot be claimed. **Atamer**, in: Kröll/Mistelis/Viscasillas, Art. 79, Nr. 32.

[170] **Staudinger/Magnus**, Art. 79, Nr. 57. According to Article 46 (2) and (3) of the CISG, Article 7.2.3 of the PICC, Article 9:102 (1) of the PECL, and III-3:302 (2) of the DCFR, the right to specific performance includes remedying the non-conforming goods. Therefore it should be accepted that if the promisee is not entitled to specific performance he cannot claim repair or replacement as well.

[171] In the same opinion see **Brunner**, p. 376.

[172] Article 28 of the CISG: "*If, in accordance with the provisions of this Convention, one party is entitled to require performance of any obligation by the other party, a court is not bound to enter a judgement for specific performance unless the court would do so under its own law in respect of similar contracts of sale not governed by this Convention.*"

[173] **Schwenzer**, EJLR 1999, 289, 292.

[174] **Brunner**, p. 363.

[175] **Brunner**, p. 349.

[176] Zimmermann states that "*Oddly, the Principles do not provide this kind of remedy. Nor does the Convention on the International Sale of Goods.*" **Zimmermann**, Breach of Contract, p. 28–29. For a similar criticism, see **Bollenberger**, p. 153 ff.

by means of analogy, the doctrine of surrogate benefits may be derived from Article 84 (2) (b) CISG,[177] which governs the effects of termination.[178]

Another issue that deserves attention is the effects of exemption from liability on the penalty or liquidated damages clauses. When the contracting parties insert penalty or liquidated damages clauses in the contract, it is debatable whether exemption from liability under Article 79 discharges the obligor from his liability to pay the amount imposed by the penalty or liquidated damages clause.[179] According to one opinion, the effect of exemption on the penalty or liquidated damages stipulated in the contract is a matter for domestic law and it is not governed under the CISG.[180] Another opinion is that unless the parties have provided otherwise in the contract, the promisor's exemption from liability also includes obligation to pay penalties and liquidated damages.[181] It is also argued that a distinction must be made between the two concepts. Accordingly, only if liquidated damages are accepted to be compensatory, then the promisor may be discharged provided the conditions of CISG Article 79 have been met. With regard to penalty clauses, it is asserted that even if reference is made to domestic law, the contractual intentions of the parties supersede CISG Article 79. If parties have not incorporated an exception in the contract to the obligation of penalty payment, the promisor will have to pay penalty even in case of exemption.[182]

The effect of exemption under Article 79 on the obligation to pay interest on money due is also debated in the doctrine. This debate bears significant importance in case of temporary impediments to performance. For instance, the promisor might be exempt from paying damages when he cannot perform due to monetary law regulations, which constitute legal impediments to performance.[183] In this case, it must be decided if the promisee is entitled to interest for the delay on money due for the period that the temporary impediment exists.

---

[177] Article 84 (2) (b) reads as follows: "(2) *The buyer must account to the seller for all benefits which he has derived from the goods or part of them:* [. . .] (*b*) *if it is impossible for him to make restitution of all or part of the goods or to make restitution of all or part of the goods substantially in the condition in which he received them, but he has nevertheless declared the contract avoided or required the seller to deliver substitutes.*"

[178] **Staudinger/Magnus**, Art. 79, Nr. 54; **Achilles**, Art. 79, Nr. 14; **Brunner**, p. 350. For the opinion that surrogates may only be claimed if it is required by the spirit and purpose of the contract, see **Stoll/Gruber**, in: Schlechtriem/Schwenzer, Art. 79, Nr. 44.

[179] Liquidated damages is a forecast of possible damages, which provide for payment of a fixed amount in the event of breach. They relieve the promisee from the duty to prove the amount of damages and limit the promisor's liability to a known amount. On the other hand, penalties are intended to guarantee the performance by the promisor and do not presuppose the occurrence of an actual loss. **Brunner**, p. 348.

[180] Secretariat Commentary, Art. 65, Nr. 9; **Stoll/Gruber**, in: Schlechtriem/Schwenzer, Art. 79, Nr. 9.

[181] **Schwenzer**, VUWLR 2008, 709, 719.

[182] **Flambouras**, PILR 2001, 261, 280–281.

[183] **Brunner**, p. 378.

Whether the promisee is entitled to ask for interest from an exempted promisor generally depends on classification of the nature of interest. Since payment of damages in case of non-performance is compensatory, if the obligation to pay interest is accepted as a form of compensation, the promisor will not have to pay interest when the promisor is exempt from compensating damages under Article 79 (5). However, the right to claim interest can hardly be characterized as a right to claim damages.[184] In other words, interest is not a form of compensation; therefore the obligation to pay interest continues even if the promisor is exempt from his liability to pay compensation for breach of contract. As a matter of fact, the CISG clearly distinguishes between interest payment obligation and damages.[185] The obligation to pay interest arises in case of a delay in payment, even if the creditor of the payment obligation has not suffered any damage from such delay.[186]

2) *PICC*

The legal effects of *force majeure* under PICC are explained under Article 7.1.7 (4). Unlike the CISG and also PECL, DCFR and CESL, PICC has preferred to list the remedies *unaffected* by *force majeure*. Accordingly, it is set forth that even if the debtor is exempt from liability, the promisee is entitled to (*i*) terminate the contract,[187] (*ii*) withhold his own performance, and (*iii*) request interest[188] in case of monetary obligations.[189] In cases, where the contract is terminated, the parties are also entitled to claim restitution, in case they have already supplied or paid under the contract. However, similar to any of Unification Instruments, the claim of surrogate benefits is not regulated as a right of the parties in case of exemption from liability.

Although Article 7.1.7 has listed the remedies, which are *available* in case of *force majeure*, Article 7.4.1 has specifically excluded the promisee's claim of

[184] **Staudinger/Magnus**, Art. 79, Nr. 61; **Brunner**, p. 378; **Honnold**, Art. 79, Nr. 435.6. Also in the opinion that interest may be claimed despite exemption from liability, see **Soergel-CISG/Lüderitz/Dettmeier**, Art. 79, Nr. 25; **Saenger**, in: Ferrari/Kieninger/Mankowski/Otte/Saenger/Schulze/Staudinger, Art. 79, Nr. 11.

[185] **Atamer**, p. 98.

[186] **Flambouras**, PILR 2001, 261, 281; **Garro**, p. 241; **Liu**, *Force majeure*, p. 1 ff.

[187] Similar to the CISG, Article 7.3.1 of the PICC states that the promisee can terminate the contract only if the breach of the debtor is fundamental.

[188] It is once again emphasized under Article 7.4.9 that the promisee is entitled to interest for monetary obligations even if the debtor's non-performance is excused under Article 7.1.7. Article 7.4.9 (1): "*If a party does not pay a sum of money when it falls due the aggrieved party is entitled to interest upon that sum from the time when payment is due to the time of payment whether or not the non-payment is excused.*"

[189] Article 7.1.7 (4): "*Nothing in this article prevents a party from exercising a right to terminate the contract or to withhold performance or request interest on money due.*"

damages if non-performance is excused under Article 7.1.7.[190] Accordingly, it is explicit that the promisee is not entitled to damages if the promisor's non-performance is excused under Article 7.1.7.

According to Article 7.2.2 of the PICC, specific performance cannot be claimed in case of impossibility of performance of non-monetary obligations. Therefore, in case of *force majeure*, where the performance is impossible and the promisor is exempt from liability under Article 7.1.7, the remedy of specific performance is automatically excluded. Therefore unlike the CISG, which leaves the promisee's right to specific performance unaffected in case of exemption of the promisor, under the PICC the promisee cannot claim specific performance if the promisor is exempt from liability. This is a successful provision, which prevents potential ambiguities regarding specific performance claim as in the CISG.

Similar to CISG, PICC contains no express provision regarding the effects of *force majeure* on contractually contemplated penalty or liquidated damages. However, it might be argued that such claims cannot be brought against the debtor if he is exempt from liability under Article 7.1.7. It must be recalled that the PICC has listed the remedies unaffected by *force majeure*. Penalty or liquidated damages are not listed among these remedies. Moreover, the issue of penalty or liquidated damages is dealt with under Article 7.4.13. It deserves an emphasis that the said Article lies under the section titled as "damages" and Article 7.4.1 rules that if the promisor is excused, he is not entitled to pay damages. Therefore, penalty or liquidated damages cannot be claimed in case of *force majeure*.[191]

The PICC is silent if the promisee is entitled to request price reduction if the promisor is exempt from liability. Price reduction remedy bears significant importance in cases of partial impediments. For instance, in case of a permanent and partial impediment, which causes fundamental breach, the promisee should be given the choice of terminating the contract if partial performance will not be of any value to him. Notwithstanding such right, in such cases, if the promisee decides not to terminate the contract but claims partial performance, the option of price reduction serves as an important tool.

Under the PICC, it is arguable that price reduction is not listed as a remedy unaffected by *force majeure*. Furthermore, it can even be argued that price reduction is not at all a remedy under the remedial scheme of the PICC.[192] Therefore, under the PICC, the promisee is not entitled to price reduction in case of the promisor's exemption from liability. On the other hand, it can also be argued that remedy of price reduction aims the maintenance of the originally agreed balance of

---

[190] Article 7.4.1: "*Any non-performance gives the aggrieved party a right to damages either exclusively or in conjunction with any other remedies except where the non-performance is excused under these Principles.*"

[191] At this point it might be argued that the issue of interest for failure to pay money is dealt with under Article 7.4.9, which lies under the section of damages as well. However, such argument would be unacceptable as the claim of interest is explicitly allowed under Articles 7.1.7 and 7.4.9.

[192] **Liu**, *Force majeure*, p. 1 ff.

the contract; hence it is not a claim of damages. Therefore the remedy of price reduction remains unaffected by the *force majeure* excuse.[193]

3) PECL

The legal effects of *force majeure* under PECL are dealt with under Article 8:101 (2). Accordingly, if the promisor is exempt from liability, the promisee cannot claim specific performance or damages.[194] However, any other remedies contemplated under Chapter 9 of the PECL is available to the promisor.[195] Due to the reference of the PECL to Chapter 9, the remaining remedies available to the promisee are (*i*) withholding performance, (*ii*) termination of the contract, and (*iii*) price reduction.[196] In cases, where the contract is terminated, the parties are also entitled to claim restitution, in case they have already supplied or paid under the contract. However, similar to any of Unification Instruments, the claim of surrogate benefits is not regulated as a right of the parties in case of exemption from liability.

Article 9:303 (4) contemplates an automatic termination mechanism if the exemption is caused by a "*total and permanent*" impediment. Accordingly, the contract would be automatically terminated at the time the impediment arises. In such cases, no notice would be required.[197] Such provision generally aims simplification of the termination process. In principle, if the promisee wants to terminate the contract he must give notice of termination to the other party under Article 9:303. However, in cases of total and permanent impediment, Article 9:303 (4) assumes that the parties will not want to be bound with a contract, which cannot be performed. Therefore the PECL contemplates an automatic termination mechanism, which at the same time eliminates the notice requirement.[198] In such cases, if one of the parties has already performed his obligation, its return would be required under the provisions regarding termination.[199]

---

[193] **Brunner**, p. 377.

[194] It is also explained under paragraph 2 (a) of Article 9:102 that specific performance cannot be claimed in case of impossibility of performance of non-monetary obligations.

[195] Article 8:101 (2): "*Where a party's non-performance is excused under Article 8:108, the aggrieved party may resort to any of the remedies set out in Chapter 9 except claiming performance and damages.*"

[196] In case of a permanent and partial impediment, which causes fundamental breach, if the promisee decides not to terminate the contract but to seek partial performance, his own obligation would be reduced proportionately under Article 9:401. PECL Commentary, Article 8:108, Comment D.

[197] Article 9:303 (4): "*If a party is excused under Article 8:108 through an impediment which is total and permanent, the contract is terminated automatically and without notice at the time the impediment arises.*"

[198] PECL Commentary, Article 8:108, Comment D.

[199] See Article 9:306 ff.

The PECL is silent as to whether the promisee is entitled to interest if the promisor of a monetary obligation is excused under Article 8:108. However, parallel to the legal reasoning regarding CISG, it would be appropriate to accept that "*Interest is not a species of ordinary damages* [. . .] *Interest is owed whether or not non-payment is excused under Article 8:108*"[200] Moreover, Article 9:508 regulates the claim of interest for default in payment of money. Within this scope, interest is one of the remedies available under Chapter 9 of the PECL. Therefore, there is no reason to argue that the promisee is not entitled to interest if the promisor is exempt from paying damages.

There is also no explicit provision in the PECL, which answers if the promisee is entitled to liquidated damages and penalty when the promisor is excused under Article 8:108. However, it is accepted that "*damages of any kind, including 'liquidated damages' and penalties, apply unless the parties have agreed otherwise.*"[201] This stance is parallel to the general view that liquidated damages and penalty are accepted as specific types of damages.

4) DCFR

The legal effects of *force majeure* under the DCFR are set forth under Articles III-3:101 and III-3:104 in a very similar way with the PECL. Accordingly, Article III-3:101 of the DCFR has expressed that if the promisor's non-performance is excused under Article III-3:104, the promisee is not entitled to specific performance[202] and damages, but the other remedies under the DCFR are available to the promisee.[203] From this provision, it can be inferred that in such cases the remedies available to the promisee are (*i*) withholding performance, (*ii*) termination of the contract, and (*iii*) price reduction. In cases, where the contract is terminated, the parties are also entitled to claim restitution, in case they have already supplied or paid under the contract. DCFR also fails to regulate the claim of surrogate benefits as a right of the parties in case of exemption from liability.

Despite the difference in wording, the provision of Article III-3:104 (4) is quite similar to Article 9:303 (4) of the PECL, which refers to an automatic termination of the contract in case of *force majeure*. In fact, in both of the cases termination of

[200] PECL Commentary, Article 9:508, Comment B.

[201] PECL Commentary, Article 8:108, Comment D.

[202] Similar to paragraph 2 (a) of Article 9:102 PECL, it is emphasized in Article III-3:302 (3) (a) of the DCFR that specific performance cannot be claimed in case of impossibility of performance regarding non-monetary obligations.

[203] III-3:101 (2): "*If the debtor's non-performance is excused, the creditor may resort to any of those remedies except enforcing specific performance and damages.*"

the contract takes place automatically without a necessity for the promisee to send a notice of termination.[204]

In Article III-3:104 (4) of the DCFR,[205] it is expressed that if the excusing impediment is permanent, obligations of both of the parties are extinguished and reference is made to the section on "Restitution".[206] In other words, neither of the parties would perform[207]; if one of the parties has already performed, it would be appropriate to accept that restitution must take place.[208]

There is no explicit reference in the DCFR if the promisee is entitled to interest and/or liquidated damages and penalty if the promisor is excused under Article III-3:104. However, the similarity between the PECL and the DCFR and a similar reasoning may be helpful to answer such questions. As a result, it can be accepted that even if the promisor's non-performance is excused due to *force majeure*, the promisee would not be entitled to liquidated damages and penalty, but interest.

5) CESL

The legal effects of *force majeure* under CESL are dealt with under Articles 88, 110 (3) (a)[209] and 106 (4) CESL. According to Article 106 (4), "*If the seller's non-performance is excused, the buyer may resort to any of the remedies referred to in paragraph 1 except requiring performance and damages.*" Within this scope, the remaining remedies in the said first paragraph are: (*i*) withholding performance, (*ii*) termination of the contract and claiming the return of any price already paid,

---

[204] There might be cases, where the obligation of the promisor is one of several obligations under the contract. In such cases, if the performance of the remaining obligations become valueless to the promisee as a result of extinction of the one obligation, the promisee would have the option to terminate the whole contractual relationship for fundamental non-performance. DCFR Commentary, Article III-3:104, Comment D.

[205] Article III-3:104 (4): "*Where the excusing impediment is permanent the obligation is extinguished. Any reciprocal obligation is also extinguished. In the case of contractual obligations any restitutionary effects of extinction are regulated by the rules in Chapter 3, Section 5, Sub-section 4 (Restitution) with appropriate adaptations.*"

[206] In cases where the obligations of both parties are extinguished, it is probable that one of the parties has already performed partially or totally. Article III-3:104 (4) expresses that in such cases restitution would take place in accordance with the provisions of Chapter 3, Section 5, Sub-section 4 of the DCFR. As a matter of fact, restitution is a result of the termination of any contractual relationship. Therefore it is also regulated under Article 81 of the CISG, Article 7.3.6 of the PICC, Article 4:115 of the PECL and Article 172 of the CESL.

[207] These rules will be subject to any specific rules on the passing of risk. For instance, there might be cases where the risk of destruction has passed to the buyer; hence counter-obligation has to be performed despite the extinguishment of the promisor's obligation to perform. DCFR Commentary, Article III-3:104, Comment D.

[208] DCFR Commentary, Article III-3:104 Comment D.

[209] The provision sets forth that performance cannot be required, where it would be impossible.

and (*iii*) price reduction.[210] The CESL is also silent regarding the claim of surrogate benefits as a right of the parties in case of exemption from liability.

Article 106/I/(a) makes it clear that the term "*requiring performance*", includes specific performance in addition to the repair or replacement of the goods. Therefore in case of the debtor's exemption from liability under Article 88, repair and replacement cannot be claimed either.[211]

The effect of the debtor's exemption on the creditor's interest claims is dealt with under Article 168 of CESL. However, such provision covers the delay of payment by a trader. Accordingly, if a trader delays the price due under the contract, interest is due unless he is excused under Article 88.[212] In other words, if a trader is excused under Article 88, no interest may be claimed from him for delay of payment.

VI) Damages in Unification Instruments

The most significant legal result of exemption from liability is that the debtor does not compensate the damages of the creditor arising from non-performance. *E contrario* if the debtor is not exempt under the exemption provision, he must compensate the damages of the creditor. Detailed explanation on the compensation regimes of Unification Instruments and the scope of recoverable damages under each Unification Instrument exceed the scope of this study. However, it would be appropriate to mention that each Unification Instrument has regulated the damage claims under one article.[213] In other words, there is no distinction in Unification Instruments for different types of breaches. Similarly, there is no distinction considering the time of occurrence of impossibility or the responsibility of the debtor.

The common premise in Unification Instruments is that the non-performing party is liable to compensate the other party in full for all pecuniary damages,

---

[210] According to Article 106/II:

If the buyer is a trader:

(a) the buyer's rights to exercise any remedy except withholding of performance are subject to cure by the seller as set out in Section 2 of this Chapter; and

(b) the buyer's rights to rely on lack of conformity are subject to the requirements of examination and notification set out in Section 7 of this Chapter.

[211] Article 116 of CESL designates a mechanism of termination for anticipated non-performance. Such mechanism may appropriately apply for cases of impossibility as well. Accordingly, in case of impossibility, the buyer may terminate the contract before due date, as it is clear that there will be non-performance.

[212] Paragraph 5 of Article 168 sets forth the method of calculation of the applicable rate of interest.

[213] See Art. 74 CISG, Art. 7.4.2 PICC, Art. 9:502 PECL, III-3:701 DCFR, Art. 160 CESL.

including the loss of profit.[214] In fact this refers to the positive interest of the aggrieved party. Within this stance, future losses—which are expected to be incurred after the time damages are assessed—are also recoverable as damages.[215] However, under no circumstances damages may be used as a tool to enrich the aggrieved party. Any interests that the aggrieved party has accrued as a result of non-performance must be deducted from the compensation.[216] In fact it is stated in Unification Instruments that the purpose of compensation is to position the aggrieved party to the place as if obligation had been duly performed.[217]

It is debatable under Unification Instruments, if the aggrieved party may claim his negative interest rather than his positive damages. However, it is widely accepted that in case of termination of the contract, the aggrieved party must be entitled to claim his negative interest.[218] Nevertheless it is generally argued that the negative interest of the creditor cannot exceed his positive interest.[219]

Under Unification Instruments the debtor is only liable for the damages, which were either foreseen or foreseeable at the time of the conclusion of the contract. Foreseeability is a tool, which sets the boundaries of the assumption of a specific risk by the breaching party.[220] The foreseeability test replaces the causal link requirement in the civil law countries including Germany, Switzerland and Turkey. In fact, the non-performing party would be deemed to have assumed the foreseeable risks of non-performance. However, as in BGB, OR and TCO, the creditor is under the obligation to prove the existence and amount of his damages.

---

[214] **Brunner**, p. 352. In addition to direct damages, consequential damages are also accepted to be recoverable under Unification Instruments, provided that they are foreseeable. **Brunner**, p. 355.

[215] See Art. 7.4.3 (1) PICC, Art. 9:501 (1) (b) PECL, III-3:701 DCFR, Art. 159 CESL. There is no express provision in the CISG regarding the matter. According to Knapp, future losses are recoverable under the CISG as well. **Knapp**, in: Bianca/Bonell, Art. 74, Nr. 3.4.

[216] Art. 7.4.2 (1) PICC; **Stoll/Gruber**, in: Schlechtriem/Schwenzer, Art. 74, Nr. 32; **Brunner**, p. 356.

[217] See Art. 9:502 PECL, III-3:702 DCFR, Art. 160 CESL.

[218] Austria 14 January 2002 Supreme Court (Cooling system case) (http://cisgw3.law.pace.edu/cases/020114a3.html); **Brunner**, p. 356.

[219] **Brunner**, p. 356.

[220] Art. 74 CISG refers to the foreseeability of damages as a *possible* consequence of the breach of contract. On the other hand, PICC, PECL, DCFR refer to foreseeability of damages, which occur as a *likely* result of non-performance. Finally, CESL refers to foreseeability *as a result* of the non-performance. It is evident that the proceeding instruments have preferred setting a more restrictive standard than the CISG. This fact points to the contemplation principle in Anglo-American law, which requires a certain degree of probability that the damage will occur. **Brunner**, p. 354.

References

Achilles, Wilhelm-Albrecht: Kommentar zum UN-Kaufrechtsübereinkommen (CISG), Luchterhand, Neuwied 2000.

Atamer, Yeşim M: Uluslararası Satım Sözleşmelerine İlişkin Birleşmiş Milletler Antlaşması (CISG) Uyarınca Satıcının Yükümlülükleri ve Sözleşmeye Aykırılığın Sonuçları, Beta, İstanbul 2005. (Cited as: Atamer, Satıcının Yükümlülükleri)

Atamer, Yeşim M: Availability of Remedies other than Damages in Case of Exemption According to Art. 79 CISG, in: Büchler, Andrea/Müller-Chen, Markus, Festschrift für Ingeborg Schwenzer zum 60. Geburtstag, Stämpfli, Bern 2011, pp. 83–98. (Cited as: Atamer)

Bar, Christian von/Clive, Eric: Principles, definitions and model rules of European private law, Sellier, München 2009. (Cited as: DCFR Commentary)

Baumgartner, Stefanie: Contract formation under the CISG and under the UNIDROIT Principles: Contract Formation under the CISG and under the UNIDROIT Principles: Special Focus on the Issue of the Battle of the Forms, VDM Verlag Dr. Müller, Saarbrücken 2008.

Bianca, Cesare Massimo/Bonell, Michael Joachim: Commentary on the International Sales Law, Giuffrè, Mailand 1987. (Cited as: Author, in: Bianca/Bonell)

Bineva, Valentina: Change of Circumstances, in: Antoniolli, Luisa/Fiorentini, Francesa, A Factual Assessment of the Draft Common Frame of Reference, Sellier, München 2011, pp. 77–96.

Bollenberger, Raimund: Das stellvertretende Commodum: die Ersatzherausgabe im österreichischen und deutschen Schuldrecht unter Berücksichtigung weiterer Rechtsordnungen, Springer, Wien 1999.

Bonell, Michael Joachim: A New Approach to International Commercial Contracts, The UNIDROIT Principles of International Commercial Contracts, Kluwer, Den Haag/Boston 1999. (Cited as: Bonell, A New Approach)

Bonell, Michael Joachim: Towards a Legislative Codification of the UNIDROIT Principles? ULR, Vol. 12, No. 2, 2007, pp. 233–246. (Cited as: Bonell)

Brunner, Christoph: Force majeure and Hardship Excuse Under General Contract Principles, Wolters Kluwer, Alphen aan den Rijn 2009.

Cerutti, Romeo: Das U.S. amerikanische Warenkaufrecht, Schulthess, Zürich 1998.

CISG Advisory Council: CISG Advisory Council Opinion No.7, ‹http://www.cisg.law.pace.edu/cisg/CISG-AC-op7.html› (Cited as: CISG Advisory Council Opinion No. 7)

Düchs, Constantin: Die Behandlung von Leistungsstörungen im Europäischen Vertragsrecht, Duncker & Humblot, Berlin 2006.

Eidenmüller, Horst/Jansen, Nils/Kieninger, Eva-Maria/Wagner, Gerhard/Zimmermann, Reinhard: Der Vorschlag für eine Verordnung über ein Gemeinsames Europäisches Kaufrecht, JZ 2012, pp. 269–289.

Enderlein, Fritz/Dietrich, Maskow: International Sales Law, Oceana, New York 1992.

Felemegas, John: Introduction, in: Felemegas, John, An International Approach to the Interpretation of the United Nations Convention on Contracts for the International Sale of Goods (1980) as Uniform Sales Law, Cambridge University Press, Cambridge/New York 2007, pp. 1–38.

Ferrari, Franco/Kieninger, Eva-Maria/Mankowski, Peter/Otte, Karsten; Saenger, Ingo/Schulze, Götz Joachim/Staudinger, Ansgar: Internationales Vertragsrecht, C.H. Beck, München 2011. (Cited as: Author, in: Ferrari/Kieninger/Mankowski/Otte/Saenger/Schulze/Staudinger)

Fischer, Nicole N.: Die Unmöglichkeit der Leistung im internationalen Kauf- und Vertragsrecht, Duncker & Humblot, Berlin 2001. (Cited as: Fischer)

Flambouras, Dionysios P.: The Doctrines of Impossibility of Performance and clausula rebus sic stantibus in the 1980 Vienna Convention on Contracts for the International Sale of Goods and the Principles of European Contract Law: A Comparative Analysis, PILR, Vol. 13, No. 1, 2001, pp. 261–293.

Flambouras, Dionysios: Exemption and hardship: Remarks on the manner in which the Principles of European Contract Law (Articles 6:111 and 8:108) may be used to interpret or supplement CISG Article 79, in: Felemegas, John, An International Approach to the Interpretation of the

United Nations Convention on Contracts for the International Sale of Goods (1980) as Uniform Sales Law, Cambridge University Press, Cambridge/New York 2007, pp. 499–505. (Cited as: Flambouras, Exemption)

Flambouras, Dionysios: Comparative Remarks on CISG Article 79 & PECL Articles 6:111, 8:108, in Guide to Article 79 - Comparison with Principles of European Contract Law (PECL), <http://cisgw3.law.pace.edu/cisg/text/peclcomp79.html>. (Cited as: Flambouras, Guide to Article 79)

Garro, Alejandro M.: Exemption of liability for damages: Comparison between provisions of the CISG (Art. 79) and the counterpart provisions of the UNIDROIT Principles (Art. 7.1.7), in: Felemegas, John, An International Approach to the Interpretation of the United Nations Convention on Contracts for the International Sale of Goods (1980) as Uniform Sales Law, Cambridge University Press, Cambridge/New York 2007. pp. 236–246.

Guillemard, Sylvette: A comparative study of the UNIDROIT Principles and the Principles of EuropeanContracts and some dispositions of the CISG applicable to the formation ofinternational contracts, in Review of the Convention for the International Sale of Goods (CISG) 2000–2001, Kluwer, Den Haag, 2000–2001, pp. 83–113.

Hondius, Ewoud: Towards an Optional Common European Sales Law, ERPL, Vol. 19, No. 6, 2011, pp. 709–715.

Honnold, John: Documentary History of the Uniform Law for International Sales : The studies, deliberations and decisions that led to the 1980 United Nations Convention; with introductions and explanations, Kluwer, Deventer 1989. (Cited as: Honnold, Documentary History)

Honnold, John: Uniform Law for International Sales under the 1980 United Nations Convention, Kluwer, Alphen aan den Rijn 2009. (Cited as: Honnold)

Honsell, Heinrich: Kommentar Zum UN-Kaufrecht: Übereinkommen der Vereinten Nationen über Verträge über den Internationalen Warenkauf (CISG), Springer, Berlin/Heidelberg 2010. (Cited as: Author, in: Honsell)

Huber, Ulrich: Handbuch des Schuldrechts, Leistungsstörungen, Band I, Die allgemeinen Grundlagen; Der Tatbestand des Schuldnersverzug; Die vom Schuldner zu vertretenden Umstände, Mohr Siebeck, Tübingen 1999. (Cited as: Huber, Leistungsstörungen I)

Huber, Peter/Mullis, Alastair: The CISG: A new textbook for students and practitioners, Sellier, München 2007.

Hudson, A. H.: Exemptions and Impossibility under the Vienna Convention, in: McKendrick, Ewan, Force majeure and Frustration of Contract Lloyd's of London Press, London 1995, pp. 267–286.

Janssen, André/Kiene, Sörren Claas: The CISG and Its General Principles, in: Janssen, André/ Meyer, Olaf, CISG Methodology, Sellier, München 2009, pp. 261–285.

Jenkins, Sarah Howard: Exemption for Nonperformance: UCC, CISG, UNIDROIT Principles – A Comparative Assessment, TLR, Vol. 72, No. 6, 1998, pp. 2015–2030.

Kallweit, Dominik: Towards a European Contract Law: For a Prosperous Future of International Trade, VUWLR, Vol. 35, No. 2, 2004, pp. 269–297.

Kröll, Stefan/Mistelis, Loukas/Perales Viscasillas, Pilar: UN Convention on Contracts for the International Sale of Goods (CISG), C.H. Beck, Oxford 2011. (Cited as: Author, in: Kröll/ Mistelis/Viscasillas)

Lando, Ole: CISG and Its Followers: A Proposal to Adopt Some International Principles of Contract Law, AJCL, Vol. 53, No. 2, 2005, pp. 379–401.

Lando, Ole/Beale, Hugh: Principles of European Contract Law, Parts I and II, Combined and Revised, Kluwer, The Hague, 2000. (Cited as: PECL Commentary)

Leyens, Patrick C.: CISG and Mistake: Uniform Law vs. Domestic Law, The Interpretative Challenge of Mistake and the Validity Loophole, <http://www.cisg.law.pace.edu/cisg/biblio/ leyens.html>.

Lindström, Niklas: Changed Circumstances and Hardship in the International Sale of Goods, NJCL, 2006/I, <http://www.njcl.fi/1_2006/commentary1.pdf>.

Liu, Chengwei: Force majeure - Perspectives from the CISG, UNIDROIT Principles, PECL and Case Law,[2nd edition: Case annotated update (April 2005)], <http://www.cisg.law.pace.edu/cisg/biblio/liu6.html>. (Cited as: Liu, Force majeure)

Liu, Chengwei: Remedies for Non-performance: Perspectives from CISG, UNIDROIT Principles & PECL, <http://article.chinalawinfo.com/Article_Detail.asp?ArticleId=24403>. (Cited as: Liu)

Lookofsyk, Joseph M.: Understanding the CISG: a compact guide to the 1980 United Nations Convention on Contracts for International Sale of Goods, Kluwer, Alphen aan den Rijn 2008.

Macgregor, Laura: Report on the Draft Common Frame of Reference: a report prepared for the Scottish Government by Laura Macgregor, University of Edinburgh, on the document known as 'Principles, Definitions and Model Rules of European Private Law' 26/09/08 <http://www.scotland.gov.uk/Resource/Doc/262952/0078639.pdf>.

Magnus, Ulrich: CISG Uyarınca Tazminat, Faiz, Sorumluluktan Kurtulma, in: Atamer, Yeşim M., Milletlerarası Satım Hukuku, XII Levha, İstanbul 2008, pp. 287–307.

Marcantonio, J. Barrigan: Unifying the Law of Impossibility, HICLR, Vol. 8, No. 1, 1984, pp. 41–59.

Maskow, Dietrich: Hardship and Force majeure, AJCL, Vol. 40, No. 3, 1992, pp. 657–669.

Mazzacano, Peter J.: Force majeure, Impossibility, Frustration & the Like: Excuses for Non-Performance; the Historical Origins and Development of an Autonomous Commercial Norm in the CISG, NJCL, Vol. 2011, No. 2, pp. 1–54.

Mitzkait, Anika: Leistungsstörung und Haftungsbefreiung, Mohr Siebeck, Tübingen 2008.

Morrissey, Joseph F./Graves, Jack M.: International Sales Law and Arbitration, Wolters Kluwer, Alphen aan den Rijn 2008.

Nicholas, Barry: Force majeure and Frustration, AJCL, Vol. 27, No. 2–3, 1979, pp. 231–245.

Nicholas, Barry: The Vienna Convention on International Sales Law, LQR, Vol. 105, No. 2, 1989, pp. 201–243.

Philippe, Denis: Book III Performance and Non-performance of Obligations and Corresponding Rights in the DCFR, in: Sagaert, Vincent/Storme, Matthias E./Terryn, Evelyne, The Draft Common Frame of Reference: national and comparative perspectives, Intersentia, Cambridge 2012, pp. 35–52.

Reinhart, Gert: UN-Kaufrecht, C.F. Müller, Heidelberg 1991.

Rimke, Joern: Force majeure and hardship: Application in international trade practice - with specific regards to the CISG and the UNIDROIT Principles of International Commercial Contracts, Pace Review of the Convention on Contracts for the International Sale of Goods, Kluwer, 1999–2000, pp. 197–243, <http://www.cisg.law.pace.edu/cisg/biblio/rimke.html>.

Saidov, Djakhongir: Cases on CISG Decided in the Russian Federation, VJ, Vol. 7, No.1, 2003, pp. 1–62.

Saidov, Djakhongir: The Law of Damages in International Sales: The CISG and other International Instruments, Hart, Oxford 2008. (Cited as: Saidov)

Schlechtriem, Peter: Uniform Sales Law – The UN-Convention on Contracts for the International Sale of Goods, Manz, Wien 1986. (Cited as: Schlechtriem, Uniform Sales Law)

Schlechtriem, Peter/Butler, Petra: UN Law on International Sales: the UN Convention on the International Sale of Goods, Springer, New York 2009.

Schlechtriem, Peter/Schwenzer, Ingeborg: Commentary on the UN Convention on the International Sale of Goods (CISG), Oxford University Press, Oxford/New York 2005. (Cited as: Author, in: Schlechtriem/Schwenzer)

Schwenzer, Ingeborg: Specific Performance and Damages According to the 1994 UNIDROIT Principles of International Commercial Contracts, EJLR, Vol. 1, No. 3, 1999, pp. 289–304.

Schwenzer, Ingeborg: Force majeure and Hardship in International Sales Contracts, VUWLR, Vol. 39, No. 3, 2008, pp. 709–771.

Schwenzer, Ingeborg/Hachem, Pascal/Kee, Christopher: Global Sales and Contract Law, Oxford University Press, Oxford 2012.

Secretariat: Commentary on the Draft Convention on Contracts for the International Sale of Goods, Prepared by the Secretariat, Document A/CONF.97/5, Art. 65, para. 7, <http://www.cnudci.org/pdf/a_conf.97_5-ocred.pdf>. (Cited as: Secretariat Commentary)

Soergel, Hans Theodor: Bürgerliches Gesetzbuch, Kohlhammer, Stuttgart 2000. (Cited as: Soergel-CISG/Author)

Southerington, Tom: Impossibility of Performance and Other Excuses in International Trade, Publication of the Faculty of Law of the University of Turku, Private law publication series B:55 <http://www.cisg.law.pace.edu/cisg/biblio/southerington.html>.

Staudenmayer, Dirk: Der Kommissionsvorschlag für eine Verordnung zum Gemeinsamen Europäischen Kaufrecht, NJW 2011, pp. 3491–3498.

Staudinger, Julius von: Kommentar zum Bürgerlichen Gesetzbuch mit Einführungsgesetz und Nebengesetzen, Wiener UN-Kaufrecht, Neuarbeitung 2005, Sellier de Gruyter, Berlin 2005. (Cited as: Staudinger/Magnus)

Study Group on a European Civil Code/Research Group on the Existing EC Private Law (Acquis Group): Principles, Definitions and Model Rules on European Private Law, <http://www.ccbe.eu/fileadmin/user_upload/NTCdocument/DCFRpdf1_1262861061.pdf>. (Cited as: DCFR Commentary)

UNCITRAL: 2008 UNCITRAL Digest of case law on the United Nations Convention on the International Sale of Goods - Digest of Article 79 case law, <http://www.cisg.law.pace.edu/cisg/text/digest-art-79.html>. (Cited as: UNCITRAL, Digest of Article 79 case law)

UNIDROIT International Institute for the Unification of Private Law: UNIDROIT Principles of International Commercial Contracts 2004, <http://www.unidroit.org/english/principles/contracts/principles2004/integralversionprinciples2004-e.pdf>. (Cited as: PICC Commentary)

Veneziano, Anna; UNIDROIT Principles and CISG: Change of Circumstances and Duty to Renegotiate according to the Belgian Supreme Court, ULR, Vol. 15, No. 1, 2010, pp. 137–151.

Viscasillas, Pilar Perales: The Role of the UNIDROIT Principles and the PECL in the Interpretation and Gap-filling of CISG, in CISG Methodology, (Janssen, André/Meyer, Olaf), Sellier, München 2009, pp. 287–317.

Vogenauer, Stefan/Kleinheisterkamp, Jan: Commentary on the UNIDROIT Principles of International Commercial Contracts (PICC), Oxford University Press, Oxford/New York 2009. (Cited as: Author, in: Vogenauer/Kleinheisterkamp)

Weitzmann, Todd: Validity and Excuse in the U.N. Sales Convention, JLC, Vol. 16, No. 2, 1997, pp. 265–290.

Whittaker, Simon: Draft Common Frame of Reference: an assessment, <http://www.justice.gov.uk/Draft_Common_Frame_of_Reference_an_assessment.pdf>.

Witz, Wolfgang/Salger, Hanns-Christian/Lorenz, Manuel: International Einheitliches Kaufrecht, Praktiker-Kommentar und Vertragsgestaltung zum CISG, Verlag Recht und Wirtschaft GmbH, Heidelberg 2000. (Cited as: Author, in: Witz/Salger/Lorenz)

Zeller, Bruno: Damages under the Convention on Contracts for the International Sale of Goods, Oceana Publications, Dobbs Ferry/New York 2005. (Cited as: Zeller, Damages)

Zeller, Bruno: CISG and the Unification of International Trade Law, Routledge-Cavendish, New York 2007 (Cited as: Zeller, CISG)

Zeller, Bruno: Four-Corners - The Methodology for Interpretation and Application of the UN Convention on Contracts for the International Sale of Goods, <http://www.cisg.law.pace.edu/cisg/biblio/4corners.html>. (Cited as: Zeller)

Part III
Comparative Assessment of the Laws

5) Utility of Impossibility as a Dogmatic Concept

One of the first and major differences of the German and Swiss—as well as Turkish—laws from Unification Instruments is that these three codes use impossibility as a dogmatic concept. Such fact deserves an emphasis because modern legal systems do not use impossibility as a dogmatic concept. Within this stance, German, Swiss and Turkish laws appear as exceptions to the modern legal trend. However, the abandonment of impossibility by Unification Instruments is not as significant as it might seem at first. At a closer look, it is apparent that the cases of impossibility constitute a sub-category within the exemption provisions of Unification Instruments.

Unification Instruments refrain from referring to the concept of impossibility. In fact under Unification Instruments, impossibility is regarded as any form of non-performance, *i.e.*, default or non-conforming delivery. Within this stance, the exemption provided in Article 79 of the CISG is designated "*for a failure to perform*". Hence, such failure to perform might either be impossibility, default, or even delivery of non-conforming goods.[1]

In different countries, the courts have accepted exemption claims for different types of breaches. For instance, in different decisions, exemption was granted to the

[1] "*The CISG adopts the idea of the unified form on non-performance, that is, a basic 'actuality' is introduced, a basic 'form in accordance with the law', a uniform and general reason for liability, where the meaning of 'contractual breach' is dominant. The term implies any breach of any form and seriousness of any main or ancillary obligation of the seller or the buyer, i.e., any case of irregular development of an obligation, on the promisor's part. In other words, the term 'contractual breach' suggests all other cases, which, within the framework of the [Greek] Civil Code, would either be characterized as inability to perform or delay by the promisor or defective performance, or they would incur the application of the provisions of the special contractual law of the Civil Code, such as in case of a legal or real defect or absence of agreed quality*" Greece 2009 Decision 4505/2009 of the Multi-Member Court of First Instance of Athens (Bullet-proof vest case) (http://cisgw3.law.pace.edu/cases/094505gr.html).

H.C. Aksoy, *Impossibility in Modern Private Law*, DOI 10.1007/978-3-319-01704-4_5,

seller's late delivery of goods[2] and the buyer's late payment of the price.[3,4] Finally, in a decision rendered by a French court, the seller, who delivered non-conforming goods, was granted exemption under Article 79.[5] As it is clearly reflected by the above examples, the scopes of the exemption provisions of Unification Instruments reach far from impossibility. Hence, impossibility may be considered as a sub-category under the exemption provisions.

At this point it may be questioned if a clear-cut impossibility rule is better than a broad exemption provision, or vice versa. In order to answer this question the perceptions of contract in the civil law and common law systems need to be compared.[6] As explained by Rheinstein, the structure of the contractual obligation in common law and civil law legal traditions are different.[7] Accordingly, the civil law doctrine accepts contract as a mutual promise of a certain behavior. On the other hand, in the common law the contract is considered as a guarantee—made by each party—of the result to be achieved through performance of his undertaking. Consequently, the breach of contract under common law consists in the divergence between the result promised under the contract and the real state of affairs. On the other hand, in civil law jurisdictions, where the focus of obligation is on the debtor's behavior, a breach can only be imputed to the debtor, if the debtor could reasonably have been expected to behave in a different way.[8]

Rheinstein's explanations may be extended as follows: Civil law countries, such as Germany, Switzerland and Turkey, accept fault liability system. This means that the creditor is entitled to damages, only if the debtor has failed to perform by fault. Otherwise, the debtor is not obliged to compensate the damages of the creditor. On the other hand, the common law system accepts a strict-liability regime.[9] In other words, the debtor is liable for non-performance, regardless of the existence of fault.[10]

---

[2] See Switzerland 10 February 1999 Commercial Court Zürich (Art books case) (http://cisgw3.law.pace.edu/cases/990210s1.html).

[3] Germany 15 September 1994 District Court Berlin (Shoes case) (http://cisgw3.law.pace.edu/cases/940915g1.html).

[4] UNCITRAL, Digest of Article 79 case law, Nr. 9.

[5] See France 19 January 1998 District Court Besançon (Flippe Christian v. Douet Sport Collections) (http://cisgw3.law.pace.edu/cases/980119f1.html).

[6] For the regulation of impossibility, impracticability and frustration in Anglo-American law, see **Treitel**, p. 1 ff.; **Reu**, p. 1 ff.; **Becker**, Unmöglichkeitslehre, p. 1 ff. For a historical background of the principle of excuse for non-performance in common law, see **Mazzacano**, NJCL 2011, 1, 12 ff.

[7] **Rheinstein**, p. 183 ff.

[8] **Basedow**, IRLE 2005, 487, 495 ff.

[9] According to Riesenhuber, "*fault, rejected at the main entrance, will sneak in through the back door*." **Riesenhuber**, p. 22. For a comprehensive study on the concept of "fault" and its decline against strict liability, see **Fauvarque-Cosson/Mazeaud**, p. 203 ff. For a comparison of the fault liability and strict liability from the perspective of law and economics, see **Ackermann**, p. 39 ff. For a review of the fault-principle and its exceptions in German law, see **Riesenhuber**, p. 3 ff.

[10] French law has a dual character as it has recognized fault liability and strict liability in different cases of non-performance. Accordingly, in French law an obligation can either be an "obligations

Such dissimilarity is closely related to the primary remedies designated for breach of contract under each system. Accordingly, civil law systems accept primary claim (performance) as the primary remedy in the case of breach of a contract. In other words, in case of non-performance of a contractual obligation, the creditor is firstly entitled to ask for the primary claim. Within this stance, damage claims are secondary in comparison to the primary claim.[11] Hence damages may be claimed only as a second choice.[12] On the other hand, in the common law system, the primary remedy for non-performance is damages. If the debtor does not perform as agreed in the contract, the creditor asks for compensation of his damages.[13]

In civil law systems, where the primary claim is the primary remedy, strict liability "*is an overreaching and unnecessary burden on the trader.*"[14] In fact, in civil law, the debtor is obliged to perform, what he has undertaken in the contract. In other words, in case of non-performance, the creditor is entitled to insist that the debtor performs the primary claim as long as primary claim is *possible*. This is already a heavy burden placed on the debtor because he must perform the primary claim even if it is very difficult or burdensome for him to perform. Therefore, in Germany, Switzerland and Turkey, where the damage compensation is regarded as a secondary remedy, the liability of the seller for non-performance is restricted with the fault-requirement. In the end, the creditor has been given the legal option of forcing the debtor for primary claim; hence there is no need to further protect the

de moyens" or an "obligations de resultat". "Obligations de moyens' impose a duty to use best efforts to perform without guaranteeing a promised result. **Pejovic**, VUWLR 2001, 817, 825; **Gordley**, p. 499. According to Article 1137/I when a person is charged with looking after an object, the required standard of care is that of a "good father of a family" (bon père de famille/ *bonus pater familias*). **Gordley**, AJCL 2004, 513, 517. Therefore, in case of "obligations de moyens" creditor is entitled to damages if he can prove the fault of the other party. **Pejovic**, VUWLR 2001, 817, 825. Such fault refers to ordinary negligence. **Gordley**, AJCL 2004, 513, 518. On the other hand, "obligations de resultat" impose a duty to achieve a promised result. Therefore, in case of "obligations de resultat" it is sufficient to prove that the promise made was not performed. **Pejovic**, VUWLR 2001, 817, 825. In such cases, Article 1147 and 1148 set forth that a party is liable whenever he cannot prove that non-performance resulted from an extrinsic cause (cause étrangere) that cannot be imputed to him, "*force majeure*' or an accident (cas fortuit). According to Gordley such dual character exists because, when they were borrowing scraps from the Roman law, the drafters of the CC "*did not have a clear idea of what they were doing*". **Gordley**, p. 500.

[11] Since the civil law remedies are primarily concerned with performance, it is accepted that someone cannot perform what is impossible, even if it is undertaken in the contract. As a result the civil lawyers traditionally rejected the idea that a party could contract to do impossible: *impossibilium nulla obligatio est*. **Mazzacano**, NJCL 2011, 1, 12.

[12] Historically, in German law, there are two cases, where damage claims may be requested prior to primary claim: (1) when performance is impossible and the debtor is responsible for impossibility; and (2) when the creditor has lost his interest in performance due to the default of the debtor. **Weidt**, p. 81; **Huber**, Leistungsstörungen II, § 36 I 5, p. 184 ff. The same principle applies for Swiss and Turkish laws as well.

[13] According to the common law approach, performance of an obligation might be impossible, but the payment of damages is always possible. **Mazzacano**, NJCL 2011, 1, 13.

[14] **Pfeiffer**, p. 54.

creditor with the debtor's strict-liability. On the other hand, as explained by Pfeiffer, in common law systems, strict liability functions "*as a legal underpinning of the contract.*"[15] In fact, in common law countries, the primary remedy is damages.[16] Therefore, the debtor is enabled not to perform his obligation undertaken in the contract (*i.e.*, primary claim) but compensate the damages of the creditor.[17] This is a clear elasticizing of the principle of *pacta sunt servanda*. If the debtor's liability was bound to a fault-requirement, this would make it even easier for the debtor to escape from his contractual undertaking. In fact, when he had no fault, the debtor would not even have to pay compensation, let alone perform. Strict liability ensures that the debtor is obliged to perform, even if his performance is in the form of compensation payment.

Unification Instruments have not followed the remedy scheme of either of the two systems but reserved specific performance as any remedy available to the creditor.[18] However, unlike civil law, specific performance is not designated as a *primary* remedy ahead of the remedy of damage compensation. In fact, such mixing of remedies is a compromise between the civil law and common law.[19] Within this stance, lack of a primary-secondary claim distinction still justifies adoption of the strict liability principle to "underpin" the contract. Otherwise, in cases where there is no fault attributable to the debtor for non-performance, the creditor would be forced to choose specific performance as the option of claiming damages would be unavailable. However in cases, where the market actors trade in the field of generic goods, the damages will almost always be the first remedy resorted to by the aggrieved party.[20] Such fact becomes more apparent in international trade of generic goods. Hence, Unification Instruments adopted the strict-liability regime of the common law system, which serves to the benefit of the creditor, who claims his damages. Within this scope, an impediment may cause an exemption of the promisor from liability and this serves as an exception to the strict-liability principle of the common law system.[21] Thus, under Unification Instruments, the breaching party is held to be liable, unless he can establish reasons for an exemption.[22]

---

[15] **Pfeiffer**, p. 54.

[16] **Reitz**, p. 270; **Schwenzer/Hachem/Kee**, Nr. 45.07.

[17] In common law, the court may grant specific performance only upon showing that the award of damages would be insufficient as a remedy to put the debtor in the position he would have been in had the breaching party performed. **Reitz**, p. 270. In fact, in common law, specific performance is an equitable remedy. **Schwenzer/Hachem/Kee**, Nr. 43.24.

[18] See Art. 28 and 46 CISG, Art. 7.2.2 PICC, Art. 9:102 PECL, III. 3:302 DCFR, Art. 110 CESL.

[19] **Fitzgerald**, JLC 1997, 291, 291.

[20] **Schwenzer/Hachem/Kee**, Nr. 43.48.

[21] "*...if the debtor fails to fulfill an obligation he is liable under Art. 74 CISG regardless of his misconduct or fault* [*Garantiehaftung*]. *This liability, which in principle is not dependent on fault, is limited by the liability exemption under Art. 79 CISG, which must be proved by the debtor.*" Austria 29 June 1999 Supreme Court (Dividing wall panels case) (http://cisgw3.law.pace.edu/cases/990629a3.html).

[22] **Maskow**, AJCL 1992, 657, 664.

An exemption provision is a broader and more flexible rule in comparison to a clear-cut impossibility rule. It releases the debtor from liability not only in case of impossibility, but also in any type of breach, which cannot be foreseen, overcome or avoided. As a result, such broad rule is more functional in terms of bringing exceptions to the strict-liability principle and elasticizing it. Moreover, since Unification Instruments adopt the unified form of non-performance with no distinction between the types of breaches, it is fully consistent and sensible that—rather than a clear-cut impossibility rule—they set one general exemption provision for all types of breaches as well. Accordingly, under Unification Instruments—like any other type of breach—performance impossibility may either result in the debtor's obligation to compensate the damages of the creditor, or the debtor may be released from his liability, provided that the conditions of the exemption/*force majeure* clauses are met. Therefore it is also sensible that Unification Instruments have accepted an exemption provision with a broad scope, rather than a clear-cut impossibility rule.

The above evaluation is valid for all common law countries, which accept strict liability principle. In such countries, exemption provisions with broad scopes might serve as a better solution. However, in civil law countries, the issue of liability (secondary claim) is already solved under the fault principle. Therefore a clear-cut impossibility rule is required to determine when primary claim cannot be asked because of impossibility. Therefore, in Germany, Switzerland and Turkey, a clear-cut impossibility rule may be more appropriate. This being the fact, it may certainly be argued that the distinction between the approaches of common law and civil law does not lead to significantly different results in practice because under both legal traditions courts use different tools to eliminate the practical significance of such difference. "*A common law court will ask for example for the precise extent of the debtor's obligation and may, by excluding certain risks, modify the final result that the debtor promised to achieve. On the basis of the fault principle, a civil law court may argue, that the debtor, in the circumstances of the case, has taken upon himself certain risks whose materialisation would otherwise have discharged him of his obligation.*"[23]

One might ask if the distinction between the approaches of common law and civil law does not lead to significantly different results in practice, why did German lawmakers prefered to keep impossibility as a dogmatic concept in the law during the reform? It should be noted that in the Discussion Draft of the reform, impossibility was abolished as a dogmatic category.[24] However, in the following discussions, it was re-introduced to the draft.[25] This may be explained by the fact

[23] **Basedow**, IRLE 2005, 487, 495 ff.

[24] For a very critical analysis of the Discussion Draft, see **Huber**, ZIP 2000, 2137, 2137 ff. According to the author, the draft "*is badly thought, immature and un-European to an extent that it is unsuitable as a basis of a legislative procedure.*" **Huber**, ZIP 2000, 2137, 2151.

[25] Although impossibility was on the verge of being abolished from the BGB, it is ironic that in the present German law impossibility plays a more important role than before. In fact, impossibility is not only used in the general provisions of the law of obligations (Allgemeines Schuldrecht) but

that the German lawmakers preferred to maintain the traditional civil law perspective. Such adherence to the fault principle may have been caused by the established nature of the fault principle in civil law tradition. In fact, in civil law countries the fault principle is a well established category of legal thinking both in private law and in criminal law. Moreover, it is accepted to be flexible enough to cover particular circumstances of any specific case.[26] Perhaps this is also the reason why the *force majeure*/exemption approach of the CISG has not been generally adopted by national laws of the civil law countries, despite being adopted by its descendants PICC, PECL, DCFR, and CESL.[27] Nevertheless, it is clear that impossibility works for fault-based systems, but not really for strict liability regimes.

References

Ackermann, Thomas: Beyond Expectation? – An Assessment of the DCFR Rules on Contractual Damages, in: Wagner, Gerhard, The Common Frame of Reference: A View from Law & Economics, Sellier, München 2009, pp. 35 - 68.

Basedow, Jürgen: Towards a Universal Doctrine of Breach of Contract: The Impact of the CISG, IRLE, Vol. 25, No. 3, 2005, pp. 487 - 500.

Becker, Joachim Christian: Die Unmöglichkeitslehre im US-amerikanischen Vertragsrecht, Dissertation, Bonn 1972. (Cited as: Becker, Unmöglichkeitslehre)

Fauvarque-Cosson, Bénédicte/Mazeaud, Denis: European Contract Law, Sellier, München 2008.

Fitzgerald, John: CISG, Specific Performance, and the Civil Law of Louisiana and Quebec, JLC, Vol. 16, No. 1, 1997, pp. 291 - 313.

Gordley, James: Impossibility and Changed and Unforeseen Circumstances, AJCL, Vol. 52, No. 3, 2004, pp. 513 - 530.

Gordley, James: Foundations of Private Law: Property, Tort, Contract, Unjust Enrichment, Oxford University Press, Oxford/New York 2006.

Huber, Ulrich: Handbuch des Schuldrechts, Leistungsstörungen, Band II, Die Folgen des Schuldnerverzugs – Die Erfüllungsverweigerung und die vom Schuldner zu vertretende Unmöglichkeit, Mohr Siebeck, Tübingen 1999. (Cited as: Huber, Leistungsstörungen II)

Huber, Ulrich: Die Unmöglichkeit der Leistung im Diskussionsentwurf eines Schuldrechtsmodernisierungsgesetzes, ZIP 2000, pp. 2137 - 2151.

Maskow, Dietrich: Hardship and Force majeure, AJCL, Vol. 40, No. 3, 1992, pp. 657 - 669.

Mazzacano, Peter J.: Force majeure, Impossibility, Frustration & the Like: Excuses for Non-Performance; the Historical Origins and Development of an Autonomous Commercial Norm in the CISG, NJCL, Vol. 2011, No. 2, pp. 1 - 54.

Pejovic, Caslav: Civil Law and Common Law: Two Different Paths Leading to the Same Goal, VUWLR, Vol. 32, No. 3, 2001, pp. 817 - 841.

---

also among the rules on sales law, with regard to the cure (Nacherfüllung) for defective goods; see §§ 437, 439 BGB.

[26] **Basedow**, IRLE 2005, 487, 497.

[27] It would not be wrong to argue that each of the Unification Instruments is a follow up of the previous one(s), which has been further developed by considering various criticisms made regarding the provisions of the said previous one(s). When the *force majeure* provisions of the Unification Instruments are comparatively studied, it can be seen that despite the difference in wording, many of the provisions and solutions have been settled on already.

Pfeiffer, Thomas: Core issues of consumer sales law, in: Schulte-Nölke, Hans/Tichy, Lubos, Perspectives for European Consumer Law: Towards a Directive on Consumer Rights and Beyond, Sellier, München 2010, pp. 45 - 58.

Reitz, John C.: Political Economy and Contract Law, in: Schulze, Reiner, New Features in Contract Law, Sellier, München 2007, pp. 247 - 276.

Reu, Fritz: Die Unmöglichkeit der Leistung im anglo-amerikanischen Recht, Enke, Stuttgart 1935.

Rheinstein, Max: Die Struktur des vertraglichen Schuldverhältnisses im anglo-amerikanischen Recht, de Gruyter, Berlin 1932.

Riesenhuber, Karl: Damages for Non-Performance and the Fault Principle, available at <http://papers.ssrn.com/sol3/papers.cfm?abstract_id=1501193>.

Schwenzer, Ingeborg/Hachem, Pascal/Kee, Christopher: Global Sales and Contract Law, Oxford University Press, Oxford 2012.

Treitel, Günter H.: Unmöglichkeit, "Impracticability" und "Frustration" im anglo-amerikanischen Recht, Nomos, Baden-Baden 1991.

UNCITRAL: 2008 UNCITRAL Digest of case law on the United Nations Convention on the International Sale of Goods - Digest of Article 79 case law, <http://www.cisg.law.pace.edu/cisg/text/digest-art-79.html>. (Cited as UNCITRAL, Digest of Article 79 case law)

Weidt, Heinz: Antizipierter Vertragsbruch, Mohr Siebeck, Tübingen 2008.

6) Scope of Impossibility

I) Generally

Although impossibility is an old concept dating back to Roman times, even in the contemporary legal world, there is not an established definition of impossibility. This fact applies for German and Swiss—as well as Turkish—legal systems, which still recognize impossibility as a dogmatic concept even after reforms to the law of obligations. Within this stance, there is no consensus on the scope of impossibility as well.

Despite the lack of a consensus regarding the definition of impossibility, there is also an attempt to classify impossibility into its types. Such classification is useful as it would enable to bind different legal results to each type. Accordingly, several classifications are made according to the source, reason, nature and time of occurrence of impossibility. The preferences of German, Swiss and Turkish laws regarding the scope and types of impossibility are explained below.

II) The Classical Distinction of Logical and Legal Impossibility

With its simplest definition, impossibility of performance refers to cases that an obligation cannot be permanently performed or it can no longer be performed by the debtor.[1] Such impossibility of performance may arise from two main sources. Accordingly, the source of impossibility may be the principles of logic or a legal provision. The first case is termed as logical impossibility. On the other hand, the latter is legal impossibility. In case of logical impossibility, the principles of science

[1] **Basler/Wiegand**, Art. 119, N. 5.

H.C. Aksoy, *Impossibility in Modern Private Law*, DOI 10.1007/978-3-319-01704-4_6,

and technology prevent performance, where as in case of legal impossibility, performance is prevented by legal norms.

1) Logical Impossibility

Logical impossibility means that performance of an obligation is not possible according to the principles of science or logic.[2] However, the boundaries of logic are difficult to determine; hence the scope of the term logical impossibility is open for both narrow and broad interpretation. As it will be discussed below, a narrow interpretation would require the prevention of performance by the law of nature, but by a broad interpretation logical impossibility may also occur just because of practical reasons, even if it is possible to perform according to the law of nature.

a) Physical Impossibility

The first case, where performance is logically impossible, is physical impossibility. Most of the time logical impossibility is caused by the law of nature. Such cases of logical impossibility are easy to figure out. For instance, the rules of logic provide that performance of an obligation to deliver destroyed goods is impossible. Suppose that the owner of a race horse sells one of the most valuable horses in his farm. However, the parties are unaware that a few minutes before the conclusion of the sales contract, the horse died. In such case, simple logic rules show that the seller cannot perform by bringing the dead horse back to life. In fact, performance is objectively impossible for everyone.

b) Practical Impossibility

In the doctrine it is argued that law of nature is not the only source of logical impossibility. With a broad interpretation of what is illogical, it has been argued that in some cases, it might be impossible to perform an obligation because of practical reasons. According to Kleineidam, similar to the amount, quality, time and place of performance, the effort to be shown for performance is included in the subject of performance. Accordingly, if performance is not possible despite the whole effort of the debtor, there is logical impossibility.[3]

As explained above, § 275 II BGB has explicitly regulated practical impossibility and the classical example of such cases is the ring that falls to the deepest point of the ocean. For the sake of argument let us expand and present the example.

---

[2] **Dural**, Batıder 1973, 11, 13; **Serozan**, § 14, Nr. 5.

[3] **Kleineidam**, p. 14 ff.

Suppose that a jeweler sells an ancient diamond ring to a wealthy business man. The parties agree that the ring will be sent to the buyer's premises in another city by plane. However, when the buyer expects to receive the ring, he hears that the plane, which carries the ring, has fallen to the ocean. The pilot is rescued but the plane and the ring are at the deepest point of the ocean. In this case, the law of nature does not prevent performance of the debtor's obligation. Indeed, the ring is not destroyed and both of the parties are aware of its location. It is possible to dive under the ocean and get the ring by the help of various machinery. Therefore the seller can still perform his obligation. However, such activity, which is possible according to the law of nature, is deemed practically impossible.

2) Legal Impossibility (Rechtliche Unmöglichkeit)

Legal impossibility refers to prevention of the debtor's performance by a legal norm. In other words, there is a legal provision which renders the performance of the obligation impossible.[4] For instance, if a governmental authority does not grant a construction permit or cancels an issued permit, performance of an obligation to construct a building is legally impossible.[5]

Anything that is impossible according to the law of nature is deemed legally impossible as well. This is natural, as it would not be logical if the legal system forced the debtor to conduct the impossible. However, while regulating the relationship between human beings, the legal order may accept impossibility of logically possible things as well. In other words, anything that is possible according to the law of nature may be subject to the results of impossibility before the law.[6] Such cases are referred as legal impossibility.

The relationship between the logical and legal impossibility is quite disputed. According to Lehmann, legal impossibility is a broader concept than logical impossibility and legal impossibility is logical impossibility as well. The author accepts that the law does not bind any results to anything that is naturally impossible. In other words, if something is logically impossible, the law also recognizes it as legally impossible. Therefore according to the author, there is no contradiction between the two concepts.[7]

In contrast to Lehmann, Kornfeld argues that there is no legal impossibility. According to the author, impossibility occurs only if one of the natural conditions of

[4] **Dural**, Batıder 1973, 11, 15; **Altunkaya**, p. 95.

[5] In one of its decisions, the Turkish Court of Appeals ruled that the construction agreement regarding establishment of a five storey building is void due to initial impossibility, since the relevant regulation, which was in effect on the date of contract formation, prohibited such construction. Yarg. 15. HD., 1981/331 E., 1981/1050 K., 7.5.1981.

[6] **Förster**, Nr. 207; **Altunkaya**, p. 92; **Berki**, p. 9; **Dural**, Batıder 1973, 11, 17.

[7] **Lehmann**, p. 232.

performance is missing. However, in cases termed as legal impossibility there is no lack of natural conditions of performance, but the legal conditions are missing since a legal norm is breached. Therefore, the obligation to perform anything illegal does not constitute impossibility, but illegality.[8]

Barth also rejects the concept of legal impossibility. According to the author such cases actually constitute illegality. The author states that legal impossibility may only occur in cases, where the state takes the necessary precautions to *physically* prevent the performance. In other words, the author states that even if the parties wanted to break the law and perform, if they are physically prevented by the precautions of the state, there is legal impossibility. For instance, an export ban may cause legal impossibility because the export activity is physically prevented at the border even for the parties willing to break the law.[9]

III) The "Ideal" Scope of Impossibility

a) Overview

There is a consensus that impossibility covers the situations where performance of the obligation is physically impossible. Since the assessment of physical impossibility is quite easy, it is recognized in German, Swiss and Turkish laws as a reason, which eliminates the primary claim. Similarly, such cases may constitute impediment under Unification Instruments. However, it must be accepted that practical impossibility and legal impossibility are also included within the ideal scope of impossibility. Moreover, accomplishment and destruction of purpose are also included in the ideal scope of impossibility. However, cases termed as interference with the basis of the transaction cannot be regarded as impossibility.

b) Practical Impossibility and Moral Impossibility

The notion of impossible under the law is not identical to impossibility in the physical sense. Therefore, some cases where performance becomes very difficult, albeit possible, may be regarded as impossibility under the law. However, this is not true for all cases where performance becomes difficult. Otherwise, the principle of *pacta sunt servanda* would be undermined. Than what could be the appropriate test for determining if performance is impossible?

---

[8] **Kornfeld**, p. 13.

[9] **Barth**, p. 27 ff.

Ideally, impossibility must be determined by a *reasonableness test*. Within this stance, leaving aside whether or not performance is logically impossible, it must be investigated **if performance cannot reasonably be expected under the circumstances of the specific case**. This would be appropriate because contractual relationships are not based on purely physical facts. There are both economic and moral parameters of obligations. The reasonableness test considers such parameters and maintains flexibility of assessment. Within this stance, it is clear that the debtor cannot reasonably be expected to perform anything that is physically impossible. Such test, however, enables to decide that the so-called practical impossibility and moral impossibility are also included in the ideal scope of impossibility.

Reasonableness is a parameter of Unification Instruments. It is used especially within the scope of foreseeability and avoidability criteria, but such test is not unknown to civil law's legal thinking on impossibility either. In fact, such test is used to decide if there is moral impossibility under § 275 III BGB. In the example of the opera singer, *reasonableness* prevents to expect performance due to moral reasons. Although BGB has accepted the reasonableness test for the cases of moral impossibility, such test is broad enough to cover the cases of practical impossibility as well. Referring back to the classical ring example, it could not be reasonably expected of the debtor to perform due to economic reasons, *i.e.*, disproportionality. Moreover, it should also be decided by a case specific reasonableness analysis if temporary impossibility is equal to permanent impossibility or if partial impossibility causes total impossibility. Such evaluation must be made from the perspective of the creditor by asking if the creditor could be expected to accept temporary or partial performance.

Practical impossibility and moral impossibility have been appropriately included in the scope of impossibility by German lawmakers. Swiss and Turkish laws, on the other hand, lack provisions, which are equivalent to § 275 II and III BGB. However, as explained above, the reasonableness test is merely a matter of perspective. Therefore, if the reasonableness test is recognized, this would constitute the legal ground for accepting such cases as impossibility even under Swiss and Turkish laws.[10]

Use of reasonableness test for determining the scope of impossibility requires granting major discretionary power to the judge. In fact, the judge would have to decide if there is impossibility in each specific case. This would not be a concern for

[10] Moral impossibility is accepted by the Swiss Federal Court. For instance, in a dispute resolved by the Swiss Federal Court, a son-in-law and his father-in-law have concluded a contract, which entitles the father-in-law to reside at the house of his son-in-law. However, after the conclusion of the contract, the son-in-law and his wife (the daughter of the father-in-law) divorced. In the decision, the Swiss Federal Court ruled that it is impossible for the son-in-law to continue performance of his obligation after the divorce. According to the decision, whether the son-in-law will be responsible for impossibility or not would be determined in accordance with the existence of his fault in divorce. BGE 82 II 332, 332 ff. In Turkish law, some authors state that sometimes performance of the obligation might cause serious negative effects on the frame of mind of the debtor, where it will be against the principle of good faith to expect his performance. **Tekinay**, p. 633–634; **Altunkaya**, p. 98; **Eren**, p. 998.

common lawyers, as in common law the judge is traditionally entrusted with extensive authority. However, the civil lawyers may be critical about extending the discretion of the judge through reasonableness test. Against such potential critique it could be argued that the reasonableness test is not less concrete than the principle of good-faith, which the civil law judges already apply. Therefore there is no reason to be afraid of the elasticity of the reasonableness test and the power it grants to the judge. Moreover, it would not be wrong to argue that case law is having an increasingly more importance in civil law countries. Lawyers are making reference to numerous court decisions not only in lawsuit petitions but also in academic studies. Hence, the role of the judge is increasing in civil law countries as well.

The cases of practical and moral impossibility are included in the scope of impossibility under Unification Instruments as well. First of all, Unification Instruments clearly rule that when performance is unreasonably burdensome or expensive for the debtor, specific performance cannot be claimed.[11] There is no doubt that such provision refers to the cases of practical and moral impossibility. For such analysis, it would be necessary to conduct reasonableness test on a case-by-case basis. CESL makes such fact further clear by making reference to the *disproportionality* requirement between the burden or expense of performance and the benefit that the buyer would obtain. Within this stance, as in German law, *burdensome* has a wider scope than financial burden which covers not only practical impossibility but also moral impossibility.[12] The provision of the PECL, which uses the term "*effort*" rather than "*burden*", also signals such fact.

Under the light of the discussions above, it is clear that practical and moral impossibility prevent the performance of the primary claim/specific performance under German, Swiss and Turkish laws as well as Unification Instruments. However, compensation of damages is a separate matter. In civil law, payment of damage compensation depends on the existence of fault. Similarly, under Unification Instruments, the debtor does not pay compensation if he is exempt from liability for impossibility. It must be emphasized that the exemption provisions are open to wide interpretation. Therefore, if the elements of exemption are met in a specific case of practical or moral impossibility, the debtor may—at least theoretically—be exempt from liability. However, it must be stated that in practice such cases would rarely cause exemption. In fact, in such cases it would be relatively difficult to argue that the debtor cannot *overcome* the impediment. Moreover, the case law on CISG shows that courts have a tendency to apply the exemption provision very narrowly, since Unification Instruments accept strict-liability system.

[11] See, Art. 7.2.2 PICC; Art. 9:102 (2) (b) PECL; III.-3:302 DCFR and Art. 110 CESL. Although there is no such express provision in the CISG, when interpreting the CISG, it would be appropriate to accept that unreasonableness constitutes a restriction of the creditor's claim of specific performance under Article 46 CISG. In the same opinion, see **Müller-Chen**, in: Schlechtriem/Schwenzer, Art. 46, Nr. 12.

[12] DCFR Commentary, III-3:302, Comment F.

c) Interference with the Basis of the Transaction

Practical impossibility and excessive performance difficulty are similar mainly in two ways: (*i*) in both cases performance is difficult, albeit physically possible; (*ii*) in both cases the reasonableness test says that performance cannot be expected from the debtor.[13] Then, it must be answered if they should be differentiated from each other. If yes, what would be the reason of such differentiation?

Despite their similarities, it would be appropriate to differentiate the two cases and accept that interference with the basis of the transaction is not included in the ideal scope of impossibility. In fact, BGB successfully differentiates between practical impossibility (§ 275 II BGB) and interference with the basis of the transaction (§ 313 BGB). As explained above, the main difference between the two cases is that in case of practical impossibility there is disproportionality between the interest of the parties in performance. However, in case of interference with the basis of the transaction, there is no such disproportion and when the value of the performance increases, the creditor's interest in receiving performance increases proportionally as well. Such difference is very important in that it affects the result of the reasonableness test. In fact, when there is a disproportion, the debtor cannot be expected to perform *at all*. On the other hand, when there is no such disproportion, it would be more difficult to accept that the debtor cannot be expected to perform at all. In such cases, reasonableness test would say that the debtor cannot be expected to perform *as undertaken* in the contract. Therefore, in BGB, TCO, the Swiss legal system and Unification Instruments—except for the CISG.[14] The latter case does not cause impossibility but adaptation of the contract. This is an effort to balance the interests of the parties. Otherwise the debtor would be excessively protected.

d) The Concept of Legal Impossibility

In contemporary legal systems, the prevention of the debtor's performance by a legal norm is deemed as impossibility. Within this stance, legal impossibility is recognized in German, Swiss and Turkish laws as a reason that eliminates the primary claim. Similarly, such cases may constitute an impediment under Unification Instruments.

[13] The reasonability test is not strange to the cases of interference with the basis of the transaction/ excessive performance difficulty as well. For instance, § 313 BGB requires an investigation if "*one of the parties cannot reasonably be expected to uphold the contract without alteration*". Similarly, Article 138 TCO asks if "*demanding performance from him—the debtor—results against the principles of good faith*".

[14] As explained above, despite the prevailing opinion, it can neither be accepted that Article 79 of the CISG covers the cases of the interference with the basis of the contract nor CISG regulates adaptation of the contract for such cases.

The concept of legal impossibility cannot be rejected and it is correct that the scope of legal impossibility is wider than physical impossibility. Legal impossibility covers the cases of physical impossibility. In the end, the law simply prescribes that there is impossibility in the cases of physical impossibility. However, the law may also create *legal* impossibility, for instance by a trade ban.

The above explained view that "*there is no legal impossibility, if the state does not take the necessary precautions to physically prevent the breach of a legal ban*" is not acceptable. Regardless of the precautions taken by the state, if performance is prevented by a legal norm, it must be deemed impossible. Within this stance, the point of reference should be the person, who obeys the law. In other words, if any performance is prohibited by law, it is impossible for the parties, who obey the law. In the end, it would be inappropriate to expect parties not to comply with the law. It must be underlined that—even if such rejections only constitute the minority opinion—these cannot be made with regard to Unification Instruments. More specifically, the sphere of control test of Unification Instruments eliminates such arguments. In fact, from the perspective of Unification Instruments legal bans are impediments, which are external to the debtor at all times. Therefore, it would not be assessed if the norm may be *physically* breached. Certainly, an exemption may be prevented if the requirements of unforeseeability and/or unavoidability are not met under the case at hand.

e) Accomplishment of Purpose (Zweckerreichung) and Destruction of Purpose (Zweckfortfall)

Accomplishment and destruction of the purpose are also included in the ideal scope of impossibility. In the classical example, where the patient dies (destruction of purpose) or gets well (accomplishment of purpose) before the arrival of the doctor, the doctor cannot cure the patient. These cases constitute physical impossibility.[15] Hence in both cases it is impossible for the debtor to perform.[16] This is accepted both in the German and Swiss—as well as Turkish—laws. A similar argument applies for Unification Instruments as well.

Even if it is accepted that such cases are included in the scope of impossibility, it would be necessary to decide if the parties may ask for compensation from each other. Within this stance, *de lege ferenda*, the "ideal" solution would be accepting that in such cases, the risk must be distributed between the parties. Accordingly, the debtor must be entitled to the counter-obligation partially. In fact, in cases, where

[15] **Hk-BGB/Schulze**, § 275, Rdnr. 10.

[16] **Sulzer**, AJP 2003, 987, 991. According to Sulzer, such cases always constitute permanent impossibility. **Sulzer**, p. 193. If the impediment is only temporary, instead of impossibility, default of the creditor may occur. **MüKo/Ernst**, § 275, Rdnr. 152.

impossibility occurs in the sphere of the debtor, the creditor's release from the counter-obligation is a *response*. More specifically, when the debtor says that he cannot perform, the creditor reacts by not performing the counter-obligation. This is an appropriate balance of the interests of the parties. However, in cases of accomplishment and destruction of purpose, impossibility occurs in the sphere of control of the creditor. Therefore, even if the debtor is eager to perform, the creditor says that he will not be able to accept performance due to impossibility. If it were accepted that the counter-obligation disappears as well, this would also be in favour of the creditor. Therefore, the interests of the debtor, who is eager to perform, would not be protected at all. This being the fact, it would also be unfair to claim full counter-obligation from the creditor because the debtor has not performed. Therefore it would be fair to distribute the risk between the parties.

In cases of accomplishment and destruction of purpose it may be a considerable solution to deduct the debtor's savings—accrued due to non-performance—from the counter-obligation agreed upon in the contract. As explained above, § 326 II BGB has accepted such risk distribution in cases, where the creditor is "*solely or very predominantly responsible*" or if impossibility for which the debtor is not responsible "*occurs at a time when the obligee is in default of acceptance*". However, when the creditor gets well before the arrival of the doctor, it can hardly be said that the creditor is *responsible* for impossibility. Within this stance, it could be accepted that there is a gap in the said provision regarding the cases of accomplishment and destruction of purpose and the provision must also cover such cases.[17] A similar solution applies for the Swiss and Turkish laws as well as Unification Instruments.[18]

From the perspective of German law, it could be argued that the above solution would create unfair results. More specifically, § 326 II BGB has accepted such rule in cases, where the creditor is "*solely or very predominantly responsible*". If the same solution is also accepted for the cases of accomplishment and destruction of the purpose when the creditor is *not* responsible, would this be unfair? In fact, there is no such unfairness: If the creditor's act constitutes a breach of duty under § 280 I BGB (or a tortuous act), the debtor can ask for compensation in addition to the counter-performance.[19] More specifically, such right would only be granted to the debtor, if the creditor is responsible for the occurrence of impossibility. In the end, where the creditor has no responsibility in the occurrence of impossibility, the debtor's claim would be restricted to the counter-obligation after deduction of savings, etc. Therefore, the effects of the existence of the creditor's responsibility would not be neglected and no unfair results would occur.

---

[17] Without referring to any gap, Ernst argues that accomplishment and destruction of purpose are within the scope of § 326 II BGB. **MüKo/Ernst**, § 275, Rdnr. 155 ff.

[18] Unification Instruments have regulated interference of the other party. Accordingly, based on the principle of exemption due to interference of the other party, a similar result may be achieved regarding Unification Instruments as well. **Brunner**, p. 467, **Achilles**, Art. 80, Nr. 6.

[19] **Staudinger/Otto**, § 326, Rdnr. C 72; **MüKo/Ernst**, § 326, Rdnr. 83.

Finally, unlike accomplishment and destruction of purpose, cases of frustration of purpose, where there is an impossibility of use are not included in the ideal scope of impossibility. In such cases, the creditor has no interest in performance as he cannot use the performance as intended. However, performance is still possible, despite being useless for the creditor. Depending on the circumstances of the case, this may constitute interference with the basis of the contract.

References

Achilles, Wilhelm-Albrecht: Kommentar zum UN-Kaufrechtsübereinkommen (CISG), Luchterhand, Neuwied 2000.

Altunkaya, Mehmet: Edimin Başlangıçtaki İmkansızlığı, Yetkin, Ankara 2005.

Barth, Hans Rudolf: Schadenersatz bei nachträglicher Unmöglichkeit der Erfüllung, Verlag H.R. Sauerländer and Co., Aarau 1958.

Berki, Şakir: Borçlar Hukuku, Kitap I, Umumi Hükümler, Güzel Sanatlar, Ankara 1958.

Brunner, Christoph: Force majeure and Hardship Excuse Under General Contract Principles, Wolters Kluwer, Alphen aan den Rijn 2009.

Dural, Mustafa: İmkansızlık Kavramı ve Türleri, Batıder, Vol. 7, No. 1, 1973, pp. 11–58.

Eren, Fikret: Borçlar Hukuku Genel Hükümler, Beta, İstanbul 2006.

Förster, Christian: Schuldrecht Allgemeiner Teil, Eine Einführung mit Fällen, C.F. Müller, Heidelberg 2011.

Honsell, Heinrich/Vogt, Nedim Peter/Wiegand, Wolfgang: Basler Kommentar zum Schweizerischen Privatrecht, Obligationenrecht I, Art. 1–529 OR, Helbing and Lichtenhahn, Basel/Genf/München 2003. (Cited as: Basler/Author)

Kleineidam, Feodor: Unmöglichkeit und Unvermögen nach dem Bürgerlichen Gesetzbuche für das Deutsche Reich, Fischer, Jena 1900.

Kornfeld, Felix: Leistungsunmöglichkeit, Manzchen, Wien 1913.

Lehmann, Heinrich: Die Unterlasungspflicht im Bürgerlichen Recht, C.H. Beck, München 1906. (Cited as: Lehmann)

Säcker, Franz Jürgen/Rixecke, Roland: Münchener Kommentar zum Bürgerlichen Gesetzbuch, Band 2, Schuldrecht, Allgemeiner Teil §§ 241–432, C.H. Beck, München 2012. (Cited as: MüKo)

Schlechtriem, Peter/Schwenzer, Ingeborg: Commentary on the UN Convention on the International Sale of Goods (CISG), Oxford University Press, Oxford/New York 2005. (Cited as: Author, in: Schlechtriem/Schwenzer)

Schulze, Reiner/Dörner, Heinrich/Ebert, Ina/Hoeren, Thomas/Kemper, Rainer/Saenger, Ingo/Schreiber, Klaus/Schulte-Nölke, Hans/Staudinger, Ansgar: Bürgerliches Gesetzbuch, Handkommentar, Nomos, Baden-Baden 2012. (Cited as: Hk-BGB/Author)

Serozan, Rona: Borçlar Hukuku Genel Bölüm Üçüncü Cilt - İfa, İfa Engelleri, Haksız Zenginleşme, Filiz, İstanbul 2006. (Cited as: Serozan)

Staudinger, Julius von: Kommentar zum Bürgerlichen Gesetzbuch mit Einführungsgesetz und Nebengesetzen, Buch 2, Recht der Schuldverhältnisse, §§ 315–326, (Leistungsstörungsrecht 2), Neuarbeitung 2009, Sellier de Gruyter, Berlin 2009. (Cited as: Staudinger/Author)

Study Group on a European Civil Code/Research Group on the Existing EC Private Law (Acquis Group): Principles, Definitions and Model Rules on European Private Law, <http://www.ccbe.eu/fileadmin/user_upload/NTCdocument/DCFRpdf1_1262861061.pdf>. (Cited as: DCFR Commentary)

Sulzer, Stefan: Zweckstörungen im schweizerischen Vertragsrecht, Schulthess, Zürich 2002. (Cited as: Sulzer)
Sulzer, Stefan: Clausula rebus sic stantibus und der gestörte Vertragszweck Zugleich Bemerkungen zu BGE 127 III (2001) 300 ff., AJP 2003, pp. 987–994.
Tekinay, Sulhi Selahattin: Borçlar Hukuku, Fakülteler Matbaası, İstanbul 1973.

7) Types of Impossibility and Their Treatment

I) Objective Impossibility – Subjective Impossibility

The first group of distinction with regard to the types of impossibility is the distinction of objective and subjective impossibility. Such classical distinction is recognized especially in civil law, but the terms are not defined in either BGB, OR and TCO or Unification Instruments.

When different legal systems are evaluated together, it appears that there are differences with regard to the criteria to be considered in differentiating the two concepts. The first criterion that differentiates objective and subjective impossibility from each other is whether performance is impossible only for the debtor, or for everyone.[1] Accordingly, if performance of the obligation is impossible for everyone, there is objective impossibility. On the other hand, in cases where performance is impossible for the debtor, but someone else can still perform, there is subjective impossibility.[2]

[1] **Berner/Becker**, Art. 20, N. 2; **Gauch/Schluep**, Band II, Nr. 2557; **Schwenzer**, Obligationenrecht, Nr. 63.08; **Esser/Schmidt**, § 22, II; **Brox/Walker**, § 22, Nr. 4; **Rampini**, Nr. 91; **Titze**, p. 59; **Huguenin**, Nr. 393; **Barth**, p. 36; **Jakobs**, p. 127; **Larenz**, p. 98; **Eckert**, Nr. 260; **Buz**, AÜSBFD 1994, 23, 24; **Topuz/Canbolat**, AÜHFD 2008, 673, 676; **Tunçomağ**, p. 179; **Eren**, p. 295.

[2] **Fikentscher/Heinemann**, § 42 III 2, Nr. 371; **Giger**, p. 10; **Witthaus**, p. 6; **Fischer**, Beitrag, p. 19 and 27; **PWW/Schmidt-Kessel**, § 275, Rdnr. 7; **Keller/Schöbi**, p. 79; **Hirsch**, Nr. 635; **Hütte/Helbron**, Nr. 377–378; **Rabel**, p. 38; **Fehre**, p. 23; **Markesinis/Unberath/Johnston**, p. 409; **Eckert**, Nr. 260; **Westermann/Bydlinski/Weber**, § 7, Nr. 7/2; **Traub**, p. 1; **Joeinig**, p. 38; **Rampini**, Nr. 81; **Brunner**, p 78; **Uygur**, p. 1021; **Altunkaya**, p. 115; **Dural**, Batıder 1973, 11, 29; **Topuz/Canbolat**, AÜHFD 2008, 673, 676; **İnan**, Bankacılar, p. 147; **Akıntürk**, p. 35; **Buz**, AÜSBFD 1994, 23, 24; **Serozan**, § 14, Nr. 9; **Tunçomağ**, p. 179; **Oğuzman/Öz**, p. 78; **Bozer**, p. 216; **Eren** p. 295. Coendet emphasizes that subjective impossibility exists only if the impediment to the performance is literally insurmountable for the debtor. **Coendet**, recht 2009, 128, 132.

H.C. Aksoy, *Impossibility in Modern Private Law*, DOI 10.1007/978-3-319-01704-4_7,

This is the common opinion in BGB and OR—as well as TCO—regarding the criteria for separating objective and subjective impossibility.[3]

Important results have been attached to the distinction of objective and subjective impossibility. Actually, § 275 BGB makes no distinction between the two types of impossibility and covers both objective and subjective impossibility. However, in Turkish and Swiss doctrines—similar to former BGB—it is accepted that initial impossibility, which causes the contract to be void must be objective in nature.[4] This being the fact, it is debated, whether subsequent impossibility under Article 119 OR—Article 136 TCO—is restricted to objective impossibility or not.[5] Finally, pursuant to Unification Instruments the impediment must be an objective one.

The difference between objective and subjective impossibility can be better illustrated with the following example: Suppose that an auctioner sells two unique paintings to two different buyers. However, while he loads the paintings to his car for delivery, a thief attempts to steal the paintings. The auctioner tries to stop the thief and during the fight between the auctioner and the thief, one of the paintings is torn into pieces by accident. However, the thief runs away with the second painting, which is not damaged. This example illustrates both objective and subjective impossibility. First of all, there is objective impossibility with regard to the delivery of the painting which is torn into pieces because the auctioner's obligation under the contract can neither be fulfilled by the auctioner himself nor anyone else. In other words, it is impossible for everyone in the universe to deliver that unique painting to the buyer. However, according to the prevailing opinion in German and Turkish/Swiss laws, the impossibility with regard to the delivery of the second painting is a subjective one.[6] Although, it is very difficult for the auctioner to find the stolen painting and deliver it to the buyer, the thief can fulfill the obligation which is subjectively impossible for the auctioner.

[3] According to the prevailing opinion, if the subject of the contract is an obligation that can only be performed by the debtor in person (Höchstpersönliche Leistung), impossibility is always objective. **Koller**, § 53, Nr. 13; **Eren**, p. 997; **Giger**, p. 23; **Schwarze**, § 4, 13; **Basler/Huguenin**, Art. 19–20, N. 46; **Huguenin**, Nr. 557; **Altunkaya**, p. 112; **Dural**, p. 35; **Bucher**, p. 418; **Gauch/Schluep**, Band I, Nr. 636. For instance, if a painter loses his hands a short time before fulfilling his obligation to draw a painting, there is objective impossibility of performance because in this contract, personal qualifications of the painter is important and no other painter has specifically the same qualifications. Since no painting by another artist can substitute the performance of the original artist, it cannot be argued that another painter can make the painting and fulfill the obligation. Contrarily, according to Serozan there is subjective impossibility in such cases. The author argues that in cases of initial impossibility, this enables the debtor to be kept bound with his undertaking, rather than applying the voidness sanction of the law. **Serozan**, § 14, Nr. 15. In the same opinion with Serozan, Tekinay further asserts that in order to accept that there is subjective impossibility in such cases, as an additional requirement, impossibility must not have been caused by any reason originating from the debtor. **Tekinay**, p. 635.

[4] **Gauch/Schluep**, Band II, Nr. 2574.

[5] **Gauch/Schluep**, Band II, Nr. 2526; **Kälin**, recht 2004, 246, 247.

[6] **Canaris**, JZ 2001, 499, 499; **Hütte/Helbron**, Nr. 378; **Serozan**, § 14, Nr. 13; **Koller**, § 53, Nr. 12; **Schwenzer**, Obligationenrecht, Nr. 63.08; **Kälin**, recht 2004, 246, 249. According to Bucher, such cases constitute objective impossibility. **Bucher**, p. 248.

If the thief were the debtor of the obligation to deliver that unique painting, he would be able to perform.

The second opinion with regard to the distinction of objective and subjective impossibility considers the source of impossibility. Accordingly, if the source of impossibility is the personality of the debtor, there is subjective impossibility. On the other hand, if the source of impossibility is the conditions, which are external to the debtor, there is objective impossibility.[7] In other words, if the facts that render performance impossible are caused by the nature of the obligation there is objective impossibility.[8] However, if an obligation, which is possible to perform, cannot be performed due to reasons arising from the debtor, there is subjective impossibility.[9] As a result, the above-explained first criterion refers to a relationship between the obligation and the third person, but the second criterion refers directly to the relationship between the obligation and the debtor.[10] This argument is similar to the beyond control criterion of Unification Instruments, where exemption may be granted if the impediment is external to the debtor.

Thirdly, there is the opinion, which rejects the concept of subjective impossibility. Kornfeld states that the concepts of objective and subjective impossibility are different in their natures. Impossibility appears only if the natural conditions of performance are missing. However, in cases which are termed as subjective impossibility, the missing element is not the natural conditions of performance, but there is a lack of ability to perform. In other words, in cases of subjective impossibility the obligation can be performed, but the debtor lacks the power to perform the obligation.[11] Therefore, according to the author, subjective impossibility is actually performance difficulty. Also according to the prevailing opinion in Swiss and Turkish doctrines, the cases termed as subjective impossibility are not impossibility in technical terms. Accordingly, subjective impossibility must be dealt with under the provisions of default[12] because when the debtor cannot perform but the same obligation can be performed by third parties, this is generally caused by the lack of necessary financial resources

---

[7] **Altunkaya**, p. 113; **Eren**, p. 296; **Barth**, p. 36.

[8] **Rabel** p. 38.

[9] An important result of this opinion is that in cases where impossibility arises from the personality of the debtor, there is subjective impossibility, even if all third persons cannot perform as well because according to this opinion, objective impossibility takes place only if everyone including the debtor cannot perform due to the same reason. **Altunkaya**, p. 113.

[10] **Altunkaya**, p. 113; **Dural**, Batıder 1973, 11, 31.

[11] **Kornfeld**, p. 19. Also according to this opinion, in case of obligations which can only be performed by the debtor in person, impossibility is always objective because in such cases ability to perform has become a natural condition of performance. In other words, the debtor's ability to perform is included in the undertaken obligation; therefore the lack thereof causes objective impossibility. **Dural**, Batıder 1973, 11, 34.

[12] **Buz**, AÜSBFD 1994, 23, 25; **von Büren**, p. 365; **Topuz/Canbolat**, AÜHFD 2008, 673, 686; **Tekinay**, p. 633. On the contrary, see, **Huguenin**, Nr. 581 ff.

by the debtor.[13] Therefore in cases where the debtor cannot perform due to subjective impossibility, the debtor would be in default.

None of the above explained opinions are appropriate to define the borders of the notion of impossibility. In fact, the distinction of impossibility as objective and subjective impossibility is an improper and unhelpful one. Therefore it must be eliminated. However, this should not mean that the so-called subjective impossibility would cause impossibility in technical terms. Otherwise, it would be very easy for the debtor to be released from the primary claim and the principle of *pacta sunt servanda* would be destroyed. On the other hand, impossibility cannot be restricted to the so-called cases of objective impossibility either. To be more precise, it might be helpful to refer back to the painting example above. In fact, for the debtor, there is hardly a difference between the likelihood of performance concerning the painting, which is torn into pieces and the painting that has been stolen. What is the likelihood for the seller finding the thief and getting the painting back? Therefore, there can be no legal reasoning for arguing that there is no impossibility regarding the stolen painting. On the other hand, it is necessary to draw the borders of impossibility. It is quite interesting that even in German law, which has eliminated the distinction of objective and subjective impossibility, it is accepted that not all cases of subjective impossibility are covered by § 275 I BGB. Accordingly, there is no impossibility in accordance with § 275 I BGB, when the debtor can overcome an existing obstacle to performance, and therefore generate or regenerate his ability to perform through procurement or replacement.[14] Such a perspective is definitely appropriate but it is also clear that even German law somewhat reserves the distinction by "objectifying" subjective impossibility. What might be the solution then?

Ideally, the distinction of objective and subjective impossibility must be rejected. As argued by Fischer, there is one single type of impossibility and its measure is equity because it cannot be expected from the debtor to show an effort that is above the level to be expected under equity.[15] Therefore, according to this opinion, impossibility includes not only the cases where the performance is impossible for everyone, but also the cases, where performance cannot be expected from the specific debtor under such circumstances. In other words, if the common opinion finds performance impossible, then there is impossibility.[16]

Fischer's opinion may be extended to argue that the criterion of impossibility is *reasonableness*. It must be noted that none of BGB, OR, TCO or Unification Instruments refers to the distinction of objective and subjective impossibility. Such distinction is the result of the efforts of courts and scholars to set the borders of the notion of impossibility. Therefore, *de lege ferenda*, there is no rule which prevents a different interpretation of impossibility based on *reasonableness*. In fact,

---

[13] **Eren**, p. 296.

[14] **Finn**, p. 141; **Zimmer**, NJW 2002, 1, 2; **Mitzkait**, p. 47; **MüKo/Ernst**, § 275, Rdnr. 52; **Staudinger/Löwisch**, § 275, Rdnr. 69; **Palandt/Grüneberg**, § 275, Rdnr. 23.

[15] **Fischer**, JJ 1897, 199, 262.

[16] **Fischer**, JJ 1897, 199, 237.

the reasonableness test would even be flexible enough to prevent unfair results regarding *subjective* impossibility. For instance, by applying such test, it would be arguable that performance of the stolen painting is impossible for the seller. As a result, German, Swiss and Turkish laws would move closer to the perspective of Unification Instruments, which uses reasonableness as an important test.

When making the reasonableness test, it would be appropriate to consider if performance cannot be expected from *any* debtor under such circumstances. In other words, the subjective sensitivities of the specific debtor and his perceptions regarding the difficulty of performance would not be taken into consideration. Otherwise, it would be almost impossible to assess, whether performance could be expected from the specific debtor under the circumstances of the case.

II) Impossibility for Which the Debtor Is Responsible – Impossibility for Which the Debtor Is Not Responsible

Another distinction regarding types of impossibility is based on the responsibility of the debtor for impossibility. Among all others, the debtor is responsible for the occurrence of impossibility if the debtor causes impossibility of performance by his intentional or negligent behavior, *i.e.*, fault.[17]

Suppose that a guitarist sells his handmade guitar to a teenager. They agree that the guitar will be delivered two days later because the seller wants to make a serenade to his girlfriend, who has her birthday in two days. However, during the serenade, the girl feels shy and humiliated and breaks up with the guitarist. Upset and angry, the guitarist smashes the guitar to a tree. Since, the handmade guitar cannot be delivered to the buyer there is impossibility of performance. There would be no doubt that the debtor is responsible for impossibility, since he gets angry and smashes the guitar intentionally. However, if the guitar was destroyed by a natural disaster, such as an earthquake, there would be non-culpable impossibility.

The importance of such distinction is that in general the debtor would be responsible only if impossibility occurs by his intentional or negligent behavior. On the other hand, if impossibility occurs due to *force majeure* or accidents (unexpected situations/cas fortuit), the debtor would not be held responsible.[18] However, the debtor's responsibility for impossibility is not restricted to cases in which he has caused impossibility by faulty behavior. In fact, there might be situations, where the law accepts the debtor's responsibility even if there is no fault in the occurrence of impossibility. For instance, § 278 BGB rules that "*The obligor is responsible for fault on the part of his legal representative, and of persons whom he uses to perform his obligation, to the same extent as for fault*

[17] **Altunkaya**, p. 138.

[18] **Reisoğlu**, p. 324; **Akıntürk**, Borçlar, p. 137.

on his own part." Such provision results in the debtor's responsibility, even if he has no fault regarding the breach of contract. A corresponding provision can be found in OR and TCO as well. On the other hand, as explained above, in cases of accomplishment and destruction of purpose, performance becomes impossible in the sphere of control of the creditor. Therefore, in such cases the debtor cannot be held responsible for impossibility.

As a result, the debtor is not responsible for impossibility of the performance, if (*i*) he has no fault liability; (*ii*) he is not liable under a guarantee arising from law or the contract; or (*iii*) if the risks lie in the sphere of control of the creditor.[19] Otherwise, the debtor is responsible for impossibility. However, it must be underlined that the distinction based on the debtor's responsibility for impossibility is not present in Unification Instruments. In fact, Unification Instruments have recognized the debtor's strict-liability in case of non-performance.

III) Partial Impossibility – Total Impossibility

The distinction of partial and total impossibility refers to the amount that has become impossible to perform within the whole of the obligation. Accordingly, if the obligation cannot be performed at all, there is total impossibility. On the other hand, if the obligation can only be partially performed, there is partial impossibility.[20] Such distinction is recognized not only under German, Swiss, and Turkish laws, but also Unification Instruments.

A distinction of total and partial impossibility requires the subject of the obligation to have a legally divisible character.[21] In fact, in cases, where the subject of the obligation is indivisible, there is total impossibility.[22] Within this context, when investigating the divisibility of the subject of the obligation, the wills of the parties, purpose of the contract and the nature of the subject of the obligation must be taken into consideration.[23]

For the occurrence of partial impossibility, the primary condition is that the subject of the obligation be physically divisible. The physical divisibility of the subject of the obligation is decided considering the nature of the obligation. If the subject of the obligation is divisible without causing any important change in its

---

[19] **Serozan**, § 15, Nr. 4.

[20] **Barth**, p. 44; **Altunkaya**, p. 127; **Topuz/Canbolat**, AÜHFD 2008, 673, 680; **Eren**, p. 999; **Dural**, Batıder 1973, 11, 37; **Oğuzman/Öz**, p. 306. For a study on the distinction of total and partial impossibility, see **Kisch**, p. 1 ff.

[21] **Fikentscher/Heinemann**, § 42 III 2, Nr. 380; **Staudinger/Otto**, § 326, Rdnr. B 40; **Fischer**, p. 102.

[22] **Mitzkait**, p. 40; **Staudinger/Otto**, § 326, Rdnr. B 40; **Altunkaya**, p. 128; **Tekinay**, p. 638; **Dural**, Batıder 1973, 11, 38.

[23] **Altunkaya**, p. 128; **Dural**, Batıder 1973, 11, 39; **Topuz/Canbolat**, AÜHFD 2008, 673, 680; **Eren**, p. 999.

character/nature, partial impossibility may occur.[24] For instance, suppose that the owner of an antique shop sells four handmade ancient chairs. One of the chairs is destroyed before the date of delivery. However, the debtor is able to deliver the remaining three chairs. Here it must be accepted that performance has become partially impossible because the three remaining chairs would still have some function without the fourth chair. However, if the subject of the same contract was delivery of one single antique chair and one of the legs of the chair was irreparably broken, this would cause total impossibility. In such case, the obligation would be physically indivisible because a chair with three legs would not function.

Divisibility of the subject of the obligation must be also evaluated in accordance with the wills of the parties because in the contract the parties may accept that a physically divisible obligation cannot be partially performed. For instance, the parties may explicitly decide in the contract that partial performance would not be accepted. In such case, even if the performance is divisible in nature, the will of the parties prevents partial performance. When there is no express provision in the contract, the hypothetical intentions of the parties must be investigated. Accordingly, it must be asked whether the parties would still conclude the contract should they be aware of partial impossibility at the time of contract formation.[25]

In cases where there is no such provision in the contract, the purpose of the contract must be considered. Accordingly, if the expectations of the parties can only be satisfied by full performance, partial impossibility would be unaccepted. For instance, in a sales contract the parties agree upon the sale and delivery of an encyclopedia composed of ten volumes. However, the last volume is damaged and the debtor can only deliver the first nine volumes. In such case, it must be accepted that there is total impossibility. In fact, as a reference material, the set of encyclopedia would lose its function without the last volume.

The final issue, which must be considered with regard to the distinction of total and partial impossibility is performance at a time and/or place different from what is specified in the contract. Accordingly, it must be answered if such cases constitute impossibility. It would be appropriate to accept that neither of the cases constitutes partial impossibility because impossibility only occurs with regard to the subject of the obligation. However, place and time of performance are outside the subject of the obligation. This being the fact, sometimes the time and/or place of performance may exceptionally become essential components of the obligation. For instance, suppose that a landowner executes a contract with a contractor for construction of a building on his property. However, after the formation of the contract, the state decides to expropriate the land. The expropriation of the land renders performance of the contract impossible because in this example the place of performance has become an essential component of performance.[26]

---

[24] **Eren**, p. 999; **Topuz/Canbolat**, AÜHFD 2008, 673, 680; **Altunkaya**, p. 128.

[25] **Bucher**, p. 243.

[26] **Dural**, Batıder 1973, 11, 40.

A similar approach is also attainable regarding the time of performance. In principle, non-performance on the definite due date (Fixgeschäft) agreed upon by the parties causes default, not impossibility. However, in some cases, non-performance on the definite due date may cause impossibility. Here a distinction has to be made between relative definite due dates (relatives Fixgeschäft), and absolute definite due dates (absolutes Fixgeschäft). In relative definite due dates, the performance of the obligation after the definite due date still satisfies the creditor. Therefore in such cases late performance constitutes default.[27] However, in absolute definite due dates, time of performance becomes an essential component of the obligation. Therefore, non-performance at the specified time causes impossibility.[28] For instance, suppose that a couple signs a contract with a famous musician to perform at their wedding. However, the musician is hit by a car in the morning of the wedding and cannot perform on the date specified in the contract. In this case the couple cannot be expected to accept performance after their wedding date. In such cases, time of performance is an essential component of the obligation and it must be accepted that the performance is impossible.

Similarly it is argued that in continuous contractual relationships non-performance at the time fixed in the contract constitutes impossibility. In fact, in such cases, it is not possible to reverse the time and have the performance made at that specific time.[29] However, if there is possibility of performance at another date, this constitutes default.[30] For instance, suppose that the seller undertakes to deliver 10 kilos of flour to a bakery. The term of the contract is 6 months and the delivery will take place on Monday morning each week. If the seller fails to deliver flour at the sixth Monday it should be accepted that there is default. As a matter of fact delivery can be made on the next day.

Within this scope, it must be underlined that in cases, where the time or place of performance has become an essential component of the obligation, impossibility is not partial but total. In fact, an obligation, which has not been performed at the date and/or place specified in the contract cannot be performed at another date and/or place. In other words, in cases where the date and/or place of the obligation is an essential component of the contract, performance at a different date and/or place does not constitute performance of the said specific obligation, not even partially.[31]

The distinction of partial and total impossibility is recognized under the German and Swiss—as well as Turkish—laws. Although there is no explicit provision in Unification Instruments, it is accepted that a distinction must be made between the two groups of cases and if the impediment impairs only part of the agreed performance, the promisor may rely on the *force majeure* provision of the relevant Unification Instrument. Such distinction is useful because depending on the circumstances of the

[27] **Altunkaya**, p. 112; **Dural**, Batıder 1973, 11, 48.

[28] **Dural**, Batıder 1973, 11, 42 ff.; **Tekinay**, p. 637. **Eren**, p. 998.

[29] **Eren**, p. 999.

[30] **Altunkaya**, p. 126; **Eren**, p. 999; **Dural**, Batıder 1973, 11, 105.

[31] **Dural**, Batıder 1973, 11, 42.

case, the creditor may have interest in partial performance. However, it must be noted that the described attempt of making a distinction between partial and total impossibility is actually a reasonableness test. Accordingly, divisibility of the subject of the obligation, expectations of the parties, the time and place of performance would serve as elements in determining if there is impossibility in accordance with the reasonableness test. Therefore, ideally, it would be appropriate to use the reasonableness test to determine the extent of impossibility.

IV) Permanent Impossibility – Temporary Impossibility

Another distinction regarding the types of impossibility is permanent impossibility and temporary impossibility. Such classification depends on whether or not impossibility is of a temporary nature.[32] Accordingly, if the events which render performance impossible are permanent and if they eliminate the possibility of performance at another time, this constitutes permanent impossibility.[33] Permanent impossibility cannot disappear by passing of time.[34] However, in cases where the events that render performance impossible may disappear in the future, this constitutes temporary impossibility.[35]

The distinction between the two concepts can be explained by reference to the previously given examples. For instance, in the above stated examples, where the sold horse died or a specific painting of an artist was torn into pieces, performance is permanently impossible. In both cases there is no chance that performance will become possible by the passing of time. On the other hand, suppose that in the above stated example, where the jeweler sent a ring to the buyer by plane, the plane did not crash but it could not fly at all for a week due to bad weather conditions. In such case, the obligation cannot be performed only temporarily because the jeweler can perform his obligation when the weather conditions get better. This constitutes temporary impossibility.

Temporary impossibility might lead to total or partial impossibility. For instance, in a lease contract if one floor of a two-storey immovable gets damaged in a fire, and the repair will take one week, it may be argued that there is temporary impossibility because the landlord will be able to fulfill his obligation arising from the contract at the end of seven days. Since only the first floor of the immovable cannot be used by the tenant this would constitute partial impossibility.

It is accepted under German and Swiss—as well as Turkish—legal systems that if temporary impossibility prevents the accomplishment of the purpose of the

---

[32] **Kotzur**, p. 209.

[33] **Barth**, p. 40; **Dural**, Batıder 1973, 11, 45; **Topuz/Canbolat**, AÜHFD 2008, 673, 679.

[34] **Barth**, p. 40; **Altunkaya**, p. 119; **Topuz/Canbolat**, AÜHFD 2008, 673, 679.

[35] **Bucher**, p. 420; **von Tuhr/Escher**, p. 96; **Altunkaya**, p. 120; **Topuz/Canbolat**, AÜHFD 2008, 673, 679; **Eren**, p. 999; **Dural**, Batıder 1973, 11, 45.

contract this must be considered as permanent impossibility. The same result applies if the time of disappearance of temporary impossibility cannot be foreseen.[36] However, this should also be required by the principle of good faith. For instance, if performance is urgent and the purpose of the contract is threatened by waiting until performance becomes possible, the creditor cannot be expected to wait until the disappearance of the temporary impossibility.[37] Moreover, it is asserted that in continuous contractual relationships, if temporary impossibility continues during the entire term of the contract there is permanent impossibility.[38] For instance, in the above example of fire, suppose that the fire breaks out in the 8th month of a 1-year-termed contract and the repair will take 4 months. It is argued that in such cases there is permanent impossibility.

It must be accepted that temporary impossibility is not impossibility in the technical sense, because the concept of impossibility has a permanent and definite nature.[39] Within this stance, if an event which prevents performance is temporary, this causes default, not impossibility.[40] However, since the debtor cannot be expected to perform during such time, claims of performance and compensation are unavailable to the creditor. In fact, this is the result recognized by Unification Instruments as well. As explained above, temporal factors cause impossibility, only if the date of performance has become an essential component of the obligation. However, it must be underlined that even in such cases impossibility is permanent in nature.

Difference between temporary and permanent impossibility is recognized in German and Turkish doctrines and by the courts. However, ideally, as in the case of practical and moral impossibility as well as objective-subjective impossibility and partial-total impossibility distinctions here reference should be made to a case-by-case analysis based on the reasonableness test. Such test would show that there is impossibility to perform for the musician after the wedding date. Similarly, in the above stated examples of fire, it would be accepted that there is impossibility.

It might occur that any performance, which is deemed as permanently impossible is later on found out to be temporarily impossible. For instance, an obligation, which is impossible to perform in today's technology, may be performed in the future as a result of technological developments. In such cases, will the obligation which has been extinguished due to impossibility automatically reappear in the future? Otherwise, in such case will the parties be under the obligation to reestablish the same contractual relationship?[41] Larenz evaluates the issue under two headings. According to the author, in contractual relationships, which create unilateral obligation for one party (the debtor) only, if it is understood that performance is not prevented permanently, the debtor must

[36] **Zürcher/Oser/Schönenberger**, Art. 119, N. 13; **Eren**, p. 998; **Barth**, p. 42; **von Tuhr/Escher**, p. 96–97; **Oğuzman/Öz**, p. 305; **Bingöl**, p. 220; **İnan**, Unmöglichkeit, p. 36.

[37] **Dural**, Batıder 1973, 11, 101; **Serozan**, § 14, Nr. 2.

[38] **Altunkaya**, p. 126; **Eren**, p. 999; **Dural**, p. 105.

[39] **Buz**, AÜSBFD 1994, 23, 24; **Eren**, p. 998; **Barth** p. 40; **von Tuhr/Escher**, p. 96.

[40] **Altunkaya**, p. 120; **Eren**, p. 998; **Tekinay**, p. 636; **Serozan**, § 14, Nr. 2.

[41] **Dural**, Batıder 1973, 11, 51.

deliver the subject matter of the contract to the creditor, when impossibility appears to be temporary. However, in contracts which create bilateral obligations, the author proposes a different solution. In such cases, the parties rightfully assume that their bilateral obligations have been extinguished and they act accordingly. In other words, none of the parties can be expected to be bound with the contract forever.[42] Within this stance, expecting the parties to reestablish the same contractual relationship would destroy especially the creditor's freedom to act. Otherwise, the creditor would have to assume that one day the debtor's performance may become possible and he may have to perform the counter-obligation as set forth in the contract as well. Therefore, in such cases the parties would not be under the obligation to reestablish the same contractual relationship.[43]

V) Initial Impossibility – Subsequent Impossibility

The last distinction between the types of impossibility is initial and subsequent impossibility. This distinction is based on the time of occurrence of the event which renders the performance of the obligation impossible. The importance of this distinction is that in some legal systems, including Swiss and Turkish laws initial impossibility causes the contract to be void. Within this stance, also in the former BGB initial impossibility was regulated as a reason of voidness.

The moment to be considered while evaluating if there is initial impossibility or subsequent impossibility is debatable under OR and TCO, which give no clue regarding the issue.[44] Accordingly, it may be argued that, in Swiss and Turkish laws, the moment, which should be taken into consideration is the time of performance. In accordance with such opinion if performance, which was impossible at the time of the contract formation, becomes possible at the time of performance, provisions of impossibility would not apply.[45]

According to the second and prevailing opinion in Swiss and Turkish laws, the moment to be considered while evaluating if there is initial impossibility or subsequent impossibility is the time of contract formation. This is the rule accepted under the BGB (§ 311a BGB) and Unification Instruments[46] as well. Within this context, initial impossibility means that performance of the obligation was already

[42] **Larenz**, p. 308.

[43] However such freedom of the parties is restricted by the principle of good faith. In case of existence of an important interest and if it can be expected from the counter party to reestablish the contract, the parties may be under the obligation to re-execute the same contract. **Dural**, Batıder 1973, 11, 51; **Larenz**, p. 308.

[44] **Rabel**, p. 47.

[45] **Altunkaya**, p. 102; **Dural**, Batıder 1973, 11, 26.

[46] PICC, PECL and DCFR have express provisions, which refer to the time of conclusion of the contract. Despite the lack of any provision in CISG and CESL, which regulate the effects of initial impossibility on the validity of the contract, a similar approach is attainable.

impossible at the time of contract formation.[47] On the other hand, if an obligation could be performed at the time of contract formation, but it becomes permanently and definitely impossible later on, this constitutes subsequent impossibility.[48]

In conditional contracts, if impossibility was already present at the time of contract formation, this constitutes initial impossibility.[49] On the other hand, in some cases impossibility of the realization of the condition takes place after the formation of the contract. In such cases, if the contract is subject to a condition subsequent, the impossibility is accepted to be subsequent. In fact, prior to the impossibility of the condition subsequent, the contract has been already formed and it has started to create legal results. Similarly, in cases where the contract is subject to a condition precedent, impossibility which arises after formation of the contract is deemed as subsequent impossibility. This opinion is consistent with the idea that the moment to be considered while evaluating whether there is initial or subsequent impossibility is the time of contract formation. Accordingly a contractual relationship has been successfully established between the parties, since the condition was not impossible at the time of contract formation. After this moment, an impossibility of realization of the condition may only cause subsequent impossibility. A similar approach is possible in transactions that are subject to consent or permission. In such contracts, if the consent/permission is not given after formation of the contract, this cannot be regarded as initial impossibility.[50]

In Swiss and Turkish laws initial impossibility is still regarded as a reason to void a contract. However, such distinction is based on coincidence. Hence it is inappropriate. The lawmakers have designated different legal results for cases of performance impossibility that occurs one second before the formation of the contract and one second after the formation of the contract.

The chronological distinction is an unfortunate remainder of Roman law and *impossibilium nulla obligation est* doctrine of Mommsen.[51] In fact, the chronological distinction does not lead to a logical distinction. More specifically, occurrence of impossibility one second before or after the formation of the contract creates different legal results. There is no legal argument to justify such different results attributed to chronological factor.

The distinction of initial and subsequent impossibility is not recognized in Unification Instruments. During the 2002 reform, such distinction was abolished from BGB as well. German lawmakers have preserved such distinction only with regard to compensation claims. More precisely, the German lawmakers have

---

[47] **Brox/Walker**, § 22, Nr. 10; **Huguenin**, Nr. 394; **Keller/Schöbi**, p. 79; **Fikentscher/Heinemann**, § 42 III 2, Nr. 375; **Larenz**, p. 98; **Zürcher/Oser/Schönenberger**, Art. 20, N. 3; **Gauch/Schluep**, Band I, Nr. 633; **Traub**, p. 1; **Kälin**, recht 2004, 246, 247; **Altunkaya**, p. 102–103; **Topuz/Canbolat**, p. 678; **Bucher**, p. 247; **Barth**, p. 32; **Dural**, Batıder 1973, 11, 25.

[48] **Zürcher/Oser/Schönenberger**, Art. 20, N. 3; **Altunkaya**, p. 105; **Buz**, AÜSBFD 1994, 23, 23; **Dural**, Batıder 1973, 11, 25.

[49] **Altunkaya**, p. 108.

[50] **Altunkaya**, p. 110; **Dural**, Batıder 1973, 11, 27.

[51] **Serozan**, § 14, Nr. 18.

differentiated the compensation requirements for initial impossibility and subsequent impossibility.

Under the light of above explanations, *de lege feranda*, cases of initial and subsequent impossibility must not be subject to different legal results. However, in civil law systems the distinction of initial and subsequent impossibility is compulsory with regard to the compensation claims. More specifically, civil law countries have accepted fault-liability. In case of subsequent impossibility fault emerges if the debtor causes impossibility. However, in case of initial impossibility fault emerges, if the debtor concludes the contract despite his awareness of the initial impossibility. Such difference is rightfully acknowledged even in the German system, which accepts that initial impossibility does not cause the contract to be void. Therefore, German lawmakers had to require in § 311a BGB that "*if the obligor was not aware of the obstacle to performance when entering into the contract and is also not responsible for his lack of awareness*" compensation cannot be claimed. However, it is a successful preference of the German lawmakers that there is no difference between the scopes of compensation in cases of initial and subsequent impossibility. In any case, the debtor is entitled to his positive interest. On the other hand, the distinction of initial and subsequent impossibility is totally insignificant for Unification Instruments, which accept strict-liability. In fact, in such systems it is important whether the debtor performs or not. A breach of obligation exists as long as the debtor does not perform. Therefore, the time of occurrence of impossibility has no effect on the compensation claim under Unification Instruments.

References

Akıntürk, Turgut: Satım Akdinde Hasarın İntikali, Sevinç, Ankara 1966.

Akıntürk, Turgut: Borçlar Hukuku – Genel Hükümler – Özel Borç İlişkileri, Sevinç, Ankara 1986. (Cited as: Akıntürk, Borçlar)

Altunkaya, Mehmet: Edimin Başlangıçtaki İmkansızlığı, Yetkin, Ankara 2005.

Barth, Hans Rudolf: Schadenersatz bei nachträglicher Unmöglichkeit der Erfüllung, Verlag H.R. Sauerländer and Co., Aarau 1958.

Becker, Hermann: Berner Kommentar, Kommentar zum Schweizerisches Zivilgesetzbuch, Band VI, Obligationenrecht, 1. Abteilung, Allgemeine Bestimmungen, Art. 1–183 OR, Stämpfli and Cie, Bern 1945. (Cited as: Berner/Becker)

Bingöl, F. Itır: Uluslararası Ticari Satım Sözleşmelerinde Mücbir Sebep (Türk Borçlar Hukuku'nda ve Viyana Satım Antlaşması'nda Mücbir Sebep), Yetkin, Ankara 2011.

Bozer, Ali: Borçlar Hukuku (Genel Hükümler), Dayınlarlı, Ankara 2002.

Brox, Hans/Walker, Wolf-Dietrich: Allgemeines Schuldrecht, C.H. Beck, München 2009.

Brunner, Christoph: Force majeure and Hardship Excuse Under General Contract Principles, Wolters Kluwer, Alphen aan den Rijn 2009.

Bucher, Eugene: Schweizerisches Obligationenrecht, Allgemeiner Teil, Schulthess, Zürich 1988. (Cited as: Bucher)

Buz, Vedat: Eser Sözleşmesinde Müteahhidin Eseri Tamamlama Borcunun İmkansızlaşması, AÜSBFD, Vol. 49, No. 1–2, 1994, pp. 23–40.

Canaris, Claus-Wilhelm: Die Reform des Rechts der Leistungsstörungen, JZ, 2001, pp. 499–524. (Also available at: <http://uni-leipzig de/wirtschaftsrecht/alt/dokumente/reform.pdf>).

Coendet, Thomas: Subjektive Unmöglichkeit als regulatives Prinzip: über die Funktion der subjektiven. Leistungsunmöglichkeit als notwendiges systematisches Regulativ gegenüber dem Schuldnerverzug, recht 2009, pp. 128–132.

Dural, Mustafa: İmkansızlık Kavramı ve Türleri, Batıder, Vol. 7, No. 1, 1973, pp. 11–58.

Eckert, Jörn: Schuldrecht, Allgemeiner Teil, Nomos, Baden-Baden 2003.

Eren, Fikret: Borçlar Hukuku Genel Hükümler, Beta, İstanbul 2006.

Esser, Josef/Schmidt, Eike: Schuldrechts, Band I, Allgemeiner Teil, C.F. Müller, Heidelberg 1984.

Fehre, Andrea: Unmöglichkeit und Unzumutbarkeit der Leistung, Voraussetzungen und Rechtsfolgen nach Inkrafttreten des Schuldrechtsmodernisierungsgesetzes, Duncker & Humblot, Berlin 2005.

Fikentscher, Wolfgang/Heinemann, Andreas: Schuldrecht, De Gruyter Recht, Berlin 2006.

Finn, Markus: Erfüllungspflicht und Leistungshindernis, die Bestimmung der Grenzen vertraglicher Primärpflichten nach §§ 275 Abs. 1 und 2, 313 BGB, Duncker & Humblot, Berlin 2007.

Fischer, Hans Albrecht: Vis major im Zusammenhang mit Unmöglichkeit der Leistung, JJ, Vol. 137, No. 1, 1897, pp. 199–300.

Fischer, Hans Albrecht: Ein Beitrag zur Unmöglichkeitslehre, Warkentien, Rostock 1904. (Cited as: Fischer, Beitrag)

Fischer, Nicole N.: Die Unmöglichkeit der Leistung im internationalen Kauf- und Vertragsrecht, Duncker & Humblot, Berlin 2001. (Cited as: Fischer)

Gauch, Peter/Schluep, Walter R.: Schweizerisches Obligationenrecht, Allgemeiner Teil, Band I, Schulthess, Zürich/Basel/Genf 2008. (Cited as: Gauch/Schluep, Band I)

Gauch, Peter/Schluep, Walter R.: Schweizerisches Obligationenrecht, Allgemeiner Teil, Band II, Schulthess, Zürich/Basel/Genf 2008. (Cited as: Gauch/Schluep, Band II)

Giger, Marcel: Die vom Gläubiger verschuldete Leistungsunmöglichkeit, Haupt, Bern 1992.

Hirsch, Christoph: Allgemeines Schuldrecht, Carl Heymanns Verlag, Köln 2009.

Honsell, Heinrich/Vogt, Nedim Peter/Wiegand, Wolfgang: Basler Kommentar zum Schweizerischen Privatrecht, Obligationenrecht I, Art. 1–529 OR, Helbing and Lichtenhahn, Basel/Genf/München 2003. (Cited as: Basler/Author)

Huguenin, Claire: Obligationenrecht, Allgemeiner Teil, Schulthess, Zürich/Basel/Genf 2006.

Hütte, Felix/Helbron, Marlena: Schuldrecht, Allgemeiner Teil, Verlag Dr. Rolf Schmidt, Grasberg bei Bremen 2005.

İnan, Ali Naim: Unmöglichkeit der Leistung im Deutschen, Schweizerischen und Türkischen Recht, Dissertation, Breisgau 1956. (Cited as: İnan, Unmöglichkeit)

İnan, Ali Naim: Bankacılar İçin Borçlar Hukuku Bilgisi, Banka ve Ticaret Hukuku Araştırma Enstitüsü, Ankara 1997. (Cited as: İnan, Bankacılar)

Jakobs, Horst Heinrich: Unmöglichkeit und Nichterfüllung, Ludwig Röhrscheid, Bonn 1969.

Joeinig, Elke: Die anfängliche Unmöglichkeit, Verlag Österreich, Wien 2006.

Kälin, Oliver: Unmöglichkeit der Leistung nach Art. 119 OR und clausula rebus sic stantibus, recht 2004, pp. 246–256.

Keller, Max/Schöbi, Christian: Allgemeine Lehren des Vertragsrecht, Band I, Helbing and Lichtenhahn, Basel/Frankfurt am Main 1982.

Kisch, Wilhelm: Die Wirkungen der nachträglich eintretenden Unmöglichkeit der Erfüllung bei gegenseitigen Verträgen nach dem Bürgerlichen Gesetzbuche für das Deutsche Reich, Fischer, Jena 1900.

Koller, Alfred: Schweizerisches Obligationenrecht, Allgemeiner Teil, Handbuch des allgemeinen Schuldrechts, Stämpfli, Bern 2009. (Cited as: Koller)

Kornfeld, Felix: Leistungsunmöglichkeit, Manzchen, Wien 1913.

Kotzur, Wolfgang: Die Auswirkungen von außergewöhnlichen Ereignissen auf vertragliche Schuldverhältnisse - Eine vergleichende Untersuchung zum deutschen und englischen Recht, Peter Lang, Frankfurt am Main 2001.

Larenz, Karl: Lehrbuch des Schuldrechts, Band I, Allgemeiner Teil, C.H. Beck'schen Buchdruckerei Nördlingen, München 1987. (Cited as: Larenz)

Markesinis, Sir Basil/Unberath, Hannes/Johnston, Angus: The German Law of Contract, A Comparative Treatise, Hart, Oregon 2006.

Mitzkait, Anika: Leistungsstörung und Haftungsbefreiung, Mohr Siebeck, Tübingen 2008.
Oğuzman, Kemal/Öz, Turgut: Borçlar Hukuku Genel Hükümler, Filiz, İstanbul 2000.
Oser, Hugo/Schönenberger, Wilhelm: Kommentar zum Schweizerischen Zivilgesetzbuch, Das Obligationenrecht, Erster Halbband: Art. 1–183, Schulthess, Zürich 1929. (Cited as: Zürcher/Oser/Schönenberger)
Palandt, Otto: Bürgerliches Gesetzbuch, C.H. Beck, München 2010. (Cited as: Palandt/Author)
Prütting, Hanns/Wegen, Gerhard/Weinreich, Gerd: BGB Kommentar, Luchterhand, Köln 2011. (Cited as: PWW/Author)
Rabel, Ernst: Unmöglichkeit der Leistung, Böhlau, Weimar 1907.
Rampini, Corrado: Die nachträgliche Leistungserschwerung, Haupt Verlag, Bern 2003.
Reisoğlu, Safa: Borçlar Hukuku Genel Hükümler, Beta, İstanbul 1998
Säcker, Franz Jürgen/Rixecke, Roland: Münchener Kommentar zum Bürgerlichen Gesetzbuch, Band 2, Schuldrecht, Allgemeiner Teil §§ 241–432, C.H. Beck, München 2012. (Cited as: MüKo)
Schwarze, Roland: Das Recht der Leistungsstörungen, de Gruyter, Berlin 2008.
Schwenzer, Ingeborg: Schweizerisches Obligationenrecht Allgemeiner Teil, Stämpfli, Bern 2006. (Cited as: Schwenzer, Obligationenrecht)
Serozan, Rona: Borçlar Hukuku Genel Bölüm Üçüncü Cilt - İfa, İfa Engelleri, Haksız Zenginleşme, Filiz, İstanbul 2006. (Cited as: Serozan)
Staudinger, Julius von: Kommentar zum Bürgerlichen Gesetzbuch mit Einführungsgesetz und Nebengesetzen, Buch 2, Recht der Schuldverhältnisse, §§ 255–304, (Leistungsstörungsrecht 1), Neuarbeitung 2009, Sellier de Gruyter, Berlin 2009. (Cited as: Staudinger/Author)
Staudinger, Julius von: Kommentar zum Bürgerlichen Gesetzbuch mit Einführungsgesetz und Nebengesetzen, Buch 2, Recht der Schuldverhältnisse, §§ 315–326, (Leistungsstörungsrecht 2), Neuarbeitung 2009, Sellier de Gruyter, Berlin 2009. (Cited as: Staudinger/Author)
Tekinay, Sulhi Selahattin: Borçlar Hukuku, Fakülteler Matbaası, İstanbul 1973.
Titze, Heinrich: Die Unmöglichkeit der Leistung nach deutschem bürgerlichen Recht, Titze, Leipzig 1900.
Topuz, Seçkin/Canbolat, Ferhat: Türk - İsviçre ve Alman Borçlar Hukukunda İmkansızlığın Düzenlenişi, AÜHFD, Vol. 57, No. 3, 2008, pp. 673–718.
Traub, Thomas: Das Allgemeine Leistungsstörungsrecht Des Bürgerlichen Gesetzbuches, Grin, Norderstedt 2001.
Tunçomağ, Kenan: Borçlar Hukuku, I. Cild, Genel Hükümler, Fakülteler Matbaası, İstanbul 1972.
Uygur, Turgut: Açıklamalı – İçtihatlı Borçlar Kanunu, Sorumluluk ve Tazminat Hukuku, Giriş ve Madde 1–40, Cilt I, Seçkin, Ankara 2003.
von Büren, Bruno: Schweizerisches Obligationenrecht, Allgemeiner Teil, Schulthess, Zürich 1964.
von Tuhr, Andreas/Escher, Arnold: Allgemeiner Teil des Schweizerischen Obligationenrechts, Band II, Schulthess Polygraphischer Verlag AG, Zürich 1974.
Westermann, Harm Peter/Bydlinski, Peter/Weber, Ralph: BGB-Schuldrecht Allgemeiner Teil, C.F. Müller, Heidelberg 2010.
Witthaus, Dieter: Störungen im Schuldverhältnis, Brockmeyer, Bochum 1986.
Zimmer, Daniel: Das neue Recht der Leistungsstörungen, NJW 2002, pp. 1–12.

Part IV
Final Conclusions

8) The Use of Impossibility as a Dogmatic Concept

1. Unification Instruments regulate non-performance in general, with no special consideration for impossibility. On the other hand, German, Swiss and Turkish laws use impossibility as a dogmatic concept. Therefore, German and Turkish laws appear to be exceptions to the modern legal trend.
2. The notion of impediment has a wider scope than the concept of impossibility. In civil law system, impossibility in the technical sense refers to an obstacle, which permanently prevents the execution of performance. Unlike impossibility, impediment refers to an obstacle, that causes either impossibility, default or defective performance. As a result, the abandonment of impossibility by Unification Instruments is not as significant as it might seem at first because cases of impossibility constitute a sub-category within exemption provisions of Unification Instruments, which refer to the notion of "impediment".
3. Unification Instruments have referred to the notion of impediment. This is aimed to prevent recourse to domestic law, which could arise by using terms such as impossibility, *force majeure* or frustration. However, such preference of the drafters has resulted in confusion, given that there is no consensus within the international arena regarding the scope of impediment. Moreover, this has caused a tendency to interpret the term very narrowly.
4. The civil law countries, including Germany, Switzerland and Turkey have recognized the primary claim and secondary claim distinction in case of non-performance. In such cases, the primary remedy of the creditor is performance. Therefore, it is appropriate that in such systems fault-liability is recognized to claim the secondary remedy. On the other hand, in common law countries, where the primary remedy is damages, strict liability works "*as a legal underpinning of the contract*." Unification Instruments have not followed the remedy scheme of either of the two systems, but reserved specific performance as *any* remedy available to the creditor. Within this stance, lack of a primary-secondary claim distinction still requires adoption of strict liability principle to "underpin" the contract. In fact, in international trade, the damages

H.C. Aksoy, *Impossibility in Modern Private Law*, DOI 10.1007/978-3-319-01704-4_8,

will almost always be the first remedy resorted to by the aggrieved party. Strict-liability serves to the benefit of the creditor, who claims his damages.

5. An exemption provision is a broader and more flexible rule in comparison to a clear-cut impossibility rule. It releases the debtor from liability not only in case of impossibility, but also in any type of breach, which cannot be foreseen, overcome or avoided. As a result, such broad rule is more functional in terms of bringing an exception to strict-liability principle and elasticizing it. Moreover, since Unification Instruments adopt the unified form of non-performance with no distinction between the types of breaches, it is fully consistent and sensible that—rather than a clear-cut impossibility rule—they set one single exemption provision for all types of breaches. Accordingly, under Unification Instruments—like any other type of breach—performance impossibility may either result in the debtor's obligation to compensate the damages of the creditor, or the debtor may be released from his liability, provided that the conditions of the exemption/*force majeure* clauses are met. Therefore it is also sensible that Unification Instruments have accepted an exemption provision with a broad scope, rather than a clear-cut impossibility rule. However, in civil law countries, the issue of liability (secondary claim) is already solved under the fault principle. Therefore a clear-cut impossibility rule is required to determine when primary claim cannot be asked because of impossibility. Hence in Germany, Switzerland and Turkey, a clear-cut impossibility rule may be more appropriate to determine the cases, where the primary claim is extinguished. This being the fact, it may certainly be argued that the distinction between the approaches of common law and civil law does not lead to significantly different results in practice.

9) Different Types and Scope of Impossibility

1. Following Mommsen's study, civil lawyers have a tendency to classify the types of non-performance and their sub-categories. However, these can never be classified in a way to cover all specific cases. Therefore, ideally impossibility must be determined by a *reasonableness test*. Within this stance, in each specific case it must be investigated **if performance cannot reasonably be expected under the circumstances of the specific case.**
2. Reasonableness is a parameter of Unification Instruments. The foreseeability and avoidability criteria are based on an evaluation of reasonableness. Nevertheless such test is not unfamiliar to the civil law's legal thinking. Such test eliminates the discussions regarding the scope of logical impossibility, as well as the distinctions of objective-subjective impossibility, partial-total impossibility and temporary-permanent impossibility. Moreover, when such perspective is taken, it becomes obvious that the impossibility regimes of civil law and Unification Instruments are quite similar to each other.
3. Civil lawyers may be critical about extending the discretion of the judge through reasonableness test. However, the reasonableness test is not less concrete than the principle of good-faith, which the civil law judges already apply. Therefore there is no reason to be afraid of the elasticity of the reasonableness test and the power it grants to the judge. Moreover, it would not be wrong to argue that case law is having an increasingly more importance in civil law countries. Hence the role of the judge is increasing in civil law countries as well.
4. After the reform of 2002, BGB has accepted that § 275 I BGB applies to any kind of impossibility with no distinction of objective-subjective impossibility, the impossibility for which the debtor is responsible or not, and initial-subsequent impossibility. As a result, it has become closer to Unification Instruments. However, Swiss and Turkish laws still fall behind the modern legal trend in this regard.
5. Physical impossibility, practical impossibility, legal impossibility and accomplishment and destruction of purpose are included in the ideal scope of impossibility. However, interference with the basis of the transaction (hardship) is not

H.C. Aksoy, *Impossibility in Modern Private Law*, DOI 10.1007/978-3-319-01704-4_9,

included in the ideal scope of impossibility. More specifically, unlike practical impossibility, in the case of interference with the basis of the transaction there is no disproportion between the interests of the parties in performance. Such difference is very important that it affects the result of the reasonableness test. In fact, when there is a disproportion, the debtor cannot be expected to perform *at all*. On the other hand, when there is no such disproportion, it would be more difficult to accept that the debtor cannot be expected to perform at all. In such cases, reasonableness test would say that the debtor cannot be expected to perform *as undertaken* in the contract.

6. In civil law systems the distinction of initial and subsequent impossibility is compulsory with regard to compensation claims only. In fact, civil law systems have accepted fault-liability and the appearance of fault differs in cases of initial and subjective impossibility. Therefore, German lawmakers have successfully differentiated the compensation requirements for initial impossibility and subsequent impossibility.
7. The impediment beyond control criterion of Unification Instruments is open to broad interpretation. This is a positive feature of the exemption regime of Unification Instruments. Together with the reasonableness test, such a broad criterion may be very useful to decide if the debtor would be exempt from liability in each specific case. However, it is seen that the courts have a tendency to interpret the concept narrowly. In fact, impediment beyond control is regarded as an objective circumstance, which is external to the debtor. As a result, in comparison to civil law it becomes very difficult for the debtor to be exempt from liability. This may be explained by the fact that Unification Instruments have recognized strict-liability and there is a tendency to narrowly interpret the exception to such rule.

10) Legal Results of Impossibility

1. Although Unification Instruments have not recognized the distinction of primary and secondary claims, they have accepted that specific performance cannot be required in case of impossibility. This is a result of the law of nature. Therefore, once impossibility is determined the matter to be discussed under BGB, OR, TCO and Unification Instruments is whether there will be compensation of damages. Within this stance, civil lawyers will make an assessment of fault, but under Unification Instruments it will be assessed if there is an exception to the strict-liability of the debtor.
2. Swiss law has recognized initial impossibility as a reason to void the contract; hence such principle has been adopted by TCO. Ironically enough, in the reasoning of the new TCO, it is emphasized that the tendencies of Unification Instruments were considered. However, based on the outdated classification of Roman law and Mommsen, in Turkish law, initial impossibility causes the contract to be void. The best solution to overcome the unfair results of initial impossibility would be elimination of the chronological distinction from the law.
3. There must be no differences between the results, especially liability regimes of initial and subsequent impossibility. Under Swiss and Turkish laws, which rule that initial impossibility causes voidness of the contract, the creditor may only have his negative damages compensated. Within this scope, positive damages may only be requested in case of subsequent impossibility. However, there is no reason to maintain further protection to any debtor, who concludes a contract despite being aware that he cannot perform it due to initial impossibility, in comparison to another debtor, who cannot perform because he is responsible for the subsequent impossibility. After the 2002 reform of BGB, the creditor is entitled to positive damages in all cases of impossibility without a time-based distinction. Such rule is also in conformity with Unification Instruments, which do not distinguish between initial and subsequent impossibility and require the compensation of positive damages.
4. BGB explicitly mandates that in cases that performance has become impossible, if the debtor acquires substitutes such as compensation claim from a third party,

H.C. Aksoy, *Impossibility in Modern Private Law*, DOI 10.1007/978-3-319-01704-4_10,

or claim arising from insurance, these may be claimed by the creditor. However, there is no explicit provision in Swiss and Turkish laws or Unification Instruments that contemplates if the creditor is entitled to claim the surrogate benefits. The concerning provision of BGB is an upholding feature of the German law.

5. Unlike BGB or Unification Instruments, OR and TCO have not regulated the creditor's right to revoke/avoid the contract in case of impossibility. However, such right must be explicitly granted to the parties, who may not want to be bound with the contract depending on the features of the case. Therefore, in this respect OR and TCO fall behind BGB and Unification Instruments.
6. Notice requirement in case of impossibility is a result of the principle of good-faith. Despite being unwritten in BGB and OR, it must be accepted to be present in these legal systems as well. However, it is an upholding rule of TCO and Unification Instruments that they explicitly require notice of impossibility to the creditor and regulate the legal results of such failure.
7. Foreseeability criterion of Unification Instruments is based on the opinion of risk assumption. Within this stance, in cases where the debtor has undertaken to perform despite the foreseeability of impossibility, the debtor would be accepted to have assumed the risk of liability. This is also the case in civil law systems, including Germany, Switzerland and Turkey. In fact, such criterion resembles the causal link requirement of civil law.
8. The avoidability criterion of Unification Instruments—together with the beyond control criterion—to some extent corresponds to the fault requirement of the civil law systems. In fact, in civil law countries—including Germany, Switzerland and Turkey—if the debtor fails to avoid an impediment that he could avoid, this would be deemed as negligence.
9. Although Unification Instruments recognize strict-liability, but BGB, OR and TCO accept fault-liability, under Unification Instruments the debtor carries the burden of proof, so that he can be exempt from liability. Similarly, in case of non-performance, civil law also requires that the debtor proves the non-existence of his fault.

Bibliography

Achilles, Wilhelm-Albrecht: Kommentar zum UN-Kaufrechtsübereinkommen (CISG), Luchterhand, Neuwied 2000.

Ackermann, Thomas: Beyond Expectation? – An Assessment of the DCFR Rules on Contractual Damages, in: Wagner, Gerhard, The Common Frame of Reference: A View from Law & Economics, Sellier, München 2009, pp. 35 - 68.

Aepli, Viktor: Kommentar zum schweizerischen Zivilrecht (Zürcher Kommentar), Band. V/1h/1, Das Erlöschen der Obligationen, Art. 114 - 126 OR, Schulthess, Zürich 1991. (Cited as: Zürcher/Aepli)

Ahrens, Martin: Der mittellose Geldschuldner: Unmöglichkeit zur Leistung und Verzug des Zahlungsverpflichteten, Duncker & Humblot, Berlin 1994.

Akıntürk, Turgut: Satım Akdinde Hasarın İntikali, Sevinç, Ankara 1966.

Akıntürk, Turgut: Borçlar Hukuku – Genel Hükümler – Özel Borç İlişkileri, Sevinç, Ankara 1986. (Cited as: Akıntürk, Borçlar)

Aksoy, Hüseyin Can/Schäfer, Hans-Bernd: Economic impossibility in Turkish contract law from the perspective of law and economics, EJLE, Vol. 34, No.1, 2012, pp.105 - 126.

Altmeppen, Holger: Schadenersatz wegen Pflichtverletzung, anfängliche Unmöglichkeit und Aufwendungsersatz im Entwurf des Schuldrechtsmodernisierungsgesetzes, DB 2001, pp. 1821 - 1824.

Altmeppen, Holger: Schadenersatz wegen Pflichtverletzung – Ein Beispiel für die Überhastung der Schuldrechtsreform, DB 2001, pp. 1131 - 1133.

Altunkaya, Mehmet: Edimin Başlangıçtaki İmkansızlığı, Yetkin, Ankara 2005.

Arık, Kemal Fikret: Borçlar Hukuku I, Genel Hükümler, Balkanoğlu, Ankara 1964.

Arp, Torsten: Anfängliche Unmöglichkeit, Ferdinand Schöningh, Paderborn 1988.

Arsebük, Esat: Borçlar Hukuku, Güney, Ankara 1950.

Asendorf, Hermann: Unmöglichkeit und Unvermögen, Triltsch & Huther, Berlin 1936.

Atamer, Yeşim M: Uluslararası Satım Sözleşmelerine İlişkin Birleşmiş Milletler Antlaşması (CISG) Uyarınca Satıcının Yükümlülükleri ve Sözleşmeye Aykırılığın Sonuçları, Beta, İstanbul 2005. (Cited as: Atamer, Satıcının Yükümlülükleri)

Atamer, Yeşim M: Availability of Remedies other than Damages in Case of Exemption According to Art. 79 CISG, in: Büchler, Andrea/Müller-Chen, Markus, Festschrift für Ingeborg Schwenzer zum 60. Geburtstag, Stämpfli, Bern 2011, pp. 83 - 98. (Cited as: Atamer)

Bamberger, Heinz Georg/Roth, Herbert: Beck'scher Online-Kommentar, C.H. Beck, München 2012. (Cited as: BeckOK)

Bar, Christian von/Clive, Eric: Principles, definitions and model rules of European private law, Sellier, München 2009. (Cited as: DCFR Commentary)

Barta, Sebastian: BGB Allgemeines Schuldrecht, Grin, Norderstedt 2011.

H.C. Aksoy, *Impossibility in Modern Private Law*, DOI 10.1007/978-3-319-01704-4,

Barth, Hans Rudolf: Schadenersatz bei nachträglicher Unmöglichkeit der Erfüllung, Verlag H.R. Sauerländer and Co., Aarau 1958.

Basedow, Jürgen: Towards a Universal Doctrine of Breach of Contract: The Impact of the CISG, IRLE, Vol. 25, No. 3, 2005, pp. 487 - 500.

Başpınar, Veysel: Borç Sözleşmelerinin Kısmı Butlanı, Batıder, Ankara 1998.

Baumgartner, Stefanie: Contract formation under the CISG and under the UNIDROIT Principles: Contract Formation under the CISG and under the UNIDROIT Principles: Special Focus on the Issue of the Battle of the Forms, VDM Verlag Dr. Müller, Saarbrücken 2008.

Baysal, Başak: Sözleşmenin Uyarlanması, XII Levha, İstanbul 2009.

Becker, Hermann: Berner Kommentar, Kommentar zum Schweizerisches Zivilgesetzbuch, Band VI, Obligationenrecht, 1. Abteilung, Allgemeine Bestimmungen, Art. 1 - 183 OR, Stämpfli and Cie, Bern 1945. (Cited as: Berner/Becker)

Becker, Joachim Christian: Die Unmöglichkeitslehre im US-amerikanischen Vertragsrecht, Dissertation, Bonn 1972. (Cited as: Becker, Unmöglichkeitslehre)

Berckemeyer, Wolfgang: Die Behebung der Unmöglichkeit, Unger, Berlin 1930.

Berghoff, Erhard: Die Unmöglichkeit und ihre Rechtsfolgen nach dem BGB und dem einheitlichen Kaufrecht, Dissertation, Münster 1980.

Berki, Şakir: Borçlar Hukuku, Kitap I, Umumi Hükümler, Güzel Sanatlar, Ankara 1958.

Beuthien, Volker: Zweckerreichung und Zweckstörung im Schuldverhältnis, J.C.B. Mohr, Tübingen 1969.

Bianca, Cesare Massimo/Bonell, Michael Joachim: Commentary on the International Sales Law, Giuffrè, Mailand 1987. (Cited as: Author, in: Bianca/Bonell)

Bineva, Valentina: Change of Circumstances, in: Antoniolli, Luisa/Fiorentini, Francesa, A Factual Assessment of the Draft Common Frame of Reference, Sellier, München 2011, pp. 77 - 96.

Bingöl, F. Itır: Uluslararası Ticari Satım Sözleşmelerinde Mücbir Sebep (Türk Borçlar Hukuku'nda ve Viyana Satım Antlaşması'nda Mücbir Sebep), Yetkin, Ankara 2011.

Blank, Wladimir: Das allgemeine Leistungsstörungsrecht in Deutschland und in der Ukraine, Lit Verlag, Berlin 2009.

Bollenberger, Raimund: Das stellvertretende Commodum: die Ersatzherausgabe im österreichischen und deutschen Schuldrecht unter Berücksichtigung weiterer Rechtsordnungen, Springer, Wien 1999.

Bonell, Michael Joachim: A New Approach to International Commercial Contracts, The UNIDROIT Principles of International Commercial Contracts, Kluwer, Den Haag/Boston 1999. (Cited as: Bonell, A New Approach)

Bonell, Michael Joachim: Towards a Legislative Codification of the UNIDROIT Principles? ULR, Vol. 12, No. 2, 2007, pp. 233 - 246. (Cited as: Bonell)

Bozer, Ali: Borçlar Hukuku (Genel Hükümler), Dayınlarlı, Ankara 2002.

Brieskorn, Konstanze: Vertragshaftung und responsabilité contractuelle, Mohr Siebeck, Tübingen 2010.

Brox, Hans/Walker, Wolf-Dietrich: Allgemeines Schuldrecht, C.H. Beck, München 2009.

Brunner, Christoph: Force majeure and Hardship Excuse Under General Contract Principles, Wolters Kluwer, Alphen aan den Rijn 2009.

Bucher, Eugene: Schweizerisches Obligationenrecht, Allgemeiner Teil, Schulthess, Zürich 1988. (Cited as: Bucher)

Buz, Vedat: Eser Sözleşmesinde Müteahhidin Eseri Tamamlama Borcunun İmkansızlaşması, AÜSBFD, Vol. 49, No. 1 - 2, 1994, pp. 23 - 40.

Canaris, Claus-Wilhelm: Die Reform des Rechts der Leistungsstörungen, JZ, 2001, pp. 499 - 524. (Also available at: <http://uni-leipzig.de/wirtschaftsrecht/alt/dokumente/reform.pdf>).

Canaris, Claus-Wilhelm: Schadenersatz wegen Pflichtverletzung, anfängliche Unmöglichkeit und Aufwendungsersatz im Entwurf des Schuldrechtsmodernisierungsgesetzes, DB 2001, pp. 1815 - 1821.

Canaris, Claus-Wilhelm: Zur Bedeutung der Kategorie der "Unmöglichkeit" für das Recht der Leistungsstörungen, in: Schulze, Reiner /Schulte-Nölke, Hans, Die Schuldrechtsreform vor

dem Hintergrund des Gemeinschaftsrechts, Mohr Siebeck, Münster 2001, pp. 43 - 67. (Cited as: Canaris, Kategorie der Unmöglichkeit)
Canaris, Claus-Wilhelm: Schuldrechtsmodernisierung 2002, C.H. Beck, München 2002. (Cited as: Canaris, Schuldrechtsmodernisierung)
Canaris, Claus-Wilhelm: Die AGB-rechtliche Leitbildfunktion des neuen Leistungsstörungsrechts, in: Habersack, Mathias/Hommelhoff, Peter/Hüffer, Uwe/Schmidt, Karsten, Festschrift für Peter Ulmer, De Gruyter Recht, Berlin 2003, pp. 1073 - 1096. (Cited as: Canaris, AGB)
Canaris, Claus-Wilhelm: Die Neuregelung des Leistungsstörungs- und des Kaufrechts-Grundstrukturen und Problemschwerpunkte, in: Lorenz, Egon, Karlsruher Forum 2002: Schuldrechtsmodernisierung, Verlag Versicherungswirtschaft, Karlsruhe 2003, pp. 5 - 100. (Cited as: Canaris, Neuregelung)
Canaris, Claus-Wilhelm: Die Behandlung nicht zu vertretender Leistungshindernisse nach § 275 Abs. 2 BGB beim Stückkauf, JZ, 2004, pp. 214 - 255.
Canaris, Claus-Wilhelm: Grundlagen und Rechtsfolgen der Haftung für anfängliche Unmöglichkeit nach § 311a Abs. 2 BGB, in: Lorenz, Stephan/Trunk, Alexander/Eidenmüller, Horst/Wendehorst, Christiane/Adolff, Johannes, Festschrift für Andreas Heldrich, C.H. Beck, München 2005, pp. 12 - 38. (Cited as: Canaris, Grundlagen)
Canaris, Claus-Wilhelm: Die einstweilige Unmöglichkeit der Leistung, in: Baums, Theodor/ Huber, Ulrich/Wertenbruch, Johannes/Lutter, Marcus/Schmidt, Karsten, Festschrift Für Ulrich Huber Zum Siebzigsten Geburtstag, Mohr Siebeck, Tübingen 2006, pp. 144 - 164. (Cited as: Canaris, Die einstweilige Unmöglichkeit)
Cekovic-Vuletic, Simonida: Haftung wegen Unmöglichkeit nach dem Schuldrechtsmodernisierungsgesetz, C.H. Beck, München 2003
Cerutti, Romeo: Das U.S. amerikanische Warenkaufrecht, Schulthess, Zürich 1998.
CISG Advisory Council: CISG Advisory Council Opinion No.7, <http://www.cisg.law.pace.edu/cisg/CISG-AC-op7.html> (Cited as: CISG Advisory Council Opinion No. 7)
Coendet, Thomas: Subjektive Unmöglichkeit als regulatives Prinzip: über die Funktion der subjektiven. Leistungsunmöglichkeit als notwendiges systematisches Regulativ gegenüber dem Schuldnerverzug, recht 2009, pp. 128 - 132.
Däubler, Wolfgang: Die vorübergehende Unmöglichkeit der Leistung, in: Lorenz, Stephan/Trunk, Alexander/Eidenmüller, Horst/Wendehorst, Christiane/Adolff, Johannes, Festschrift für Andreas Heldrich, C.H. Beck, München 2005, pp. 55 - 66.
Dauner-Lieb, Barbara/Arnold, Arnd: Kein Rücktrittsrech des Käufers bei von ihm verschuldeter Unmöglichkeit der Nacherfüllung?, in: Häuser, Franz/Steinbeck, Anja/Hammen, Horst/Siebel, Ulf R./Hennrichs, Joachim/Welter, Reinhard, Festschrift für Walter Hadding, De Gruyter Recht, Berlin 2004, pp. 25 - 31.
Dauner-Lieb, Barbara/Langen, Werner: BGB Schuldrecht, Nomos, Baden-Baden 2012. (Cited as: Author, in: Dauner-Lieb/Langen)
Dauner-Lieb, Barbara/Heidel, Thomas/Lepa, Manfred/Ring, Gerhard: Das neue Schuldrecht in der anwaltlichen Praxis, Deutscher Anwaltverlag, Bonn 2002. (Cited as: Author, in: Dauner-Lieb/ Heidel/Lepa/Ring, Das neue Schuldrecht)
Dauner-Lieb, Barbara/Heidel, Thomas/Lepa, Manfred/Ring, Gerhard: Schuldrecht, Deutscher Anwaltverlag, Bonn 2002. (Cited as: Author, in: Dauner-Lieb/Heidel/Lepa/Ring, Schuldrecht)
Der Bundesminister der Justiz: Diskussionsentwurf eines Schuldrechtsmodernisierungsgesetzes, Der Bundesminister der Justiz, Berlin 2000. (Cited as Discussion Draft)
Döll, Yves: Rückgewährstörungen beim Rücktritt, Mohr Siebeck, Tübingen 2011.
Dörner, Heinrich/Staudinger, Ansgar: Schuldrechtsmodernisierung: systematische Einführung und synoptische Gesamtdarstellung, Nomos, Baden-Baden 2002.
Dötterl, Sebastian: Wann ist der Gläubiger für die Unmöglichkeit verantwortlich?, Nomos, Baden-Baden 2008.
Dullinger, Silvia: Bürgerliches Recht, Band II, Schuldrecht Allgemeiner Teil, Springer, Wien 2008.

Dural, Mustafa: İmkansızlık Kavramı ve Türleri, Batıder, Vol. 7, No. 1, 1973, pp. 11 - 58.

Dural, Mustafa: Borçlunun Sorumlu Olmadığı Sonraki İmkansızlık (BK. 117), Fakülteler Matbaası, İstanbul 1976. (Cited as: Dural, Sonraki İmkansızlık)

Düchs, Constantin: Die Behandlung von Leistungsstörungen im Europäischen Vertragsrecht, Duncker & Humblot, Berlin 2006.

Eckert, Jörn: Schuldrecht, Allgemeiner Teil, Nomos, Baden-Baden 2003.

Eidenmüller, Horst/Jansen, Nils/Kieninger, Eva-Maria/Wagner, Gerhard/Zimmermann, Reinhard: Der Vorschlag für eine Verordnung über ein Gemeinsames Europäisches Kaufrecht, JZ 2012, pp. 269 - 289.

Emmerich, Volker: Das Recht der Leistungsstörungen, C.H. Beck, München 2005.

Emmert, Jochen: Auf der Suche nach den Grenzen vertraglicher Leistungspflichten, Mohr Siebeck, Tübingen 2001.

Enderlein, Fritz/Dietrich, Maskow: International Sales Law, Oceana, New York 1992.

Eren, Fikret: Borçlar Hukuku Genel Hükümler, Beta, İstanbul 2006.

Ergüne, Mehmet Serkan: Reform Sonrasında Alman Medeni Kanununda İmkansızlık Halleri ve Sonuçları, İÜHFM, Vol. 62, No. 1 - 2, 2004, pp. 351 - 380.

Ergüne, Mehmet Serkan: Olumsuz Zarar, Beta, İstanbul 2008.

Esser, Josef/Schmidt, Eike: Schuldrechts, Band I, Allgemeiner Teil, C.F. Müller, Heidelberg 1984.

Fauvarque-Cosson, Bénédicte/Mazeaud, Denis: European Contract Law, Sellier, München 2008.

Fehre, Andrea: Unmöglichkeit und Unzumutbarkeit der Leistung, Voraussetzungen und Rechtsfolgen nach Inkrafttreten des Schuldrechtsmodernisierungsgesetzes, Duncker & Humblot, Berlin 2005.

Feldhahn, Peer: Die Störung der Geschäftsgrundlage im System des reformierten Schuldrechts, NJW 2005, pp. 3381 - 3383.

Felemegas, John: Introduction, in: Felemegas, John, An International Approach to the Interpretation of the United Nations Convention on Contracts for the International Sale of Goods (1980) as Uniform Sales Law, Cambridge University Press, Cambridge/New York 2007, pp. 1 - 38.

Ferrari, Franco/Kieninger, Eva-Maria/Mankowski, Peter/Otte, Karsten; Saenger, Ingo/Schulze, Götz Joachim/Staudinger, Ansgar: Internationales Vertragsrecht, C.H. Beck, München 2011. (Cited as: Author, in: Ferrari/Kieninger/Mankowski/Otte/Saenger/Schulze/Staudinger)

Fikentscher, Wolfgang/Heinemann, Andreas: Schuldrecht, De Gruyter Recht, Berlin 2006.

Finn, Markus: Erfüllungspflicht und Leistungshindernis, die Bestimmung der Grenzen vertraglicher Primärpflichten nach §§ 275 Abs. 1 und 2, 313 BGB, Duncker & Humblot, Berlin 2007.

Fischer, Hans Albrecht: Vis major im Zusammenhang mit Unmöglichkeit der Leistung, JJ, Vol. 137, No. 1, 1897, pp. 199 - 300.

Fischer, Hans Albrecht: Ein Beitrag zur Unmöglichkeitslehre, Warkentien, Rostock 1904. (Cited as: Fischer, Beitrag)

Fischer, Nicole N.: Die Unmöglichkeit der Leistung im internationalen Kauf- und Vertragsrecht, Duncker & Humblot, Berlin 2001. (Cited as: Fischer)

Fischer, Otto: Unmöglichkeit als Nichtigkeitsgrund bei Urteilen und Rechtsgeschäften, C.H. Beck, München 1913. (Cited as: Fischer, Unmöglichkeit)

Fitzgerald, John: CISG, Specific Performance, and the Civil Law of Louisiana and Quebec, JLC, Vol. 16, No. 1, 1997, pp. 291 - 313.

Flambouras, Dionysios P.: The Doctrines of Impossibility of Performance and clausula rebus sic stantibus in the 1980 Vienna Convention on Contracts for the International Sale of Goods and the Principles of European Contract Law: A Comparative Analysis, PILR, Vol. 13, No. 1, 2001, pp. 261 - 293.

Flambouras, Dionysios: Comparative Remarks on CISG Article 79 & PECL Articles 6:111, 8:108, in Guide to Article 79 - Comparison with Principles of European Contract Law (PECL), <http://cisgw3.law.pace.edu/cisg/text/peclcomp79.html>. (Cited as: Flambouras, Guide to Article 79)

Flambouras, Dionysios: Exemption and hardship: Remarks on the manner in which the Principles of European Contract Law (Articles 6:111 and 8:108) may be used to interpret or supplement CISG Article 79, in: Felemegas, John, An International Approach to the Interpretation of the United Nations Convention on Contracts for the International Sale of Goods (1980) as Uniform Sales Law, Cambridge University Press, Cambridge/New York 2007, pp. 499 - 505. (Cited as: Flambouras, Exemption)

Förster, Christian: Schuldrecht Allgemeiner Teil, Eine Einführung mit Fällen, C.F. Müller, Heidelberg 2011.

Furrer, Andreas/Schnyder, Anton K.: Handkommenar zum Schweizer Privatrecht, Obligationenrecht Allgemeine Bestimmungen, Schulthess, Zürich 2012. (Cited as: CHK/Author)

Garro, Alejandro M.: Exemption of liability for damages: Comparison between provisions of the CISG (Art. 79) and the counterpart provisions of the UNIDROIT Principles (Art. 7.1.7), in: Felemegas, John, An International Approach to the Interpretation of the United Nations Convention on Contracts for the International Sale of Goods (1980) as Uniform Sales Law, Cambridge University Press, Cambridge/New York 2007, pp. 236 - 246.

Gauch, Peter/Schluep, Walter R.: Schweizerisches Obligationenrecht, Allgemeiner Teil, Band I, Schulthess, Zürich/Basel/Genf 2008. (Cited as: Gauch/Schluep, Band I)

Gauch, Peter/Schluep, Walter R.: Schweizerisches Obligationenrecht, Allgemeiner Teil, Band II, Schulthess, Zürich/Basel/Genf 2008. (Cited as: Gauch/Schluep, Band II)

Giger, Marcel: Die vom Gläubiger verschuldete Leistungsunmöglichkeit, Haupt, Bern 1992.

Gordley, James: Impossibility and Changed and Unforeseen Circumstances, AJCL, Vol. 52, No. 3, 2004, pp. 513 - 530.

Gordley, James: Foundations of Private Law: Property, Tort, Contract, Unjust Enrichment, Oxford University Press, Oxford/New York 2006.

Gruber, Urs Peter: Schuldrechtsmodernisierung 2001/2002 – Die beiderseits zu vertretende Unmöglichkeit, JuS 2002, pp. 1066 - 1071.

Grunewald, Barbara: Vorschläge für eine Neuregelung der anfänglichen Unmöglichkeit und des anfänglichen Unvermögens, JZ 2001, pp. 433 - 436.

Gsell, Beate: Zeitweilige Unmöglichkeit und prozessuale Durchsetzung des Leistungsanspruchs, in: Bauer, Jobst-Hubertus/Kort, Michael/Möllers, Thomas M.J./Sandmann, Bernd, Festschrift für Herbert Buchner, C.H. Beck, München 2009, pp. 267 - 280.

Guhl, Theo: Das Schweizerische Obligationenrecht, Schulthess, Zürich 2000. (Cited as: Guhl/Author)

Guillemard, Sylvette: A comparative study of the UNIDROIT Principles and the Principles of European Contracts and some dispositions of the CISG applicable to the formation of international contracts, in Review of the Convention for the International Sale of Goods (CISG) 2000 - 2001, Kluwer, The Hague, 2000 - 2001, pp. 83 - 113.

Haake, Benno: Inwieweit steht das Unvermögen des Schuldners zur Leistung der Unmöglichkeit der Leistung gleich?, Dissertation, Rostock 1903.

Hamburger, Georg: Das Recht aus der Haftung und die Unmöglichkeit der Leistung, Vahlen, Berlin 1915.

Hammen, Horst: Stellvertretendes commodum bei anfänglicher Unmöglichkeit für jedermann?, in: Häuser, Franz/Steinbeck, Anja/Hammen, Horst/Siebel, Ulf R./Hennrichs, Joachim/Welter, Reinhard, Festschrift für Walter Hadding, De Gruyter Recht, Berlin 2004, pp. 41 - 56. (Cited as: Hammen, Stellvertretendes)

Harke, Jan Dirk: Unmöglichkeit und Pflichtverletzung: Römisches Recht, BGB und Schuldrechtsmodernisierung, in: Helms, Thobias/Neumann, Daniela/Caspers, Georg/Sailer, Rita/Schmidt-Kessel, Martin, Das neue Schuldrecht, Richard Boorberg Verlag, Stuttgart 2001, pp. 29 - 61.

Henssler, Martin/Graf von Westphalen, Friedrich: Praxis der Schuldrechtreform, ZAP Verlag, Recklinghausen 2001. (Cited as: Author, in: Henssler/Graf von Westphalen)

Hirsch, Christoph: Allgemeines Schuldrecht, Carl Heymanns Verlag, Köln 2009.

Hohmeister, Frank Udo: Die Einordnung anfänglichen Unvermögens des Schuldners zur Leistung in die Unmöglichkeitslehre des BGB, Dissertation, Göttingen 1982.

Hondius, Ewoud: Towards an Optional Common European Sales Law, ERPL, Vol. 19, No. 6, 2011, pp. 709 - 715.
Honnold, John: Documentary History of the Uniform Law for International Sales : The studies, deliberations and decisions that led to the 1980 United Nations Convention; with introductions and explanations, Kluwer, Deventer 1989. (Cited as: Honnold, Documentary History)
Honnold, John: Uniform Law for International Sales under the 1980 United Nations Convention, Kluwer, Alphen aan den Rijn 2009. (Cited as: Honnold)
Honsell, Heinrich: Kommentar Zum UN-Kaufrecht: Übereinkommen der Vereinten Nationen über Verträge über den Internationalen Warenkauf (CISG), Springer, Berlin/Heidelberg 2010. (Cited as: Author, in: Honsell)
Honsell, Heinrich: 100 Jahre Schweizerisches Obligationenrecht, ZSR 2011 II, pp. 5 - 115.
Honsell, Heinrich/Vogt, Nedim Peter/Wiegand, Wolfgang: Basler Kommentar zum Schweizerischen Privatrecht, Obligationenrecht I, Art. 1 - 529 OR, Helbing and Lichtenhahn, Basel/Genf/München 2003. (Cited as: Basler/Author)
Huber, Peter/Faust, Florian: Schuldrechtsmodernisierung Einführung in das neue Recht, C.H. Beck, München 2002.
Huber, Peter/Mullis, Alastair: The CISG: A new textbook for students and practitioners, Sellier, München 2007.
Huber, Ulrich: Handbuch des Schuldrechts, Leistungsstörungen, Band I, Die allgemeinen Grundlagen; Der Tatbestand des Schuldnersverzug; Die vom Schuldner zu vertretenden Umstände, Mohr Siebeck, Tübingen 1999. (Cited as: Huber, Leistungsstörungen I)
Huber, Ulrich: Handbuch des Schuldrechts, Leistungsstörungen, Band II, Die Folgen des Schuldnerverzugs – Die Erfüllungsverweigerung und die vom Schuldner zu vertretende Unmöglichkeit, Mohr Siebeck, Tübingen 1999. (Cited as: Huber, Leistungsstörungen II)
Huber, Ulrich: Die Pflichtverletzung als Grundtatbestand der Leistungsstörung im Diskussionsentwurf eines Schuldrechtsmodernisierungsgesetzes, ZIP 2000, pp. 2273 - 2284.
Huber, Ulrich: Die Unmöglichkeit der Leistung im Diskussionsentwurf eines Schuldrechtsmodernisierungsgesetzes, ZIP 2000, pp. 2137 - 2151.
Hudson, A. H.: Exemptions and Impossibility under the Vienna Convention, in: McKendrick, Ewan, Force majeure and Frustration of Contract Lloyd's of London Press, London 1995, pp. 267 - 286.
Huguenin, Claire: Obligationenrecht, Allgemeiner Teil, Schulthess, Zürich/Basel/Genf 2006.
Hütte, Felix/Helbron, Marlena: Schuldrecht, Allgemeiner Teil, Verlag Dr. Rolf Schmidt, Grasberg bei Bremen 2005.
Immenhauser, Martin: Das Dogma von Vertrag und Delikt, Böhlau, Köln 2006.
İnan, Ali Naim: Unmöglichkeit der Leistung im Deutschen, Schweizerischen und Türkischen Recht, Dissertation, Breisgau 1956. (Cited as: İnan, Unmöglichkeit)
İnan, Ali Naim: Borçlar Hukuku, Genel Hükümler, Birinci Kitap, Ankara Üniversitesi Hukuk Fakültesi Yayınları, Ankara 1971. (Cited as: İnan)
İnan, Ali Naim: Bankacılar İçin Borçlar Hukuku Bilgisi, Banka ve Ticaret Hukuku Araştırma Enstitüsü, Ankara 1997. (Cited as: İnan, Bankacılar)
Jagielski, Boleslaus: Die Grundsätze über die ursprüngliche Unmöglichkeit und das ursprüngliche Unvermögen in dem Bürgerlichen Gesetzbuche, Noske, Borna-Leipzig 1910.
Jakobs, Horst Heinrich: Unmöglichkeit und Nichterfüllung, Ludwig Röhrscheid, Bonn 1969.
Janssen, André/Kiene, Sörren Claas: The CISG and Its General Principles, in: Janssen, André/ Meyer, Olaf, CISG Methodology, Sellier, München 2009, pp. 261 - 285.
Jauernig, Othmar: Bürgerliches Gesetzbuch mit Allgemeinen Gleichbehandlungsgesetzes, C.H. Beck, München 2011.
Jenkins, Sarah Howard: Exemption for Nonperformance: UCC, CISG, UNIDROIT Principles – A Comparative Assessment, TLR, Vol. 72, No. 6, 1998, pp. 2015 - 2030.
Joachim, Willi: "Personale" Unmöglichkeit – Die Zumutbarkeit pflichtgemässen Verhaltens, in Zivil- und Wirtschaftsrecht im Europäischen und Globalen Kontext, De Gruyter Recht, Berlin 2006, pp. 49 - 65.

Joeinig, Elke: Die anfängliche Unmöglichkeit, Verlag Österreich, Wien 2006.
Joussen, Jacob: Schuldrecht I - Allgemeiner Teil, Kohlhammer, Stuttgart 2008.
Junker, Markus/Beckmann, Roland Michael/Rüssmann, Michael: juris PraxisKommentar, BGB, Schuldrecht, juris, Saarbrücken 2004. (Cited as: jurisPK-BGB/Author)
Kaiser, Dagmar: Zeitweilige Unmöglichkeit, in: Häuser, Franz/Steinbeck, Anja/Hammen, Horst/ Siebel, Ulf R./Hennrichs, Joachim/Welter, Reinhard, Festschrift für Walter Hadding, De Gruyter Recht, Berlin 2004, pp. 121 - 143. (Cited as: Kaiser, Zeitweilige)
Kaiser, Gisbert A.: Das allgemeine Leistungsstörungsrecht als Kernpunkt des Diskussionsentwurfs eines Schuldrechtsmodernisierungsgesetzes. Die Bedeutung für das Private Baurecht, ZfBR 2001, pp. 147 - 154.
Kalbhen, Kurt: Das Surrogationsprinzip bei Unmöglichkeit der Leistung, Dissertation, Erlangen 1937.
Kallweit, Dominik: Towards a European Contract Law: For a Prosperous Future of International Trade, VUWLR, Vol. 35, No. 2, 2004, pp. 269 - 297.
Kaplan, Felix: Die ürsprüngliche teilweise Unmöglichkeit der versprochenen Leistung, insbesondere die teilweise Nichtexistenz des geschuldeten Gegenstandes nach dem Gemeinen Recht und dem Recht des Bürgerlichen Gesetzbuches, Schade, Berlin 1903. (Cited as: Kaplan, Ürsprüngliche)
Kaplan, Felix: Die teilweise Unmöglichkeit der Leistung nach dem Recht des Bürgerlichen Gesetzbuches, Struppe & Winckler, Berlin 1904. (Cited as: Kaplan)
Kälin, Oliver: Unmöglichkeit der Leistung nach Art. 119 OR und clausula rebus sic stantibus, recht 2004, pp. 246 - 256.
Käunicke, Anja: Die Schadensersatzpflicht des Rückgewährschuldners wegen anfänglicher Unmöglichkeit, Duncker & Humblot, Berlin 2011.
Keller, Max/Schöbi, Christian: Allgemeine Lehren des Vertragsrecht, Band I, Helbing and Lichtenhahn, Basel/Frankfurt am Main 1982.
Kırca, Çiğdem: Örtülü (Gizli) Boşluk ve Bu Boşluğun Doldurulması Yöntemi Olarak Amaca Uygun Sınırlama (Teleologische Reduktion), AÜHFD, Vol. 50, No. 1, 2001, pp. 91 - 120.
Kisch, Wilhelm: Die Wirkungen der nachträglich eintretenden Unmöglichkeit der Erfüllung bei gegenseitigen Verträgen nach dem Bürgerlichen Gesetzbuche für das Deutsche Reich, Fischer, Jena 1900.
Klausch, Sebastian: Unmöglichkeit und Unzumutbarkeit im system des allgemeinen Leistungsstörungsrecht nach der Schuldrechtsmodernisierung 2002, Peter Lang, Frankfurt am Main 2004.
Kleineidam, Feodor: Unmöglichkeit und Unvermögen nach dem Bürgerlichen Gesetzbuche für das Deutsche Reich, Fischer, Jena 1900.
Kley, Britta: Unmöglichkeit und Pflichtverletzung, Duncker & Humblot, Berlin, 2001.
Knütel, Christian: Zur Gleichstellung von zu vertretender und nicht zu vertretender Unmöglichkeit in § 275 BGB im Regierungsentwurf zur Schuldrechtsmodernisierung, JR 2001, pp. 353 - 355.
Kocayusufpaşaoğlu, Necip: Borçlar Hukukuna Giriş, Hukuki İşlem, Sözleşme, Filiz, İstanbul 2008.
Kohte, Wolfhard/Micklitz, Hans-W/Rott, Peter/Tonner, Klaus/Willingmann, Armin: Das neue Schuldrecht, Kompaktkommentar, Luchterhand, München 2003. (Cited as: Author, in: Kohte/Micklitz/Rott/Tonner/Willingmann)
Koller, Alfred: Schweizerisches Obligationenrecht, Allgemeiner Teil, Handbuch des allgemeinen Schuldrechts, Stämpfli, Bern 2009. (Cited as: Koller)
Koller, Ingo: Recht der Leistungsstörungen, in: Koller, Ingo/Roth, Herbert/Zimmermann, Reinhard, Schuldrechtsmodernisierungsgesetz 2002, C.H. Beck, München 2002, pp. 45 - 65. (Cited as: Koller, Leistungssörungen)
Kornfeld, Felix: Leistungsunmöglichkeit, Manzchen, Wien 1913.
Kotzur, Wolfgang: Die Auswirkungen von außergewöhnlichen Ereignissen auf vertragliche Schuldverhältnisse - Eine vergleichende Untersuchung zum deutschen und englischen Recht, Peter Lang, Frankfurt am Main 2001.

Kollmann, Andreas: Allgemeines Geschäftsbedingungen und Individualvereinbarungen, in: Kroiss, Ludwig, Klausel Schuldrecht, Deutscher Anwaltverlag, Bonn 2003, pp. 19 - 163.

Köhler, Helmut: Unmöglichkeit und Geschäftsgrundlage bei Zweckstörungen im Schuldverhältnis, C.H. Beck, München 1971.

Köhler, Helmut/Lorenz, Stephan: Schuldrecht I, Allgemeiner Teil, C.H. Beck, München 2005.

Köndgen, Johannes: Die Entlastung des Schuldners wegen Unmöglichkeit der Leistung - Versuch einer Ehrenrettung des § 275 Abs. 2 BGB, in: Eger, Thomas/Ott, Claus/Bigus, Jochen/von Wangenheim, Georg, Internationalisierung des Rechts und seine ökonomische Analyse, Festschrift für Hans-Bernd Schäfer zum 65. Geburtstag, Gabler, Wiesbaden 2008, pp. 275 - 298.

Kötz, Hein: Vertragsrecht, Mohr Siebeck, Tübingen 2009.

Krajewski, Markus: The New German Law of Obligations, EBLR, Vol. 14, No. 2, 2003, pp. 201 - 216.

Kramer, Ernst A.: Berner Kommentar, Kommentar zum schweizerischen Privatrecht, Band VI: Das Obligationenrecht, 1. Abteilung: Allgemeine Bestimmungen, 2. Teilband, Unterteilband 1a: Inhalt des Vertrages, Kommentar zu Art. 19 - 20 OR, Stämpfli, Bern 1991. (Cited as: Berner/Kramer)

Kramer, Ernst A.: Obligationenrecht Allgemeiner Teil, Helbing Lichtenhahn Verlag, Basel 2009. (Cited as: Kramer, Obligationenrecht)

Kröll, Stefan/Mistelis, Loukas/Perales Viscasillas, Pilar: UN Convention on Contracts for the International Sale of Goods (CISG), C.H. Beck, Oxford 2011. (Cited as: Author, in: Kröll/ Mistelis/Viscasillas)

Krückmann, Paul: Unmöglichkeit und Unmöglichkeitsprozess, Mohr Siebeck, Tübingen 1907.

Kuhlmann, Kai/Nauen, Bernd: Neues und Altes von der vorübergehenden Unmöglichkeit – Primärleistungspflicht und Sekundäransprüche, in: Sutschet, Holger, Tradition und Moderne - Schuldrecht und Arbeitsrecht nach der Schuldrechtsreform, Duncker & Humblot, Berlin 2005, pp. 31 - 94.

Laimer, Simon: Durchführung und Rechtsfolgen der Vertragsaufhebung bei nachträglichen Erfüllungsstörungen, Mohr, Tübingen 2009.

Lando, Ole: CISG and Its Followers: A Proposal to Adopt Some International Principles of Contract Law, AJCL, Vol. 53, No. 2, 2005, pp. 379 - 401.

Lando, Ole/Beale, Hugh: Principles of European Contract Law, Parts I and II, Combined and Revised, Kluwer, The Hague, 2000. (Cited as: PECL Commentary)

Larenz, Karl: Lehrbuch des Schuldrechts, Band I, Allgemeiner Teil, C.H. Beck'schen Buchdruckerei Nördlingen, München 1987. (Cited as: Larenz)

Larenz, Karl: Methodenlehre der Rechtswissenschaft, Springer, Berlin 1991. (Cited as: Larenz, Methodenlehre)

Lehmann, Berthold: Inwieweit können die allgemeinen Vorschriften des BGB über die Unmöglichkeit der Leistung mit den speziellen über die Gewährleistung des Verkäufers für Sachmängel gegebenen Normen konkurrieren?, Dissertation, Greifswald 1910. (Cited as: Lehmann, Unmöglichkeit)

Lehmann, Heinrich: Die Unterlasungspflicht im Bürgerlichen Recht, C.H. Beck, München 1906. (Cited as: Lehmann)

Lenczyk, Harry: Teilweise Unmöglichkeit, Dissertation, Breslau 1936.

Leyens, Patrick C.: CISG and Mistake: Uniform Law vs. Domestic Law, The Interpretative Challenge of Mistake and the Validity Loophole, <http://www.cisg.law.pace.edu/cisg/biblio/ leyens.html>.

Lindström, Niklas: Changed Circumstances and Hardship in the International Sale of Goods, NJCL, 2006/I, <http://www.njcl.fi/1_2006/commentary1.pdf>.

Liu, Chengwei: Force majeure - Perspectives from the CISG, UNIDROIT Principles, PECL and Case Law, [2nd edition: Case annotated update (April 2005)], <http://www.cisg.law.pace.edu/ cisg/biblio/liu6.html>. (Cited as: Liu, Force majeure)

Liu, Chengwei: Remedies for Non-performance: Perspectives from CISG, UNIDROIT Principles & PECL, <http://article.chinalawinfo.com/Article_Detail.asp?ArticleId=24403>. (Cited as: Liu)

Lookofsyk, Joseph M.: Understanding the CISG: a compact guide to the 1980 United Nations Convention on Contracts for International Sale of Goods, Kluwer, Alphen aan den Rijn 2008.
Looschelders, Dirk: Schuldrecht, Allgemeiner Teil, Carl Heymanns Verlag, Köln 2006.
Lorenz, Stephan: Neues Leistungsstörungs- und Kaufrecht: Eine Zwischenbilanz, De Gruyter Recht, Berlin 2004. (Cited as Lorenz Kaufrecht)
Lorenz, Stephan: Schuldrechtsreform 2002: Problemschwerpunkte drei Jahre danach, NJW 2005, pp. 1889 - 1896.
Lorenz, Stephan: Schuldrechtsmodernisierung- Erfahrungen seit dem 1. Januar 2002, in: Lorenz, Egon, Karlsruher Forum 2005: Schuldrechtsmodernisierung- Erfahrungen seit dem 1. Januar 2002, Verlag Versicherungswirtschaft, Karlsruhe 2006, pp. 5 - 139. (Cited as: Lorenz, Schuldrechtsmodernisierung)
Lorenz, Stephan/Riehm, Thomas: Lehrbuch zum neuen Schuldrecht C.H. Beck, München 2002.
Lorenz, Werner: Reform of the German Law of Breach of Contract, ELR, Vol. 1, No. 3, 1997, pp. 317 - 344.
Löwisch, Manfred: Neues Schuldrecht in Deutschland, RLR, No. 20, 2003, pp. 157 - 179, <www.ritsumei.ac.jp/acd/cg/law/lex/rlr20/Manfred157.pdf>.
Lutz, Achim: Die Berücksichtigung persönlicher Leistungshindernisse in vertraglichen Schuldverhältnissen, Cuvillier Verlag, Göttingen 2002.
Lüttringhaus, Jan D.: Verhandlungspflichten bei Störung der Geschäftsgrundlage – Ein Beitrag zur Dogmatik und Durchsetzung von Anpassungsanspruch und Verhandlungspflichten nach § 313 Abs. 1 BGB, AcP, Vol. 213, No. 2, 2013, pp. 266 - 298.
Macgregor, Laura: Report on the Draft Common Frame of Reference: a report prepared for the Scottish Government by Laura Macgregor, University of Edinburgh, on the document known as 'Principles, Definitions and Model Rules of European Private Law' 26/09/08 <http://www.scotland.gov.uk/Resource/Doc/262952/0078639.pdf>.
Magnus, Ulrich: CISG Uyarınca Tazminat, Faiz, Sorumluluktan Kurtulma, in: Atamer, Yeşim M., Milletlerarası Satım Hukuku, XII Levha, İstanbul 2008, pp. 287 - 307.
Maile-Zinser, Tanja: Auswirkungen der Unmöglichkeit auf den Erfüllungsanspruch, Logos Verlag, Berlin 2006.
Marcantonio, J. Barrigan: Unifying the Law of Impossibility, HICLR Vol. 8, No. 1, 1984, pp. 41 - 59.
Markesinis, Sir Basil/Unberath, Hannes/Johnston, Angus The German Law of Contract, A Comparative Treatise, Hart, Oregon 2006.
Marquardt, Rudolf: Die teilweise Unmöglichkeit der Leistung nach deutschem bürgerlichem Recht, Vater, Breslau 1925.
Maskow, Dietrich: Hardship and Force majeure, AJCL, Vol. 40, No. 3, 1992, pp. 657 - 669.
Mathias, Reimann: The Good, the Bad, and the Ugly: The Reform of the German Law of Obligations, TLR, Vol. 83, No. 4, 2009, pp. 877 - 919.
Mazzacano, Peter J.: Force majeure, Impossibility, Frustration & the Like: Excuses for Non-Performance; the Historical Origins and Development of an Autonomous Commercial Norm in the CISG, NJCL, Vol. 2011, No. 2, pp. 1 - 54.
Medicus, Dieter: Bemerkungen zur "vorübergehenden Unmöglichkeit", in: Lorenz, Stephan/Trunk, Alexander/Eidenmüller, Horst/Wendehorst, Christiane/Adolff, Johannes, Festschrift für Andreas Heldrich, C.H. Beck, München 2005, pp. 347 - 357. (Cited as: Medicus, Unmöglichkeit)
Medicus, Dieter: Schuldrecht I, Allgemeiner Teil, C.H. Beck, München 2006. (Cited as: Medicus)
Mitzkait, Anika: Leistungsstörung und Haftungsbefreiung, Mohr Siebeck, Tübingen 2008.
Mommsen, Friedrich: Die Unmöglichkeit der Leistung in ihrem Einfluss auf obligatorische Verhältnisse, Schwetschke, Braunschweig 1853.
Morrissey, Joseph F./Graves, Jack M.: International Sales Law and Arbitration, Wolters Kluwer, Alphen aan den Rijn 2008.
Motsch, Richard: Risikoverteilung im allgemeinen Leistungsstörungsrecht, JZ 2001, pp. 428 - 433.
Mousourakis, George: Fundamentals of Roman Private Law, Springer, Berlin/Heidelberg 2012.

Nicholas, Barry: Force majeure and Frustration, AJCL, Vol. 27, No. 2 - 3, 1979, pp. 231 - 245.
Nicholas, Barry: The Vienna Convention on International Sales Law, LQR, Vol. 105, No. 2, 1989, pp. 201 - 243.
Oğuz, Arzu: Türk Medeni Hukuku'nun Gelişim Çizgisi ve Karşılaştırmalı Hukukun Rolü, AÜHFD, Vol. 55, No. 1, 2006, pp. 195 - 206.
Oğuzman, Kemal/Barlas, Nami: Medeni Hukuk, Beta, İstanbul 2007.
Oğuzman, Kemal/Öz, Turgut: Borçlar Hukuku Genel Hükümler, Filiz, İstanbul 2000.
Olgaç, Senai: Kazai ve İlmi İçtihatlarla Türk Borçlar Kanunu Genel Hükümler, İsmail Akgün Matbaası, İstanbul 1970.
Oser, Hugo/Schönenberger, Wilhelm: Kommentar zum Schweizerischen Zivilgesetzbuch, Das Obligationenrecht, Erster Halbband: Art. 1 - 183, Schulthess, Zürich 1929. (Cited as: Zürcher/Oser/Schönenberger)
Pakuscher, Ernst: Die allgemeinen Grundsätze des Bürgerlichen Gesetzbuchs über die anfängliche Unmöglichkeit der Leistung, J. Pakuscher, Berlin 1907.
Palandt, Otto: Bürgerliches Gesetzbuch, C.H. Beck, München 2010. (Cited as: Palandt/Author)
Pejovic, Caslav: Civil Law and Common Law: Two Different Paths Leading to the Same Goal, VUWLR, Vol. 32, No. 3, 2001, pp. 817 - 841.
Pels Leusden, Hans Heinrich: Besteht ein Anspruch auf Leistung trotz Unmöglichkeit der Erfüllung?, Trute, Quakenbrück 1929.
Peres, Daniel: Haftung, Zurechnung und Beweisführung bei anfänglicher und nachträglicher Unmöglichkeit, Duncker & Humblot, Berlin 2012.
Petersen, Jens: Examens-Repetitorium, Allgemeines Schuldrecht, C.F. Müller, Heidelberg 2002.
Pfeiffer, Thomas: Core issues of consumer sales law, in: Schulte-Nölke, Hans/Tichy, Lubos, Perspectives for European Consumer Law: Towards a Directive on Consumer Rights and Beyond, Sellier, München 2010, pp. 45 - 58.
Philippe, Denis: Book III Performance and Non-performance of Obligations and Corresponding Rights in the DCFR, in: Sagaert, Vincent/Storme, Matthias E./Terryn, Evelyne, The Draft Common Frame of Reference: national and comparative perspectives, Intersentia, Cambridge 2012, pp. 35 - 52.
Popescu, Paul: Kein positives Interesse bei anfänglicher Unmöglichkeit und anfänglich unbehebbaren Mängeln, Nomos, Baden-Baden 2012.
Poszewiecki, Adam: Perspective of Unification of Obligation Law in Aspect of Impossibility of Performance, <http://www.law.muni.cz/sborniky/cofola2008/files/pdf/mps/poszewiecki_adam.pdf>.
Prütting, Hanns/Wegen, Gerhard/Weinreich, Gerd: BGB Kommentar, Luchterhand, Köln 2011. (Cited as: PWW/Author)
Quass, Guido: Die Nutzungsstörung, Duncker & Humblot, Berlin 2003.
Rabel, Ernst: Unmöglichkeit der Leistung, Böhlau, Weimar 1907.
Rampini, Corrado: Die nachträgliche Leistungserschwerung, Haupt Verlag, Bern 2003.
Reinke, Alwin: Die allgemeinen Grundsätze über die anfängliche Unmöglichkeit der Leistung, R. Noske, Borna-Leipzig 1905.
Reinhard, Thorsten: Die beiderseits zu vertretende Unmöglichkeit im Synallagma, Duncker & Humblot, Berlin 1998.
Reinhart, Gert: UN-Kaufrecht, C.F. Müller, Heidelberg 1991.
Reisoğlu, Safa: Borçlar Hukuku Genel Hükümler, Beta, İstanbul 1998.
Reitz, John C.: Political Economy and Contract Law, in: Schulze, Reiner, New Features in Contract Law, Sellier, München 2007, pp. 247 - 276.
Reu, Fritz: Die Unmöglichkeit der Leistung im anglo-amerikanischen Recht, Enke, Stuttgart 1935.
Rheinstein, Max: Die Struktur des vertraglichen Schuldverhältnisses im anglo-amerikanischen Recht, de Gruyter, Berlin 1932.
Riesenhuber, Karl: Damages for Non-Performance and the Fault Principle, available at <http://papers.ssrn.com/sol3/papers.cfm?abstract_id=1501193>.

Rimke, Joern: Force majeure and hardship: Application in international trade practice - with specific regards to the CISG and the UNIDROIT Principles of International Commercial Contracts, Pace Review of the Convention on Contracts for the International Sale of Goods, Kluwer, 1999 - 2000, pp. 197 - 243, <http://www.cisg.law.pace.edu/cisg/biblio/rimke.html>.
Rohde, Gerd: Die Unmöglichkeit der Leistung bei Gattungsschulden, P & S Sofortdr., Würzburg 1972.
Rödl, Julia: Die Spannung der Schuld, Duncker & Humblot, Berlin 2002.
Rüssmann, Helmut: Die vom Gläubiger und vom Schuldner zu vertretende Unmöglichkeit, in: Brüggemeier, Gert, Liber Amicorum Eike Schmidt, C.F. Müller, Heidelberg 2005, pp. 281 - 301.
Säcker, Franz Jürgen/Rixecke, Roland: Münchener Kommentar zum Bürgerlichen Gesetzbuch, Band 2, Schuldrecht, Allgemeiner Teil §§ 241 - 432, C.H. Beck München 2012. (Cited as: MüKo)
Sarrazin, Wilfried: Die Zweckerreichung als Erlöschungsgrund des Schuldverhältnisses : Zugleich ein Beitrag zur Lehre von der Abgrenzung der Zweckerreichung von der Unmöglichkeit, Vater, Breslau 1935.
Saidov, Djakhongir: Cases on CISG Decided in the Russian Federation, VJ, Vol. 7, No.1, 2003, pp. 1 - 62.
Saidov, Djakhongir: The Law of Damages in International Sales: The CISG and other International Instruments, Hart, Oxford 2008. (Cited as: Saidov)
Scheer, Günther: Die zeitweilige und die beseitigte Unmöglichkeit der Vertragsleistung, R. Noske, Borna-Leipzig 1906.
Scheller, Adolf: Die zeitweilige Unmöglichkeit der Leistung nach dem Rechte des Bürgerlichen Gesetzbuches, Dissertation, Heidelberg 1908.
Schimmel, Roland/Buhlmann, Dirk: Frankfurter Handbuch zum neuen Schuldrecht, Luchterland, Neuwied/Kriftel 2002.
Schlechtriem, Peter: Uniform Sales Law – The UN-Convention on Contracts for the International Sale of Goods, Manz, Vienna 1986. (Cited as: Schlechtriem, Uniform Sales Law)
Schlechtriem, Peter: Die Unmöglichkeit – ein Wiedergänger, in: Coester, Michael/Martiny, Dieter/von Sachsen Gessaphe, Karl August Prinz, Privatrecht in Europa, C.H. Beck, München 2004, pp. 125 - 133. (Cited as: Schlechtriem, Unmöglichkeit)
Schlechtriem, Peter: The German Act to Modernize the Law of Obligations in the Context of Common Principles and Structures of the Law of Obligations in Europe, <http://ouclf.iuscomp.org/articles/schlechtriem2.shtml>. (Cited as: Schlechtriem, German Act)
Schlechtriem, Peter/Butler, Petra: UN Law on International Sales: the UN Convention on the International Sale of Goods, Springer, New York 2009.
Schlechtriem, Peter/Schmidt-Kessel, Martin: Schuldrecht: Allgemeiner Teil, Mohr Siebeck, Tübingen 2005.
Schlechtriem, Peter/Schwenzer, Ingeborg: Commentary on the UN Convention on the International Sale of Goods (CISG), Oxford University Press, Oxford/New York 2005. (Cited as: Author, in: Schlechtriem/Schwenzer)
Schmidt, Patrick: Die Unmöglichkeit der Erfüllung in Ansehung der Zeit, Duncker & Humblot, Berlin 2007.
Schmidt-Kessel, Baldus: Prozessuale Behandlung des Wegfalls der Geschäftsgrundlage nach neuem Recht, NJW 2002, pp. 2076 - 2078.
Schmidt-Räntsch, Jürgen: Das neue Schuldrecht, Carl Heymanns Verlag, Köln 2002.
Schmidt-Recla, Adrian: Echte, faktische, wirtschaftliche Unmöglichkeit und Wegfall der Geschäftsgrundlage, in: Kern, Bernd-Rüdiger/Wadle, Elmar/Schroeder, Klaus-Peter/Katzenmeier, Christian, Humaniora, Springer, Berlin 2006, pp. 641 - 668.
Schneider, Susanne: Wechselwirkungen zwischen Irrtum und Unmöglichkeit: ein Beitrag zur Haftung des Schuldners bei anfänglichen Leistungshindernissen, Duncker & Humblot, Berlin 2008.

Schulte-Nölke, Hans: The New German Law of Obligations: an Introduction, <http://www.iuscomp.org/gla/literature/schulte-noelke.htm>.

Schultz, Michael: Leistungsstörungsrecht, in: Westermann, Harm Peter, Das Schuldrecht 2002, Richard Boorberg Verlag, Stuttgart 2002, pp. 17 - 105.

Schulze, Reiner: Common European Sales Law (CESL) – Commentary -, C.H. Beck/Hart/Nomos, Baden-Baden 2012.

Schulze, Reiner/Dörner, Heinrich/Ebert, Ina/Hoeren, Thomas/Kemper, Rainer/Saenger, Ingo/Schreiber, Klaus/Schulte-Nölke, Hans/Staudinger, Ansgar: Bürgerliches Gesetzbuch, Handkommentar, Nomos, Baden-Baden 2012. (Cited as: Hk-BGB/Author)

Schwab, Dieter/Löhnig, Martin: Einführung in das Zivilrecht: Einschliesslich BGB- Allgemeiner Teil, C.F. Müller, Heidelberg 2010.

Schwarz, Andreas B.: Borçlar Hukuku Dersleri, I. Cilt, Kardeşler Basımevi, İstanbul 1948.

Schwarze, Roland: Das Recht der Leistungsstörungen, de Gruyter, Berlin 2008.

Schweitzer, Herbert: Die ursprüngliche Unmöglichkeit der Leistung bei einseitigen Verpflichtungen nach dem Rechte des Bürgerlichen Gesetzbuches, Henning, Greiz 1911.

Schwenzer, Ingeborg: Specific Performance and Damages According to the 1994 UNIDROIT Principles of International Commercial Contracts, EJLR, Vol. 1, No. 3, 1999, pp. 289 - 304.

Schwenzer, Ingeborg: Schweizerisches Obligationenrecht Allgemeiner Teil, Stämpfli, Bern 2006. (Cited as: Schwenzer, Obligationenrecht)

Schwenzer, Ingeborg: Force majeure and Hardship in International Sales Contracts, VUWLR, Vol. 39, No. 3, 2008, pp. 709 - 771.

Schwenzer, Ingeborg/Hachem, Pascal/Kee, Christopher: Global Sales and Contract Law, Oxford University Press, Oxford 2012.

Schwingenheuer, Yasmine-Lee: Die Geschichte der Unmöglichkeitslehre - Die Unmöglichkeit im Wandel der Zeit, Grin, Norderstedt 2001.

Secretariat: Commentary on the Draft Convention on Contracts for the International Sale of Goods, Prepared by the Secretariat, Document A/CON~9V5, Art. 65, para. 7, <http://www.cnudci.org/pdf/a_conf.97_5-ocred.pdf>. (Cited as: Secretariat Commentary)

Seichter, Detlef Karl-Heinz: Beiderseits zu vertretende Unmöglichkeit beim Gegenseitigen Vertrag, Schmacht, Bamberg, Hamburg 1971.

Serozan, Rona: Sözleşmeden Dönme, İstanbul Üniversitesi Hukuk Fakültesi, İstanbul 1975. (Cited as: Serozan, Dönme)

Serozan, Rona: Medeni Hukuk Genel Bölüm, Vedat, İstanbul 2004. (Cited as: Serozan, Medeni Hukuk)

Serozan, Rona: Borçlar Hukuku Genel Bölüm Üçüncü Cilt - İfa, İfa Engelleri, Haksız Zenginleşme, Filiz, İstanbul 2006. (Cited as: Serozan)

Soergel, Hans Theodor: Bürgerliches Gesetzbuch, Kohlhammer, Stuttgart 2000. (Cited as: Soergel-CISG/Author)

Southerington, Tom: Impossibility of Performance and Other Excuses in International Trade, Publication of the Faculty of Law of the University of Turku, Private law publication series B:55 <http://www.cisg.law.pace.edu/cisg/biblio/southerington.html>.

Staudenmayer, Dirk: Der Kommissionsvorschlag für eine Verordnung zum Gemeinsamen Europäischen Kaufrecht, NJW 2011, pp. 3491 - 3498.

Staudinger, Julius von: Kommentar zum Bürgerlichen Gesetzbuch mit Einführungsgesetz und Nebengesetzen, Wiener UN-Kaufrecht, Neuarbeitung 2005, Sellier de Gruyter, Berlin 2005. (Cited as: Staudinger/Magnus)

Staudinger, Julius von: Kommentar zum Bürgerlichen Gesetzbuch mit Einführungsgesetz und Nebengesetzen, Buch 2, Recht der Schuldverhältnisse, §§ 311, 311a, 312, 312a - f, (Vertragsschluss), Neuarbeitung 2005, Sellier de Gruyter, Berlin 2005. (Cited as: Staudinger/Author)

Staudinger, Julius von: BGB Eckpfeiler des Zivilrechts, Sellier de Gruyter, Berlin 2005. (Cited as: Staudinger, Eckpfeiler)

Staudinger, Julius von: Kommentar zum Bürgerlichen Gesetzbuch mit Einführungsgesetz und Nebengesetzen, Buch 2, Recht der Schuldverhältnisse, §§ 255 - 304, (Leistungsstörungsrecht 1), Neuarbeitung 2009, Sellier de Gruyter, Berlin 2009. (Cited as: Staudinger/Author)

Staudinger, Julius von: Kommentar zum Bürgerlichen Gesetzbuch mit Einführungsgesetz und Nebengesetzen, Buch 2, Recht der Schuldverhältnisse, §§ 315 - 326, (Leistungsstörungsrecht 2), Neuarbeitung 2009, Sellier de Gruyter, Berlin 2009. (Cited as: Staudinger/Author)

Stelzer, Alfred: Die Abgrenzung zwischen Verzug und zeitweiliger Unmöglichkeit der Leistung, Mauser, Forchheim Ofr., 1933.

Stipanski, Eckart: Die zeitweilige und die beseitigte nachfolgende Unmöglichkeit der Leistung nach dem Recht des bürgerlichen Gesetzbuches, Höfer & Limmert, Erlangen 1931.

Study Group on a European Civil Code/Research Group on the Existing EC Private Law (Acquis Group) Principles, Definitions and Model Rules on European Private Law, <http://www.ccbe.eu/fileadmin/user_upload/NTCdocument/DCFRpdf1_1262861061.pdf>. (Cited as: DCFR Commentary)

Sulzer, Stefan: Clausula rebus sic stantibus und der gestörte Vertragszweck Zugleich Bemerkungen zu BGE 127 III (2001) 300 ff., AJP 2003, pp. 987 - 994.

Sulzer, Stefan: Zweckstörungen im schweizerischen Vertragsrecht, Schulthess, Zürich 2002. (Cited as: Sulzer)

Sutschet, Holger: Haftung für anfängliches Unvermögen, NJW 2005, pp. 1404 - 1406.

Sutschet, Holger: Garantiehaftung und Verschuldenshaftung im gegenseitigen Vertrag, Mohr Siebeck, Tübingen 2006. (Cited as: Sutschet, Garantiehaftung)

Sy, Ilaria: Pflichtverletzung und Vertretenmüssen beim Schadensersatz statt der Leistung, Dr. Kovač, Hamburg 2010.

Tekinay, Sulhi Selahattin: Borçlar Hukuku, Fakülteler Matbaası, İstanbul 1973.

Tekinay, Sulhi Selahattin/Akman, Sermet/Burcuoğlu, Haluk/Altop, Atilla: Borçlar Hukuku Genel Hükümler, Filiz, İstanbul 1993.

Titze, Heinrich: Die Unmöglichkeit der Leistung nach deutschem bürgerlichen Recht, Titze, Leipzig 1900.

Tonner, Klaus/Willingmann, Armin/Tamm, Marina: Vertragsrecht. Kommentar: Luchterhand, Köln 2010. (Cited as: Author, in: Tonner/Willingmann/Tamm)

Topuz, Seçkin/Canbolat, Ferhat: Türk - İsviçre ve Alman Borçlar Hukukunda İmkansızlığın Düzenlenişi, AÜHFD, Vol. 57, No. 3 2008, pp. 673 - 718.

Traub, Thomas: Das Allgemeine Leistungsstörungsrecht Des Bürgerlichen Gesetzbuches, Grin, Norderstedt 2001.

Treitel, Günter H.: Unmöglichkeit, "Impracticability" und "Frustration" im anglo-amerikanischen Recht, Nomos, Baden-Baden 1991.

Tunçomağ, Kenan: Borçlar Hukuku, I. Cild, Genel Hükümler, Fakülteler Matbaası, İstanbul 1972.

UNCITRAL: 2008 UNCITRAL Digest of case law on the United Nations Convention on the International Sale of Goods - Digest of Article 79 case law, <http://www.cisg.law.pace.edu/cisg/text/digest-art-79.html>. (Cited as: UNCITRAL, Digest of Article 79 case law)

UNIDROIT International Institute for the Unification of Private Law: UNIDROIT Principles of International Commercial Contracts 2004, <http://www.unidroit.org/english/principles/contracts/principles2004/integralversionprinciples2004-e.pdf>. (Cited as: PICC Commentary)

Uygur, Turgut: Açıklamalı – İçtihatlı Borçlar Kanunu, Sorumluluk ve Tazminat Hukuku, Giriş ve Madde 1 - 40, Cilt I, Seçkin, Ankara 2003.

Veneziano, Anna; UNIDROIT Principles and CISG: Change of Circumstances and Duty to Renegotiate according to the Belgian Supreme Court, ULR, Vol. 15, No. 1, 2010, pp. 137 - 151.

Viscasillas, Pilar Perales: The Role of the UNIDROIT Principles and the PECL in the Interpretation and Gap-filling of CISG, in CISG Methodology, (Janssen, André/Meyer, Olaf), Sellier, München 2009, pp. 287 - 317.

Vogenauer, Stefan/Kleinheisterkamp, Jan: Commentary on the UNIDROIT Principles of International Commercial Contracts (PICC), Oxford University Press, Oxford/New York 2009. (Cited as: Author, in: Vogenauer/Kleinheisterkamp)

Vogt, Patrick: Gesetzliche und rechtsgeschäftliche Beschränkungen der Mängelrechte des Käufers, Unmöglichkeit und Unzumutbarkeit der Leistung im kaufrechtlichen Mängelrecht und rechtsgeschäftliche Disponibilität der 437 ff. BGB, Peter Lang, Frankfurt am Main 2005.

von Büren, Bruno: Schweizerisches Obligationenrecht, Allgemeiner Teil, Schulthess, Zürich 1964.

von Tuhr, Andreas/Escher, Arnold: Allgemeiner Teil des Schweizerischen Obligationenrechts, Band II, Schulthess Polygraphischer Verlag AG, Zürich 1974.

Wagner, Eric: Studien zum Recht der Unmöglichkeit, Nomos, Baden-Baden 2007.

Wallow, Astrid: Risikozuweisung und Vertragshaftung: Anfängliche Leistungshindernisse vor den Gerichten in den U.S.A. und in Deutschland, Lit Verlag, Berlin 2008.

Weber, Rolf H.: Berner Kommentar, Kommentar zum schweizerischen Privatrecht, Band VI: Das Obligationenrecht, 1. Abteilung: Allgemeine Bestimmungen, 5. Teilband: Die Folgen der Nichterfüllung (Art. 97 - 109 OR), Stämpfli, Bern 2000. (Cited as: Berner/Weber)

Weidt, Heinz: Antizipierter Vertragsbruch, Mohr Siebeck, Tübingen 2008.

Weitzmann, Todd: Validity and Excuse in the U.N. Sales Convention, JLC, Vol. 16, No. 2, 1997, pp. 265 - 290.

Westermann, Harm Peter/Bydlinski, Peter/Weber, Ralph: BGB-Schuldrecht Allgemeiner Teil, C.F. Müller, Heidelberg 2010.

Whittaker, Simon: Draft Common Frame of Reference: an assessment, <http://www.justice.gov.uk/Draft_Common_Frame_of_Reference_an_assessment.pdf>.

Wieser, Eberhard: Schuldrechtsreform – Die Unmöglichkeit der Leistung nach neuem Recht, MDR 2002, pp. 858 - 862.

Wilhelm, Jan/Deeg, Peter: Nachträgliche Unmöglichkeit und nachträgliches Unvermögen, JZ 2001, pp. 223 - 233.

Witthaus, Dieter: Störungen im Schuldverhältnis, Brockmeyer, Bochum 1986.

Witz, Wolfgang/Salger, Hanns-Christian/Lorenz, Manuel: International Einheitliches Kaufrecht, Praktiker-Kommentar und Vertragsgestaltung zum CISG, Verlag Recht und Wirtschaft GmbH, Heidelberg 2000. (Cited as: Author, in: Witz/Salger/Lorenz)

Wollschläger, Christian: Die Entstehung der Unmöglichkeitslehre, Böhlau, Köln, Wien 1970.

Zeller, Bruno: Damages under the Convention on Contracts for the International Sale of Goods, Oceana Publications, Dobbs Ferry/New York 2005. (Cited as: Zeller, Damages)

Zeller, Bruno: CISG and the Unification of International Trade Law, Routledge-Cavendish, New York 2007 (Cited as: Zeller, CISG)

Zeller, Bruno: Four-Corners - The Methodology for Interpretation and Application of the UN Convention on Contracts for the International Sale of Goods, <http://www.cisg.law.pace.edu/cisg/biblio/4corners.html>. (Cited as: Zeller)

Zerres, Thomas: Bürgerliches Recht, Ein einführendes Lehrbuch in das Zivil- und Zivilprozessrecht, Springer, Berlin/Heidelberg 2005.

Ziegler, Antje: Die anfängliche Unmöglichkeit der Leistung in der schweizerischen Lehre, Paul Haupt, Bern 1992.

Zimmer, Daniel: Das neue Recht der Leistungsstörungen, NJW 2002, pp. 1 - 12.

Zimmermann, Reinhard: Law of Obligations: Roman foundations of the civilian tradition, Oxford University Press, Oxford 1996. (Cited as: Zimmermann, Law of Obligations)

Zimmermann, Reinhard: The New German Law of Obligations, Oxford University Press, Oxford/New York 2005. (Cited as: Zimmermann, New German Law)

Zimmermann, Reinhard: Breach of Contract and Remedies under the New German Law of Obligations, <http://www.cisg.law.pace.edu/cisg/biblio/zimmerman.html>. (Cited as: Zimmermann, Breach of Contract)

Zweigert, Konrad/Kötz, Hein: Einführung in die Rechtsvergleichung auf dem Gebiete des Privatrechts, Mohr Siebeck, Tübingen 1996.

The manufacturer's authorised representative in the EU is Springer Nature Customer Service Centre GmbH, Europaplatz 3, 69115 Heidelberg, Germany. If you have any concerns regarding our products, please contact ProductSafety@springernature.com

Printed and bound by CPI Group (UK) Ltd, Croydon, CR0 4YY
30/09/2026
02225566-0008